RU Apr 13
OrOCT 15

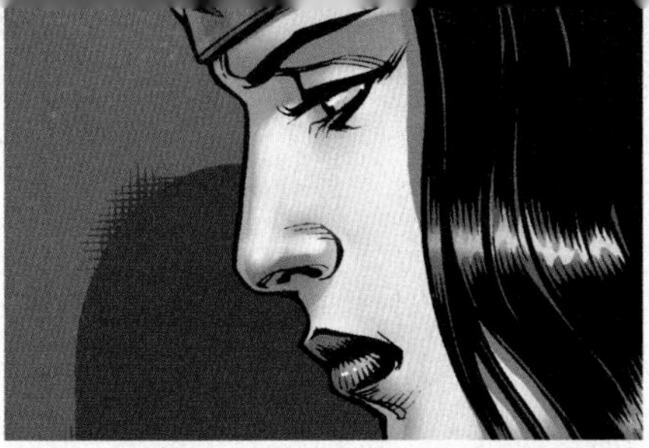

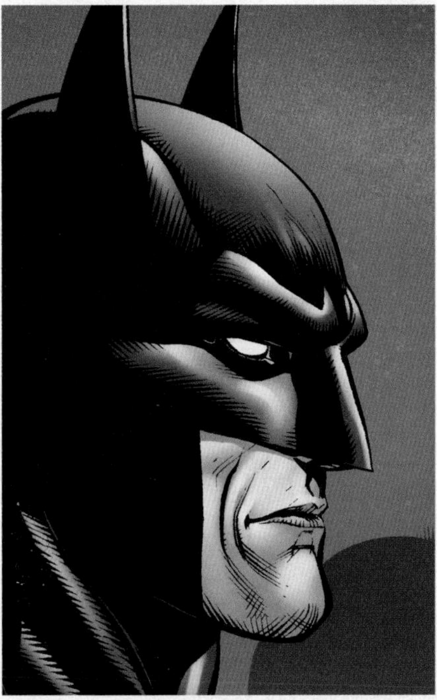

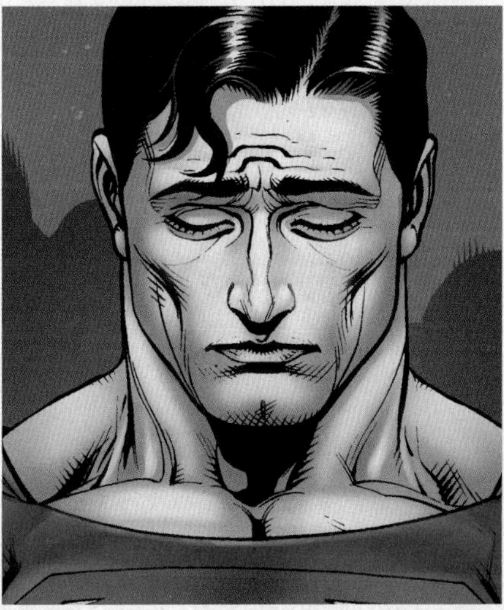

FINAL CRISIS COMPANION

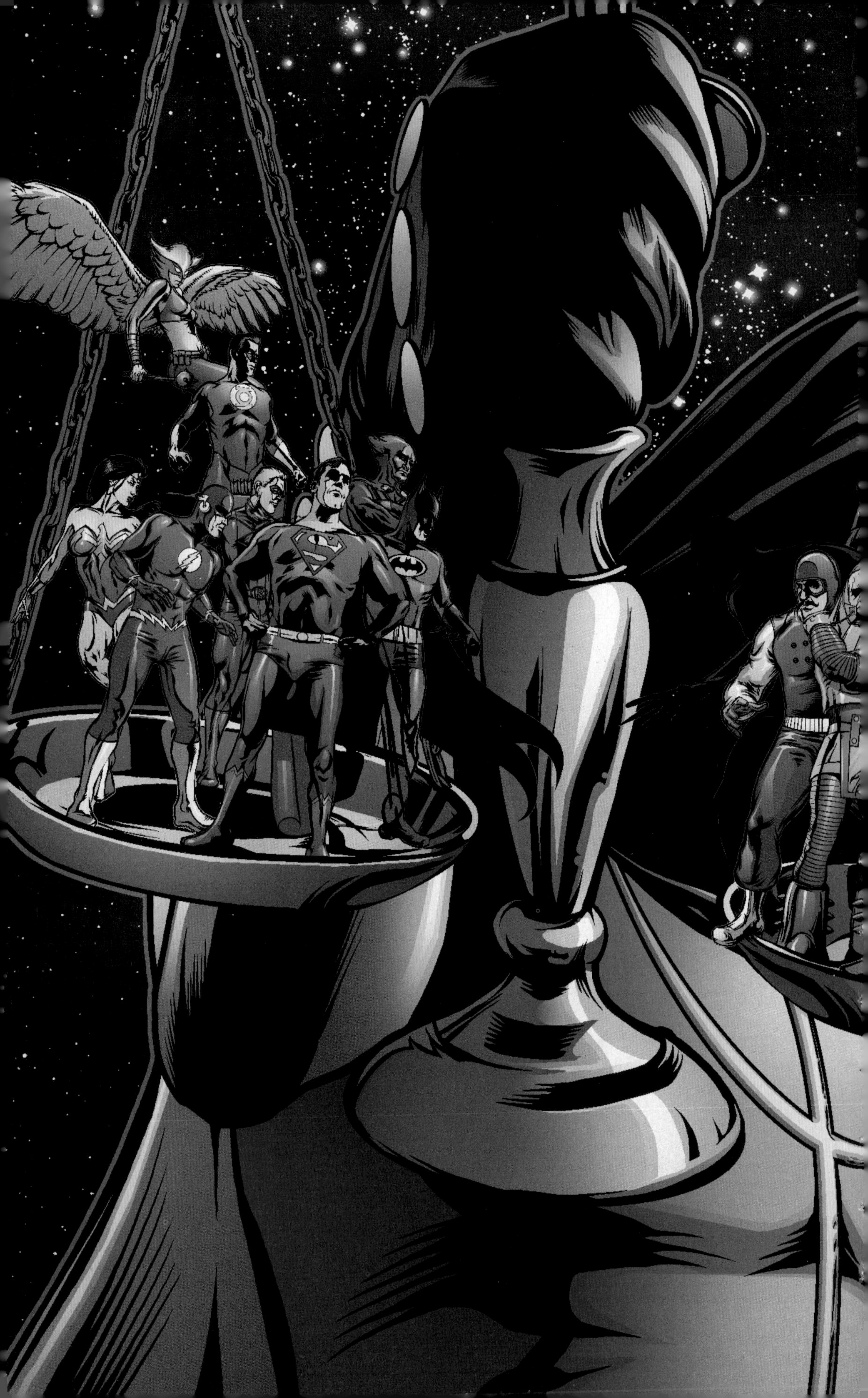

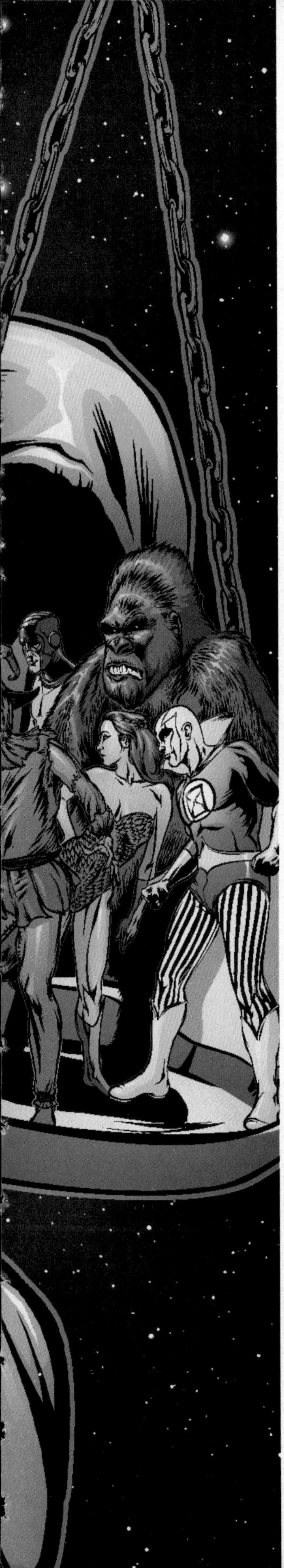

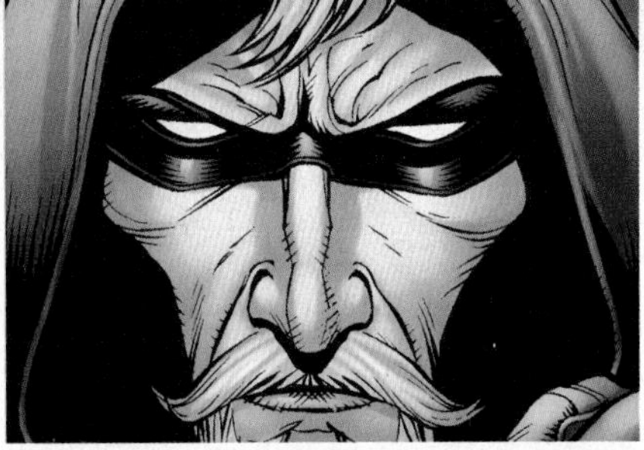

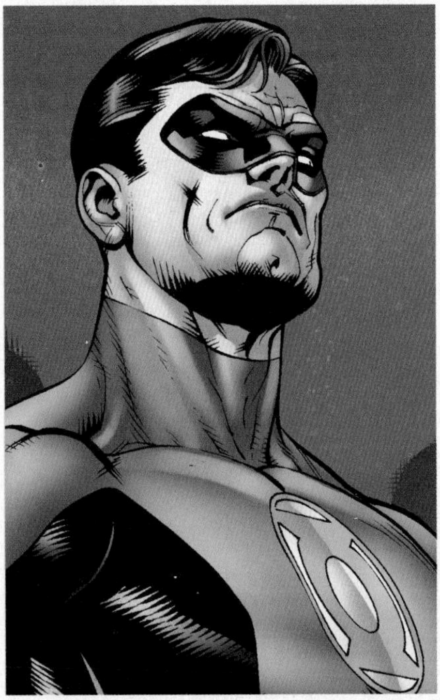

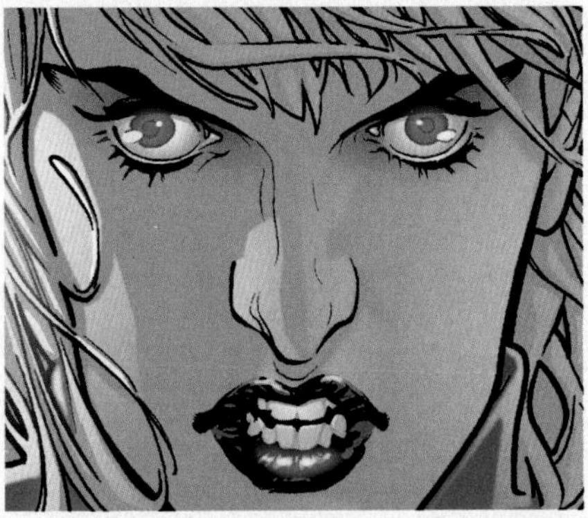

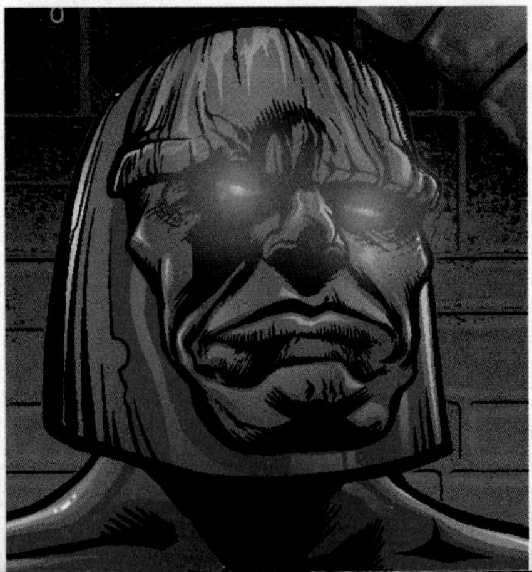

FINAL CRISIS COMPANION

DIRECTOR'S CUT

Grant Morrison
Writer

J.G. Jones
Artist

BALANCING ACT

Len Wein
Writer

Tony Shasteen
Artist

Alex Bleyaert
Colorist

Rob Leigh
Letterer

REQUIEM: CARETAKERS OF MARS

Peter J. Tomasi
Writer

Doug Mahnke
Penciller

Christian Alamy
Rodney Ramos
Inkers

Nei Ruffino
Colorist

John J. Hill
Letterer

RESIST

Greg Rucka &
Eric Trautmann
Writers

Ryan Sook
Marco Rudy
Artists

Jeromy Cox
Colorist

John J. Hill
Letterer

Dan DiDio   Senior VP-Executive Editor

Eddie Berganza   Editor-original series

Adam Schlagman   Associate Editor-original series

Sean Mackiewicz   Editor-collected edition

Robbin Brosterman   Senior Art Director

Paul Levitz   President & Publisher

Georg Brewer   VP-Design & DC Direct Creative

Richard Bruning   Senior VP-Creative Director

Patrick Caldon   Executive VP-Finance & Operations

Chris Caramalis   VP-Finance

John Cunningham   VP-Marketing

Terri Cunningham   VP-Managing Editor

Amy Genkins   Senior VP-Business & Legal Affairs

Alison Gill   VP-Manufacturing

David Hyde   VP-Publicity

Hank Kanalz   VP-General Manager, WildStorm

Jim Lee   Editorial Director-WildStorm

Gregory Noveck   Senior VP-Creative Affairs

Sue Pohja   VP-Book Trade Sales

Steve Rotterdam   Senior VP-Sales & Marketing

Cheryl Rubin   Senior VP-Brand Management

Alysse Soll   VP-Advertising & Custom Publishing

Jeff Trojan   VP-Business Development, DC Direct

Bob Wayne   VP-Sales

Cover by J.G. Jones

FINAL CRISIS COMPANION

DC Comics, 1700 Broadway, New York, NY 10019
A Warner Bros. Entertainment Company
Printed in Canada. First Printing.
ISBN: 978-1-4012-2274-1

SUSTAINABLE FORESTRY INITIATIVE

Certified Fiber
Sourcing
www.sfiprogram.org

Fiber used in this product line meets the sourcing requirements
of the SFI program. www.sfiprogram.org PWC-SFICOC-260

FINAL CRISIS: DIRECTOR'S CUT cover by J.G. Jones

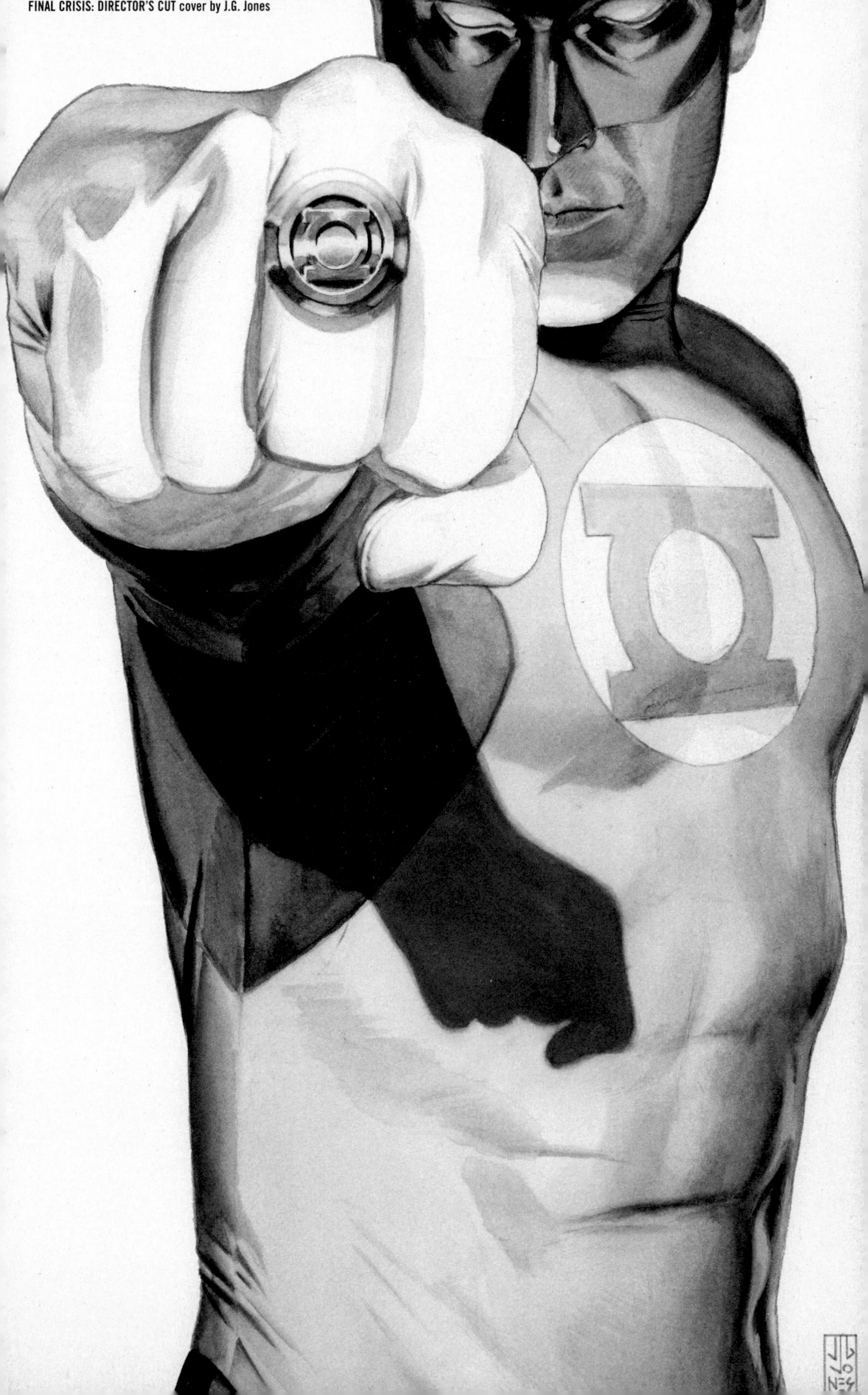

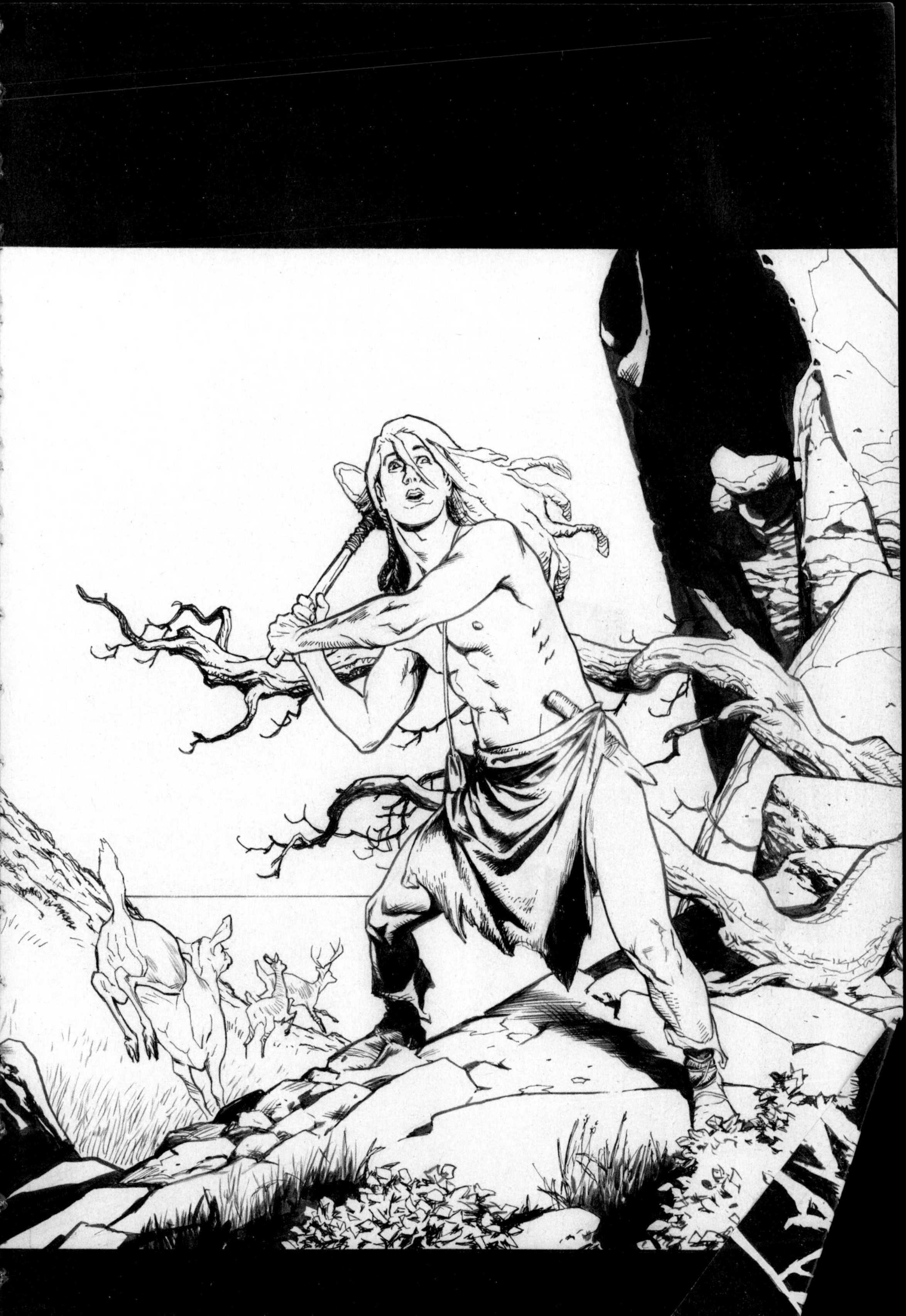

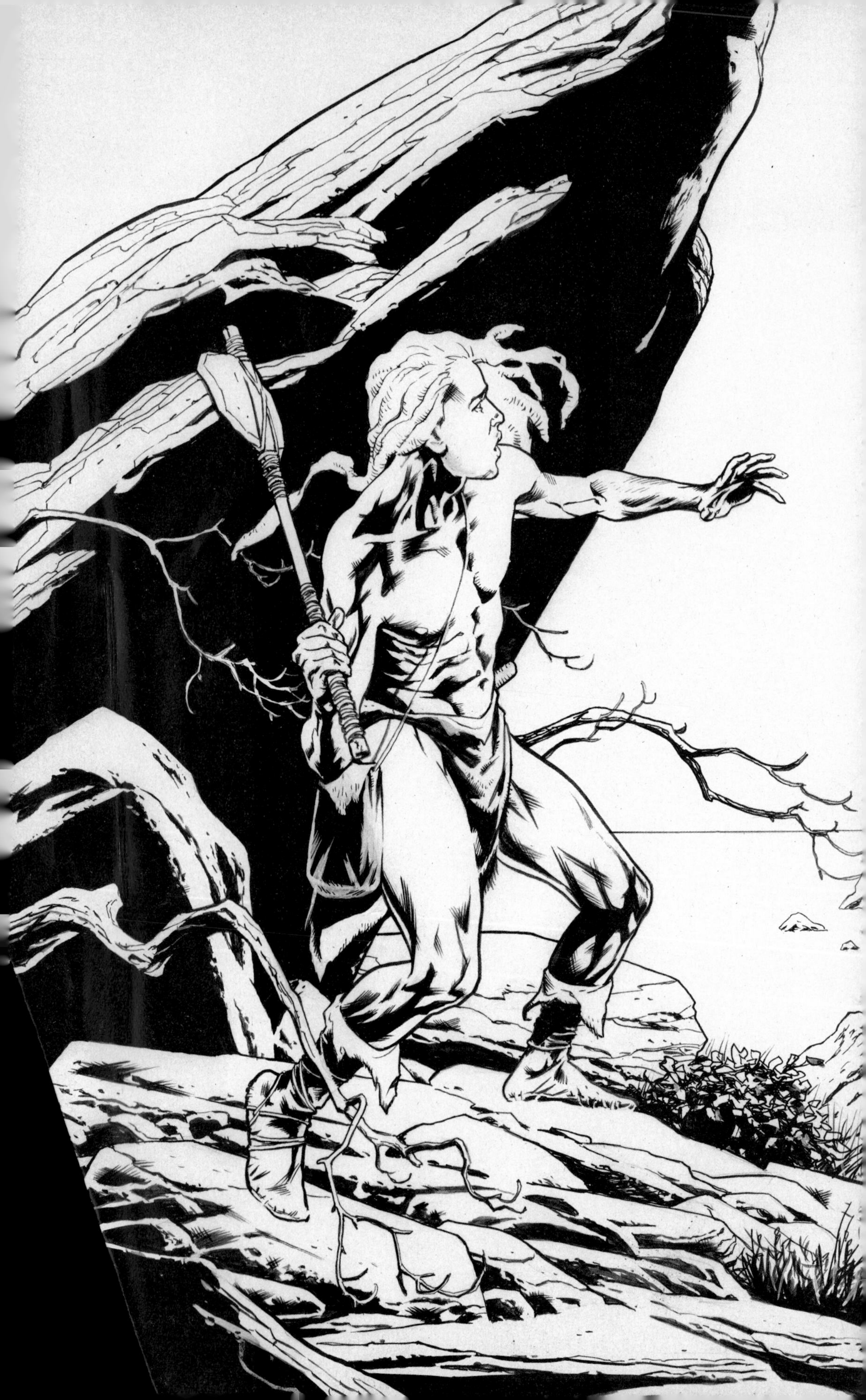

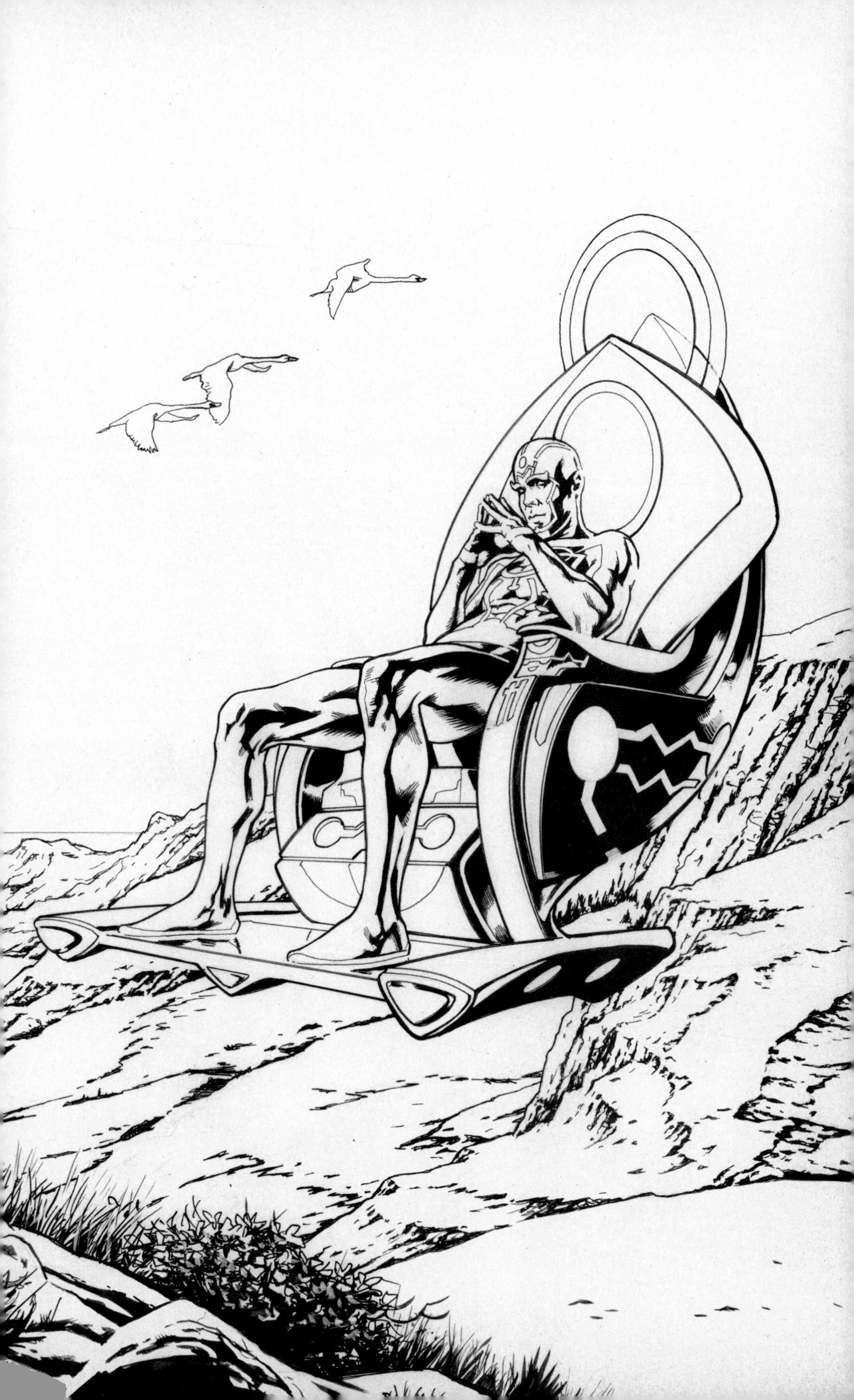

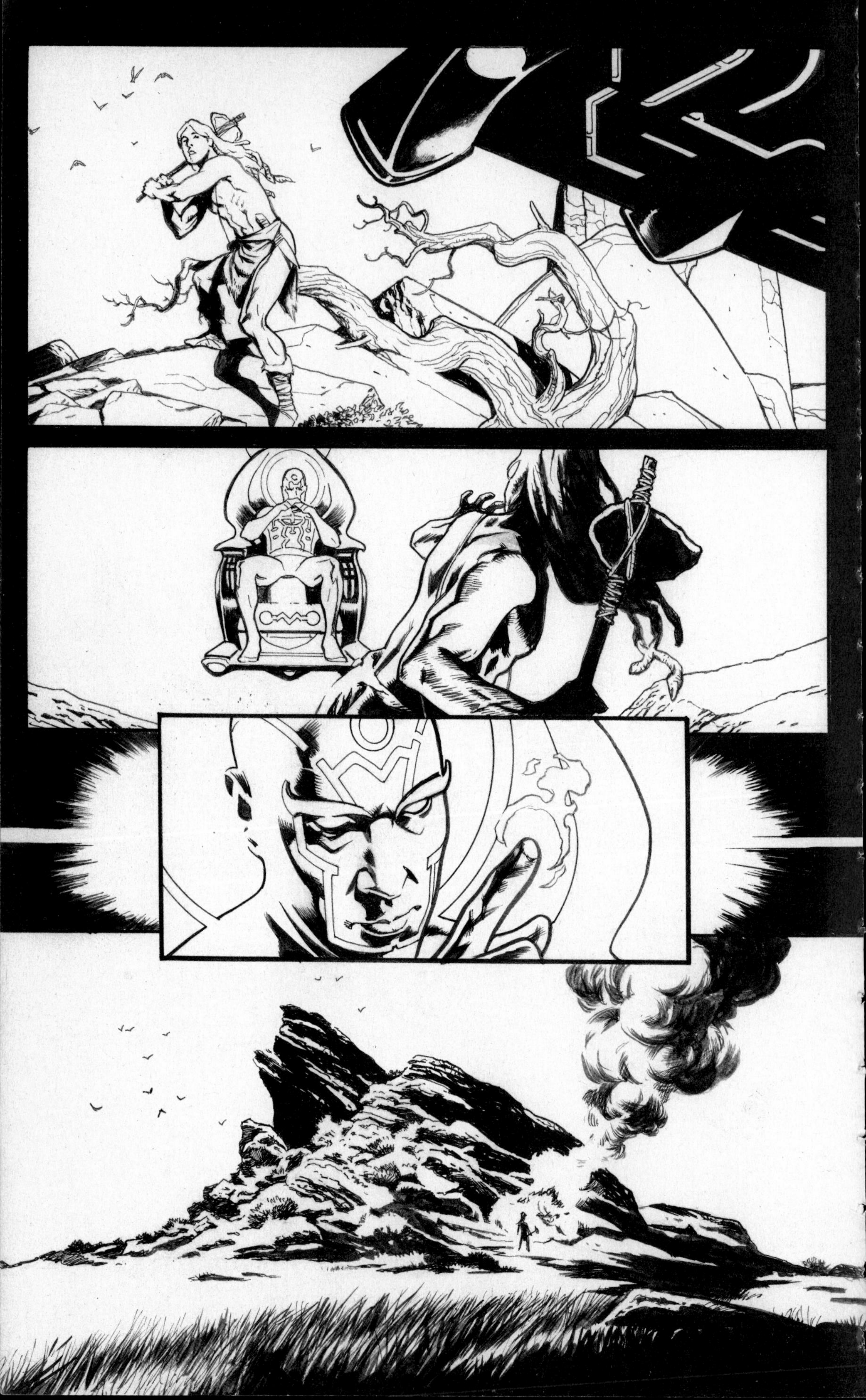

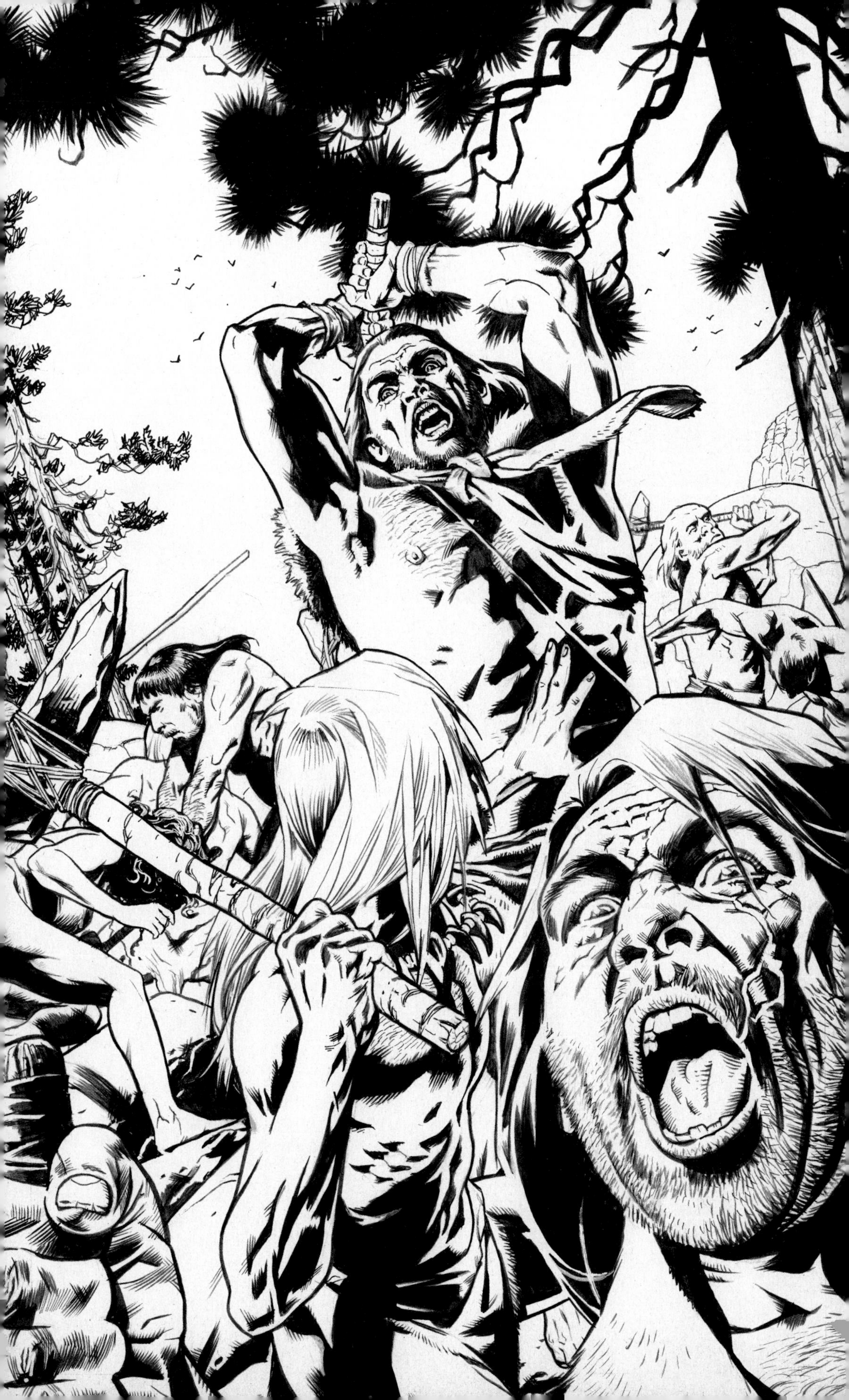

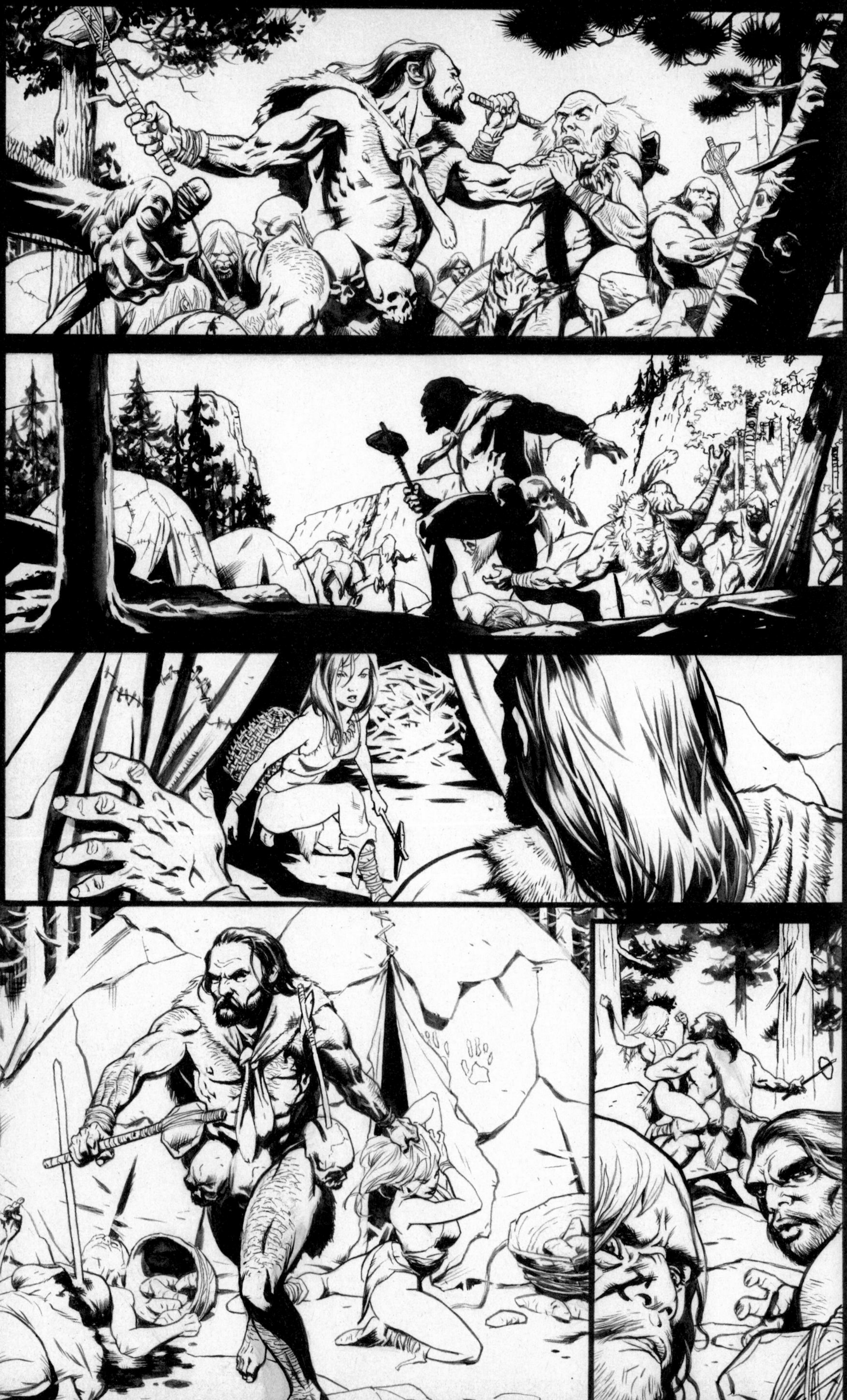

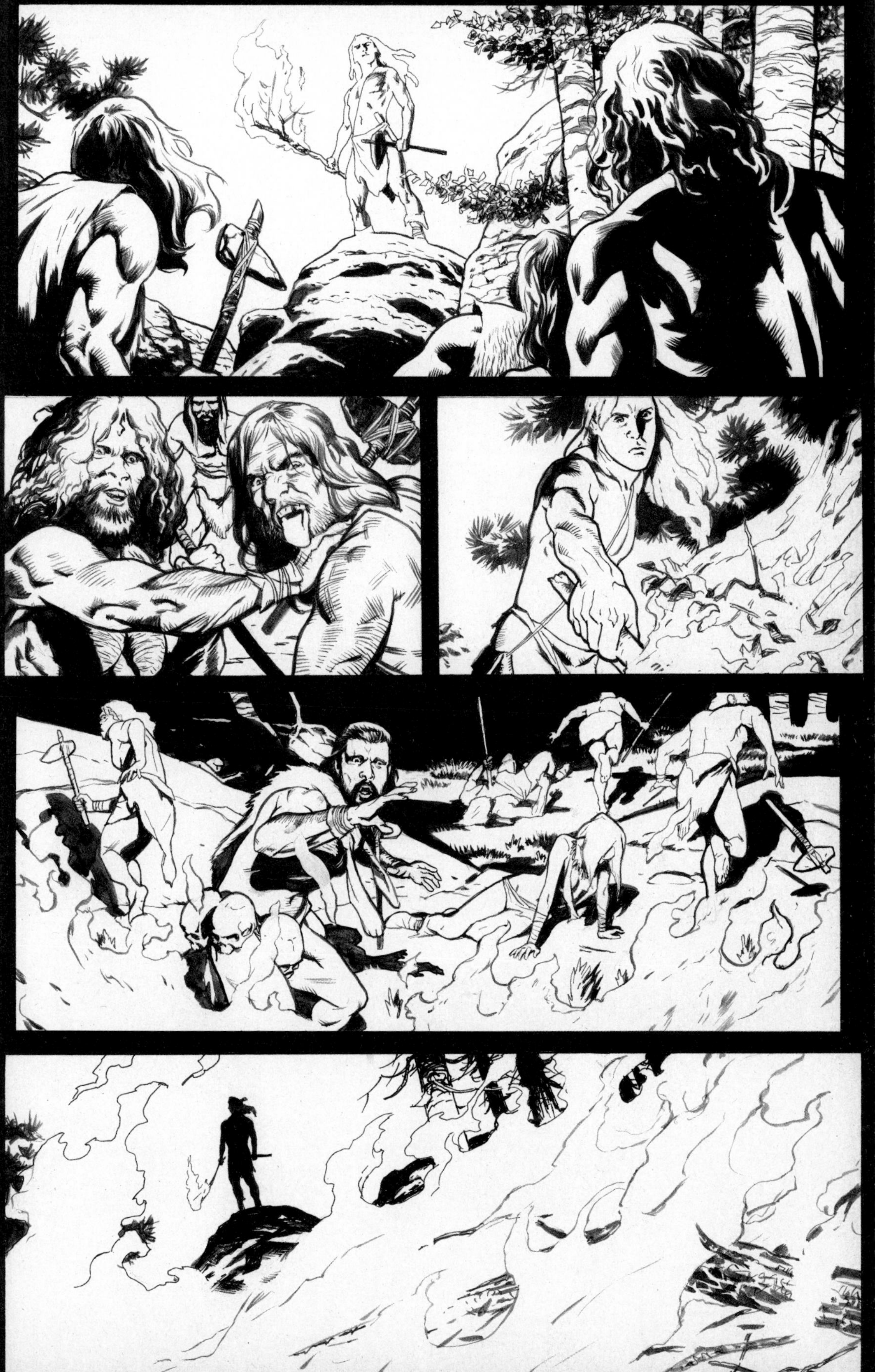

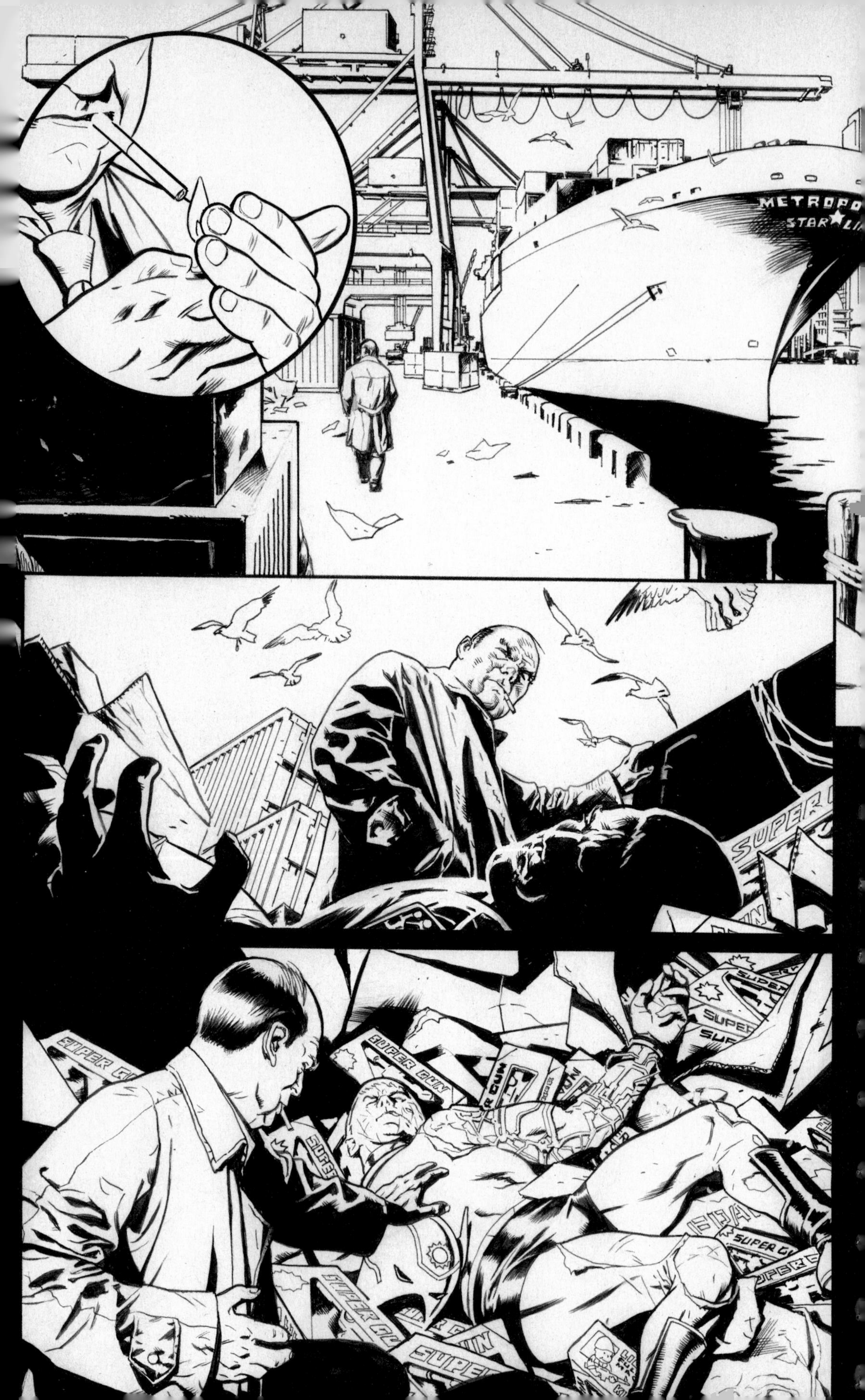
METROPO
STAR

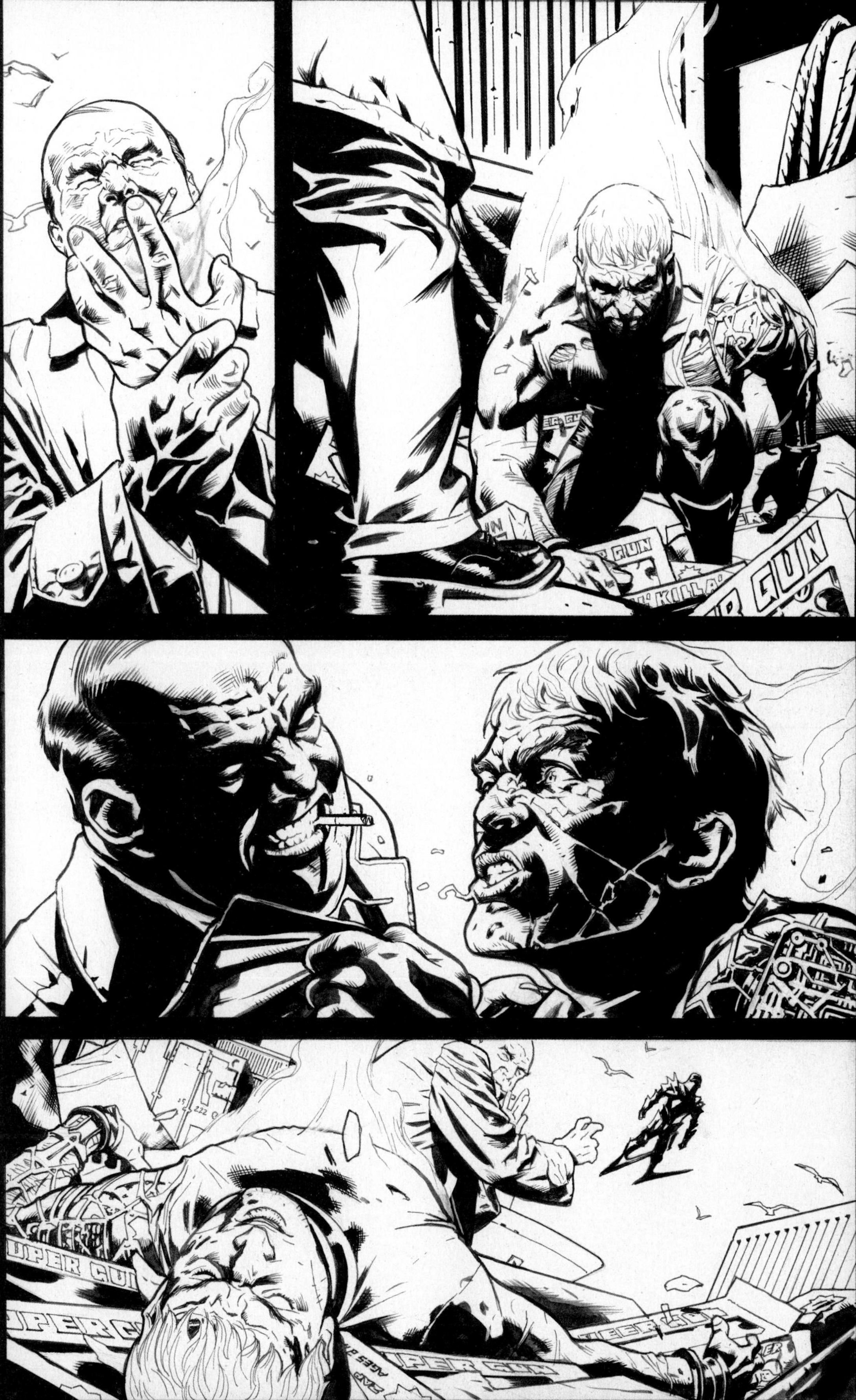

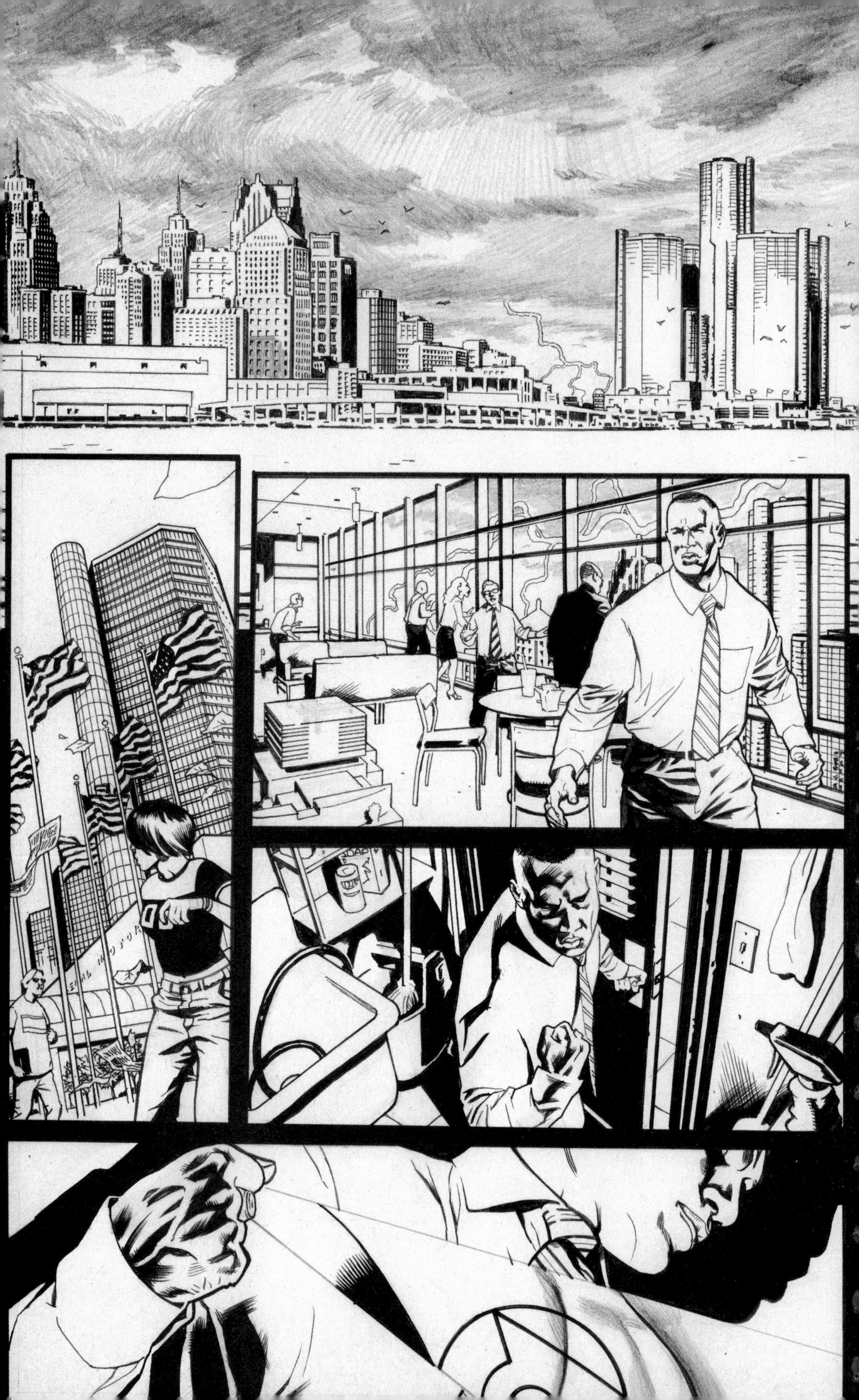

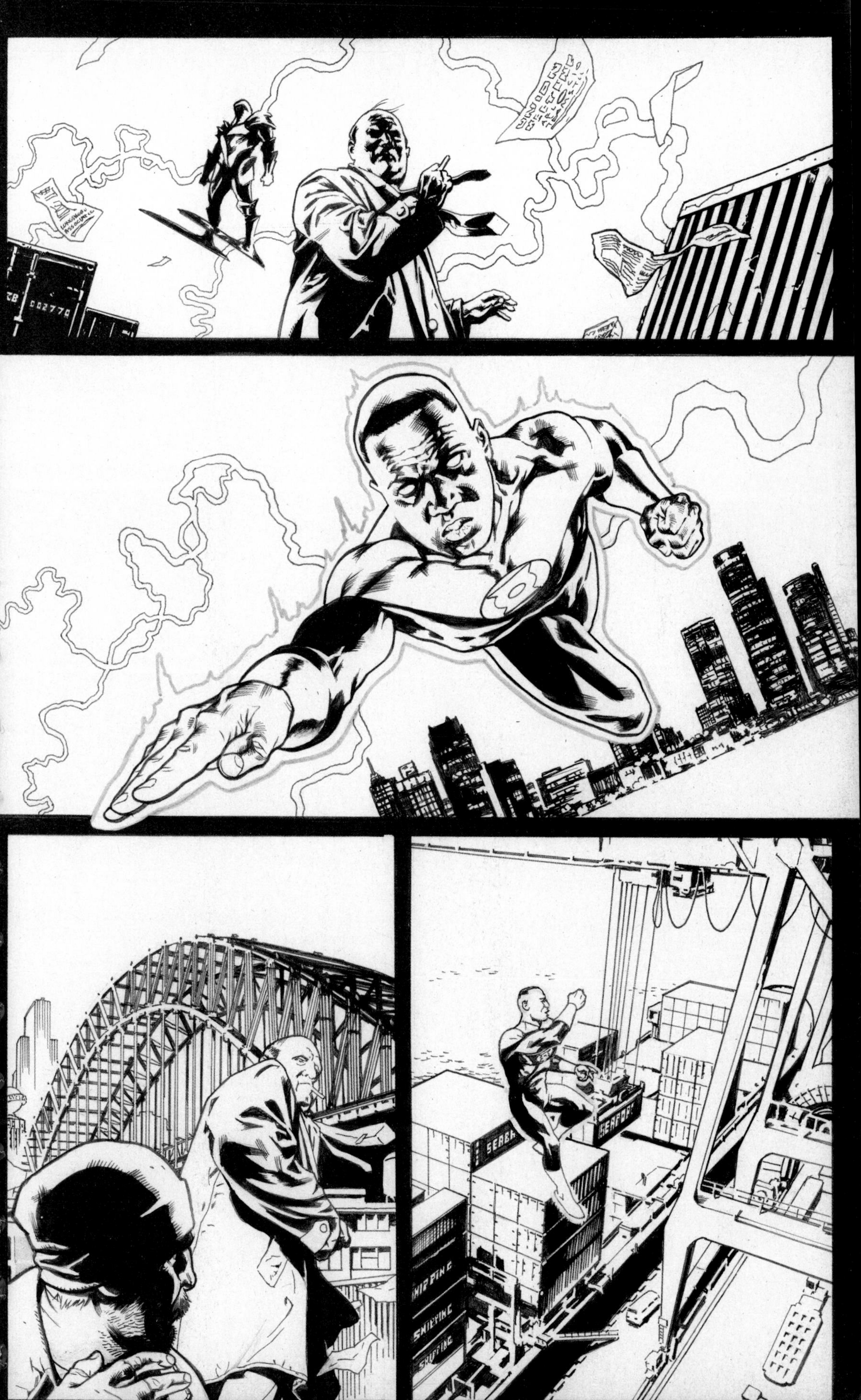

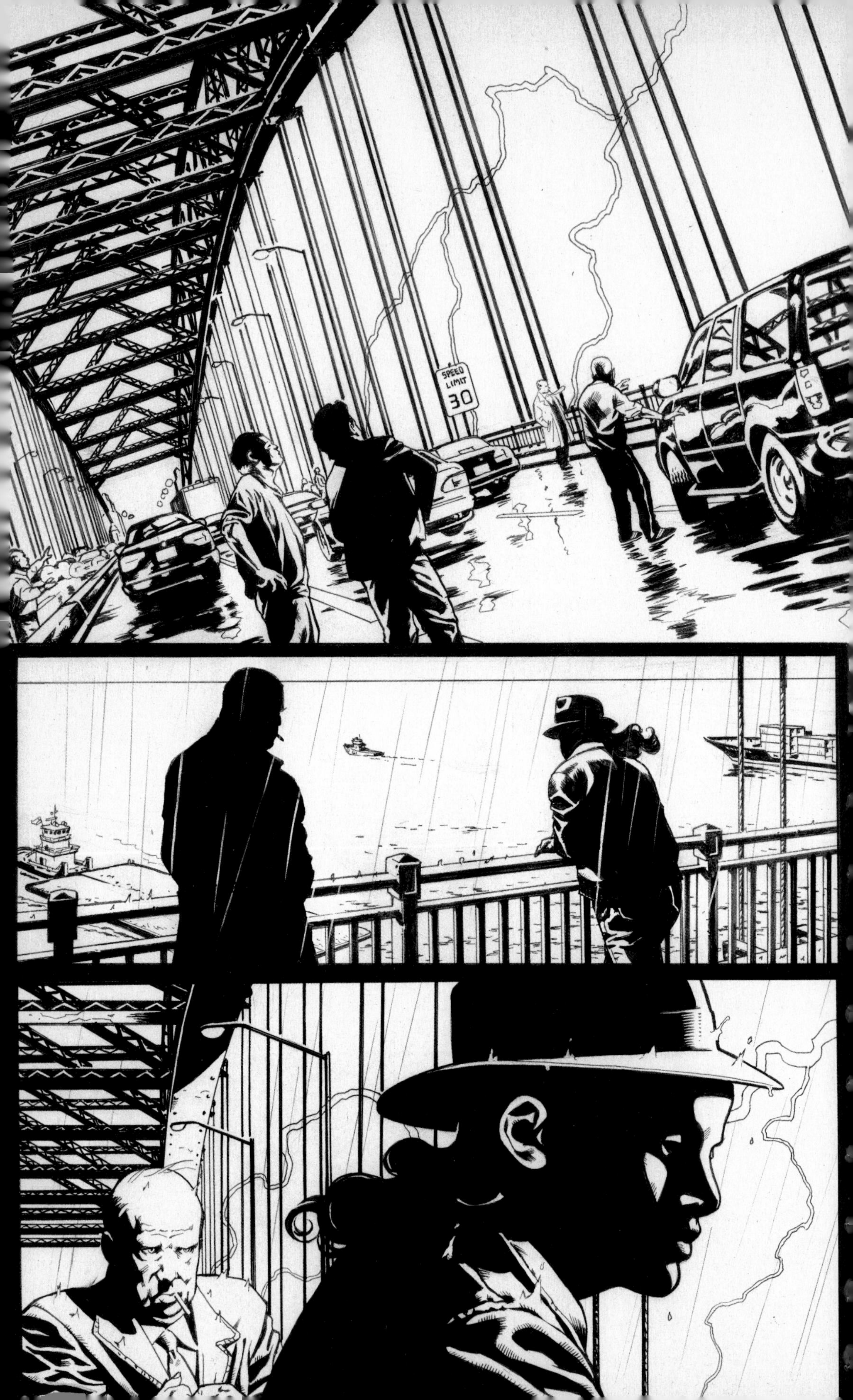
SPEED
LIMIT
30

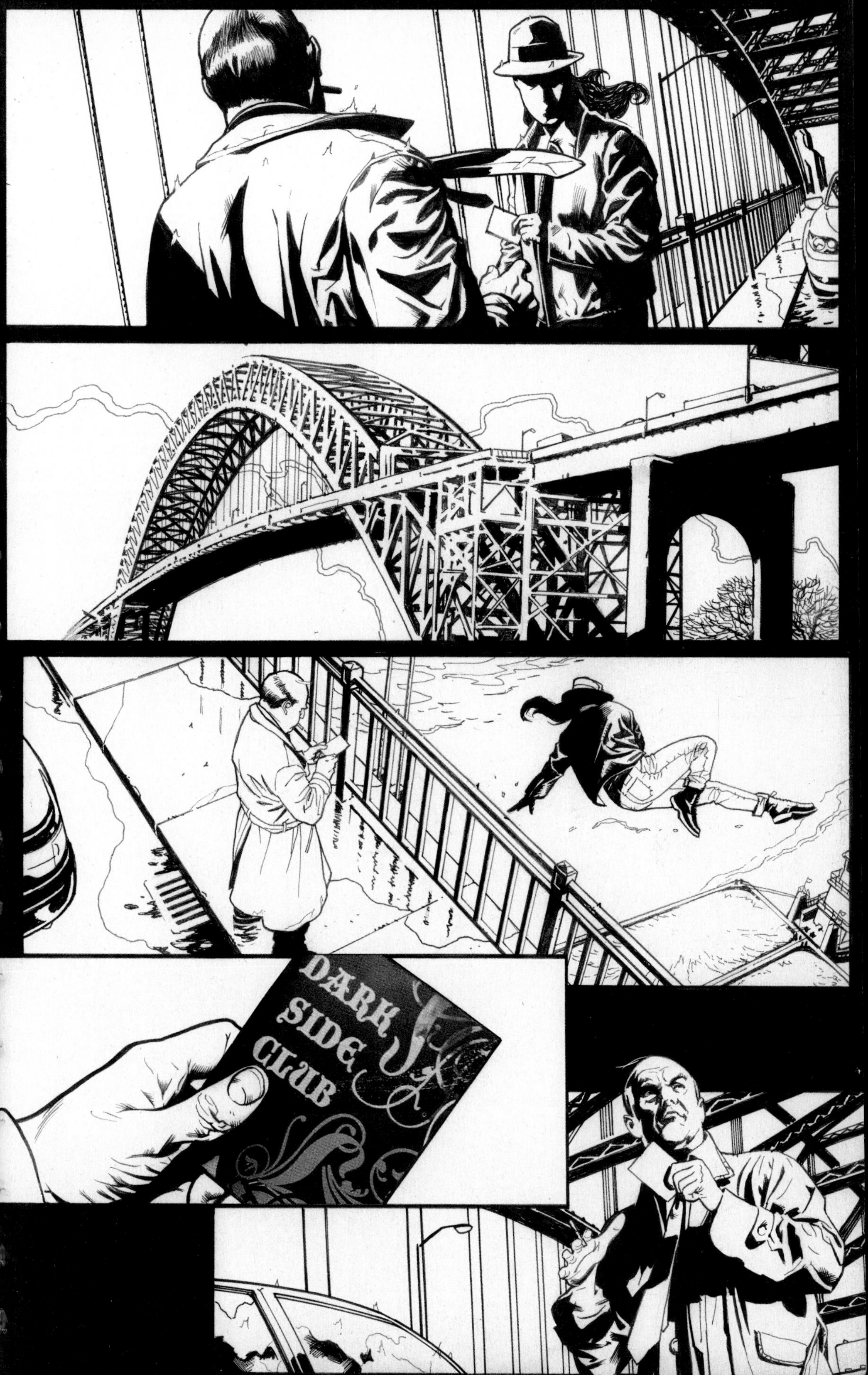
DARK
SIDE
CLUB

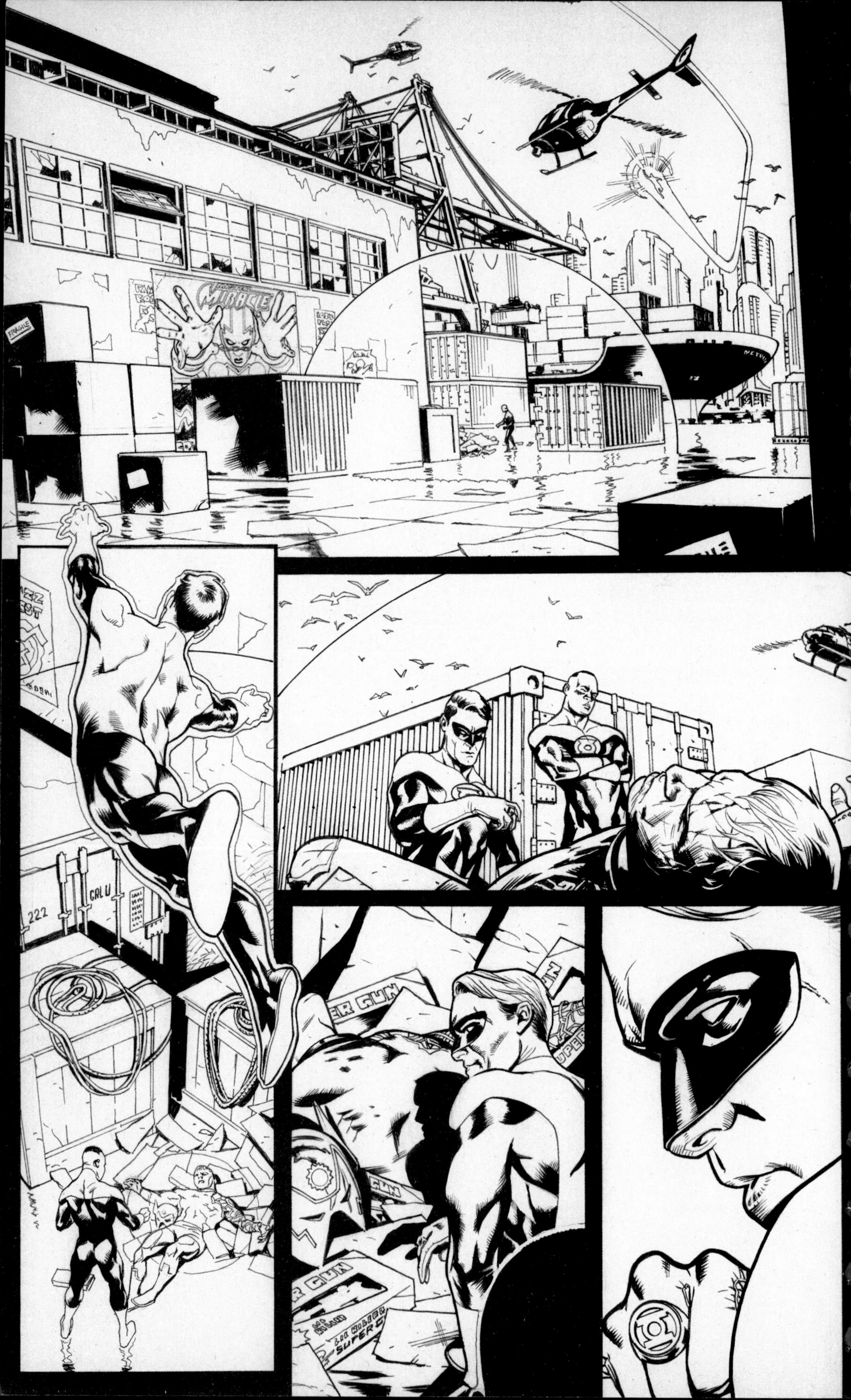
FRAGILE
MIRACLE

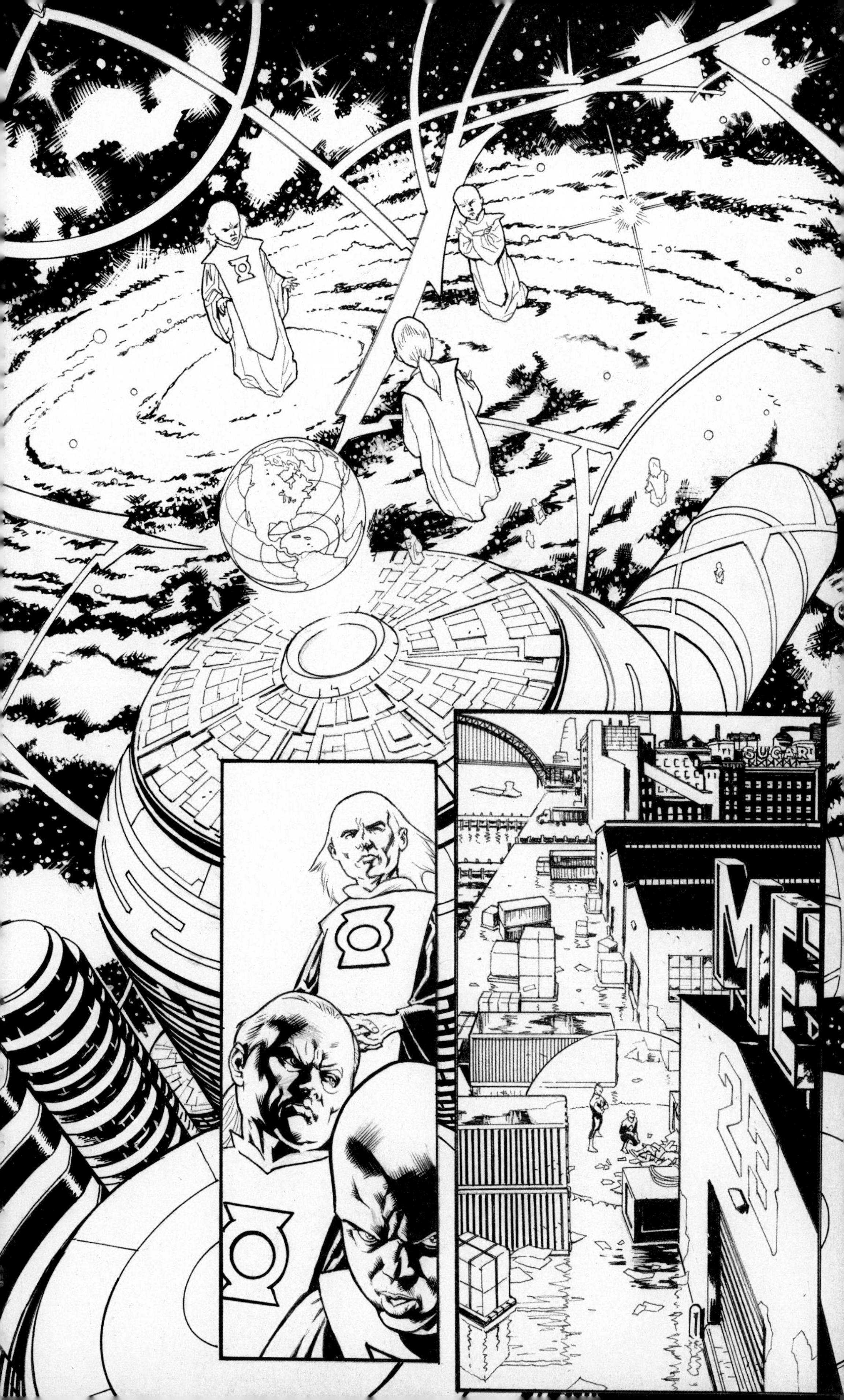
SUGAR

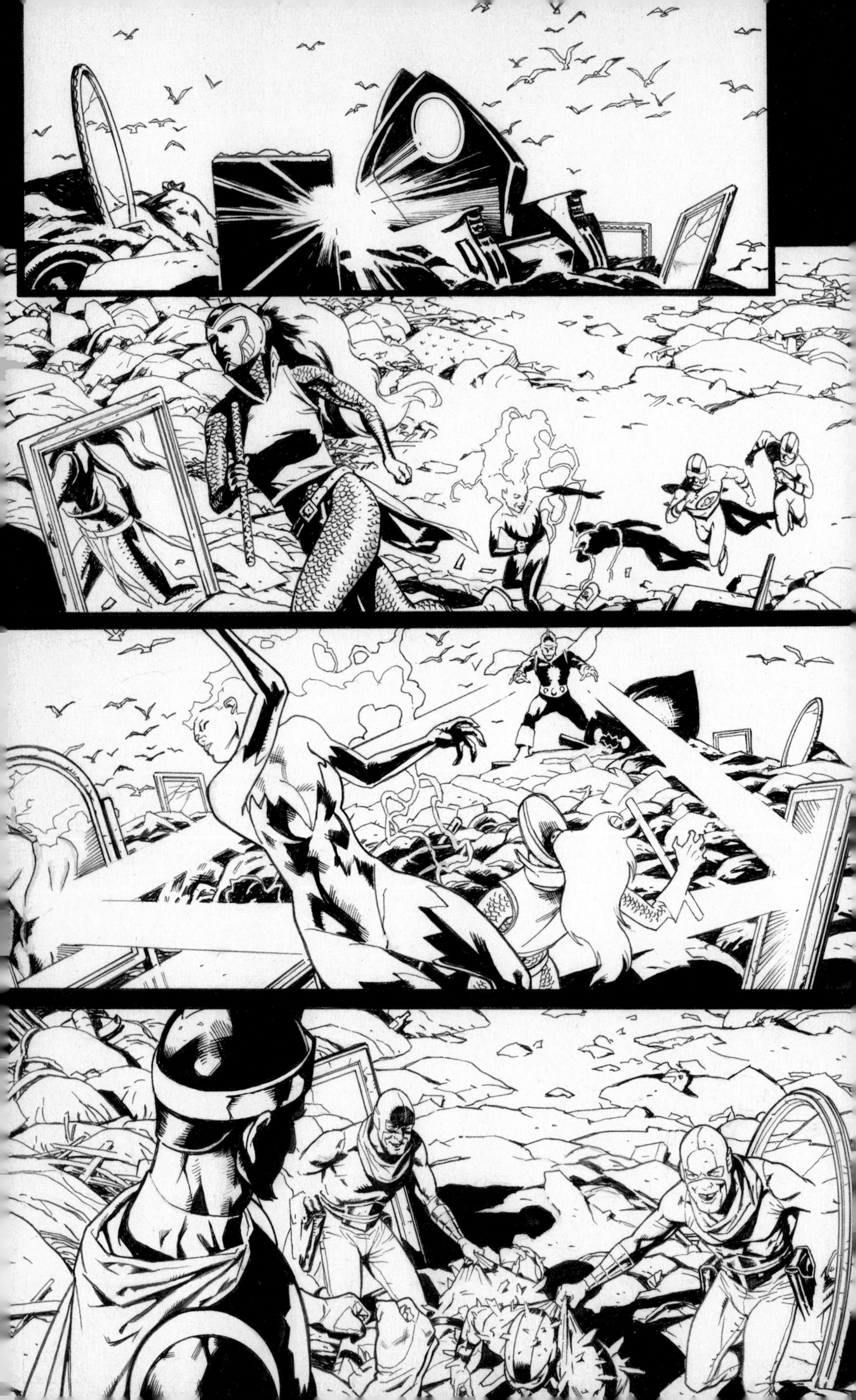

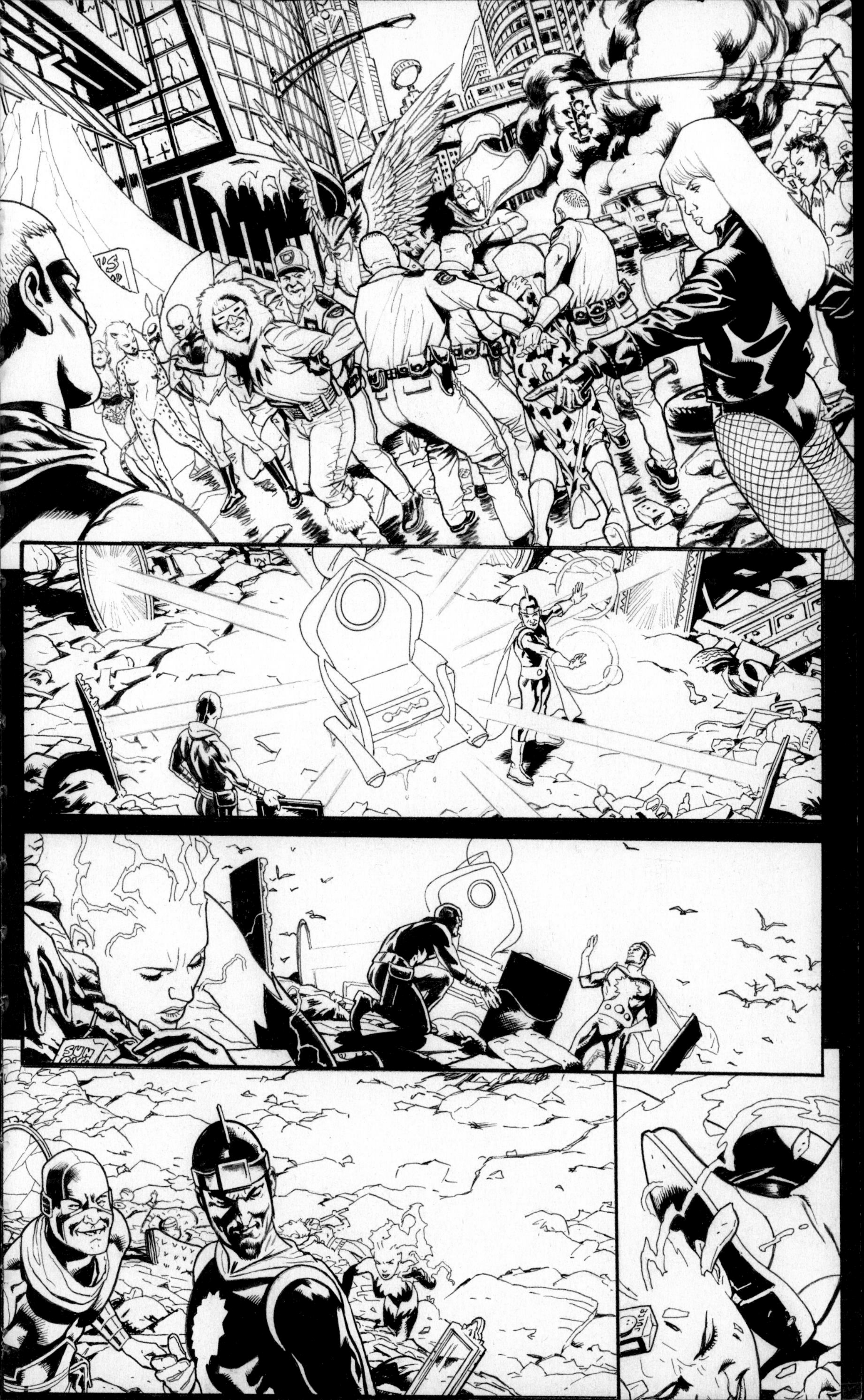

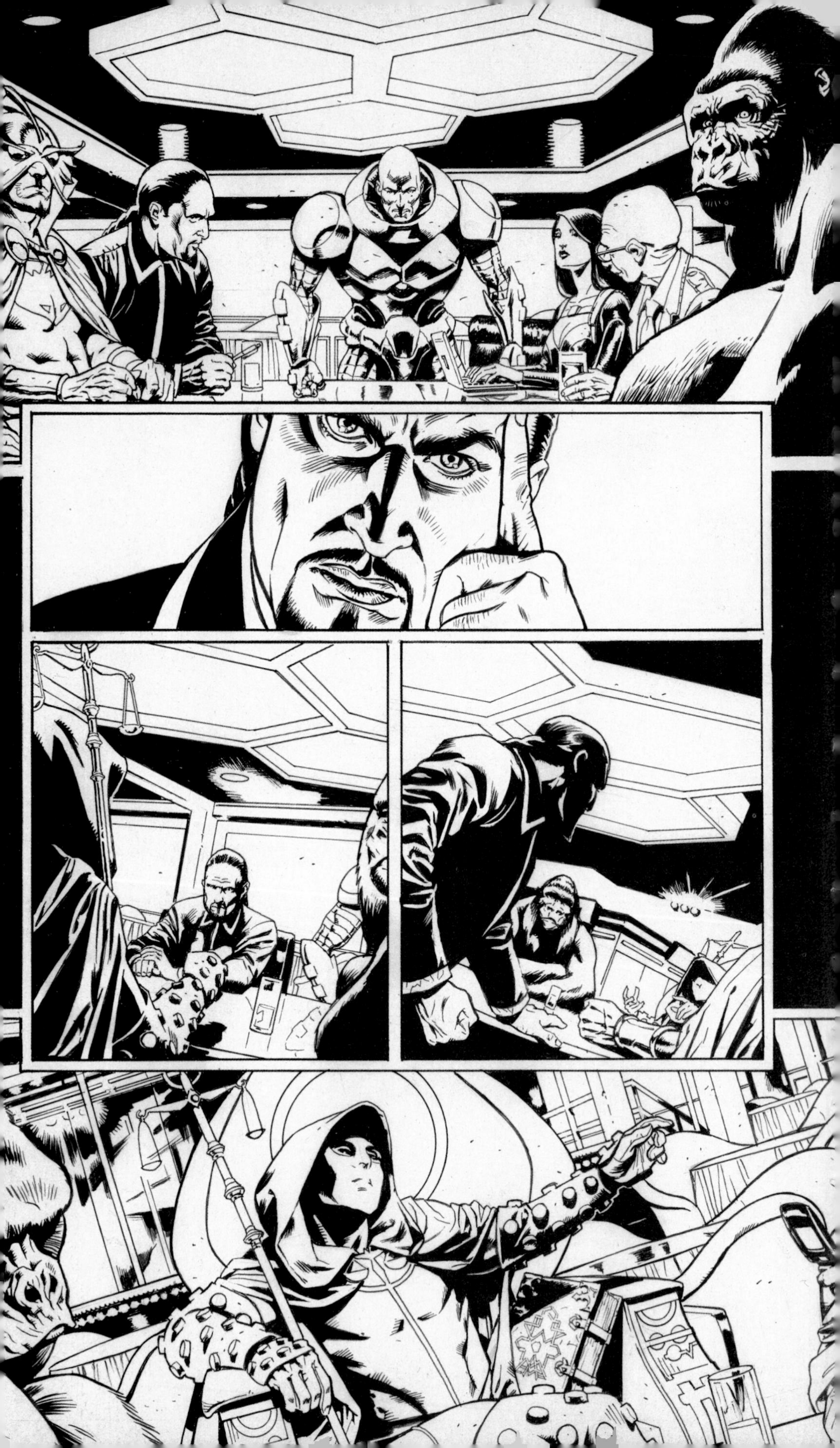

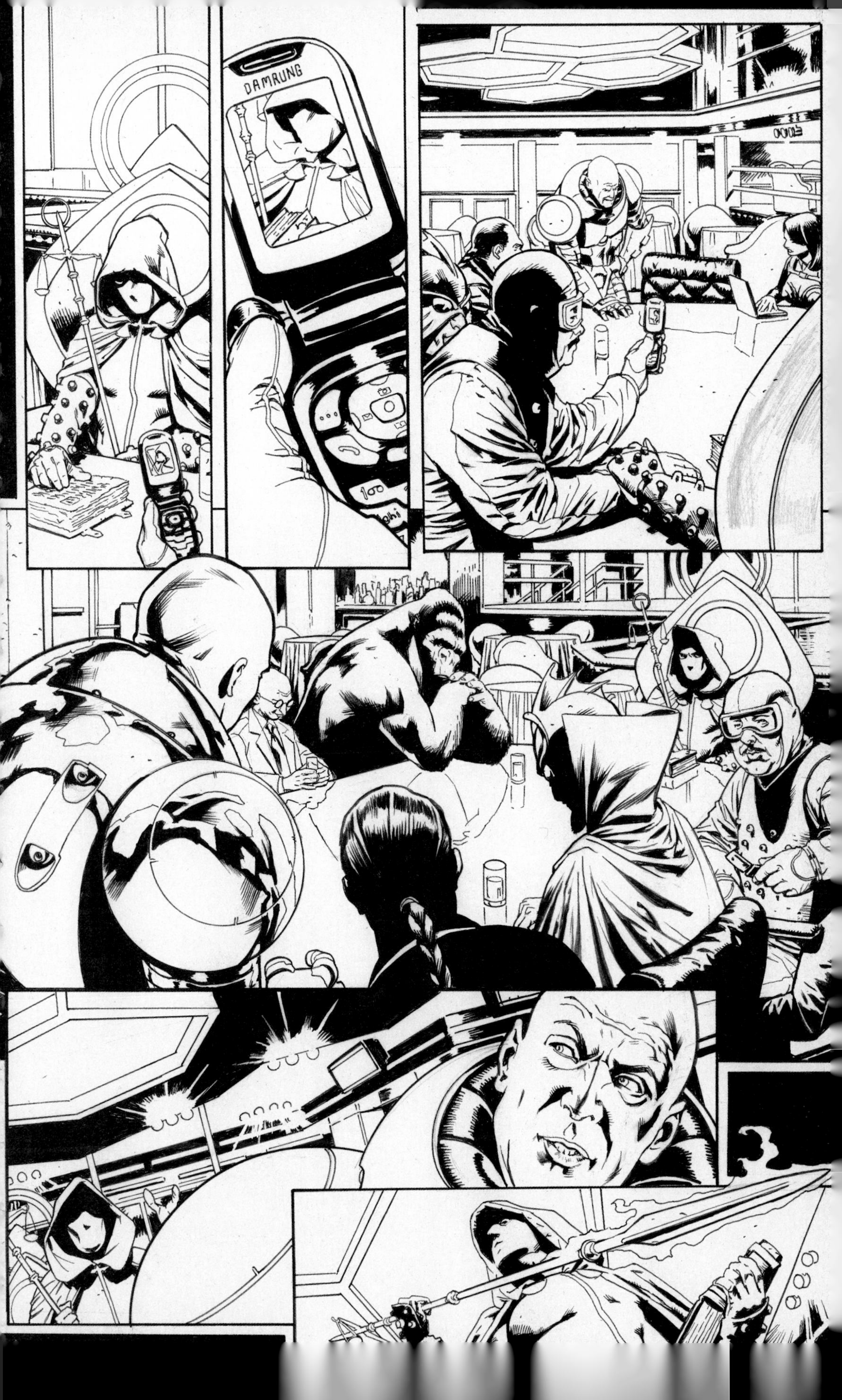
DAMRUNG

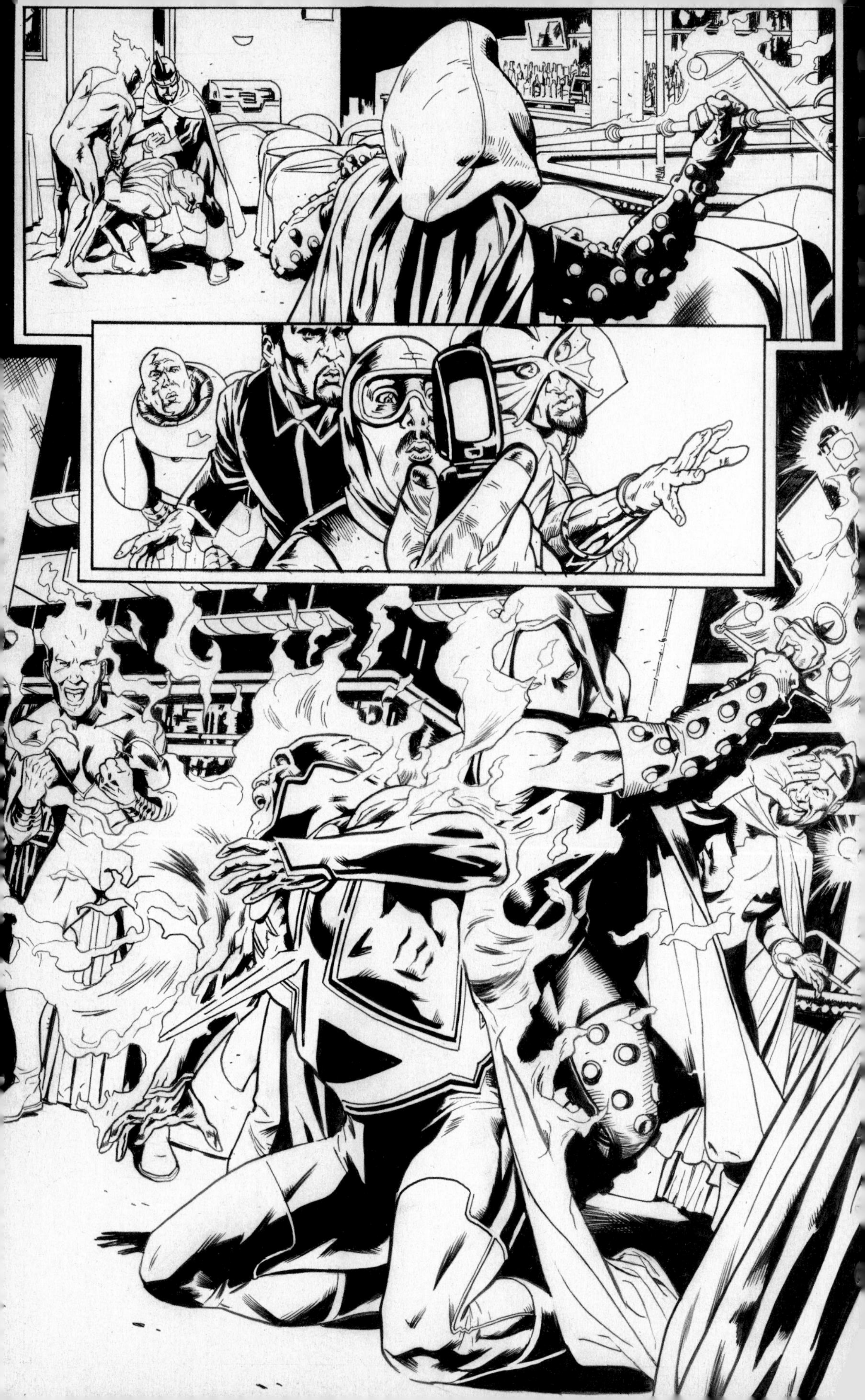

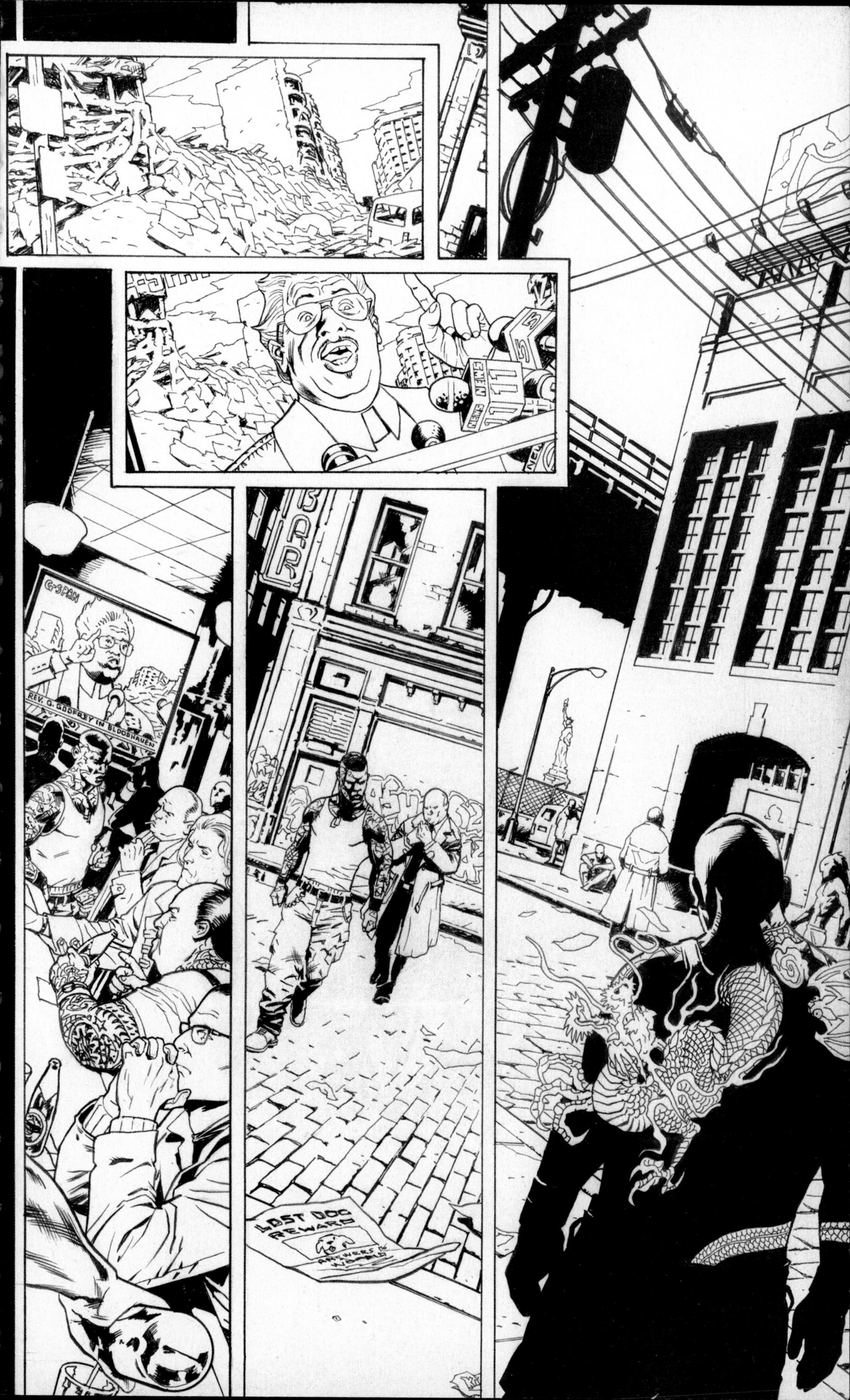
C-SPAN
REV. G. GODFREY IN BLOODHAVEN
BAR
LOST DOG
REWARD
ANSWERS TO

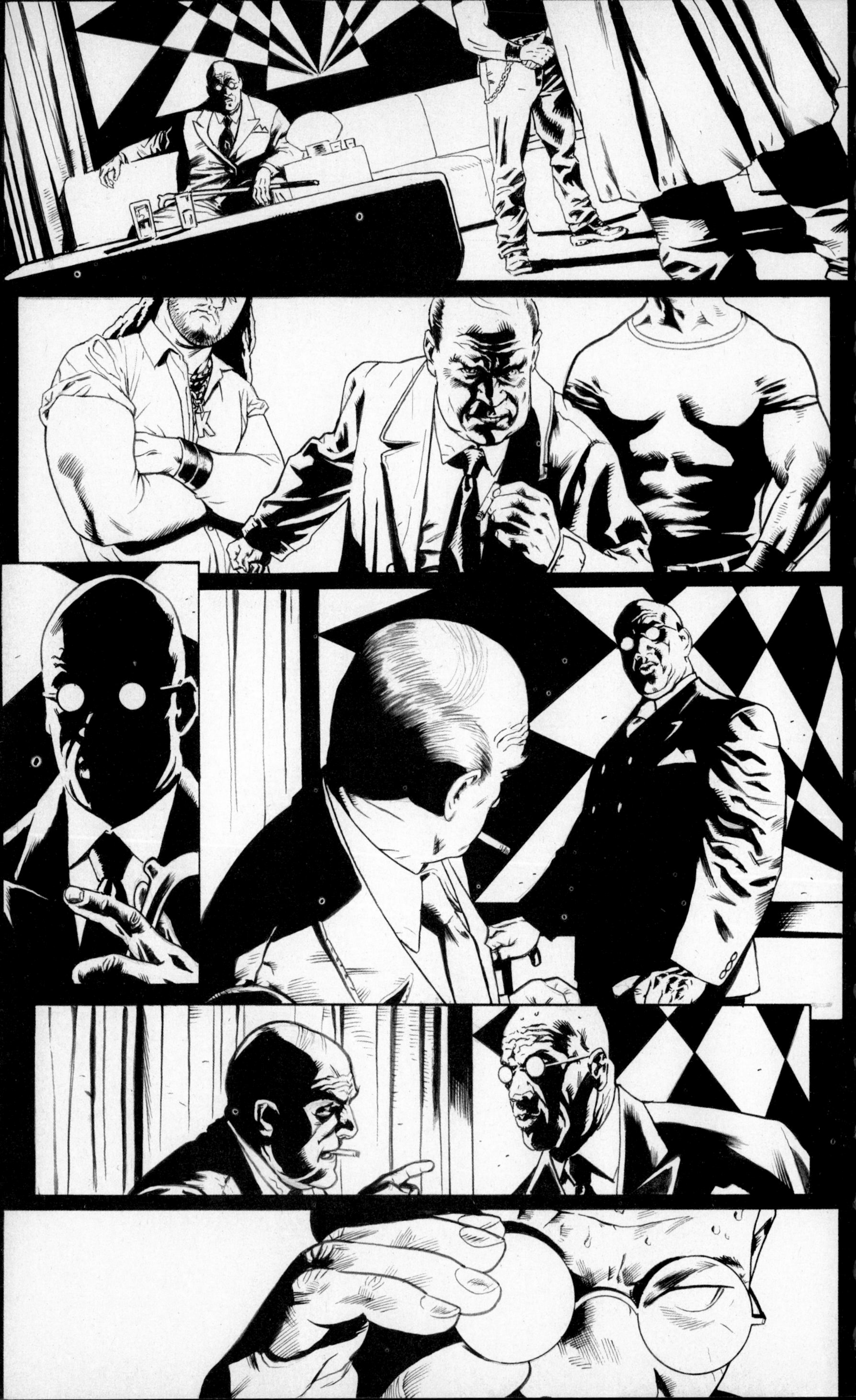

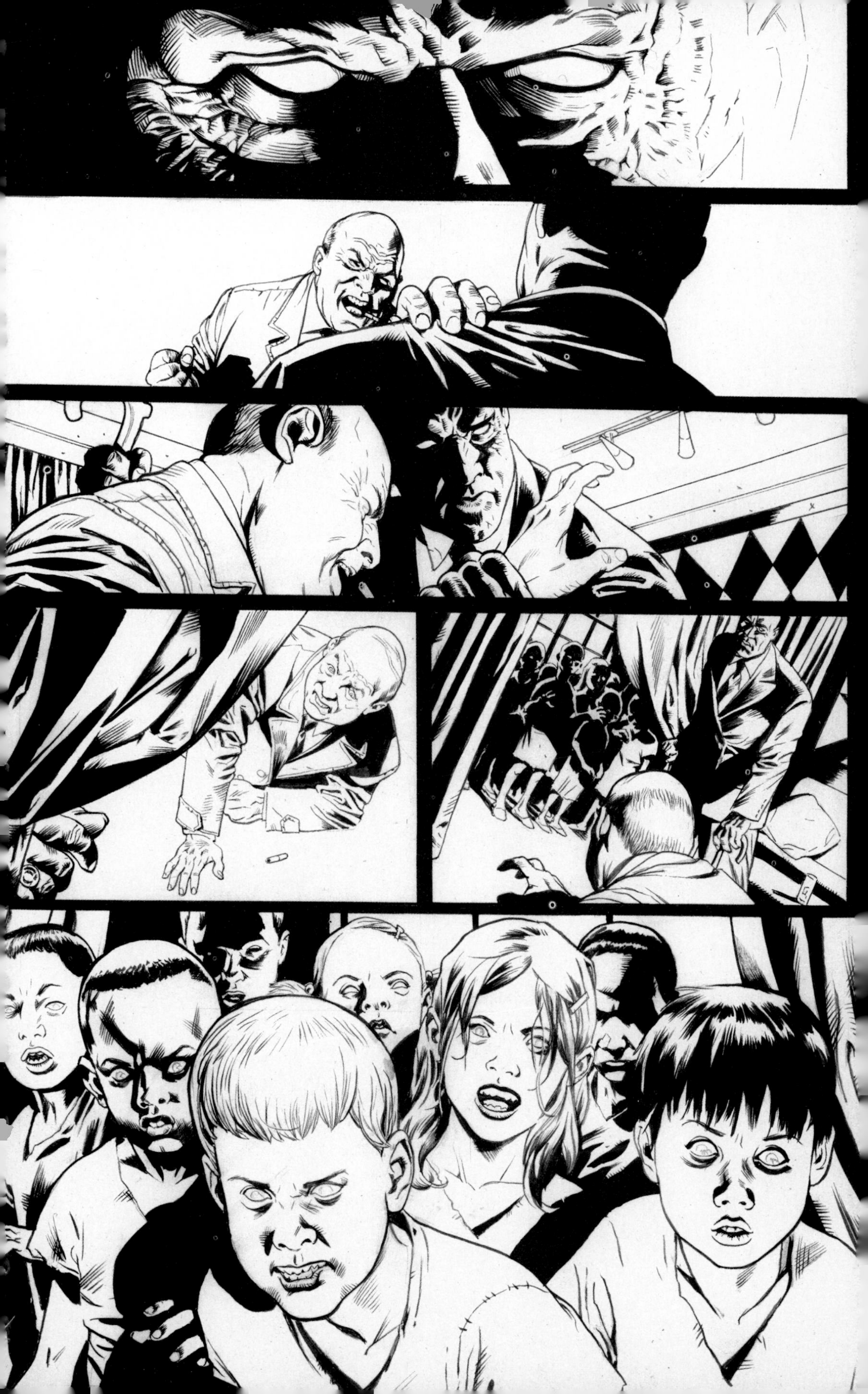

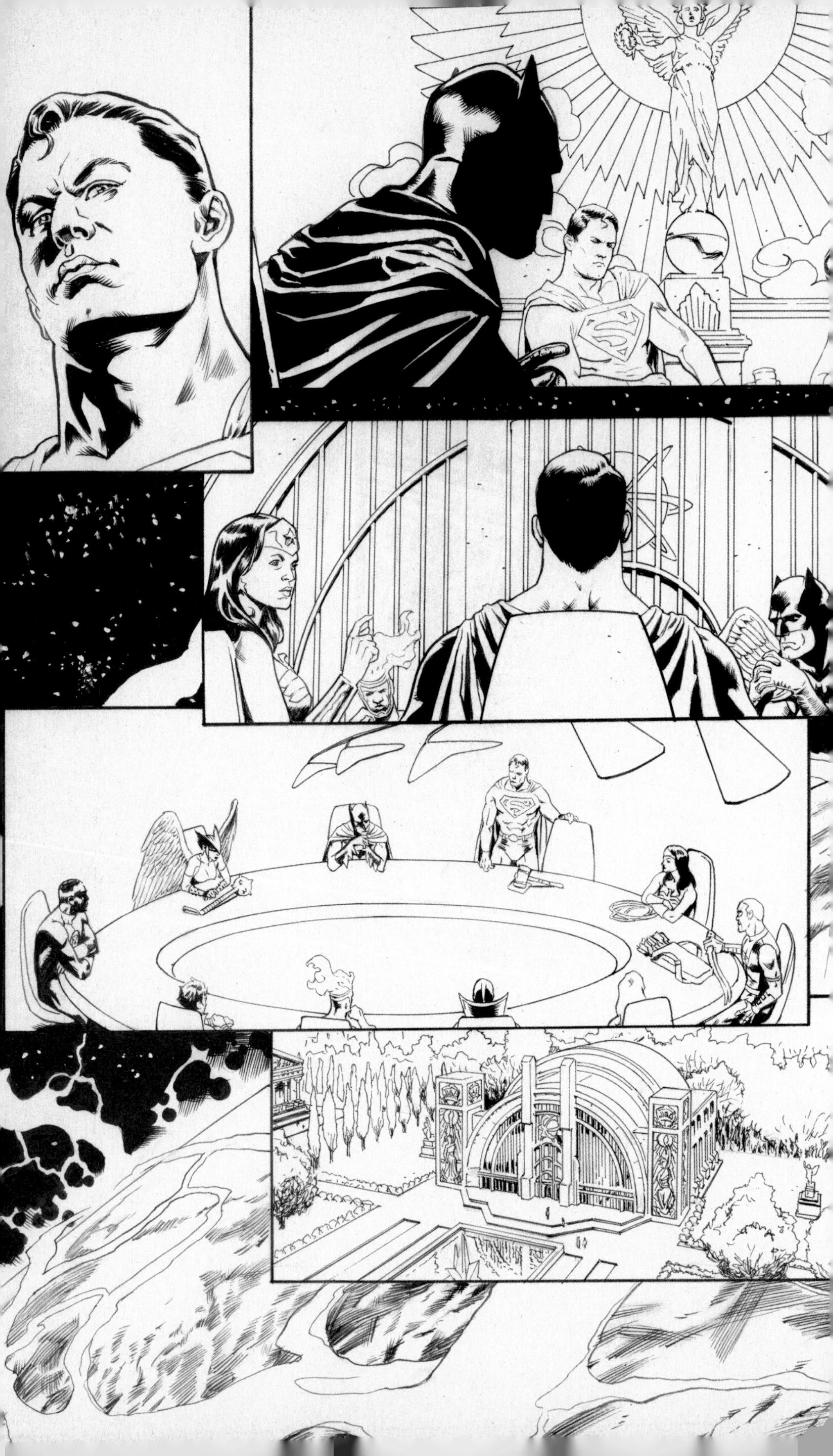

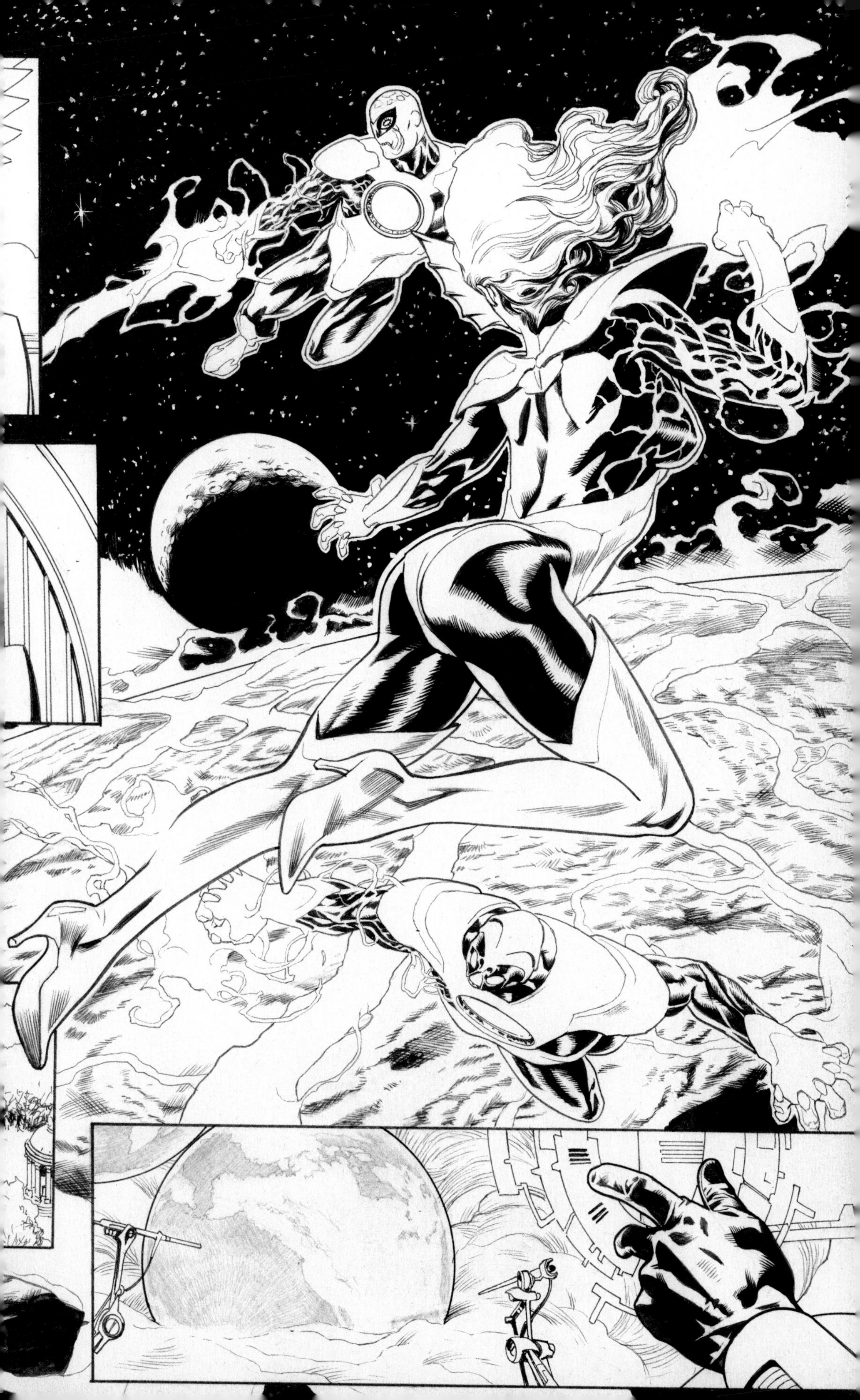

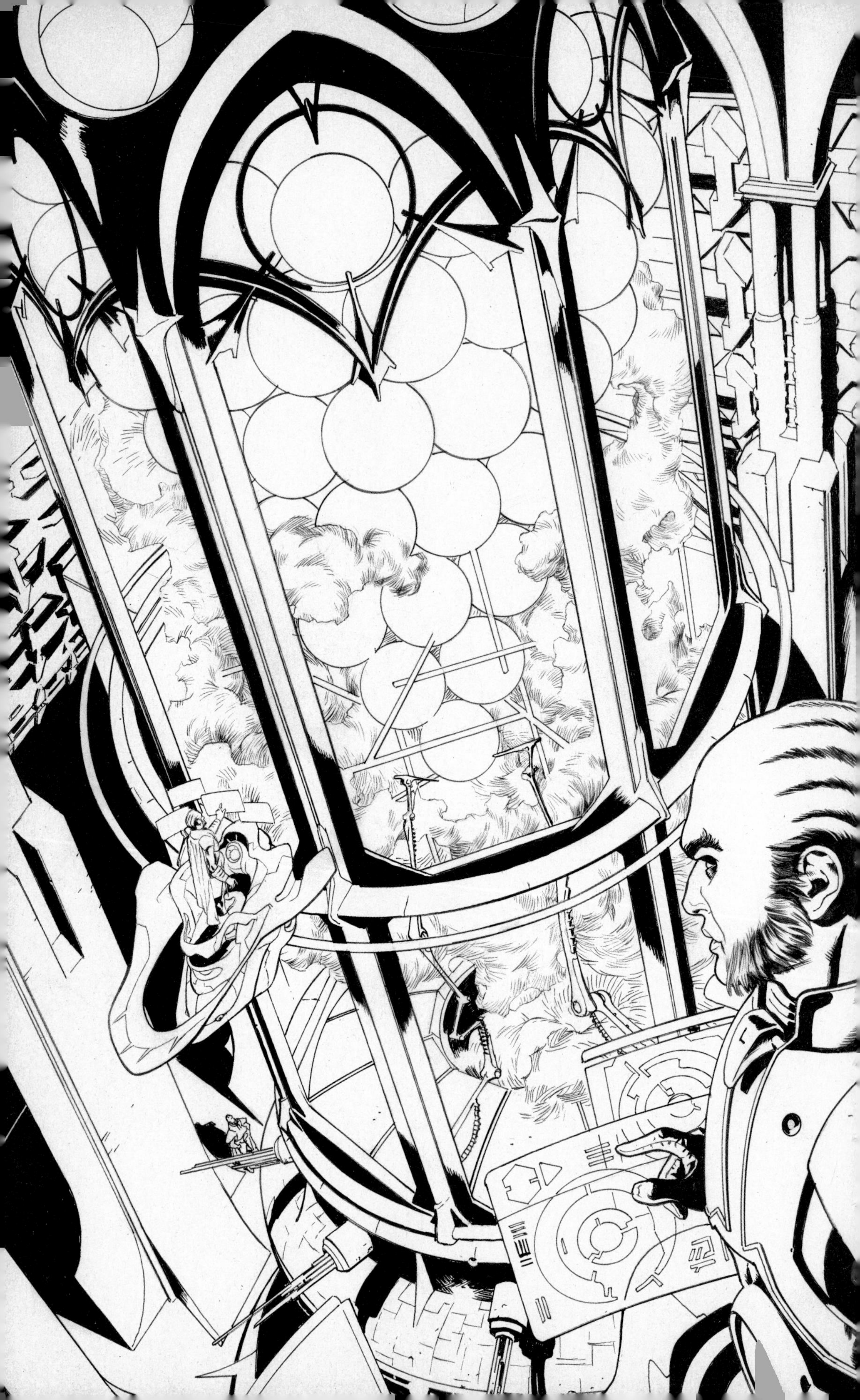

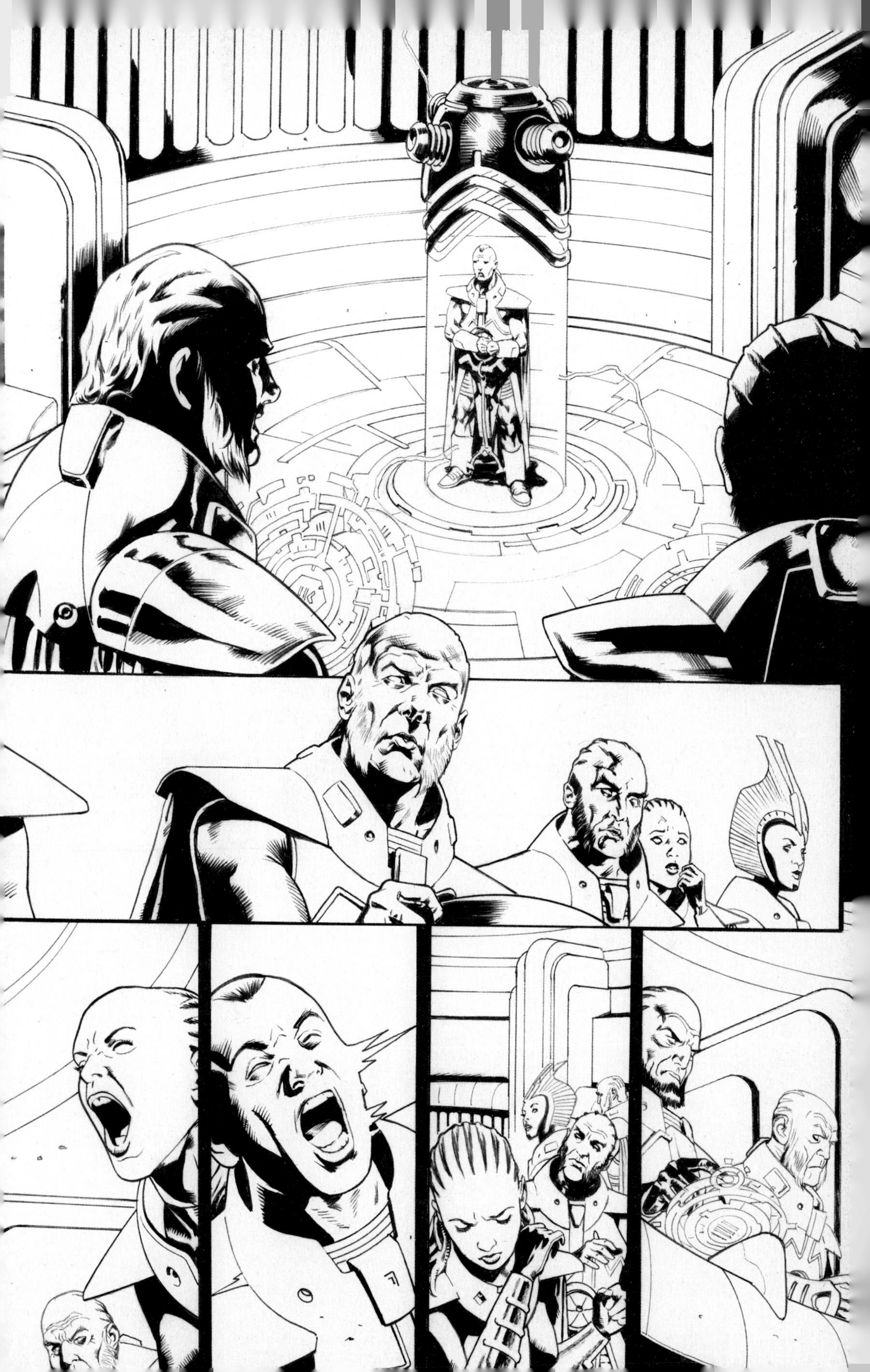

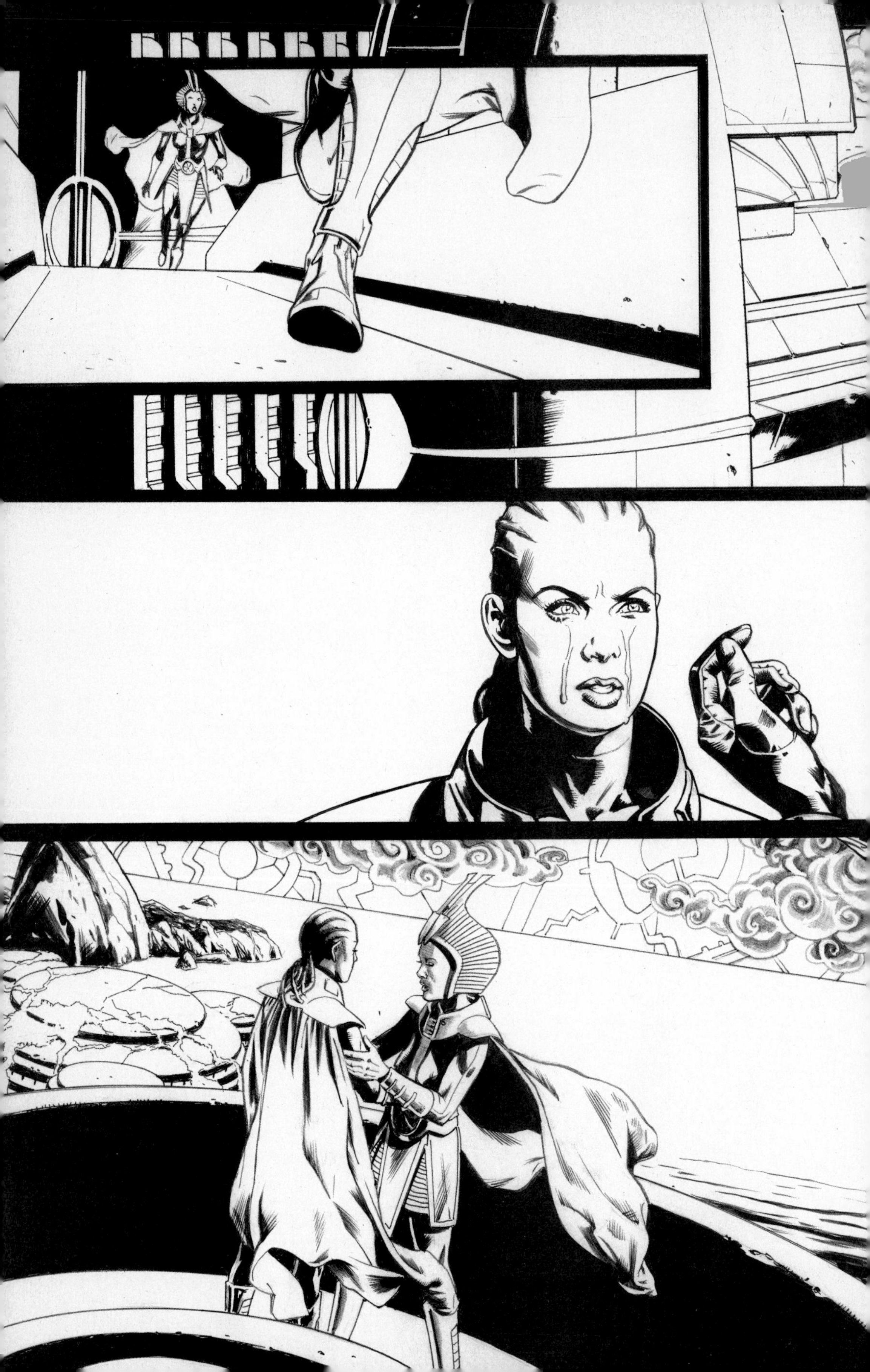

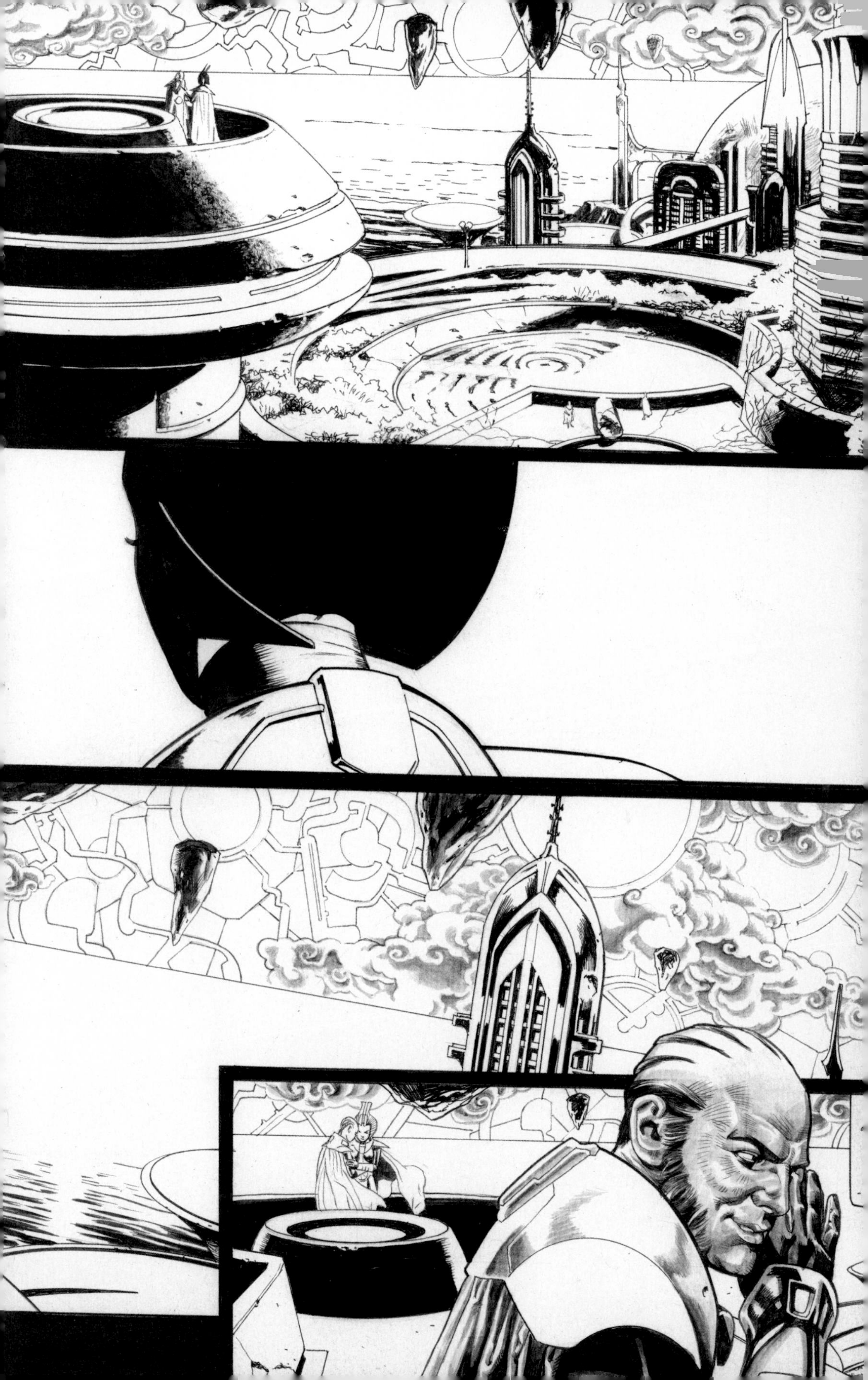

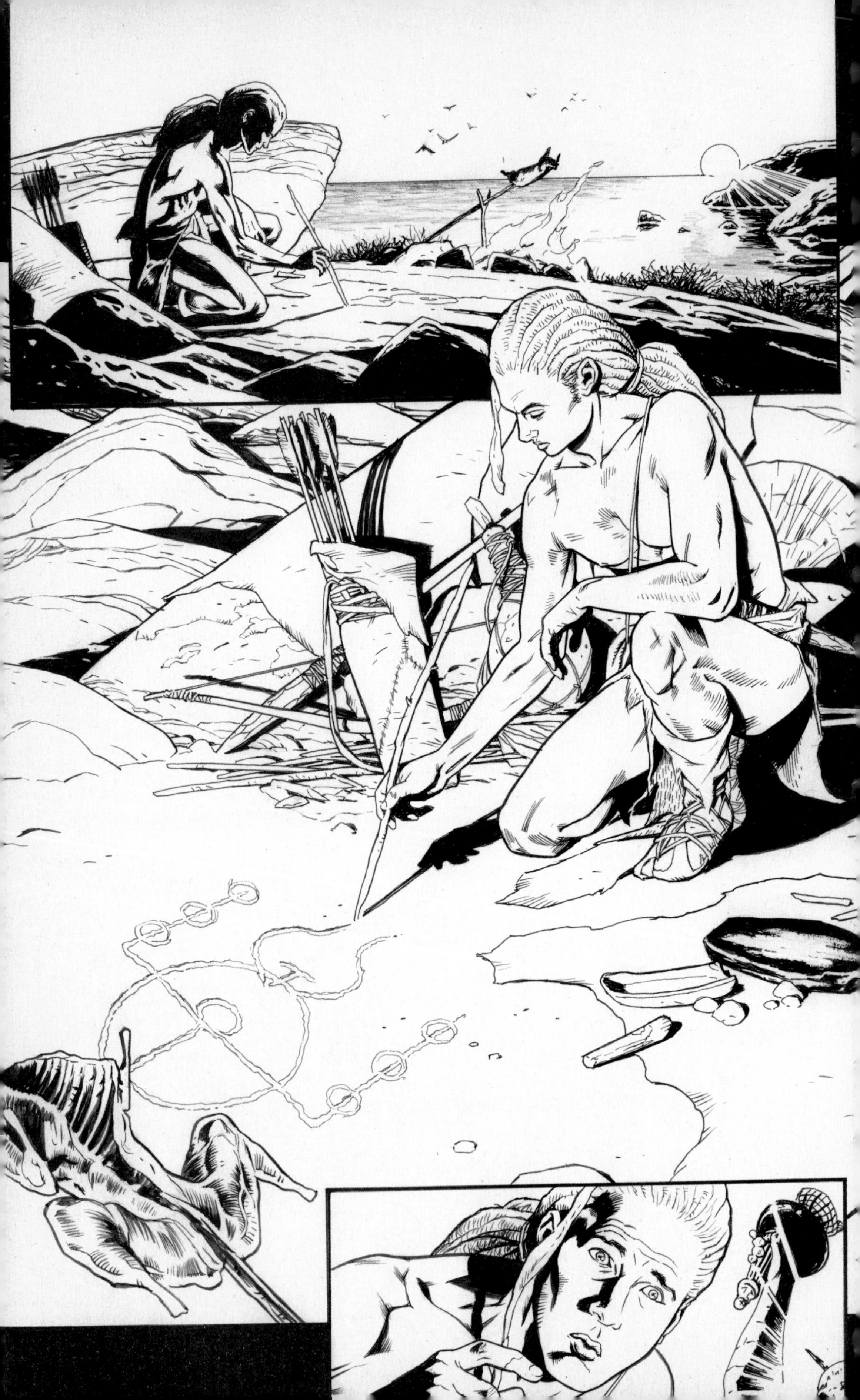

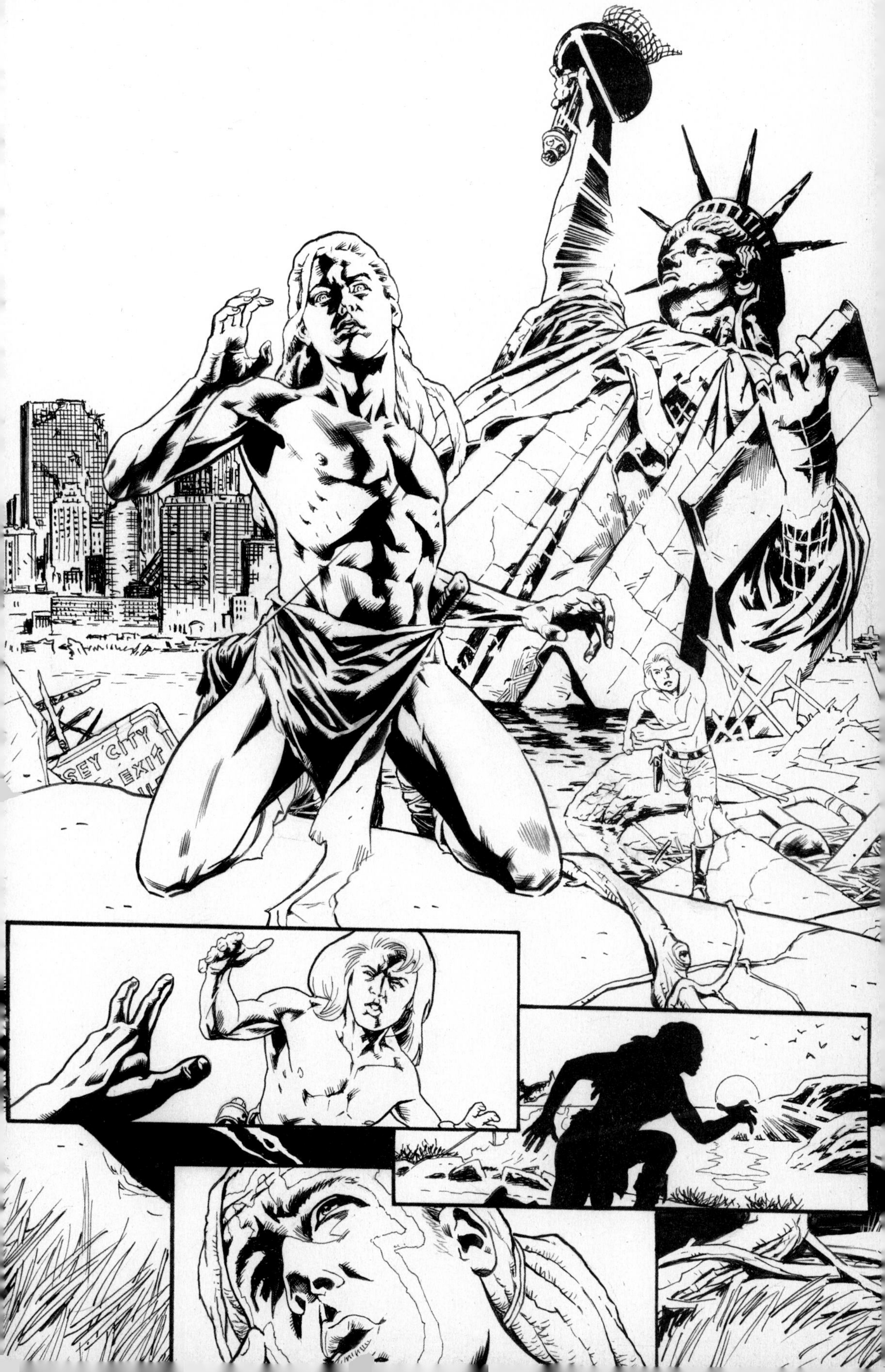
SEY CITY
EXIT

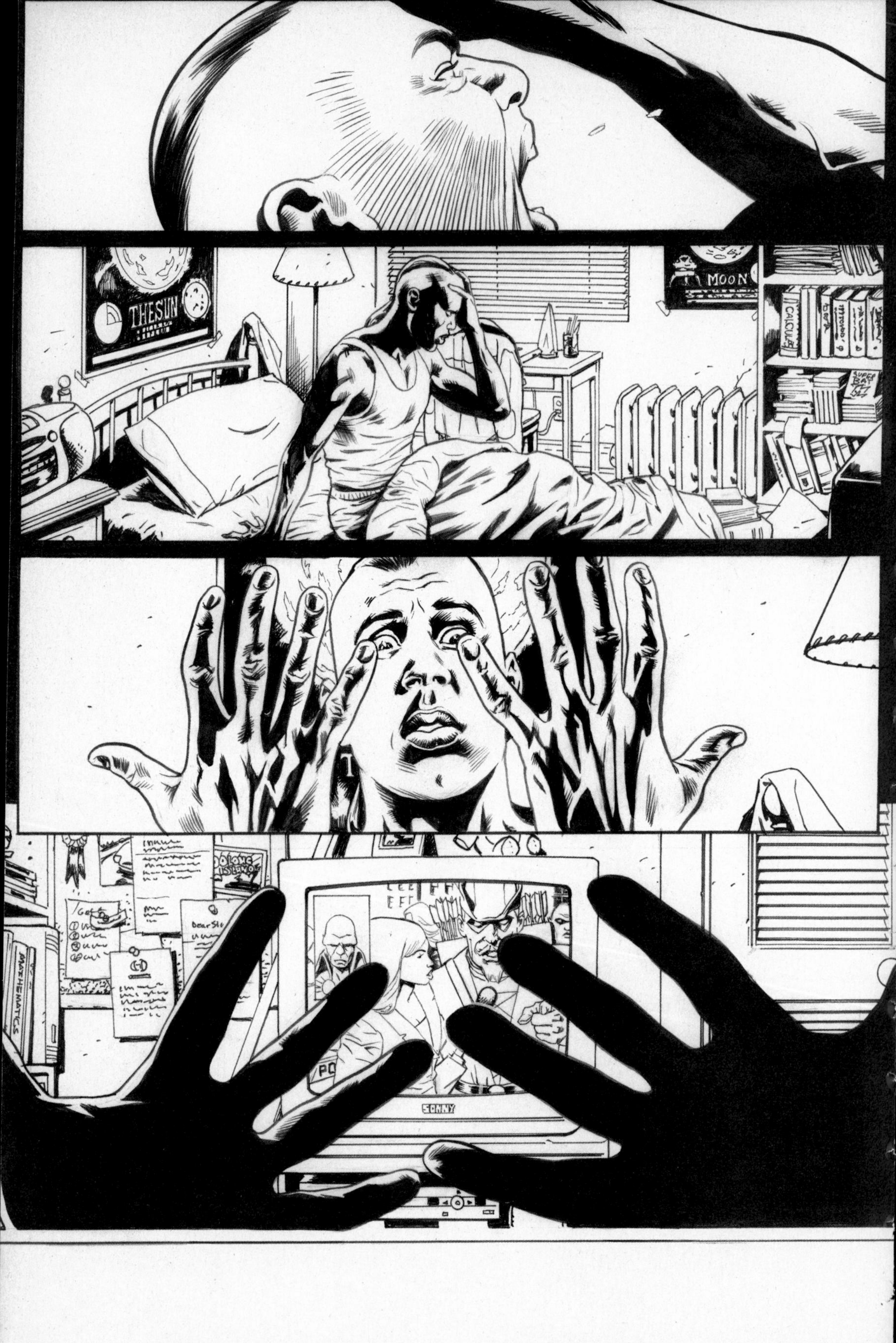
THE SUN
MOON
MATHEMATICS
SONNY

FINAL CRISIS

Title: FINAL CRISIS 1 -
Frame 1

D.O.A.: the god of war!

Full page. Bright sunlight on the veldt at the Dawn of Man. Here's DC's caveboy Anthro – shaggy brown hair, handsome, white and probably not much like any caveman who ever lived, but let's just deal with it and play with the idea of Anthro as the First Boy on Earth and Kamandi as the Last. A full figure shot of Anthro in the center of the page. Astonished, he stares past us at something off panel. Panicked animals run past him, heading away from us, as Anthro stands his ground, fighting his terror. He has his bound stone axe raised in both hands. This place we are in is where, 40,000 years from now, Manhattan will be.

1) BALLOON:

MAN.

PAGE 2/3
Frame 1

Double-page panoramic splash. Metron of the New Gods is here, hovering serenely in his Mobius Chair five feet above the grass. Everything else is normal - the sun shines, the landscape stretches into the vast horizon. There are a few bushes around. Anthro faces the god.

1) BALLOON:

I AM <u>METRON</u>.

PAGE 4
Frame 1

Anthro is afraid but does not back down. He holds his club in both hands like a baseball bat as he faces the uncanny hovering chair and its occupant.

Frame 2

Anthro cocks his head, curious, and slowly lowers his axe.

1) BALLOON:

HAVE NO FEAR.

Frame 4

Go in closer on Metron, concentrating on his eyes, and one finger which is raised to enter the shot – a flame burns there at the tip. His expression is that of a scientist studying a specimen.

2) BALLOON:

HERE IS KNOWLEDGE.

Frame 5

Long shot. Suddenly Metron is gone. The day is still. Anthro stands alone – with a burning bush.

PAGE 5
Frame 1

Cut to a full-page shot of Anthro's Cro-Magnon Bear Tribe fighting Vandal Savage's Neanderthal Wolf Tribe. It's much later now, just before twilight. Savage's men use brutal heavy clubs and jagged jawbones as weapons. The Cro-Magnons have axes. It is the end of the era of Neanderthals and we're seeing how it happened...

PAGE 6
Frame 1

Vandal slaughters the chief of the tribe — recognisable by his graying, maned magnificence and his necklace of shells and feathers.

1) VANDAL:

!

Frame 2

Vandal throws the broken body of the Chief aside as he heads into a fur and hide tent. Women and children cower before Vandal and his monstrous horde.

2) VANDAL:

!!

Frame 3

Vandal grins horribly as he closes in on the Chief's daughter – and Anthro's main squeeze. She picks up an axe and grips it in both hands to defend herself.

3) VANDAL:

!

Frame 4

Then Vandal is dragging the girl out of her tent by the hair. Her axe is stuck in the muscle and meat of his pectoral.

4) VANDAL:

(just a thick black scribble of primitive emotion)

5) GIRL:

!

Frame 5

As Vandal stands over the girl, his men are reacting to a sound from off panel. They turn to point, wild-eyed. The survivors of Anthro's tribe are suddenly filled with hope.

6) GIRL:

!

7) ANTHRO:

! *(from off, in a big jagged shout balloon)*

PAGE 7
Frame 1

Anthro appears on the brow of the hill. He has a blazing, burning brand in his hand.

1) CAVEMAN:

? *(the question mark very small in the center of the balloon to suggest a barely whispered utterance)*

Frame 2

Vandal's men snarl. Eyes widen as if they've seen a flying saucer land.

2) CAVEMAN:

!

3) CAVEMAN 2:

?

Frame 3

Anthro — his face lit by hot light – he sets the bushes alight.

Frame 4

Fear in Savage's eyes. His men back off shielding their faces from the light that springs up off panel. Something uncanny and unforeseen has come among them.

4) CAVEMAN:	**?**
5) VANDAL:	**?**
6) FLEEING CAVEMAN:	**?**

Frame 5
Move closer into the flickering, crackling flames as they sweep across the panel.

7) CAP.:
YOU ASK ME, FIRE WAS OUR <u>FIRST</u> BIG MISTAKE.

PAGE 8
Frame 1
Now cut to a close-up on a match lighting a cigarette.

1) CAP.:
LIKE EVERYTHIN' ELSE THE SAD, STINKIN' HUMAN RACE EVER THOUGHT OF...

2) CAP.:
WE TAKE A GOOD IDEA.

Frame 2
Here's Dan "Terrible" Turpin, ex of Metropolis Special Crimes Unit. Grimy modernity. Gritty street realism now. Turpin's getting on now but he's hard as nails, like a Frank Miller hero. He sucks down on the cigarette and flips the match away. Maybe this would be good down at the docks, Jeff? For some extra atmosphere, with the bridge in background? What do you think? We're in METROPOLIS.

3) CAP.:
AND WE USE IT TO <u>KILL</u> OURSELVES.

Frame 3
Overhead shot as he reaches down into the splintered remains of a big crate, to pull aside a debris of spilled boxes with toy guns and stuff bound from China to stores in the USA. Smoke rises from the disturbed pile.

4) CAP.:
HERE'S <u>ME</u>, WAY PAST RETIREMENT AND <u>THREE WEEKS</u> OUT ON THE TRAIL OF SIX MISSING KIDS.

5) CAP.:
BRIGHT KIDS, GIFTED KIDS WHO WENT OUT ONE DAY AND NEVER CAME <u>HOME</u>.

Frame 4
He finds stricken, dying Orion there in the wreckage. Orion's skin is burned. His body seems broken. The Mother Box is fused and blown out on his arm. His clothes torn.

6) CAP.:
LAST THING I EXPECTED WAS TO FIND ME A <u>SUPER MUK MUK</u> IN THE GARBAGE.

PAGE 9
Frame 1
Turpin jerks his finger back, trailing smoke. His fingertips are burned.

1) TURPIN:
<u>TZZAOW!</u>

Frame 2
Side shot. Suddenly Orion raises himself – spooky – like a dead man – face all shadows.

2) ORION:
<u>...HEAVEN...CRACKED AND BROKEN...</u>

3) ORION:
YOU! *(Orion's lettering is bigger and bolder than normal, as befits even a dying god)*

Frame 3
Looking over Turpin's head as Orion uses his last breath to snarl into his face, hauling himself up using Turpin's lapels which smoke at Orion's touch.

4) TURPIN:
GET YOUR HANDS OFFA ME!

5) ORION:
<u>THEY DID NOT DIE!</u>

6) ORION:
<u>HE IS IN YOU ALL...</u>

Frame 4
Orion falls back out of Turpin's grip, towards us, chin pointing at the sky. Turpin lets go looking up as the wind starts up. Things erupt all around...garbage explodes from bags. Something stands there – the Black Racer glimpsed in the tumult, he simply stands there, floating in the air in background.

7) ORION:
FIGHT.

8) ORION:
✕

PAGE 10
Frame 1
DETROIT. Sky goes dark - stuff blowing everywhere. Papers and fast food litter. Blood-red rain and black boiling clouds that tumble across the sky blotting out the sun.

Frame 2
Interior. An architect's office in Detroit. People are looking out of a big window lashed by rain. This is happening everywhere. While they're all looking out, John Stewart slips away.

1) WOMAN:
JOHN, YOU <u>HAVE</u> TO CHECK THIS OUT.

2) WOMAN:
THE WEATHER'S GONE <u>NUTS</u>!

3) JOHN STEWART:
HOLD ON A SECOND.

4) JOHN STEWART:
I HAVE A <u>MESSAGE</u> COMING IN.

Frame 3
John opens a door and ducks into a dark closet. His ring glows.

5) RING:
LANTERN JOHN STEWART 2814.2

6) RING:
<u>1011</u> IN PROGRESS.

7) RING:
<u>1011</u> IN PROGRESS

Frame 4
John Stewart aims his ring at himself, erasing his work clothes to reveal the Green Lantern uniform underneath.

8) JOHN STEWART:	1011?
9) JOHN STEWART:	WHAT THE HELL'S 1011?

PAGE 11

Frame 1

Turpin is backing away from the flying debris, out of the alley. The Black Racer is still there motionless at the center of the storm.

1) CAP.: BACK IN THE DAY WITH THE METROPOLIS SPECIAL CRIMES UNIT I LEARNED HOW TO STOP A SUPERHUMAN DEAD.

2) CAP.: BUT ME SEEING THIS...

3) CAP.: ME BEING HERE...

Frame 2

Incredible shot of John Stewart flashing through the stormy sky. Rain vaporises on his green force field.

Frame 3

Some weird homeless guy looks up past Turpin to where a faint green light grows from above.

4) CAP.: IT FEELS LIKE...SACRILEGE.

5) CAP.: LET THE SPACE COPS HANDLE THE FALLOUT.

6) CAP.: I'M GONE.

Frame 4

John Stewart lands. Lightning forks across the sky. Everything is all elemental fury, J.G.

7) JOHN STEWART: MY BACKUP ON THE WAY YET?

8) RING: LANTERN JORDAN 2814.1 HAS BEEN ALERTED.

9) RING: HIS RING IS NOT RESPONDING AT THIS TIME.

PAGE 12

Frame 1

Panoramic shot of the Bridge. Turpin walks towards us. Cars stopped, people get out and point at the sky. It's red. It's suspended over one of those huge Metropolis drops with a waterfall behind – everything is heightened, magnificent.

Frame 2

Follow Turpin across the bridge. Up ahead there's a woman with a stylish cut standing at the rail, looking over. She's tall and wears a long coat to hide her costume. Faceless. It's RENEE MONTOYA, the Question.

1) TURPIN: WE USED TO FIGHT IN THE ALLEYS.

2) TURPIN: GUYS THESE DAYS FIGHT IN THE CLOUDS.

3) QUESTION: PROGRESS?

Frame 3

Turpin joins THE QUESTION who doesn't turn her head to look at the detective yet – instead she faces the whipping winds as if enjoying them on her skin. She wears a pair of shades – and she has no face.

4) TURPIN: YOU TELL ME.

5) TURPIN: DIDN'T THE QUESTION USED TO BE A GUY?

6) QUESTION: LUNG CANCER.

7) QUESTION: FROM SMOKING.

PAGE 13

Frame 1

Question turns to look at Turpin.

1) TURPIN: LIGHTWEIGHT.

2) TURPIN: SORRY! I'M SORRY!

3) TURPIN: WHAT YOU GOT?

4) QUESTION: A QUESTION, YOU IGNORANT OLD @%#&$%

5) QUESTION: WHAT DID YOUR SIX HAVE IN COMMON, APART FROM BEING POOR AND SMART?

6) QUESTION: ANY EVIDENCE OF SUPERPOWER METAGENE ACTIVITY, FOR INSTANCE?

Frame 2

Long shot of the bridge. The red skies above. Stuff blowing past on the wind.

7) QUESTION: SOMEBODY'S BEEN TARGETING META KIDS.

8) QUESTION: I KEEP TURNING UP LINKS TO THIS PLACE.

9) QUESTION: BUT YOU BE CAREFUL IN THE SHADOWS, DANNY BOY.

Frame 3

The Question vanishes in a curl of question mark smoke that hovers quizzically in the air. Turpin looks at the card in his hand.

10) TURPIN: WHY ARE YOU HELPING ME ANYWAY?

11) TURPIN: HEY!

12) TURPIN: HEY!

Frame 7

The card in Turpin's hand – it reads DARK SIDE CLUB in Deco lettering.

Frame 8

Then Turpin looks up. He's alone on the bridge, hunched in the wind.

13) TURPIN: SUPER MUK MUKS.

PAGE 14
Frame 1

Long shot – a green plasma dome above the murder site. Film crews are watching from the helicopters which buzz around — WGBS and any others, etc. There's a distant green light coming down like a flare towards the dome as Hal Jordan arrives.

1) JOHN: WHAT <u>KEPT</u> YOU, FLYBOY?

2) JOHN: BLONDE OR REDHEAD?

Frame 2

Hal Jordan arrives, landing lightly beside John as John scans Orion's body with his ring. There's a Mister Miracle poster torn on the wall showing Shilo Norman as MISTER MIRACLE - the poster's in the style of a rap album cover with Shilo hanging upside down in a straitjacket.

3) HAL: DEEP AND DREAMLESS.

4) HAL: WHAT'S THE STORY, JOHN?

5) JOHN: COOLING RAPIDLY.

6) JOHN: YOU EVER HEAR ABOUT <u>1011</u>, HAL?

7) JOHN: APPARENTLY IT DOESN'T HAPPEN TOO OFTEN.

Frame 3

Hal crouches to examine the dead god. Fumes still rise from Orion's body as it cools. John is still standing. He looks down, as if noticing something strange about Hal.

8) HAL: 1011?

9) JOHN STEWART: <u>DEICIDE</u>?

10) JOHN STEWART: SOMEBODY JUST MURDERED A <u>GOD</u> ON OUR WATCH.

11) JOHN STEWART: TAKE A LOOK FOR YOURSELF.

12) JOHN STEWART: RECOGNIZE HIM ?

Frame 4

Hal turns to look back over his shoulder at us. Behind, we can see Orion. Hal has a small but noticeable scar which starts at the tip of his left eyebrow and cuts diagonally up across his temple. Part of the scar is hidden by his mask.

13) HAL: <u>ORION</u>!

14) HAL: THE <u>SOLDIER GOD</u> OF <u>NEW GENESIS.</u>

15) HAL: <u>A-NUMBER ONE</u>, COSMIC <u>HARD-ASS</u>.

16) JOHN: YUP.

Frame 5

Hal looks back over his shoulder at us.

17) HAL: I'LL REPORT TO THE <u>GUARDIANS ON OA</u>.

18) HAL: YOU ALERT THE <u>JUSTICE LEAGUE</u>.

PAGE 15
Frame 1

Cut to the Guardians of the Universe — an incredible shot of three of them standing together in a green-lit chamber with an incredible view of the center of the galaxy where there are thousands of suns, radiating an incredible brightness.

1) GUARDIAN: SEAL THE CRIME SCENE OUT TO THE PLANET'S LaGRANGE POINT.

2) GUARDIAN: NO ONE MUST ENTER OR LEAVE THE GRAVITY WELL.

3) GUARDIAN 2:   DUST FOR RADIATION PRINTS.

4) GUARDIAN: INTERROGATE <u>ALL</u> POTENTIAL SUSPECTS.

5) GUARDIAN 3:   1011 REQUIRES A <u>VAST</u> ENERGY EXPENDITURE.

6) GUARDIAN: LOCATE THE WEAPON.

Frame 2

Close on the Guardians as they confer telepathically without speaking.

7) GUARDIAN 2:   WE REPEAT: THIS IS A MATTER OF <u>UTMOST</u> CONCERN. LANTERN JORDAN 2814.1

8) GUARDIAN 3:   A <u>SPECIAL OPERATIONS ALPHA LANTERN UNIT</u> IS ON ITS WAY.

Frame 3

Hal and John stand in the rain in the dirty alley, looking somehow human and vulnerable in the face of the storm.

9) RING: PREPARE TO MAKE CONTACT.

10) JOHN: SPECIAL OPERATIONS?

11) JOHN: HAL...THESE <u>NEW</u> GODS.

12) JOHN: THEY COME WITH <u>BAD</u> GODS TOO.

PAGE 16
Frame 1

Cut to a municipal garbage dump on the outskirts of Metropolis. Steamy orange dawn of a new day. Metron's Mobius Chair is here, tilted and grimy, discarded in the junk. Old mirrors jutting out of the debris seem to surround the chair in a rough circle, pointing towards it.

1) EMPRESS: KEEP UP, <u>SPARX</u>!

2) EMPRESS: IT'S JUST OVER THIS RISE...

Frame 2

EMPRESS is running up the slope, pointing ahead excitedly. Behind her, crackling with electrical arcs, is the young hero SPARX. Sparx is looking back over his shoulder for his teammates. QUITE A FEW old mirrors in fact...

3) EMPRESS: YOU BELIEVE ME <u>NOW</u>?

4) EMPRESS: MY VISIONS <u>TOLD</u> ME WE'D FIND IT HERE.

5) SPARX: BUT IF IT'S LITERALLY FROM ANOTHER <u>WORLD</u>, ANOTHER <u>REALITY</u>...EMPRESS...

6) SPARX: I MEAN, THIS IS TOTALLY A <u>MAJOR LAUNCH</u> FOR T<u>HE LEAGUE OF TITANS</u>!

7) SPARX: *MAS Y MENOS?* <u>GO</u>, TITANS!..

Frame 3

Suddenly it's all going wrong. DOCTOR LIGHT rises up from behind the Mobius Chair and shoots light — TWO beams of light split from him and shoot in different angles. One beam strikes an old mirror sticking up on one side of the panel. The other beam strikes off of a mirror on a discarded dressing table. Both beams reflect back from the mirrors to blast EMPRESS and SPARX with deadly radiance. Their bodies turn white as if bleached by super-bright light.

8) SPARX: <u>GUHHH</u>!

9) DOCTOR LIGHT: <u>HA</u>!

10) DOCTOR LIGHT: THE <u>FIRST</u> INNOCENT VICTIMS OF THE BLINDINGLY OBVIOUS <u>DOCTOR LIGHT/ MIRROR MASTER</u> TEAM!

Frame 4

Looking pleased with himself, grinning his wicked, gap-toothed grin, MIRROR MASTER emerges from the smoking surface of the tall old mirror Doctor Light just shot at. Mirror Master throws out the limp, unconscious and smoldering body of MAS of MAS Y MENOS. Elsewhere in the picture we see a second Mirror Master emerging from another mirror, throwing MENOS to the ground. Both MAS Y MENOS have hundreds of small, jagged shards of glass embedded in their skin. Their costumes are torn. They look like they ran straight into a hail of glass. Which they did.

11) DOCTOR LIGHT: <u>GAD</u>! THEY'RE <u>ASKING</u> FOR IT IN THESE OUTFITS!

12) MIRROR MASTER: AYE, AWRIGHT. THERE'S A <u>TIME AN' THERE'S A PLACE</u>, KNOW?

13) MIRROR MASTER: WE'RE NOT A BAD <u>TEAM</u> BUT...

14) MIRROR MASTER: THIS WEE MISSION GOT US WELL AWAY FROM THE BIG RAMMY WI' THE <u>JUSTICE LEAGUE</u>, EH?

PAGE 17
Frame 1

Cut to a big pic of the JLA mopping up members of the Secret Society after what looks like a big battle which has clearly damaged cars and property vehicles melted to slag. most of the villains — KILLER MOTH, POISON IVY, THE CHEETAH, SIGNALMAN - are being rounded up by heroes including RED TORNADO, BLACK CANARY, RED ARROW, BLACK LIGHTING AND VIXEN — or taken away in ambulances. The cops are here, too, trying to make sense of the whole scene as CAPTAIN COLD and SIGNALMAN argue vehemently with HAWKGIRL. This is all taking place in METROPOLIS so it's with that distinctive skyline in background.

1) CAPTAIN COLD: <u>...YOU ATTACKED US WITH ZERO PROVOCATION, FASCIST!</u>

2) HAWKWOMAN: <u>THIRTY</u> SUPERVILLAINS MARCHING UP MAIN STREET IS ZERO PROVOCATION?

3) SIGNALMAN: THIS WAS A <u>PROTEST MARCH</u> AGAINST VIGILANTE BRUTALITY.

4) SIGNALMAN: AND <u>YOU'LL</u> BE HEARING FROM MY <u>LAWYER</u>!

5) BLACK CANARY: YOU <u>BELIEVE</u> THIS?

Frame 2

Cut back to Mirror Master and Doctor Light. Caught in the crisscrossing beams from the mirrors which have all been put in place and angled towards it, the Chair is lifting up off the ground and beginning to fade. Mirror Master checks one of the teleport mirrors and jerks his thumb in the direction of the Mobius Chair. Doctor Light is glancing at Mirror Master, shifty-eyed.

6) MIRROR MASTER: WHAT'S THIS PIECE A' JUNK FOR ANYWAY?

7) DOCTOR LIGHT: SOMETHING <u>LIBRA</u> WANTS.

8) DOCTOR LIGHT: LOOK HERE, <u>McCULLOCH</u>...I WAS JUST HAVING A WORD WITH THE <u>REVERSE-FLASH</u> AND <u>HE</u> SAID YOU WERE THE SORT OF MAN WHO MIGHT BE ABLE TO LAY YOUR HANDS ON CERTAIN...YOU KNOW...

9) DOCTOR LIGHT: <u>PHARMACEUTICAL</u> REQUISITES...

Frame 3

In foreground, Sparx raises his head. Little crackles run across his skin.
Mirror Master and Doctor Light chat in background as the Mobius Chair vanishes in the crisscrossing mirror rays. Mirror Master bends down to angle a mirror just right. He has a wry, world-weary expression. Doctor Light in background, is irritable, embarrassed and sweating, nervously looking off panel, like he's expecting someone to come and get him.

10) MIRROR MASTER: AYE. AYE. WHIT YEH WANTIN'?

11) MIRROR MASTER: I'VE GOT A WEE BITTIE <u>PERUVIAN FLAKE</u>'LL STRAIGHTEN OOT THE FIN ON YER HEID NAY BOTHER.

12) DOCTOR LIGHT: NO, <u>NO!</u>

13) DOCTOR LIGHT: DO I LOOK LIKE SOME <u>JUNKIE</u>?

14) DOCTOR LIGHT: I HAVE A DATE WITH <u>GIGANTA</u>, IF YOU <u>MUST</u> KNOW AND, WELL... <u>ARTHUR LIGHT</u> NEVER LIKES TO LET A LADY DOWN.

Frame 4

Light in foreground, head and shoulders. His eyes dart back. Behind him, Sparx is getting up on one elbow, crackling with electricity, as he weakly tries to mount a counterattack.

15) MIRROR MASTER: A DATE WI' <u>GIGANTA</u>!

16) MIRROR MASTER: THE <u>MONSTER WUMMIN</u>?

17) DOCTOR LIGHT: <u>ENOUGH</u>...OR I'M NEVER TEAMING UP WITH YOU <u>AGAIN</u>!

18) DOCTOR LIGHT: HOW ABOUT WE JUST DELIVER THE CHAIR TO <u>LIBRA</u> AND KEEP OUR PERSONAL LIVES <u>PERSONAL</u>!

19) DOCTOR LIGHT: WE'RE WORKING FOR <u>LIBRA</u> NOW AND WHAT LIBRA <u>WANTS</u>, LIBRA GETS.

Frame 5

Doctor Light's boot strikes down to mash poor Sparx's head, face first into the garbage in a burst of electrical energy.

20) DOCTOR LIGHT: REMEMBER?

PAGE 18
Frame 1

Cut to Secret Society temporary meeting place – Luthor and others around a table. Luthor sits back, arms crossed, unconvinced, with a "Show me the money" expression. Beside him is Vandal Savage and on his other side, TALIA. They look like the judges on American Idol. They're in a strip joint in Keystone City which used to be the Community Center building almost a decade ago. Here, an elite group of master villains is called to witness: LUTHOR, VANDAL SAVAGE, TALIA, OCEAN MASTER, GRODD.

1) LUTHOR: DO I HAVE TO OUTLINE THIS IN TEDIOUS DETAIL <u>ONE MORE TIME</u> BEFORE I WALK?

2) LUTHOR: YOU MAY HAVE DAZZLED THE <u>RANK AND FILE,</u> BUT THE <u>REST</u> OF US...

3) LUTHOR   DO WE LOOK LIKE THE SORT OF PEOPLE WHO'D BE INCLINED TO <u>FOLLOW</u> ORDERS?

Frame 2

Vandal Savage looks up off panel. We recognise him from the opening scenes – the savage Neanderthal bone structure, the hair and beard now trimmed neatly, almost prissily.

4) SAVAGE: LUTHOR'S RIGHT.

5) SAVAGE   YOU INVITE US TO SOME ABANDONED <u>THEATER</u> RIGHT IN THE HEART OF <u>FLASH TERRITORY</u> THEN EXPECT US TO HAND OVER THE REINS OF THE <u>SECRET SOCIETY</u>!

6) SAVAGE: WE ARE ORGANIZED SUPERCRIME <u>SPECIALISTS</u>...

Frame 3

Looking down over Libra's head. His scales in shot. Holds his arms apart.

7) LIBRA: I DON'T WANT TO TAKE YOUR <u>PLACE</u> AT ALL, PLEASE...

8) LIBRA   BUT PEOPLE <u>HAVE</u> BEEN WAITING <u>50,000</u> YEARS FOR <u>VANDAL SAVAGE</u> TO CRUSH CIVILIZATION BENEATH HIS BOOTHEEL.

9) LIBRA: EXCUSE ME IF I...<u>HEH</u>...STIFLE A <u>YAWN</u>.

Frame 4

Savage snarls and stands, hunched over the table, leaning on his fists. Libra is unfazed.

10) SAVAGE: <u>I AM NOT AVERSE TO THE TASTE OF HUMAN FLESH, SIR!</u>

11) LIBRA: SPOKEN LIKE A <u>TRUE</u> GENTLEMAN.

12) LIBRA: AND WHO SAYS I'M <u>HUMAN</u>, ANYWAY ?

13) LIBRA: STRIKES <u>ME</u> YOUR ENEMIES FIGHT AND WIN AGAIN AND AGAIN BECAUSE THEY <u>TRULY</u> BELIEVE THEIR ACTIONS ARE IN ACCORDANCE WITH A <u>HIGHER MORAL ORDER.</u>

Frame 4

Libra sits in the Mobius Chair — his posture is expansive, commanding. The man in the face-concealing blue hood is pleased with himself.

14) LIBRA: BUT WHAT HAPPENS IN A WORLD WHERE <u>GOOD</u> HAS <u>LOST</u> ITS PERPETUAL STRUGGLE AGAINST EVIL?

15) LIBRA:	GENTLEMEN, YOU CAN CALL ME <u>LIBRA</u>.
16) LIBRA:	I BALANCE THE <u>SCALES</u>. I EVEN THE ODDS.

PAGE 19
Frame 1

Libra close-up.

1) LIBRA: IN RETURN FOR YOUR <u>PARTICIPATION</u> IN MY GRAND EXPERIMENT THERE'S REALLY ONLY <u>ONE LITTLE THING</u> I CAN ABSOLUTELY <u>GUARANTEE</u> EACH AND EVERY ONE OF YOU...

Frame 2

Libra leans forward, drawing them into his web.

2) LIBRA: YOUR <u>HEART'S DESIRE</u>.

3) LIBRA: HOW DOES <u>THAT</u> SOUND?

Frame 3

Luthor sneers. Libra is sure of himself.

4) LUTHOR: <u>MY</u> "HEART'S DESIRE"?

5) LUTHOR: I DON'T IMAGINE <u>THAT</u> BEING WITHIN <u>YOUR</u> POWER TO DELIVER.

6) LIBRA: WHAT DO YOU WANT ME TO <u>SAY</u>, LUTHOR?

7) LIBRA: THE <u>HUMAN FLAME</u> HERE BELIEVED IN ME.

8) LIBRA: MIKE WANTED THE <u>MANHUNTER FROM MARS</u> DEAD JUST AS MUCH AS <u>YOU</u> DREAM OF DANCING ON <u>SUPERMAN'S</u> GRAVE.

Frame 4

Luthor gets to his feet, smug. Beside him, The HUMAN FLAME speaks up.

9) LUTHOR: YOU IMAGINE THIS <u>HALFWIT</u>, "MIKE," THIS <u>NONENTITY'S</u> HATE MATCHES MINE?

10) LUTHOR: YOU PRESUME I HAVE NO CREED?

11) LUTHOR: MY CREED IS <u>LUTHOR</u>.

12) FLAME: HEY! HEY! MR. LUTHOR...

13) FLAME: YOU DON'T UNDERSTAND!

14) FLAME: HE'S <u>SERIOUS</u>!

Frame 5

Libra and Luthor face one another. Luthor with coat slung over shoulders, arrogant and self-assured.

15) LIBRA: DON'T <u>LEAVE</u>. LUTHOR.

16) LIBRA: CAN'T WE MURDERERS, MADMEN, AND MASTERMINDS WORK IN <u>HARMONY</u> JUST THIS <u>ONCE</u>, TO ACHIEVE SOMETHING <u>NONE</u> OF US EVER HAVE BEFORE ?

17) LUTHOR: WHAT'S IN THIS FOR <u>YOU</u>?

Frame 6

Libra gets to his feet and takes his lance-like scales in his hands, as if testing the weight of a spear.

18) LIBRA: AN <u>END</u> TO THE AGE OF <u>SUPERHEROES</u>.

19) LIBRA: A FULL-ON, NO BULL$@!&, <u>TWILIGHT OF THE GODS</u>.

20) LIBRA: HOW DOES <u>THAT</u> SOUND?

PAGE 20
Frame 1

Out comes MANHUNTER FROM MARS dragged to his knees, looking up. Libra prepares to strike with the sharp end of his scales. The scales themselves have burst into dramatic blue flame, making the whole thing look like a spear with a blade at one end and wings of fire at the other.

1) DOCTOR LIGHT: HEH!

2) DOCTOR LIGHT: HE'S STILL GROGGY FROM THE <u>PYRO-TRANQUILISERS</u>.

3) LIBRA: KEEP HIM THAT WAY.

4) LIBRA: I'D HATE TO TAKE <u>THIS ONE</u> ON IN A <u>FAIR</u> FIGHT!

Frame 2

Luthor's eyes widen. Savage leans forward in his chair. Human Flame can't believe what he's seeing.

5) HUMAN FLAME: HOLY $@!#%

6) FLAME: CAN EVERYBODY <u>SEE</u> THIS?

7) FLAME: THIS, MY FRIENDS, IS WHAT HAPPENS TO ANYBODY WHO %@&S WITH THE <u>HUMAN FLAME</u>!

Frame 3

The kill shot.

8) MANHUNTER: M'YRI'AH!

PAGE 21
Frame 1

Cut to a TV screen showing the ruins of Blüdhaven, glowing eerily in the twilight.

1) TV: I CALL THIS A <u>*BONA FIDE*</u> AMERICAN DISASTER!

Frame 2

Then on comes the Reverend Godfrey - it's GLORIOUS GODFREY here as a charismatic black preacher. His name REVEREND G. GODFREY GOOD as we can see from the banner across the screen. He's in a typically militant mood. Behind him we see an Atomic Knights dog being prepared for its rider.

2) TV:

A DEAD CITY! A SUPPURATIN' WOUND ON THE FLANK OF AN IDLE NATION!

3) TV:

MY HEART EXTENDS TO EMBRACE ALL THOSE POOR CITIZENS OF BENIGHTED BLUDHAVEN.

4) TV:

ANOTHER YEAR ON, AND NOT ONE DAY CLOSER TO SALVATION.

Frame 3

Pull out again. Turpin is in a sleazy bar filled with small-time, lowlife superhoods - including the Tattooed Man (in fact, all of the various Tattooed Men are here. Let's discuss who might be appropriate to be propping up at the bar here — any proper scummy types you can think of will be welcome).

5) TV:

MAKE NO MISTAKE, THE MESSAGE RINGS CLEAR!

6) TV:

IF YOU'RE POOR, IF YOU'RE HOMELESS, THEN YOU CAN RASSLE THE MUTATIONS OUT OF YOUR OWN BACKYARD!

7) TATTOOED MAN:

YOU TURPIN?

Frame 4

Turpin leaves the bar with Tattooed Man and they cross the street.
We're in NEW YORK now - as established in SEVEN SOLDIERS.

8) TATTOOED MAN:

SO.

9) TATTOOED MAN:

YOU KNOW MUCH ABOUT WHAT GOES ON AT THE DARK SIDE CLUB, BUD ?

10) TURPIN:

I AIN'T YOUR "BUD" AND IF YOU CALL ME THAT ONE MORE TIME YOU'LL BE CHOWING DOWN ON YOUR OWN LAST, BEST HOPE OF FATHERING AN HEIR TO THE TATTOOED MAN FORTUNE.

11) TURPIN:

LEMME GUESS: IT'S SOMETHIN' SAD AND STUPID WITH WHIPS AND LEATHER.

Frame 5

Establishing shot of the Dark Side Club in this weird, run-down part of town – bizarre people hang around, and there's a seedy atmosphere. Tattooed Man stops in the street with his tattoos coiling around him, floating off his skin and back onto it. Turpin at the steel door of the club glances back. There's only a tiny discreet little sign to identify the place. All of the windows have bars.

12) TATTOOED MAN:

>tt<

13) TATTOOED MAN:

YOU'LL SEE.

PAGE 22
Frame 1

Boss Dark Side, sweating, leaning on a stick. His head and shoulders are in shadow. Just two little bright dots where his eyes are.

1) DARK SIDE:

....AHHH, THERE YOU ARE. COME IN, SIT DOWN.

2) DARK SIDE:

TELL ME, MISTER TURPIN. >KAFF<

3) DARK SIDE:

HAVE WE MET?

Frame 2

Turpin, stocky and tough, fixes on Dark Side off panel. Darkseid's men behind (see MISTER MIRACLE issue 3 for KALIBAK and KANTO). While keeping his gimlet eye on his man, he takes the cigarette butt from his mouth.

4) TURPIN:

CALL THE GOONS OFF.

5) TURPIN:

I'M AN OLD MAN.

6) TURPIN:

THESE BOYS WOULD HATE TO HAVE THEIR ASSES HANDED TO 'EM BY AN OLD MAN.

Frame 3

Dark Side lifts a hand. Film-noirish light. Shadow across his face so that just the little pinpoints of eyes show. The single anglepoise lamp on his desk floods the room with shadow.

7) DARK SIDE:

KALIBAK.

8) DARK SIDE:

KANTO.

9) DARK SIDE:

OUTSIDE.

Frame 4

Dark Side and Turpin confront one another. Dark Side leaning heavily on sticks comes into the light now. He's much older looking than he was at the end of SEVEN SOLDIERS.

10) TURPIN:

BOSS "DARK SIDE," HUH?

11) TURPIN:

GUESS I EXPECTED SOMEBODY YOUNGER.

12) DARK SIDE:

BODIES – KURRF - THEY WEAR OUT HARD IN HERE.

13) DARK SIDE:

AND ME, I WAS HURT IN A FALL, YOU MIGHT SAY.

14) DARK SIDE:

BUT IT'S WHAT WE ENDURE THAT MAKES US STRONG, DON'T YOU THINK ?

Frame 5

Closer on the two as Turpin refuses to back down from Boss Dark Side's intimidating, unholy presence. His suit makes him seem to blend into the blackness of the shadows as he cuts Turpin short with his own curt reply.

15) TURPIN: MY FATHER USED TO SAY THE SAME THING.

16) TURPIN: SO YOU WANNA TELL ME HOW COME MY MISSING KIDS TRAIL LEADS RIGHT TO <u>YOU</u>?

17) DARK SIDE: HOW COULD IT <u>NOT</u>?

18) DARK SIDE: AS FOR THE CHILDREN...

19) DARK SIDE: I GAVE <u>THEM</u> TO <u>GRANNY</u>.

Frame 6

Dark Side's awful face, emotionless, tilted back so that he gazes down his nose at us and begins to remove his little shades. His is a hatred without emotion, a cold, utterly inhuman and destructive thing. Nothing is real in his world but Darkseid. He would feel perfect if it weren't for the whole universe hating him, so he obviously has to bring the universe into line with his viewpoint or he'll never feel comfortable. Darkseid has no experience of love, tenderness, sorrow. He is monstrously, sociopathically at odds with all free, living things. Everything that is not Darkseid is a thorn in his side and must be converted. Only when the whole universe is an expression of Darkseid's will can it ever feel comfortable to him. He does terrible things because...he MUST.

20) DARK SIDE: HUMANITY'S BEST <u>HOPE</u> FOR THE FUTURE.

21) DARK SIDE: ITS <u>YOUNG</u>.

22) DARK SIDE: ITS <u>LIFE FORCE</u>.

23) DARK SIDE: AHHH.

PAGE 23
Frame 1

The glasses are off. Go closer until it's unbearable to look at this man's eyes anymore. There is nothing there. A flat, onionskin-colored void.

1) DARK SIDE: THERE WAS A <u>WAR</u> IN HEAVEN, MISTER TURPIN, AND I <u>WON</u>.

2) DARK SIDE: YOUR <u>FUTURE</u> BELONGS TO <u>DARK SIDE</u> NOW.

Frame 2

Turpin frowns. His hackles are rising as he grips Dark Side's lapels.

3) TURPIN: <u>WHAT DID YOU DO TO THOSE KIDS, YOU SICK BASTARD!</u>

4) DARK SIDE: <u>REMOVE YOUR HAND.</u>

Frame 3

Dark Side removes Turpin's hands with a shockingly powerful grip.

5) TURPIN: <u>GHHNN!</u>

6) DARK SIDE: WE TAUGHT THEM HOW TO SAY THE <u>EQUATION</u>.

7) DARK SIDE: HOW TO BE STUNTED, MALFORMED <u>SLAVES</u>.

8) DARK SIDE COME <u>CLOSER</u>, TURPIN.

Frame 4

Turpin, eyes wide, looks over Dark Side's shoulders.

9) DARK SIDE: I <u>CAN</u> USE YOU.

10) DARK SIDE: THERE.

11) DARK SIDE: IT'S BEST THAT YOU SEE THE FACE OF THE <u>NEW MODEL HUMAN</u> FROM YOUR KNEES.

12) TURPIN: NO.

Frame 5

Turpin POV. Eyes come out of the darkness behind Dark Side, figures emerging from the dense shadows that seem deeper than they should be.

13) DARK SIDE: THEY ARE <u>BEYOND</u> SALVATION.

14) DARK SIDE: CHILDREN...

Frame 6

Close on the horrible dead eyes, with heavy shadows underneath and sagging bags making the children's faces monstrous. Sharp little teeth show between lips as the children of Darkseid come forth.

15) DARK SIDE: SHOW HIM WHAT YOU'VE LEARNED ABOUT <u>ANTI-LIFE</u>.

PAGE 24/25
Frame 1

Superman stands at the Justice League meeting table. He's grave in dramatic lighting. A hushed emergency meeting.

1) SUPERMAN: AS <u>GREEN LANTERN</u> JUST EXPLAINED <u>GUARDIAN</u> ARCHIVES DESCRIBE <u>ORION</u> AND HIS PEOPLE AS "<u>NEW GODS</u>," WHICH OUGHT TO GIVE YOU <u>SOME</u> INDICATION OF THE <u>POWER LEVELS</u> WE'RE DEALING WITH.

Frame 2

Superman sits down again. Batman is at his left side.

2) BATMAN: EVIL GODS, EVIL PEOPLE.

3) BATMAN: DIFFERENT UNIVERSES, SAME DUMB.

4) BATMAN: I'VE PREPARED A DETAILED DOSSIER FOR THOSE OF YOU WHO HAVEN'T ENCOUNTERED THESE BEINGS BEFORE.

5) SUPERMAN:

UNFORTUNATELY, ORION'S MURDER SEEMS TO CONFIRM SOME OF OUR FEARS.

6) SUPERMAN:

INCIDENCES OF CONTACT WITH THE GODS OF NEW GENESIS AND APOKOLIPS HAVE BEEN ON THE INCREASE.

Frame 3

Pull back again. Superman, Batman and Wonder Woman too, on Superman's right side. Mythic.

7) WONDER WOMAN:

IF THE EVIL GODS ARE ANYWHERE ON EARTH, IT'S IMPERATIVE THAT WE FIND THEM BEFORE THEY STRIKE.

8) BATMAN:

AGREED.

9) SUPERMAN:

THESE ARE CELESTIALS CAPABLE OF CRACKING THE PLANET IN HALF AND ENSLAVING BILLIONS.

Frame 4

Pull back to see the whole group at the table. Green Lantern is there.

10) SUPERMAN:

JUSTICE LEAGUE CONDITION AMBER.

Frame 5

Pull back right out of the door and across the plaza for a cool exterior of the Hall of Justice. In foreground, Sparx, Empress and *Mas y Menos* page limp into view heading for the Hall..

Frame 6

Pull back again, on an infinite zooming recede as we go right out of the atmosphere and into Earth orbit, looking at the horizon of the planet spread out across the breadth of the whole panel. The entire Earth is being sealed with crisscrossing bands of green energy. In foreground, as if they're coming in from all sides of the panel and we're in among them, comes a group of four uber-Green Lanterns – the Alpha Lanterns have the same kind of relationship to the regular Corps that the FBI have to normal policemen. They're the super-elite, the upgraded version – with hearts replaced by power batteries and implanted rings on each hand. Led by the female Alpha Lantern KRAKEN, this team of shiny fetish-Lanterns moves toward the widescreen horizon of planet Earth.

11) CAP.:

ALPHA LANTERN GREEN MAN.

12) CAP.:

ALPHA LANTERN BOODIKKA.

13) CAP.:

ALPHA LANTERN VARIX.

14) CAP.:

SECURE THE CRIME SCENE!

Frame 7

Pull back further. We can see the whole Earth – its top hemisphere is rising out of some mercury-like liquid which ripples as the pincers of strange machines – like laser pointers mounted on insectile articulated limbs (which hang from a sci-fi rig above the Multiverse Machine cooling in its Well). The laser pointers are all arranged to fire at various hotspots on the top hemisphere of the Earth. In foreground, there's a HAND on a rail.

15) MONITOR HERMUZ:

THERE.

16) HERMUZ:

NEW EARTH.

17) HERMUZ:

THE FOUNDATION STONE OF ALL EXISTENCE.

PAGE 26

Frame 1

Cut to a spectacular Monitor world shot. Looking down – MONITOR ZIP HERMUZ (whose hand it was) stands on a platform operating buttons and levers on the rig, withdrawing the laser feelers in an elegant clench of machine limbs. Hermuz looks down into the Multiverse Machine. Imagine a huge, industrial chimney-sized tube, open at the top and with huge rounded cathedral windows down the sides so that we get a glimpse into the glowing, mysterious working of the Multiverse. Below the rig and Hermuz's jutting operator's platform (of which there are several arranged around the rig on all sides of the PIT) the open top of the tube reveals a circular surface of mercurial silver liquid with the upper hemisphere of New Earth sticking up. We can now see there are various other Earths, little floating Earths of various sizes arranged in meaningful patterns around the central hub of New Earth. There are as many as you fancy, in a fractal crown around the partially submerged New Earth. But more of this perfectly arranged structure of Earths can be seen through the blue glass of the cathedral-style windows which allow us to peek into the uncanny depths of the machine.

In foreground, we're looking down the head and shoulders of a second Monitor – ROX OGAMA by name.

1) HERMUZ:

NEW EARTH IS SECURE.

2) HERMUZ:

THE BLEED DRAINS ARE INTACT.

3) HERMUZ:

THE MULTIVERSAL ORRERY HAS SURVIVED REPAIR AFTER THE LOSS OF MOVING PART: UNIVERSE 51.

4) OGAMA:

AND YOUNG UOTAN...

5) OGAMA:

I HEAR HE IS TO FACE ABSOLUTE SANCTION FOR HIS FAILURE.

6) OGAMA:

WHEN DID WE BECOME SO SEVERE?

Cut to NIX UOTAN – a young Monitor, the youngest in fact. He's in the center of a circular floor, inside a big kind of tube like a teleport tube in glass and chrome Deco - Yellow Submarine/Peter Max hybrid style. He's shackled inside as the light seems to grow more intense. Steam pours out of valves or funnels on the side. He's surrounded by a court of Monitors in judgment. His girl, WEEJA DELL, watches, appalled. And at his lectern of judgment stands the eldest of the group -- MONITOR TAHOTEH.

1) MONITOR TAHOTEH: MULTIVERSAL MONITOR NIX UOTAN.

2) TAHOTEH: THERE IS ONLY ONE PENALTY FOR A MONITOR WHOSE NEGLECT ENDANGERS THE ORRERY OF WORLDS.

3) UOTAN: I ARRIVED TOO LATE TO SAVE EARTH 51.

4) UOTAN: THERE WAS SABOTAGE, I SWEAR.

Frame 2

Monitor Tahoteh is grave. At his side on the Council Ogama tries to intercede on the boy's behalf.

5) TAHOTEH: THE SENTENCE IS EXILE.

6) TAHOTEH: YOU WILL BE STRIPPED OF YOUR DUTIES, YOUR POWERS AND YOUR WORD OF ATTENTION.

7) TAHOTEH: YOU WILL LIVE OUT YOUR DAYS AS A HUMBLE, MORTAL GERM...AND DIE TO FEED THE ORRERY.

8) OGAMA: BUT CONSIDER HIS YOUTH, PRIME MONITOR TAHOTEH!

Frame 3

Uotan's lover WEEJA DELL is reacting badly. Tahoteh extends his arm for judgment.

9) WEEJA: NO!

10) WEEJA: IT'S NOT HIS FAULT!

11) TAHOTEH: SILENCE!

12) TAHOTEH: WE ARE MULTIVERSAL MONITORS, ANCIENT AND WISE!

Frame 4

Nix reaches out to her. Something is already beginning to happen to him.

13) NIX: I'LL FIND A WAY BACK TO YOU, WEEJA DELL!

14) NIX: I PROMISE I'LL FIND A WAY BACKKKKKkkkk

Frame 5

She covers her face. Ogama is impassive behind her.

15) WEEJA DELL: I CAN'T WATCH THIS!

16) OGAMA: FORGIVE ME, WEEJA DELL.

17) OGAMA: I TRIED TO SPEAK IN HIS DEFENSE.

Frame 6

Hermuz lit from below closes his eyes. Sets his dials.

18) TAHOTEH: JUSTICE IS DONE.

19) TAHOTEH: MAY THE ORRERY ENDURE.

20) HERMUZ: AS IT WAS EVER DONE, SO SHALL IT BE DONE AGAIN!

Cut to Weeja and ZILLO VALLA another, older female Monitor, coming out of the courtroom onto a wide terrace. It's a kind of "THINGS TO COME" architecture, Jeff. A monumental sci-fi retro Deco style. Combining the wide spaces of Greek architecture with a Pulp-y Planet Krypton vibe. To add to the solemn, heavy grandeur, most of the vast city that hugs the rocky coastline and fills the background to the horizon, is in runs. Only the nearer parts of the city are still intact and lit. The broad plazas and stairs have cracked. Alien weeds force their way up through the fissures. The fountains are dry and broken. The atmosphere is mournful and melancholy. The last gasp of an ancient civilization. Zillo Valla catches up to the distraught Weeja Dell, taking her arm.

1) ZILLO VALLA: WEEJA DELL, WAIT!

2) WEEJA DELL: WHY?

Frame 2

Long shot of the women at the sweeping ramparts high above the sullen sea. Heavy gloomy atmosphere of an ancient society at last gasp. Vast floating mountains over the horizon, like broken, fragmented Rock of Eternity pieces in a surrealist sky. These floating massifs are glimpsed through the fine soot which falls, grainy, across the red sky. More broken columns and cracked marble floors with weeds growing up through them. Like the Getty Center falling helplessly into ruin with no one left to maintain its overgrown gardens or pick up its fallen statuary.

3) WEEJA DELL: HE TRIED TO SAVE THE ORRERY, NOT TO HARM IT!

4) WEEJA DELL: WHY THIS?

5) WEEJA DELL:	WHY DO I CARE?
6) ZILLO VALLA:	WEEJA DELL, BEHOLD: WE MONITORS, WHO WERE FACELESS ONCE...
7) ZILLO VALLA:	WE ALL NOW HAVE NAMES AND STORIES.
8) ZILLO VALLA:	THERE ARE HEROES AND VILLAINS...SECRETS AND LOVERS.
Frame 3	They look out across the terraces...Zillo Valla holds Weeja. Under the dreadful broken sky.
9) WEEJA DELL:	IT'S TRUE...I... NEVER FELT ANYTHING BEFORE!
10) WEEJA DELL:	NOW I... I'M...CRYING...
11) WEEJA DELL:	ZILLO VALLA?
12) ZILLO VALLA:	OGAMA FEARS WE HAVE BECOME CONTAMINATED DURING CONTACT WITH THE OBSCURE LIFEFORMS THAT GROW WITHIN THE WORKINGS OF THE ORRERY.
13) ZILLO VALLA:	THROUGH THEM, TIME HAS ENTERED OUR TIMELESS WORLD.
14) ZILLO VALLA:	BEGINNINGS AND ENDINGS.
Frame 4	They look out across the red ocean to the vast uncanny sky beyond. Weirdly colored clouds – like in those Nepalese thanka paintings we looked at, Jeff - float across what looks like a Kirby kollage sky. Liquid bursts, gouting like geysers from the ocean surface as though it was boiling. Rising from the sea are the broken, ruined remains of a once great civilization, haunting shapes against a fantastic sky.
15) ZILLO VALLA:	CONSIDER OUR DIVINE ENGINE, OUR CELESTIAL FOUNTAIN OF INTERLOCKING UNIVERSES...
16) ZILLO VALLA:	ALL EXISTENCE DEPENDS ON ITS SURVIVAL.
17) ZILLO VALLA:	SAVE YOUR LOVE FOR THE ORRERY.
Frame 5	Three suns are setting in blood-red ancient twilight. In foreground the evil Monitor Ogama turns from watching the women out on the terrace and addresses us directly from behind his hand like the villain in a Shakespeare play.
18) OGAMA:	ATTENTIONS WANDER.
19) OGAMA:	UOTAN, MY ONLY OBSTACLE, IS GONE.
20) OGAMA:	WE'RE ON...

PAGE 30

Frame 1	Cut to Anthro once more as flame snaps across foreground - his food is cooking - he draws in the dirt on the east coast where New York will one day be - in the swamps...he's walked here. He has all kinds of new invented technology now. He sits as the sun goes down. Smoke rises. In a visionary trance, he draws with a stick.
Frame 2	Anthro's drawn image on the ground – it's the pattern on Metron's costume – that engraved circuit pattern he has on his chest.
Frame 3	Anthro looks up. Awestruck...his eyes swivel back as he realises the sun is rising behind him he raises his hand to point...THIS SHOULD BE THE SAME PLACE WHERE HE MET METRON IN THE OPENING SCENE.
1) ANTHRO:	!

PAGE 31

Frame 1	Full-page pic with inserts. He's facing us but his eyes shift backwards as he realises the whole world has changed behind him. The background is an incredible, apocalyptic shot of future New York as seen on the cover to KAMANDI issue 1. Kamandi stands in middle distance, looking at Anthro's back, like an out-of-register copy of Anthro. Beyond is the wrecked Statue of Liberty half toppled in the sea which laps these "rocks" – what appear to be rocks are the remains of buildings which once were the Battery Park district. The sky is like blood and soot.
2) ANTHRO:	!
Frame 2	Anthro's POV as his hand reaches away from us towards Kamandi. Kamandi reaches out towards us, yelling. Their hands almost touch one another, frozen in a desperate outreach.
3) KAMANDI:	METRON GAVE YOU A WEAPON AGAINST THE GODS!
4) KAMANDI:	WE NEED IT NOW!
Frame 3	We're behind Anthro. The incredible vision is gone. The flame has gone out. There is only dawn beyond. His hand lowers from the sun.
Frame 4	Close on Anthro, puzzled, looking past us at the infinite. He has drawn on his brow with paint the pattern of the design on Metron's hood.

5) ANTHRO: ?

PAGE 32
Frame 1

Cut to a boy waking up in bed, sweating as if from a startling dream.
It's Nix Uotan – we can recognise his distinctive hairstyle, his face but he's no longer a
godlike coordinator of worlds, he's an 18-year-old black kid waking to the "real" world.

1) BOY: AHHH

Frame 2

Pull back. Uotan sits up in bed, a little dazed as he stares at his own hands. On the wall
behind him is a picture of the sun. His clothes lie on the floor next to his bed – a mat-
tress. A stack of books, CDs and a beatbox. He seems to be just a normal teenaged kid
living in cheap rented digs somewhere in the cheap outer boroughs of Metropolis.

2) UOTAN: AWW, MAN.

3) UOTAN: 9:15?

4) UOTAN: I AM IN SUCH DEEP...

Frame 3

Close on Uotan. He looks up past his hands, past us and towards the
TV, off panel. His eyes get wider as it all starts to dawn on him.

5) UOTAN: ...DEEP...

6) TV BALLOON: *(letters blurring in...)* AND HE WAS A VALUED FRIEND AND COMRADE...

7) TV: &%@ THAT! WHOEVER <u>DID</u> THIS TO <u>J'ONN</u> WILL <u>SUFFER</u>, YOU <u>HEAR</u> ME!
                              WILL SUFFER! *(from off panel)*

Frame 4

Uotan POV. Looking between his fingers at the TV on a table under
the window. The news is on and it looks pretty important.

8) TV: THE SUPERHERO COMMUNTY REACTS TO THE HORRIFIC <u>MURDER</u>
                              OF <u>J'ONN J'ONZZ</u>, THE <u>MANHUNTER FROM MARS</u>.

9) TV: MORE AFTER THE BREAK...

Frame 5

Titles bar – simple sans serif font black on white – doomy and official.

TITLE: **D.O.A.: The God of War!**

FINAL CRISIS DIRECTOR'S CUT COMMENTARY

June 26th, 2008

Grant Morrison & JG Jones

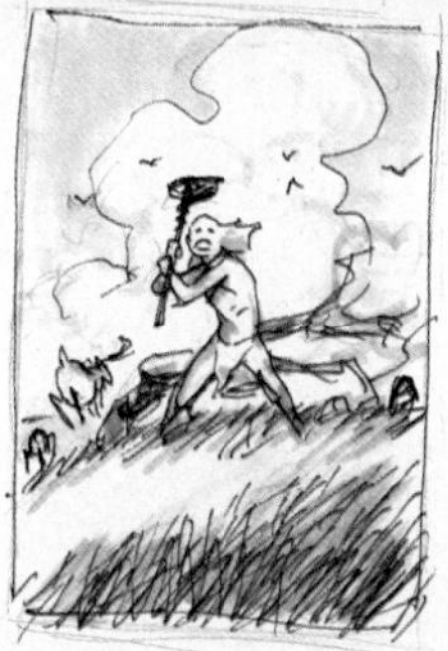

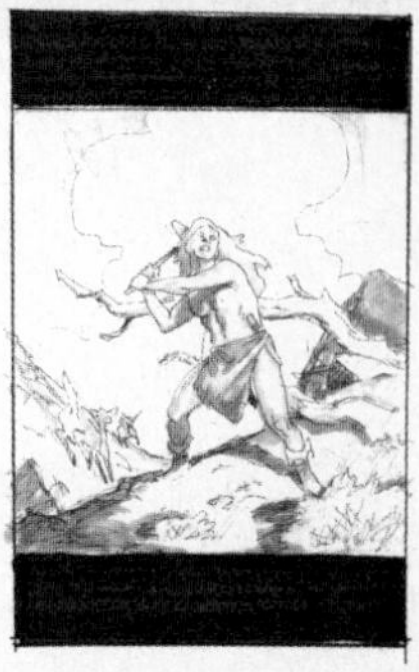

Read forth and behold the hidden secrets of the first issue of the galaxy spanning epic that could only be titled FINAL CRISIS. Discover mysteries of the remaining issues of this, the final part of the Crisis trilogy. Prepare to enter the minds of Grant Morrison and JG Jones, the architects behind this masterpiece. Read on. It could be the only way to save yourself from the Anti-Life Equation.

PAGE 1

Grant: This is one of my favorite pages ever. It's beautiful! It's amazing! The animals are running away. We know that something big's happening off page.

JG: It's a great image. It was all there in the script. I did so many sketches for this first page. I really wanted the reader to turn the page wanting more.

Grant: Anthro represents the first human being in civilization with a higher intelligence. The first DC prototype hero.

PAGES 2-3

JG: This page is sort of like my first meeting with Grant. Meeting with a higher intelligence.

Grant: This flips the entire idea of the first page. It's the first meeting between man and a God. The contrast between the two characters is incredible. This is the first story you find in all mythologies. The story of the first contact with a higher being.

JG: In regard to the new design for Metron I just kept thinking to myself, don't %*# it up! Grant and I sat together and went through all the New Gods.

I went back to look at the Kirby chair, it's changed so many times. The shape of the chair is taken from the lotus seats in Tibetan Thangka paintings.

Grant: The chair takes in all the elements of things from Buddhism and higher deities that we see.

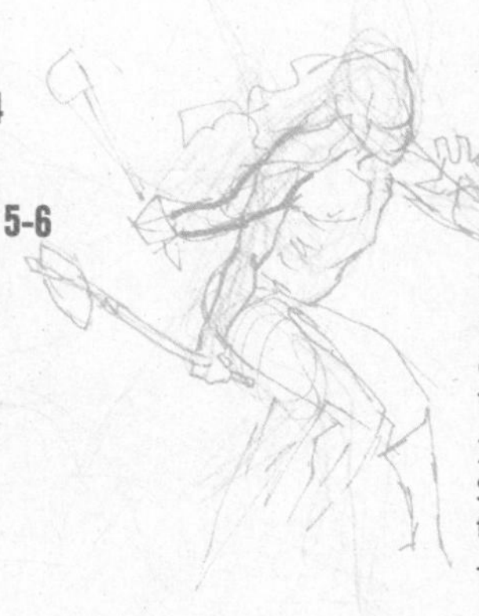

PAGE 4

Grant: The big clue to the end of Final Crisis is right here.

PAGES 5-6

Grant: We move from one primal scene to one of war, which has haunted mankind from the beginning and has always held us back. This is the first war as we see the last war at the end of Final Crisis.

It doesn't really matter if you don't know who Vandal Savage is; it's what he represents that's important and that's the first evil in the universe.

This is DC's version of GENESIS.

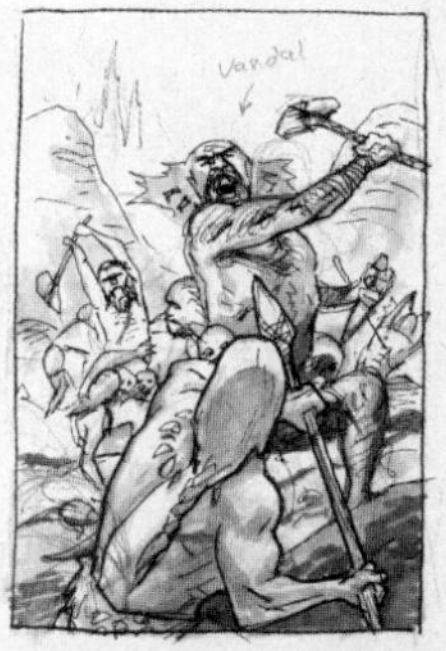
Vandal

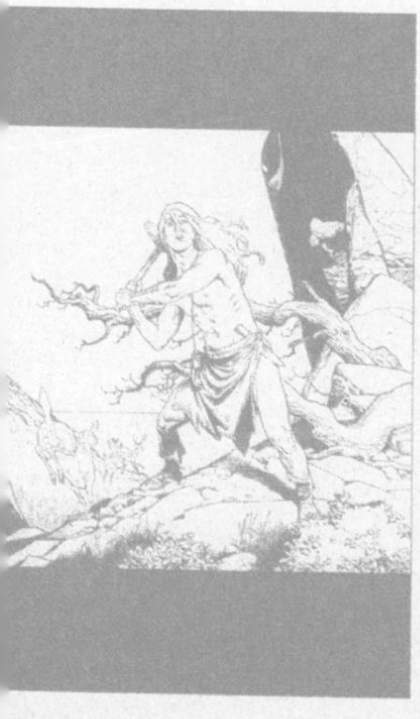

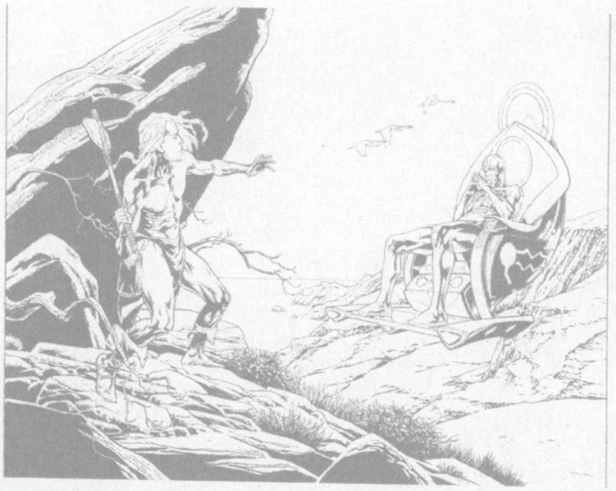

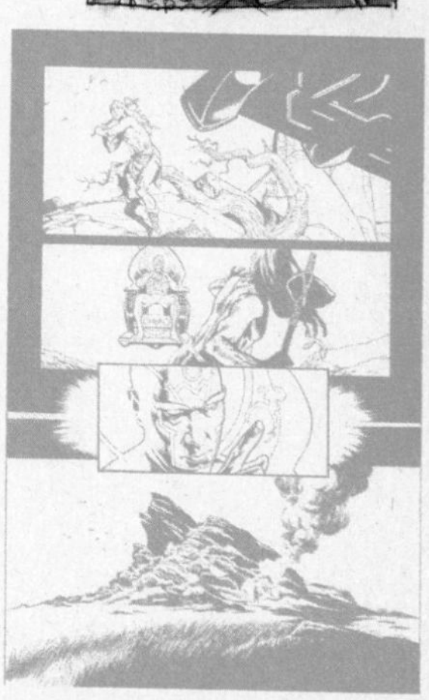

PAGE 7

Grant: It's the world's first superhero with the first super weapon...FIRE.

Makes you wonder if we never accepted the weapon, if there'd still be war.

PAGES 8-9

Grant: Fire goes from the dawn of the world to something that's just used to light up a cigarette so you can poison your lungs and kill yourself.

JG: That's why I used that circular panel to zero in on that. And you get the death of a god on the same page. How cool is that?

Grant: The rules have all changed. We don't see the fall from the skies, we just see him lying in the dirt.

JG: You can't get any lower than dying in a gutter on Earth surrounded by toy guns.

Grant: And then there's the Black Racer who we see for the first time. He no longer swoops in but floats there ominously waiting to grab your soul as it leaves your body.

PAGES 10-11

Grant: John Stewart is the first hero you see in the book.

JG: Stewart always seems to be the heart of the DC Universe for me. He was in the Marines and is always the guy out there fighting in the trenches.

Eddie: I love what you did with John in that last panel on page 10 showing the costume through his shirt with the light from his ring.

JG: It surprised me that no one had ever done that before, it just seemed so obvious to me.

Grant: And the Red Skies have returned. They're a sign of the Multiverse dying à la previous Crises. Wait until you see what the Red Skies actually are and how they tie into DC lore.

PAGES 12-13

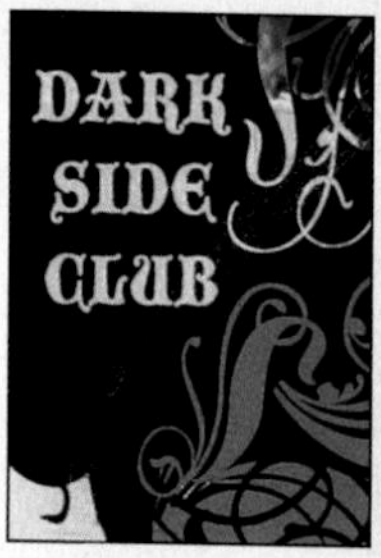
DARK
SIDE
CLUB

Grant: It was really important for us to start with the human connection. I didn't want to begin with big Super Heroes. We start desolate and build up the tension from the ground level. The connections Greg Rucka has been building with Montoya in 52 and the Crime Bible are all coming to fruition. Wait until you see Darkseid's connection to the Crime Bible.

And that Dark Side Club flyer that JG designed is so Gothy and creepy.

JG: I drew that separately and really wanted to get the feel of a Goth invitation. The members of these kinds of clubs all want to pretend they're evil, but they buy their counterculture stuff at the mall.

PAGES 14-15

Grant: What would you do if you found the dead body of a god? What would the police procedure be? It seemed like a really good idea to push this forward into a CSI sort of take. I thought it was great to have an FBI type of organization that would be a special branch of the Green Lantern Corps, and the Alpha Lanterns were created. Geoff Johns helped further develop the Alpha Lanterns in Green Lantern retroactively.

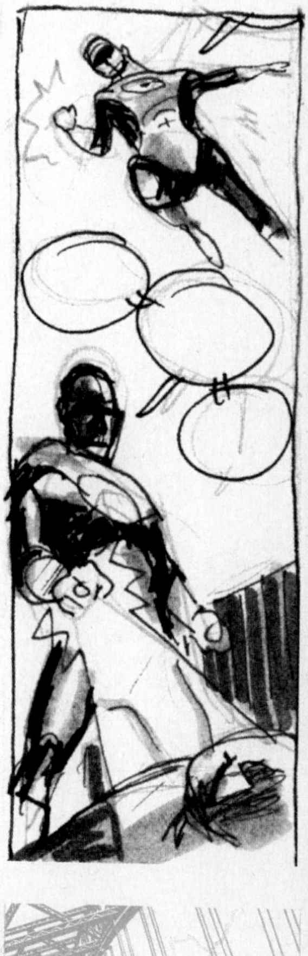

JG: And what's with that scar on Hal's face? Why is that there?

Grant: I can't tell you that! Wait until future issues!

PAGE 16

Grant: This was one of the first images I ever had for this series. With the mobius chair in the dump, with the sun rising behind. And JG added the seagulls.

JG: I do live close to Staten Island. Had some great reference.

Grant: Here's the first hint of Libra's gang with Dr. Light and Mirror Master.

JG: I love the dialog between these two.

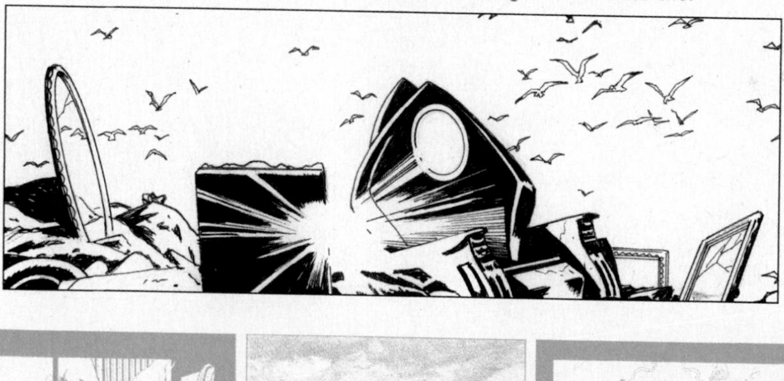

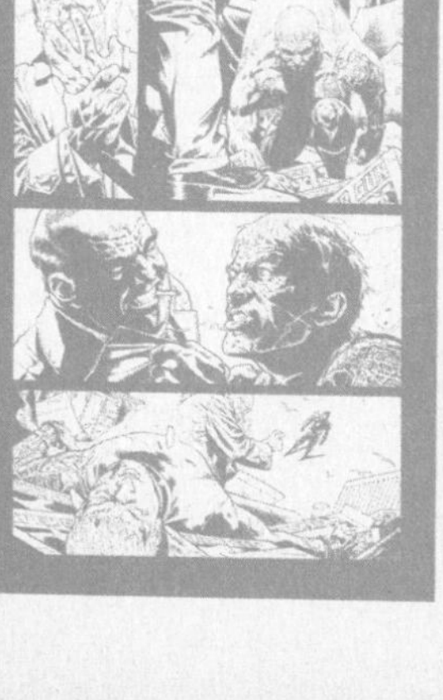

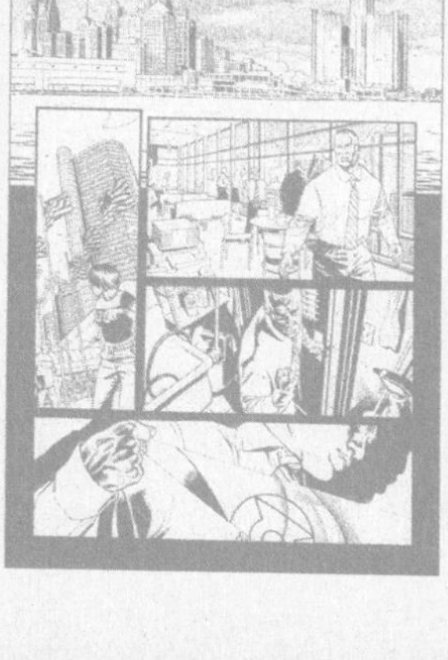

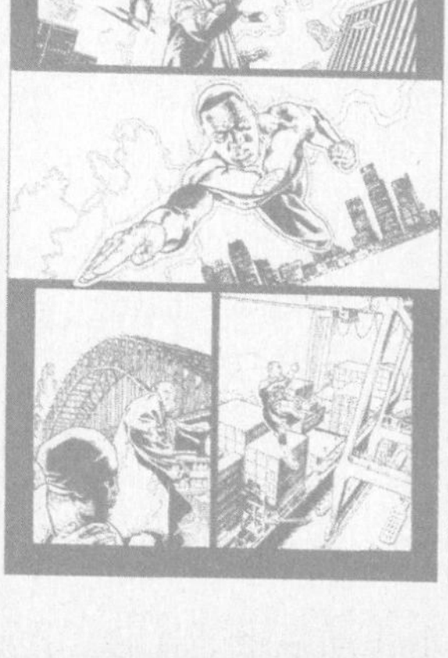

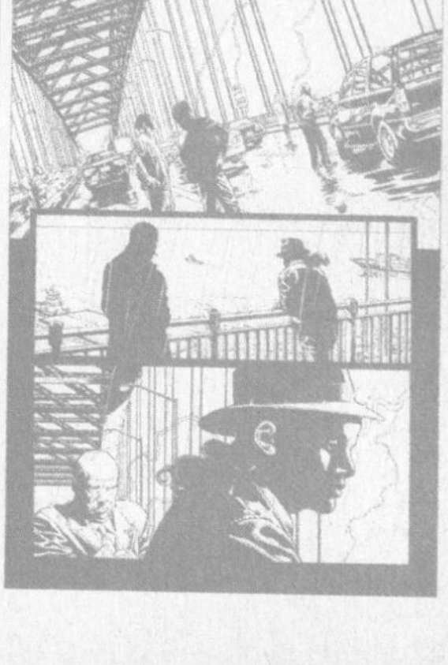

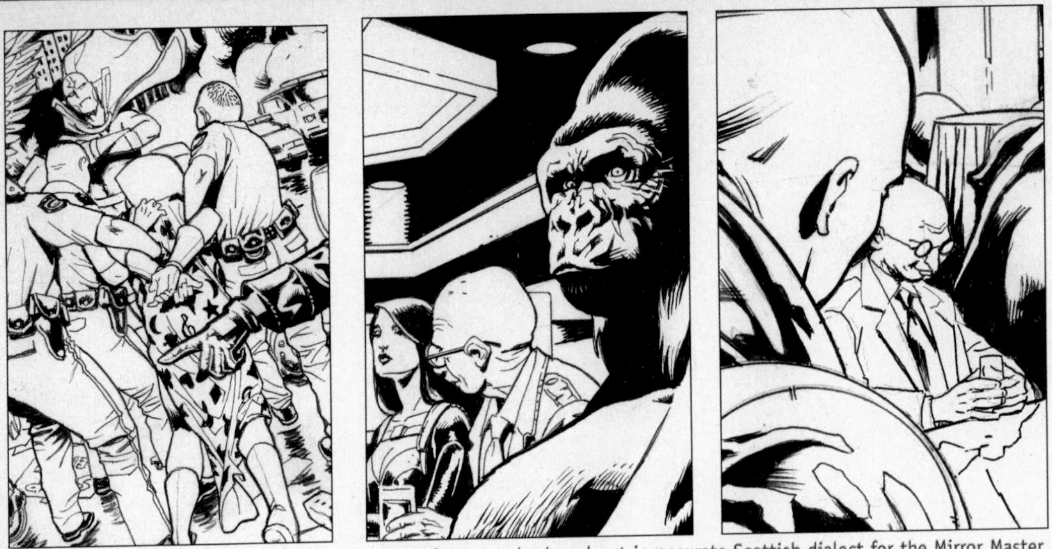

Grant: It was fun to go back and put in accurate Scottish dialect for the Mirror Master. I loved writing him back when I scripted Animal Man.

PAGE 17

JG: And here's the first shot of lots of heroes in one panel.

Grant: The shot is from the street angle, and we realize that these guys walk around in costumes because the superheroes do it. I love Signal Man with his feet dragging and his costume between his legs. Plus he's got a lawyer.

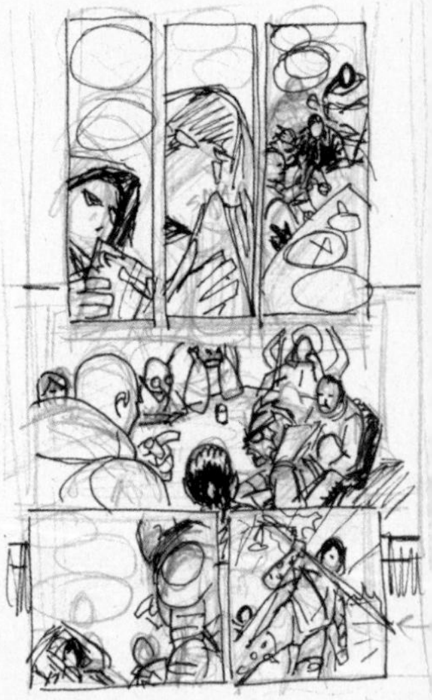

JG: Signal Man is such a loser. He runs around in a bed sheet.

Grant: Then we got Dr. Light's date with Giganta.

JG: That's a whole lot of woman.

I thought it was interesting that people were interpreting this as Light wanting a date rape drug, but I thought it was Super Viagra.

Grant: Yeah, I don't want to be encouraging people to use date rape drugs or anything.

PAGES 18-19

Grant: I love that Grodd looks like he's thinking, "I can't believe you humans talk so much."

JG: I love drawing Gorilla Grodd so much. He's so fun.

Grant: The villains all look like real people here sitting around a table. And you can feel Sivana sitting there thinking of ways to kill Captain Marvel.

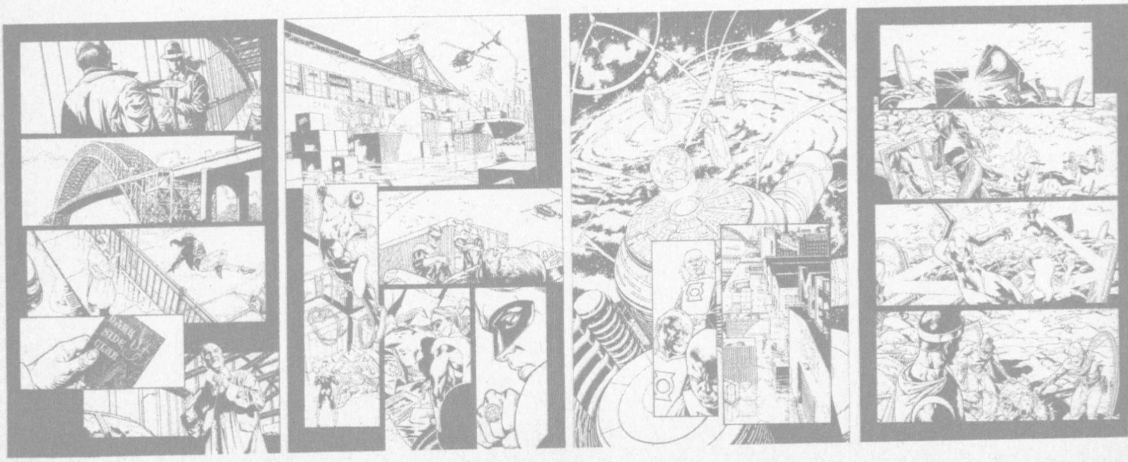

JG: Yep, he's playing through scenarios in his head.

I loved redesigning Libra too off the Len Wein design. That hood really helps.

PAGE 20

Grant: And then J'onn is killed, and people either loved it or hated it. This was the first signal that this wasn't your dad's crossover.

JG: I love the way he's dragged in and just bang, you're gone.

Grant: I think no one was expecting it, and even if you were, you weren't expecting it like this. It was done so horribly without even a struggle.

JG: That's why this scene is so effective, just walk into the house and you're dead.

Grant: And check out the villains' reactions. The ones who don't have anything are loving it. Those who have a power base and influence are just surprised by this new way.

JG: They're going to have to reevaluate the way they do things. We're playing by new rules now.

Grant: We're going to see a real test of the villains. Luthor in particular.

JG: You're not a nice person, Grant.

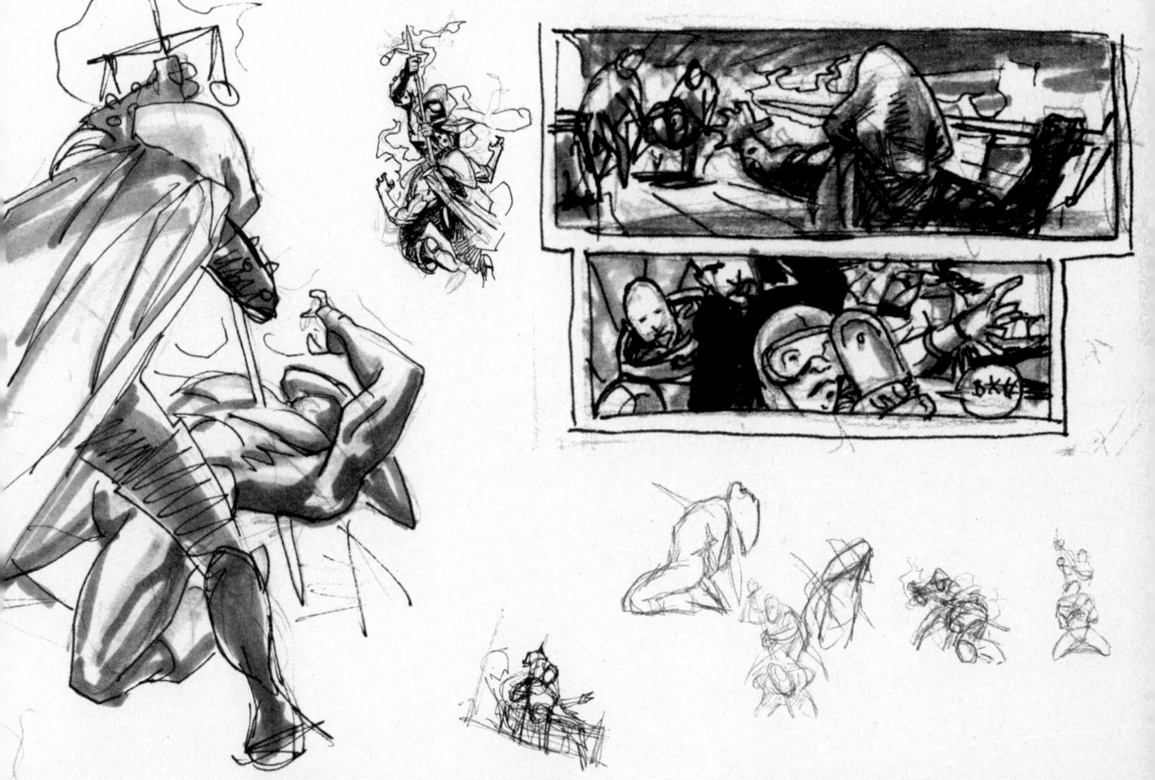

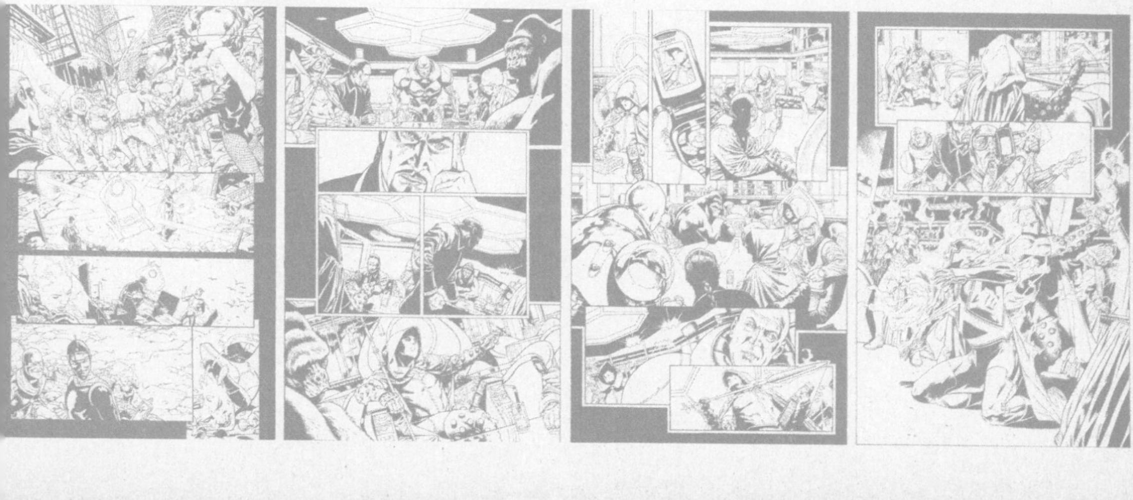

Grant:	Scary a world can produce such monsters, eh?

PAGE 21

JG:	I liked that next page; I didn't do too many vertical pages.
Grant:	Blüdhaven is like New Orleans. The government didn't respond properly. There's anarchy now and it reminds us of Apokolips.
	Watch out for the Tattoo Man. His role in Final Crisis: Submit sets him up for the role he'll play later in Final Crisis.

PAGES 22-23

JG:	Enter the Dark Side Club.
Grant:	I love that you make this look like David Lynch. It's "Twin Peaks."
JG:	I was thinking "Blue Velvet" here, but it's just so Lynch.
Grant:	I love him.
	Turpin walks into hell without realizing it. Darkseid is able to bring Turpin to his knees effortlessly.
JG:	Grant talked about how shadows follow Darkseid no matter where he is. So I played with that, which is why nothing's ever 100% clear. I kept the camera spinning in this scene, it's never still.

PAGES 24-25

Grant:	Again the idea was to go from the ground level where we've been, to god level. And we suddenly enter the world of the Justice League again. I wanted to distance the Justice League from the New Gods. It needs to seem like it's out of their league.
	We pull out from Superman, to the Trinity, to the JLA, to the Hall of Justice, to Earth, to the whole Multiverse. I think JG did the most ultimate zoom out in the history of anything.

JG: In only 6 panels.

Grant: Just shows what can be done. And then you see the Alpha Lanterns and you realize there's so much more going on here than the JLA, and you realize they're in big trouble.

JG: With a name like Final Crisis, they'd better be in big trouble.

Grant: This is the end of the DC Universe, and we're actually going to see it.

PAGES 26

Grant: The Orrery of Worlds. Stark, cone-shaped with one Earth on top of another. An almost Victorian structure.

JG: I did not have a clue of what Grant was visualizing in the script, but his little sketch brought it all together for me. It was still a bitch to draw, though.

Like a Victorian butterfly collection in a glass watched over by the Monitors.

PAGES 27-29

Grant: Then you're just thrust into the world of an ancient race with old rules and old customs.

The monitor world is the inspiration for all sci-fi universes. It's a dark, elegiac sort of feeling that this world is coming to an end. So what's going to happen to the Multiverse when the Monitor's world ends? I wanted to get to the world beyond the gods, outside of the Multiverse, and a world that we all know from our dreams.

JG: And that spread turned out so beautiful. Thank you Alex Sinclair (colorist), for being the guy. He fixes all my little screwups.

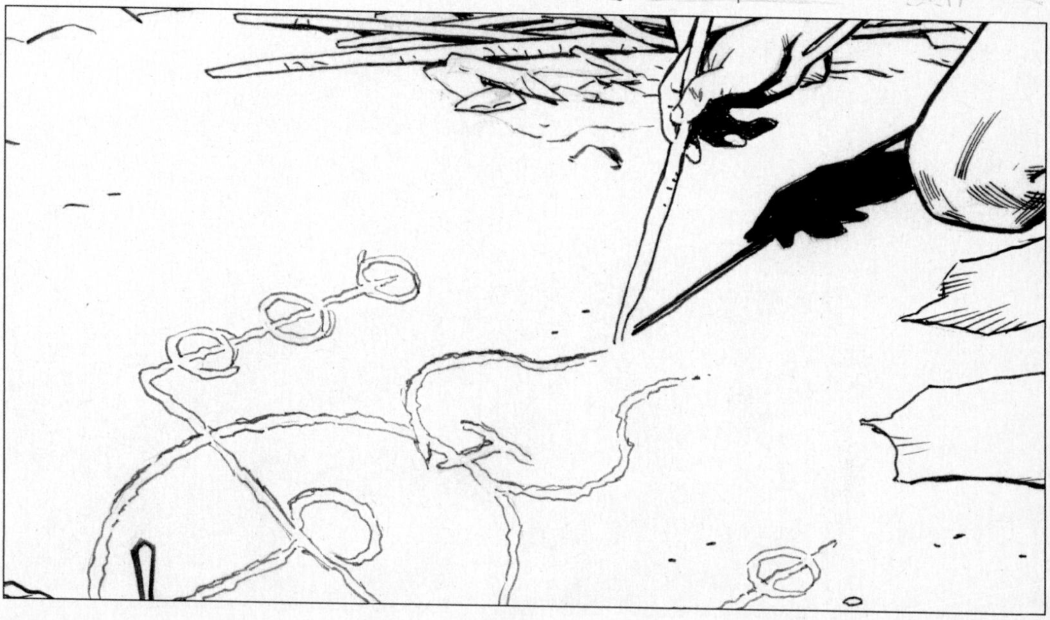

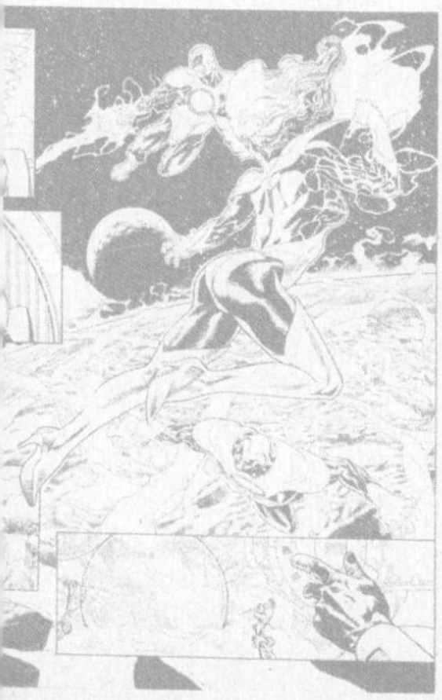

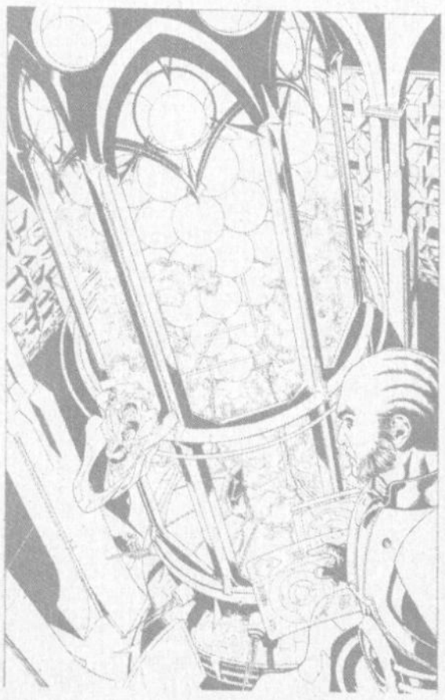

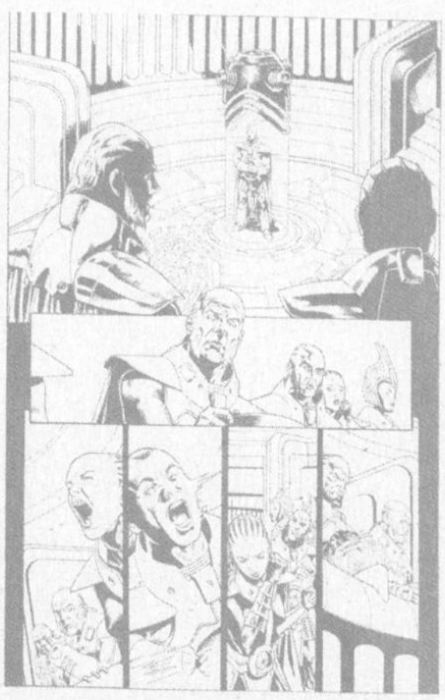

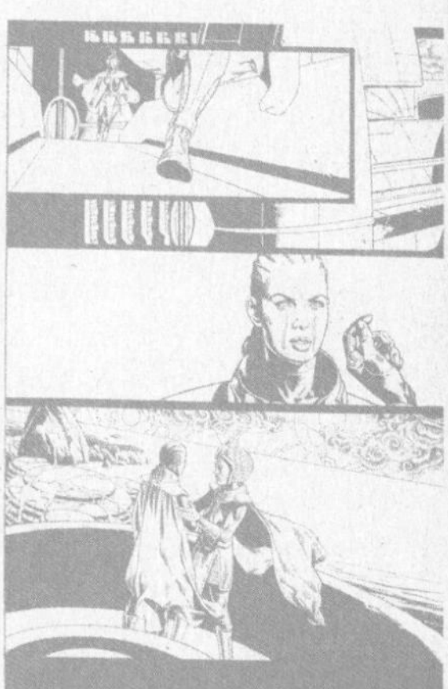

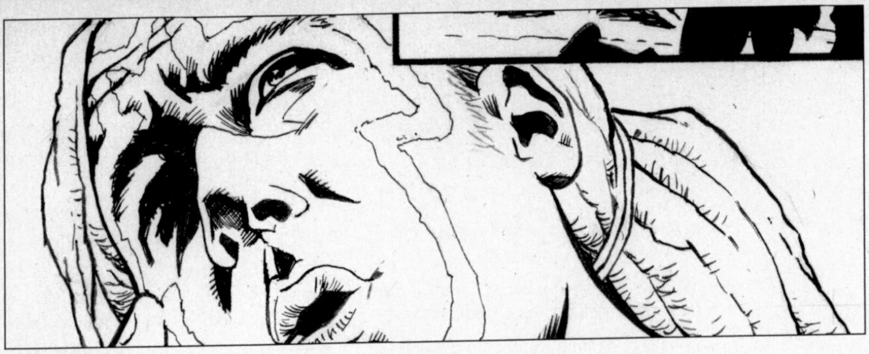

PAGES 30-31

Grant: We shoot back to Anthro in the place where he met Metron and he has better weapons and technology plus he's drawing a symbol in the sand which shows him visions of the future and there's Kamandi. But Kamandi's also in issue #2. How's he in both places? Wait until issue #6. And that design on his face is an important defense against Darkseid. It's the same design that's on Metron's mask.

JG: I've always loved that first Kamandi cover so much, and this was sort of an homage to that with the Statue of Liberty.

PAGE 32

JG: But wait, there's more!

Grant: It's the former Monitor, Nix Uotan, waking up as if he's just dreamed the entire comic, which he probably did.

JG: I wanted to treat that room as I did the Monitor world, with all the elements of the entire world wrapped up in this small little space.

Grant: And we end with the reader POV shot, oh God, where am I?

JG: Hey, good comic there, Grant.

Grant: You too, JG.

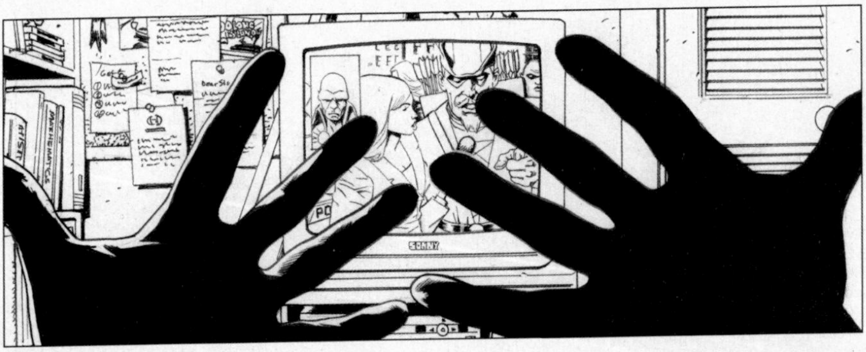

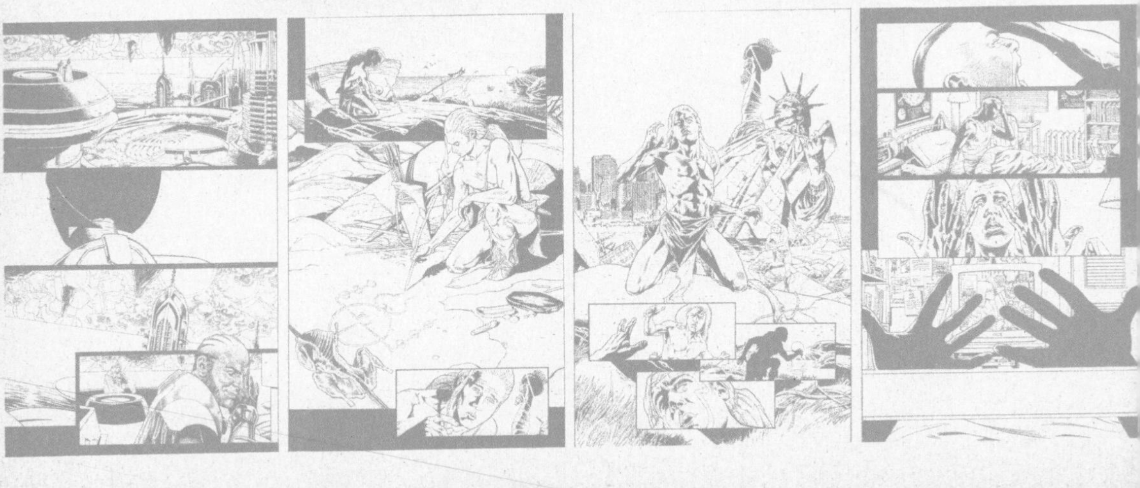

FINAL CRISIS SECRET FILES cover by Frank Quitely

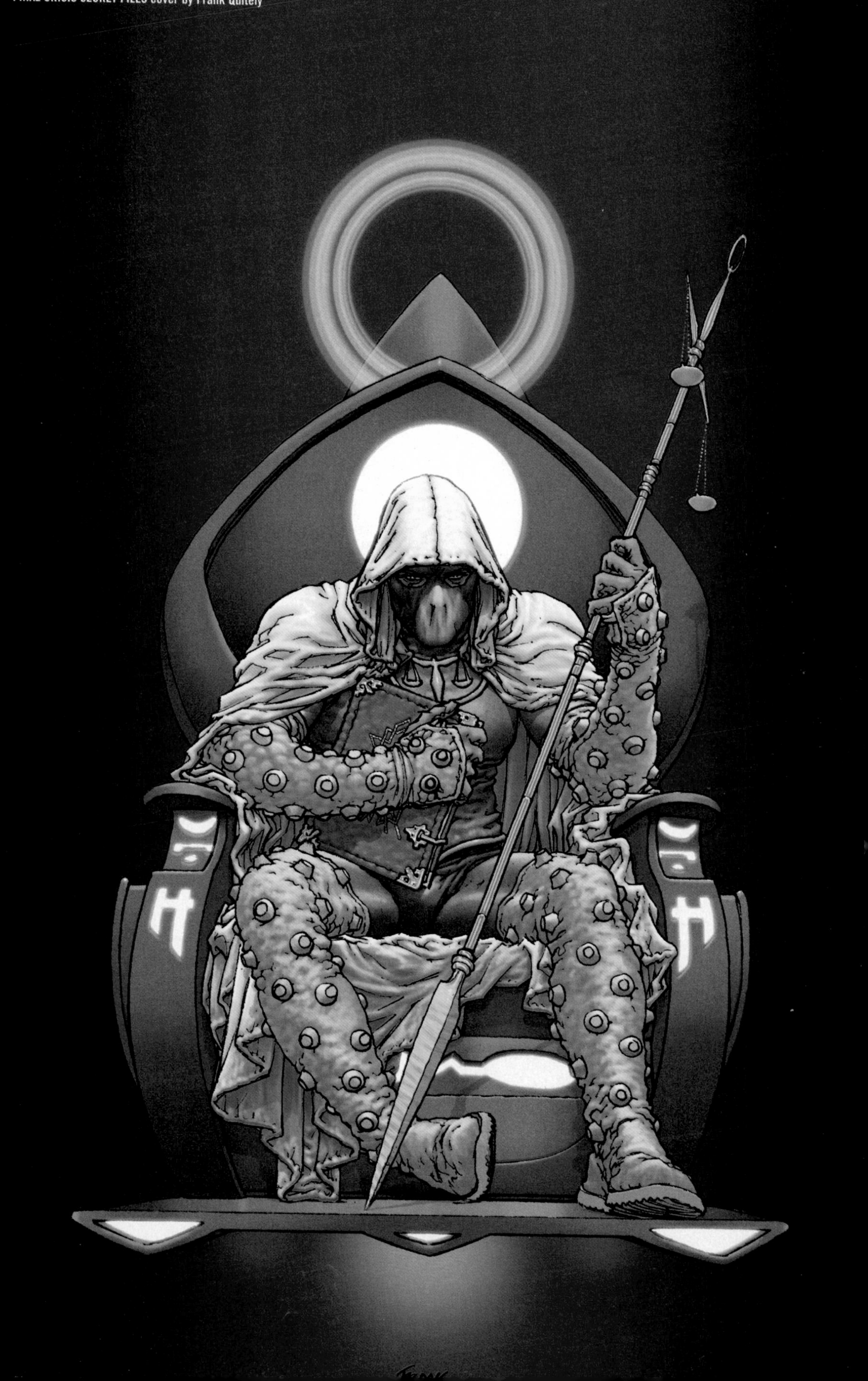

Sliver cover by Jim Lee, Richard Friend and Randy Mayor

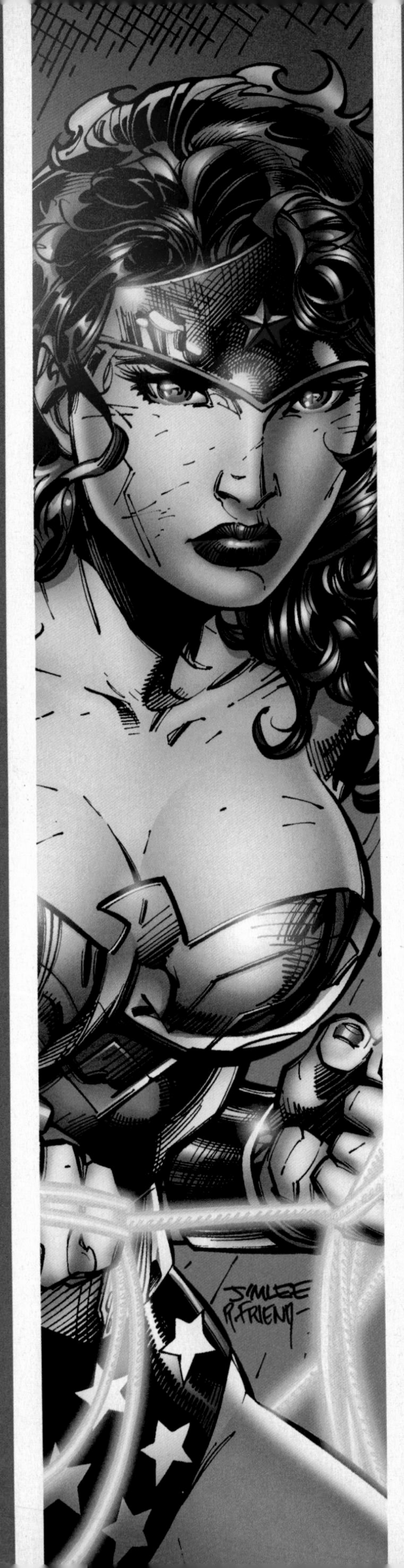

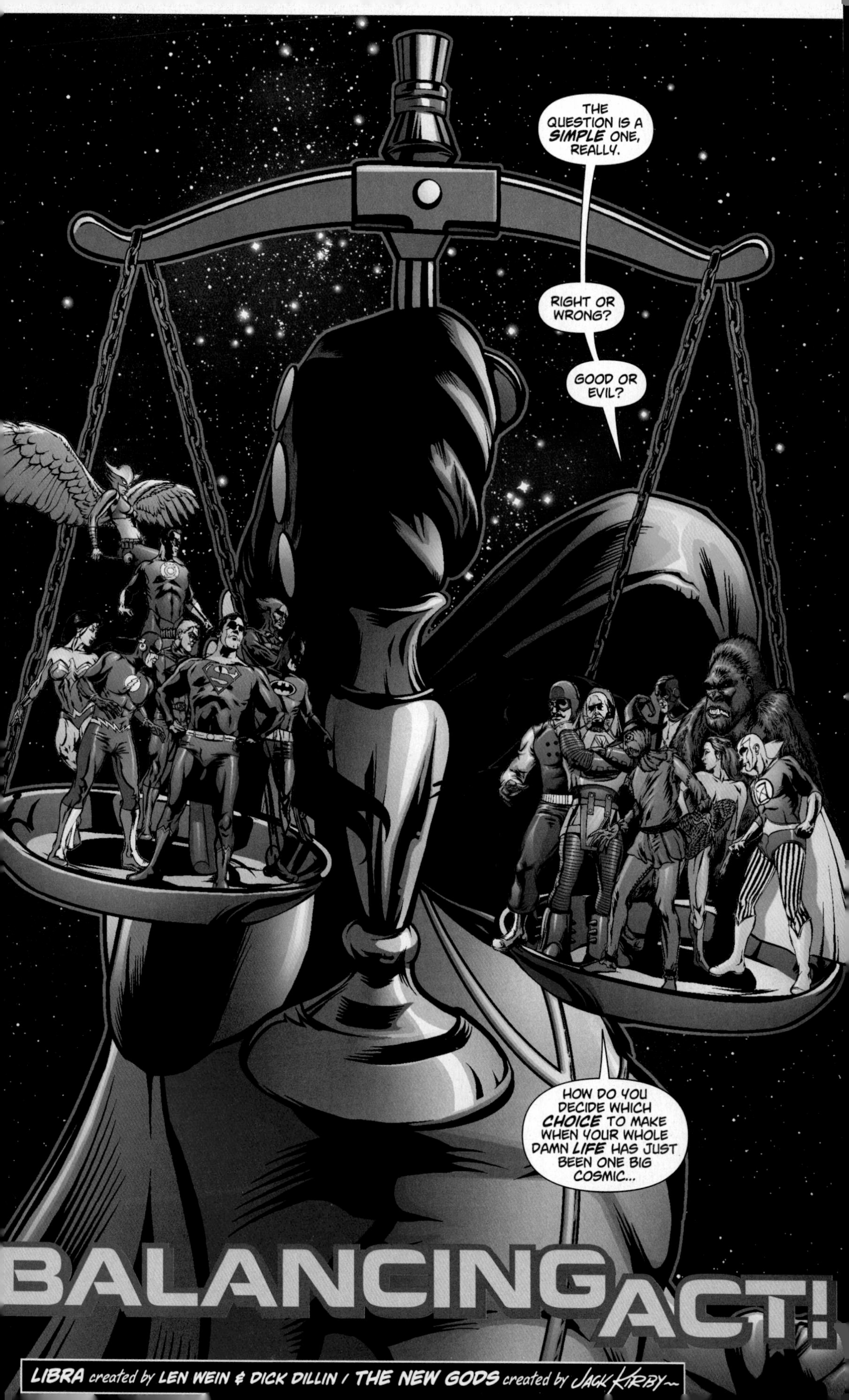
THE QUESTION IS A SIMPLE ONE, REALLY.
RIGHT OR WRONG?
GOOD OR EVIL?
HOW DO YOU DECIDE WHICH CHOICE TO MAKE WHEN YOUR WHOLE DAMN LIFE HAS JUST BEEN ONE BIG COSMIC...
BALANCING ACT!
LIBRA created by LEN WEIN & DICK DILLIN / THE NEW GODS created by JACK KIRBY

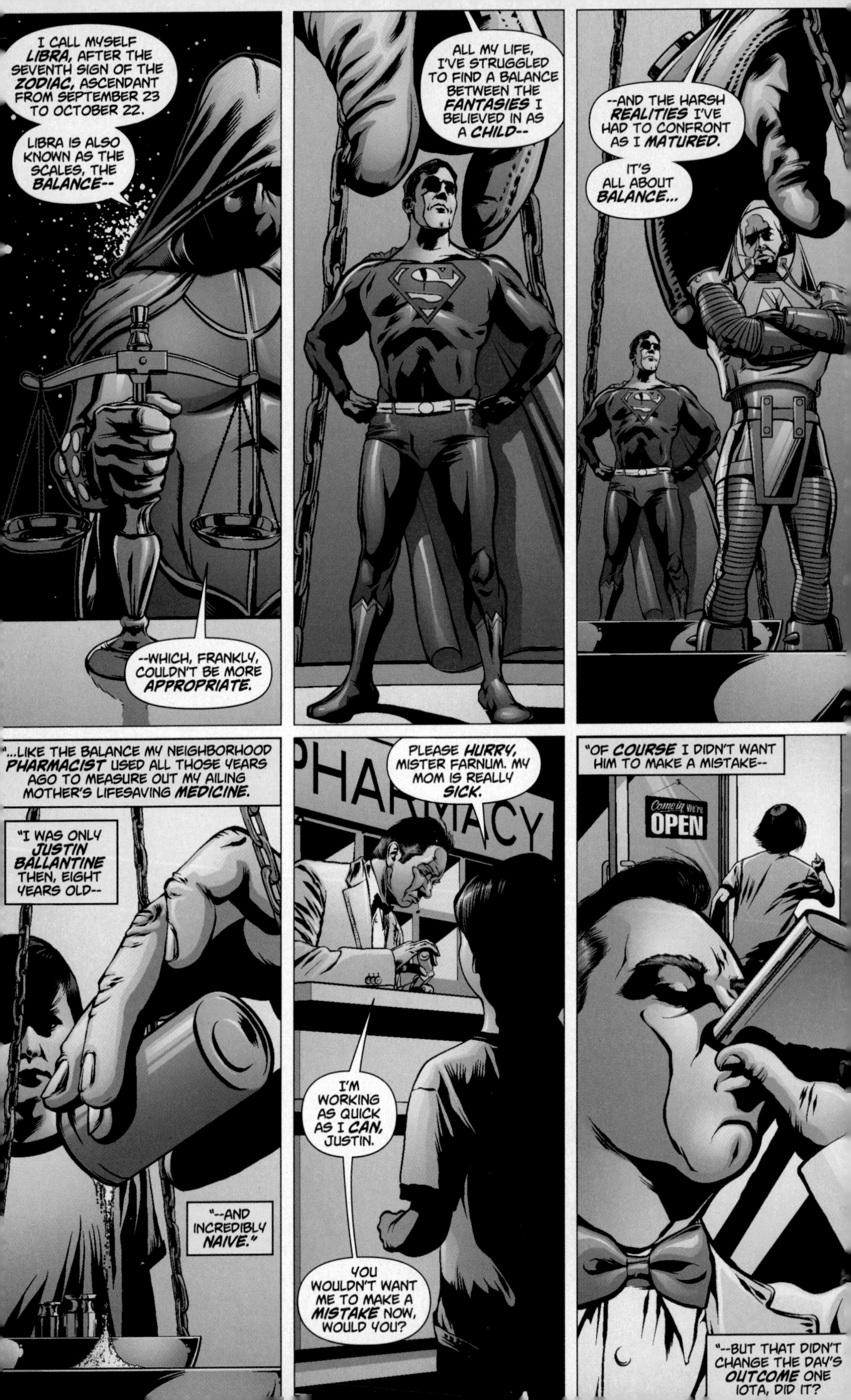
I CALL MYSELF LIBRA, AFTER THE SEVENTH SIGN OF THE ZODIAC, ASCENDANT FROM SEPTEMBER 23 TO OCTOBER 22.
LIBRA IS ALSO KNOWN AS THE SCALES, THE BALANCE--
--WHICH, FRANKLY, COULDN'T BE MORE APPROPRIATE.
ALL MY LIFE, I'VE STRUGGLED TO FIND A BALANCE BETWEEN THE FANTASIES I BELIEVED IN AS A CHILD--
--AND THE HARSH REALITIES I'VE HAD TO CONFRONT AS I MATURED.
IT'S ALL ABOUT BALANCE...
"...LIKE THE BALANCE MY NEIGHBORHOOD PHARMACIST USED ALL THOSE YEARS AGO TO MEASURE OUT MY AILING MOTHER'S LIFESAVING MEDICINE.
"I WAS ONLY JUSTIN BALLANTINE THEN, EIGHT YEARS OLD--
"--AND INCREDIBLY NAIVE."
PHARMACY
PLEASE HURRY, MISTER FARNUM. MY MOM IS REALLY SICK.
I'M WORKING AS QUICK AS I CAN, JUSTIN.
YOU WOULDN'T WANT ME TO MAKE A MISTAKE NOW, WOULD YOU?
"OF COURSE I DIDN'T WANT HIM TO MAKE A MISTAKE--
Come in We're OPEN
"--BUT THAT DIDN'T CHANGE THE DAY'S OUTCOME ONE IOTA, DID IT?

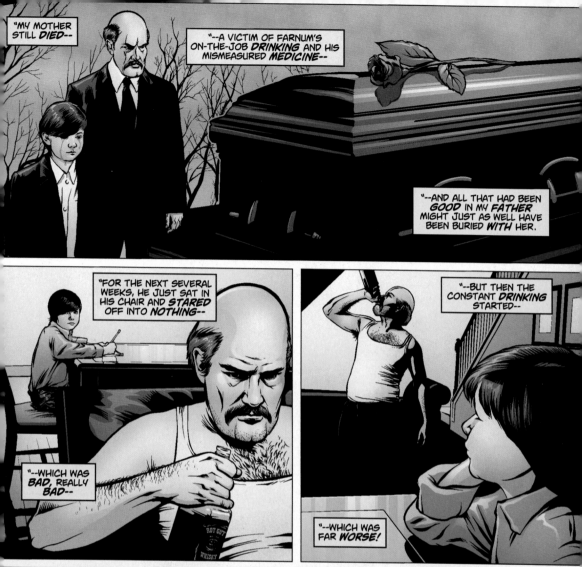

"MY MOTHER STILL *DIED*--

"--A VICTIM OF FARNUM'S ON-THE-JOB *DRINKING* AND HIS MISMEASURED *MEDICINE*--

"--AND ALL THAT HAD BEEN *GOOD* IN MY *FATHER* MIGHT JUST AS WELL HAVE BEEN BURIED *WITH* HER.

"FOR THE NEXT SEVERAL WEEKS, HE JUST SAT IN HIS CHAIR AND *STARED* OFF INTO *NOTHING*--

"--WHICH WAS *BAD*, REALLY *BAD*--

"--BUT THEN THE CONSTANT *DRINKING* STARTED--

"--WHICH WAS FAR *WORSE!*

"WITH NO *OTHER* OUTLET FOR HIS RAGE AND FRUSTRATION, I BECAME MY FATHER'S *WHIPPING BOY*--"

LOUSY, STUPID *KID!*

WAK

"--AND I SOON FOUND *MYSELF* STARING AS WELL--

"--INTO THE *DARK*, INTO THE *NIGHT*--

"--INTO THE INFINITE VASTNESS OF *SPACE*--

"--AND THE *COMFORT* OF THE BECKONING STARS

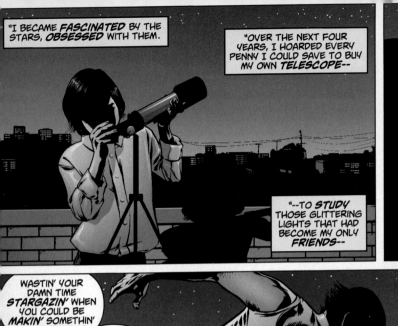

"I BECAME *FASCINATED* BY THE STARS, *OBSESSED* WITH THEM.

"OVER THE NEXT FOUR YEARS, I HOARDED EVERY PENNY I COULD SAVE TO BUY MY OWN *TELESCOPE*--

"--TO *STUDY* THOSE GLITTERING LIGHTS THAT HAD BECOME MY ONLY *FRIENDS*--

"--FRIENDS WHO WERE STILL TOO FAR AWAY TO EVER *PROTECT* ME!"

KNEW I'D *FIND* YOU UP HERE, BOY!

WASTIN' YOUR DAMN TIME *STARGAZIN'* WHEN YOU COULD BE *MAKIN'* SOMETHIN' OF YOURSELF!

WELL, I'M *DONE* WITH THIS, Y'HEAR?

THIS TIME I'M GONNA *POUND* SOME SENSE INTO YOUR DAMN--

--huh?

"FOR A MOMENT, HE *TEETERED* AT THE ROOFTOP'S *EDGE*--

NO.

"--STRUGGLING TO REGAIN HIS *EQUILIBRIUM*..."

"THEN, *SCREAMING* PITIFULLY, HE DROPPED OUT OF MY LIFE *FOREVER*--

"--A VICTIM OF *GRAVITY* AND HIS OWN BLIND *HATRED!*

NOOOOOO!

"I DON'T KNOW HOW LONG I JUST STOOD LOOKING DOWN AT MY FATHER'S BROKEN *BODY*, AS THE WAIL OF SIRENS GREW CLOSER, BUT ALL I CAN REMEMBER *THINKING* IS:

"LIFE IS ALL JUST A MATTER OF *BALANCE*."

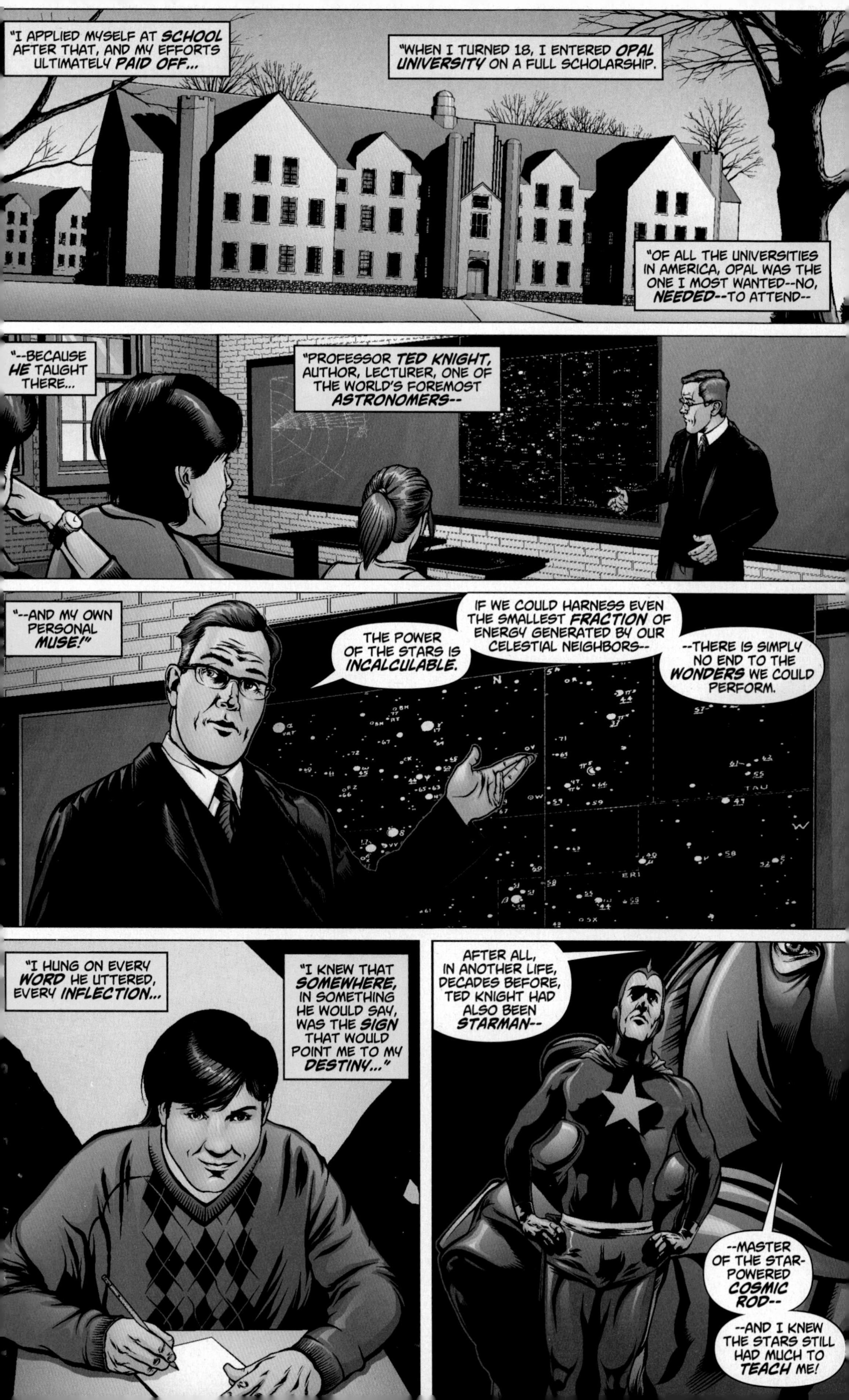
"I APPLIED MYSELF AT SCHOOL AFTER THAT, AND MY EFFORTS ULTIMATELY PAID OFF...
"WHEN I TURNED 18, I ENTERED OPAL UNIVERSITY ON A FULL SCHOLARSHIP.
"OF ALL THE UNIVERSITIES IN AMERICA, OPAL WAS THE ONE I MOST WANTED--NO, NEEDED--TO ATTEND--
"--BECAUSE HE TAUGHT THERE...
"PROFESSOR TED KNIGHT, AUTHOR, LECTURER, ONE OF THE WORLD'S FOREMOST ASTRONOMERS--
"--AND MY OWN PERSONAL MUSE!"
THE POWER OF THE STARS IS INCALCULABLE.
IF WE COULD HARNESS EVEN THE SMALLEST FRACTION OF ENERGY GENERATED BY OUR CELESTIAL NEIGHBORS--
--THERE IS SIMPLY NO END TO THE WONDERS WE COULD PERFORM.
"I HUNG ON EVERY WORD HE UTTERED, EVERY INFLECTION...
"I KNEW THAT SOMEWHERE, IN SOMETHING HE WOULD SAY, WAS THE SIGN THAT WOULD POINT ME TO MY DESTINY..."
AFTER ALL, IN ANOTHER LIFE, DECADES BEFORE, TED KNIGHT HAD ALSO BEEN STARMAN--
--MASTER OF THE STAR-POWERED COSMIC ROD--
--AND I KNEW THE STARS STILL HAD MUCH TO TEACH ME!

"BY THE END OF MY SENIOR YEAR, I'D TAKEN ALL THE *COURSES* HE TAUGHT, AND THERE WAS NOTHING LEFT FOR PROFESSOR KNIGHT TO *OFFER* ME--"

"--AT LEAST, NOT IN THE *CLASSROOM*..."

"...WHICH IS WHY, LATE ONE NIGHT DURING SPRING BREAK, I FORCED MY WAY INTO THE PROFESSOR'S *PRIVATE* OFFICE--"

"--AND CAREFULLY *RIFLED* THROUGH HIS *FILING CABINETS*--"

"--UNTIL I FINALLY *FOUND* WHAT I HAD KNOWN IN MY HEART ALL ALONG HAD TO *BE* THERE..."

"THE FILE WAS MARKED *PRIVATE* AND *CONFIDENTIAL*--"

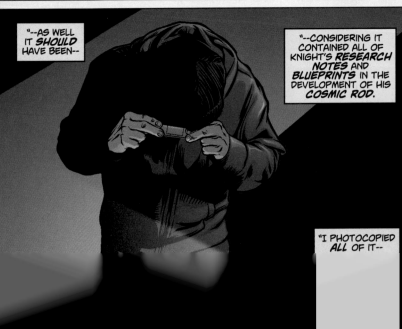

"--AS WELL IT *SHOULD* HAVE BEEN--"

"--CONSIDERING IT CONTAINED ALL OF KNIGHT'S *RESEARCH NOTES* AND *BLUEPRINTS* IN THE DEVELOPMENT OF HIS *COSMIC ROD*."

"I PHOTOCOPIED *ALL* OF IT--"

"--AND THEN STOLE *OUT* OF THE ROOM AS QUIETLY AS I'D FIRST GOTTEN *IN*..."

"...MY *FUTURE* NOW IN MY OWN *HANDS*..."

"I SPENT THE NEXT SEVERAL YEARS AFTER GRADUATION EVOLVING AND REFINING KNIGHT'S *DESIGNS* INTO SOMETHING UNIQUELY *MY OWN*..."

"...THEN PUT EVERY PENNY I COULD BEG, BORROW OR STEAL INTO THE CONSTRUCTION OF A DEVICE I CALLED MY *ENERGY-TRANSMORTIFIER*--"

"--A MECHANISM DESIGNED TO *ABSORB* HALF THE ENERGY IN THE ENTIRE *GALAXY*--"

"--AND TRANSFER IT INTO *ME!*"

"BUT HOW BEST TO *TEST* THE MACHINE BEFORE USING IT ON MYSELF WITH POSSIBLY *FATAL* RESULTS?

"I PONDERED THE PROBLEM FOR *DAYS*--

"--UNTIL A QUICK GLANCE AT A WEEKS-OLD *NEWSPAPER* SUDDENLY GAVE ME THE *ANSWER*..."

LASH CAPTURES CAPTAIN COLD

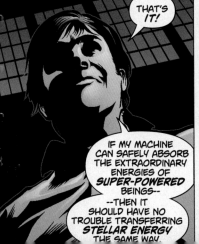

THAT'S IT!

IF MY MACHINE CAN SAFELY ABSORB THE EXTRAORDINARY ENERGIES OF *SUPER-POWERED* BEINGS--

--THEN IT SHOULD HAVE NO TROUBLE TRANSFERRING *STELLAR ENERGY* THE SAME WAY.

"BUT IF I WAS GOING TO *WALK* AMONG THESE MASKED MYSTERYMEN, IT SEEMED ONLY RIGHT THAT I SHOULD *LOOK* LIKE ONE OF THEM...

"CONSIDERING MY TWO *PASSIONS*, THERE WAS REALLY NEVER ANY QUESTION ABOUT WHAT *SORT* OF ROLE I WOULD ASSUME...

"I BECAME *LIBRA*, THE *BALANCER*--

"--AND MY *LIFE* WOULD NEVER AGAIN BE THE *SAME*.

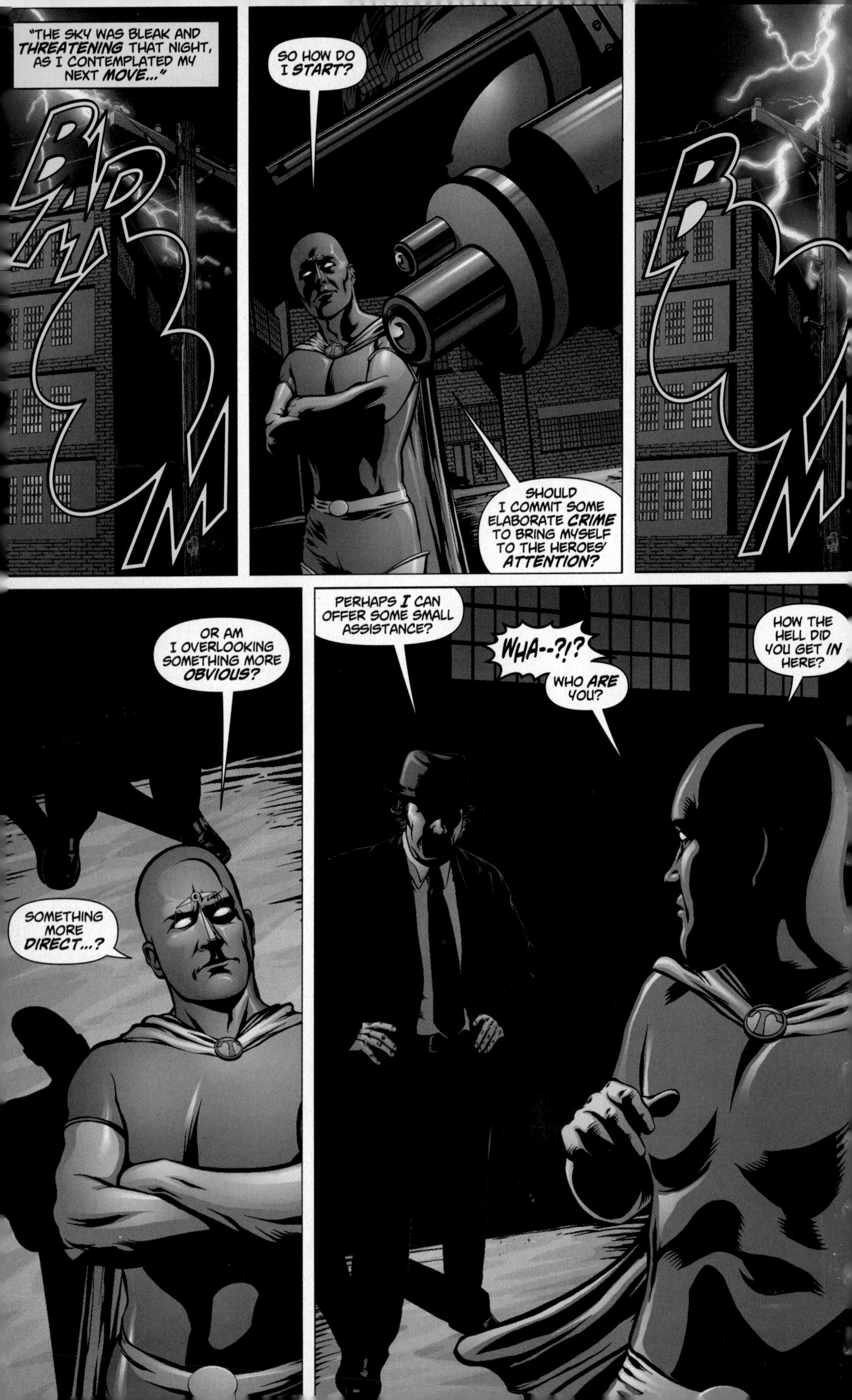
"THE SKY WAS BLEAK AND THREATENING THAT NIGHT, AS I CONTEMPLATED MY NEXT MOVE..."
BADOOM
SO HOW DO I START?
SHOULD I COMMIT SOME ELABORATE CRIME TO BRING MYSELF TO THE HEROES' ATTENTION?
BOOM
OR AM I OVERLOOKING SOMETHING MORE OBVIOUS?
SOMETHING MORE DIRECT...?
PERHAPS I CAN OFFER SOME SMALL ASSISTANCE?
WHA--?!?
WHO ARE YOU?
HOW THE HELL DID YOU GET IN HERE?

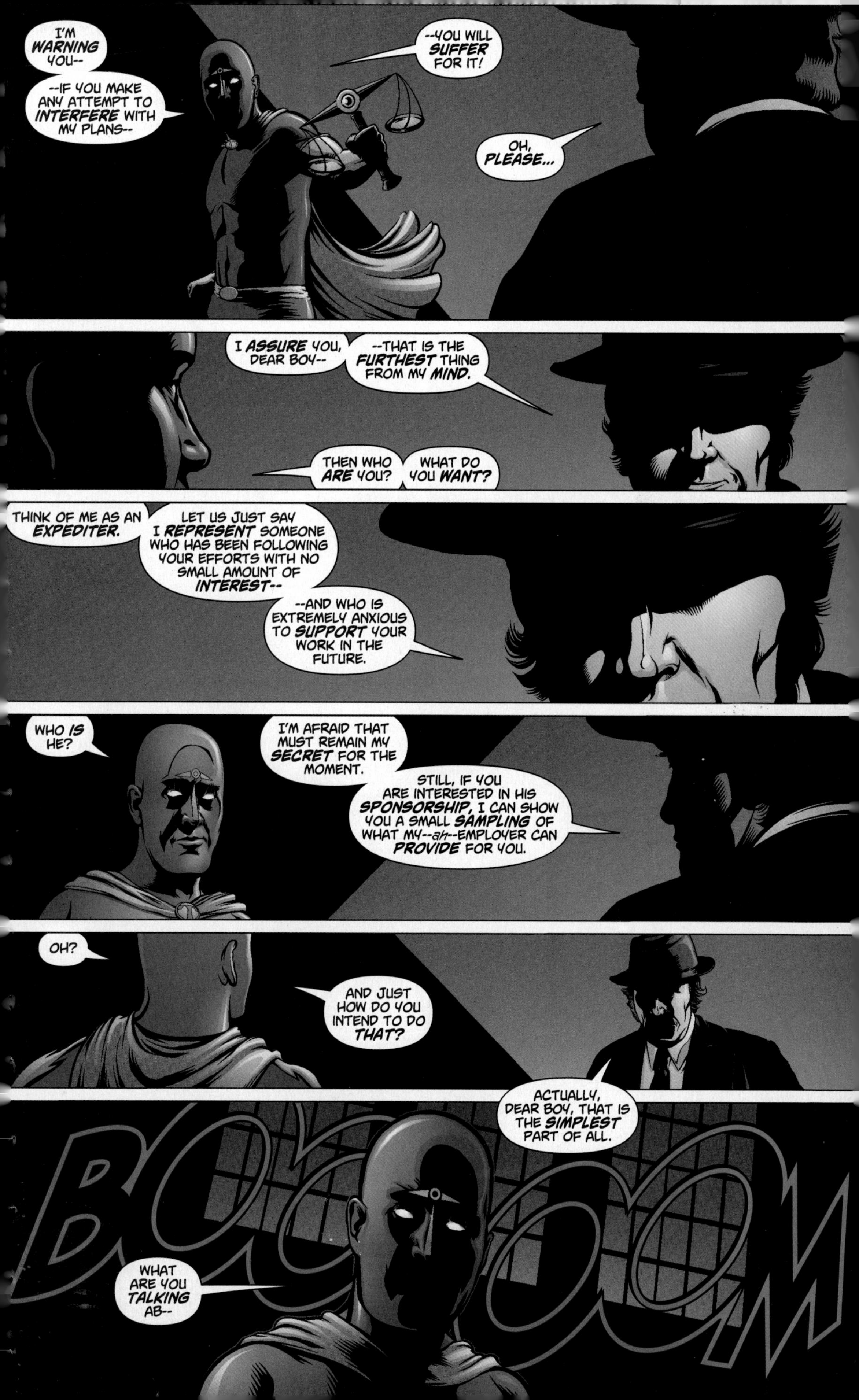
I'M WARNING YOU--
--IF YOU MAKE ANY ATTEMPT TO INTERFERE WITH MY PLANS--
--YOU WILL SUFFER FOR IT!
OH, PLEASE...
I ASSURE YOU, DEAR BOY--
--THAT IS THE FURTHEST THING FROM MY MIND.
THEN WHO ARE YOU?
WHAT DO YOU WANT?
THINK OF ME AS AN EXPEDITER.
LET US JUST SAY I REPRESENT SOMEONE WHO HAS BEEN FOLLOWING YOUR EFFORTS WITH NO SMALL AMOUNT OF INTEREST--
--AND WHO IS EXTREMELY ANXIOUS TO SUPPORT YOUR WORK IN THE FUTURE.
WHO IS HE?
I'M AFRAID THAT MUST REMAIN MY SECRET FOR THE MOMENT.
STILL, IF YOU ARE INTERESTED IN HIS SPONSORSHIP, I CAN SHOW YOU A SMALL SAMPLING OF WHAT MY--ah--EMPLOYER CAN PROVIDE FOR YOU.
OH?
AND JUST HOW DO YOU INTEND TO DO THAT?
ACTUALLY, DEAR BOY, THAT IS THE SIMPLEST PART OF ALL.
BOOOOOM
WHAT ARE YOU TALKING AB--

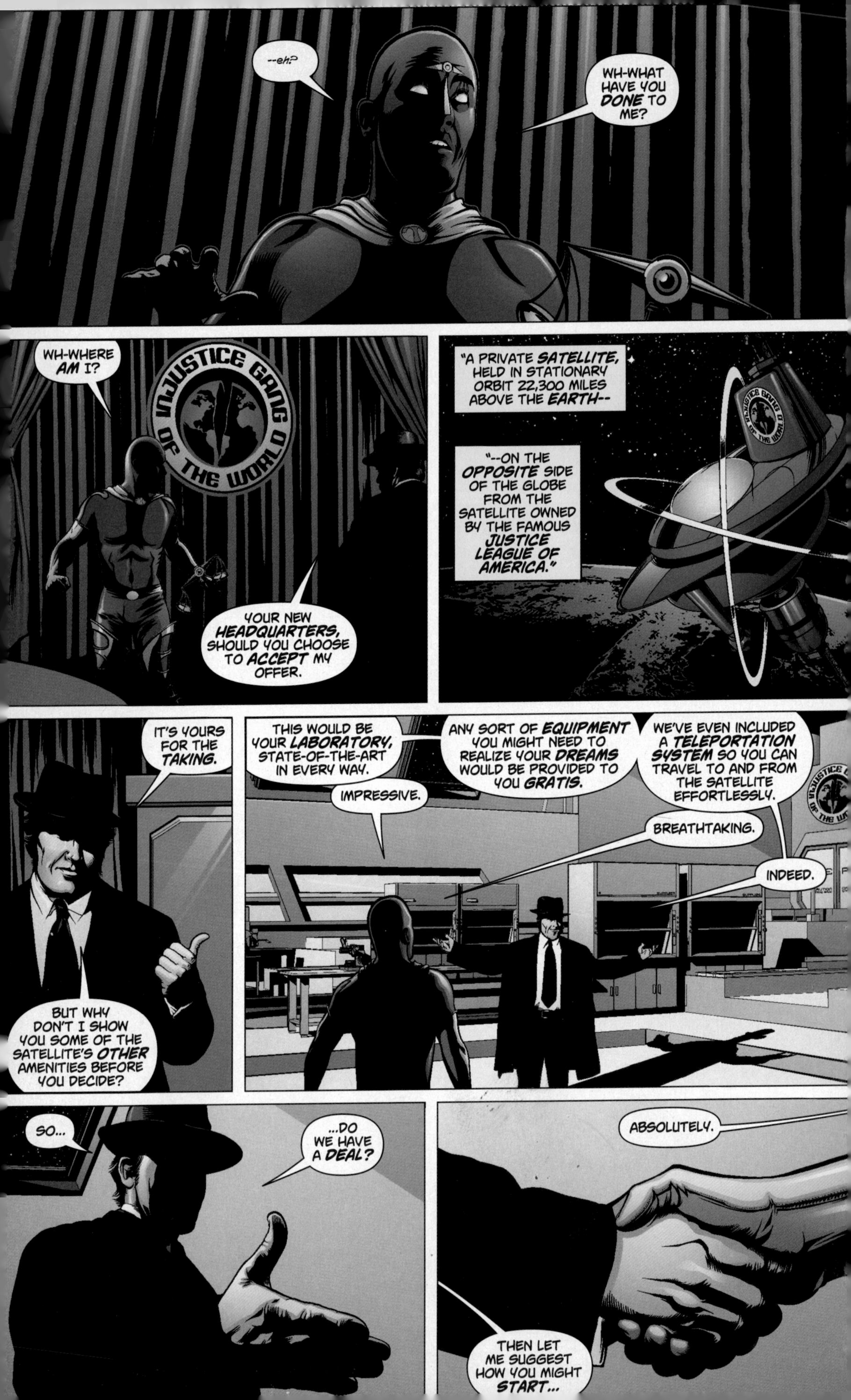
--eh?
WH-WHAT HAVE YOU DONE TO ME?
WH-WHERE AM I?
INJUSTICE GANG OF THE WORLD
YOUR NEW HEADQUARTERS, SHOULD YOU CHOOSE TO ACCEPT MY OFFER.
"A PRIVATE SATELLITE, HELD IN STATIONARY ORBIT 22,300 MILES ABOVE THE EARTH--
"--ON THE OPPOSITE SIDE OF THE GLOBE FROM THE SATELLITE OWNED BY THE FAMOUS JUSTICE LEAGUE OF AMERICA."
IT'S YOURS FOR THE TAKING.
BUT WHY DON'T I SHOW YOU SOME OF THE SATELLITE'S OTHER AMENITIES BEFORE YOU DECIDE?
THIS WOULD BE YOUR LABORATORY, STATE-OF-THE-ART IN EVERY WAY.
IMPRESSIVE.
ANY SORT OF EQUIPMENT YOU MIGHT NEED TO REALIZE YOUR DREAMS WOULD BE PROVIDED TO YOU GRATIS.
BREATHTAKING.
WE'VE EVEN INCLUDED A TELEPORTATION SYSTEM SO YOU CAN TRAVEL TO AND FROM THE SATELLITE EFFORTLESSLY.
INDEED.
SO...
...DO WE HAVE A DEAL?
ABSOLUTELY.
THEN LET ME SUGGEST HOW YOU MIGHT START...

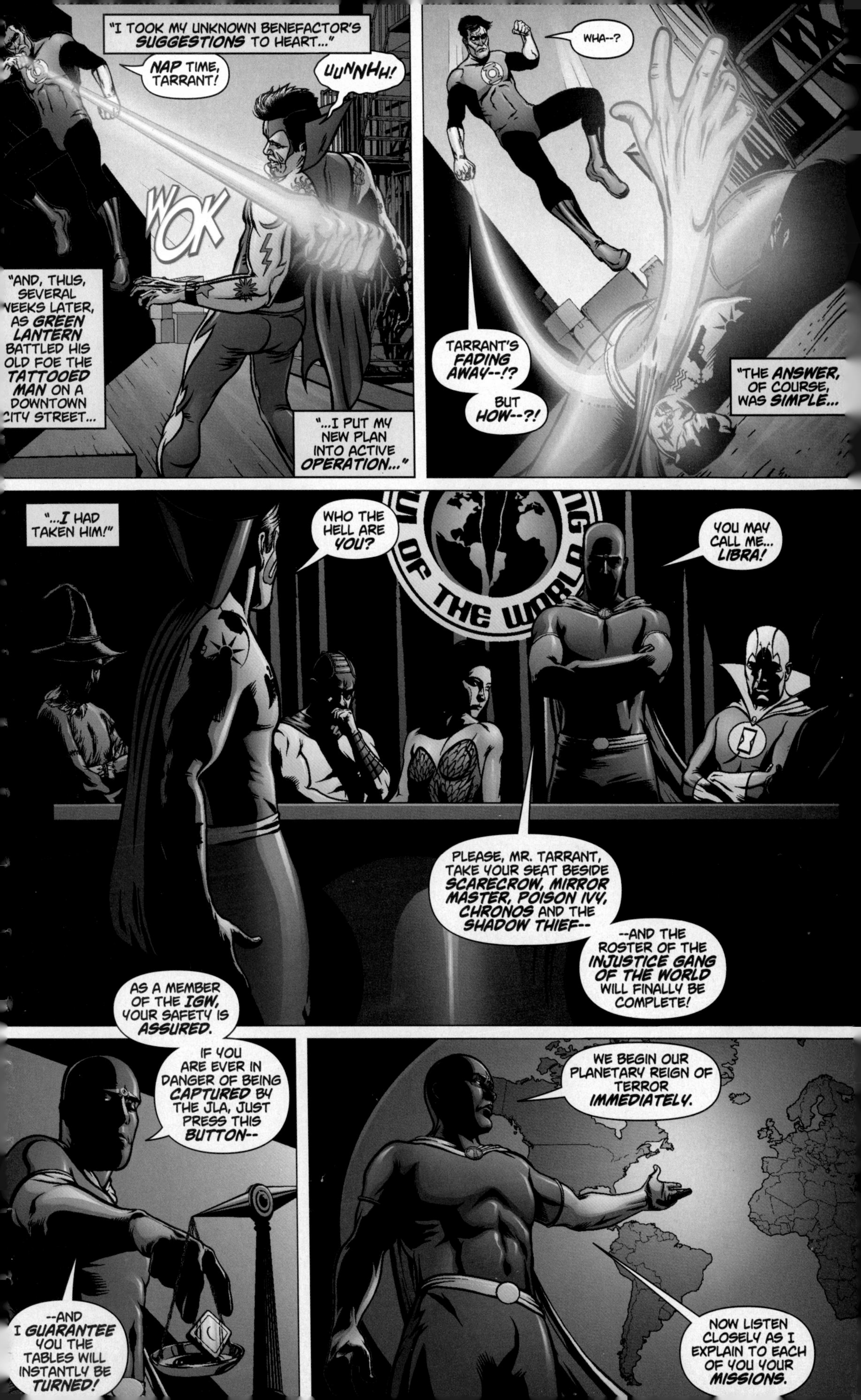
"I TOOK MY UNKNOWN BENEFACTOR'S SUGGESTIONS TO HEART..."
NAP TIME, TARRANT!
UUNNHH!
WOK
"AND, THUS, SEVERAL WEEKS LATER, AS GREEN LANTERN BATTLED HIS OLD FOE THE TATTOOED MAN ON A DOWNTOWN CITY STREET...
"...I PUT MY NEW PLAN INTO ACTIVE OPERATION..."
WHA--?
TARRANT'S FADING AWAY--!?
BUT HOW--?!
"THE ANSWER, OF COURSE, WAS SIMPLE...
"...I HAD TAKEN HIM!"
WHO THE HELL ARE YOU?
YOU MAY CALL ME... LIBRA!
OF THE WORLD
PLEASE, MR. TARRANT, TAKE YOUR SEAT BESIDE SCARECROW, MIRROR MASTER, POISON IVY, CHRONOS AND THE SHADOW THIEF--
--AND THE ROSTER OF THE INJUSTICE GANG OF THE WORLD WILL FINALLY BE COMPLETE!
AS A MEMBER OF THE IGW, YOUR SAFETY IS ASSURED.
IF YOU ARE EVER IN DANGER OF BEING CAPTURED BY THE JLA, JUST PRESS THIS BUTTON--
--AND I GUARANTEE YOU THE TABLES WILL INSTANTLY BE TURNED!
WE BEGIN OUR PLANETARY REIGN OF TERROR IMMEDIATELY.
NOW LISTEN CLOSELY AS I EXPLAIN TO EACH OF YOU YOUR MISSIONS.

"AND SO IT BEGAN..."

"...IN SINGAPORE..."

"...MY UNWITTING MINIONS DID *BATTLE* WITH THE HEROES OF THE *JUSTICE LEAGUE*..."

"...IN HOLLYWOOD..."

"...AND WHEN, AS EVER, THEY FOUND THEMSELVES OVERWHELMED AND *OUTMATCHED* AND PRESSED THEIR *BUTTONS* AS INSTRUCTED..."

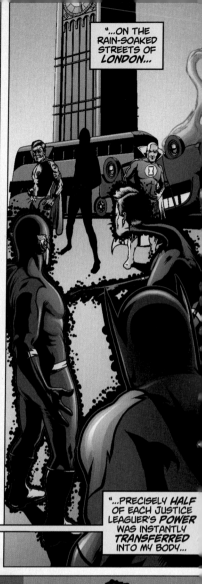

"...ON THE RAIN-SOAKED STREETS OF *LONDON*..."

"...PRECISELY *HALF* OF EACH JUSTICE LEAGUER'S *POWER* WAS INSTANTLY *TRANSFERRED* INTO MY BODY..."

"...ENABLING ME TO QUICKLY *DEFEAT* EACH AND EVERY ONE OF THEM..."

"...AND LEAVE THEM *SPRAWLED* SENSELESS AT MY *FEET.*"

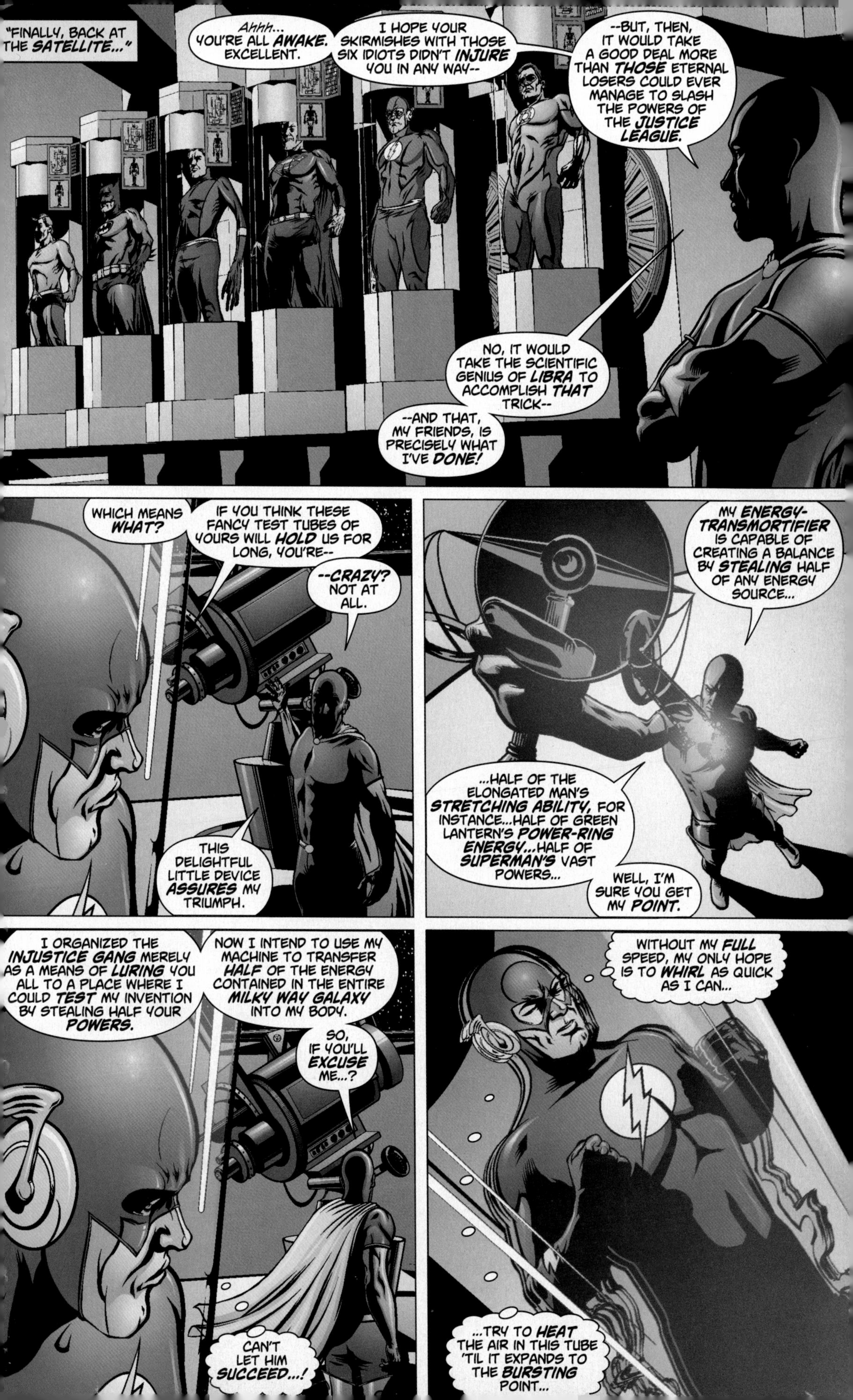
"FINALLY, BACK AT THE SATELLITE..."
Ahhh... YOU'RE ALL AWAKE. EXCELLENT.
I HOPE YOUR SKIRMISHES WITH THOSE SIX IDIOTS DIDN'T INJURE YOU IN ANY WAY--
--BUT, THEN, IT WOULD TAKE A GOOD DEAL MORE THAN THOSE ETERNAL LOSERS COULD EVER MANAGE TO SLASH THE POWERS OF THE JUSTICE LEAGUE.
NO, IT WOULD TAKE THE SCIENTIFIC GENIUS OF LIBRA TO ACCOMPLISH THAT TRICK--
--AND THAT, MY FRIENDS, IS PRECISELY WHAT I'VE DONE!
WHICH MEANS WHAT?
IF YOU THINK THESE FANCY TEST TUBES OF YOURS WILL HOLD US FOR LONG, YOU'RE--
--CRAZY? NOT AT ALL.
THIS DELIGHTFUL LITTLE DEVICE ASSURES MY TRIUMPH.
MY ENERGY-TRANSMORTIFIER IS CAPABLE OF CREATING A BALANCE BY STEALING HALF OF ANY ENERGY SOURCE...
...HALF OF THE ELONGATED MAN'S STRETCHING ABILITY, FOR INSTANCE...HALF OF GREEN LANTERN'S POWER-RING ENERGY...HALF OF SUPERMAN'S VAST POWERS...
WELL, I'M SURE YOU GET MY POINT.
I ORGANIZED THE INJUSTICE GANG MERELY AS A MEANS OF LURING YOU ALL TO A PLACE WHERE I COULD TEST MY INVENTION BY STEALING HALF YOUR POWERS.
NOW I INTEND TO USE MY MACHINE TO TRANSFER HALF OF THE ENERGY CONTAINED IN THE ENTIRE MILKY WAY GALAXY INTO MY BODY.
SO, IF YOU'LL EXCUSE ME...?
CAN'T LET HIM SUCCEED...!
WITHOUT MY FULL SPEED, MY ONLY HOPE IS TO WHIRL AS QUICK AS I CAN...
...TRY TO HEAT THE AIR IN THIS TUBE 'TIL IT EXPANDS TO THE BURSTING POINT...

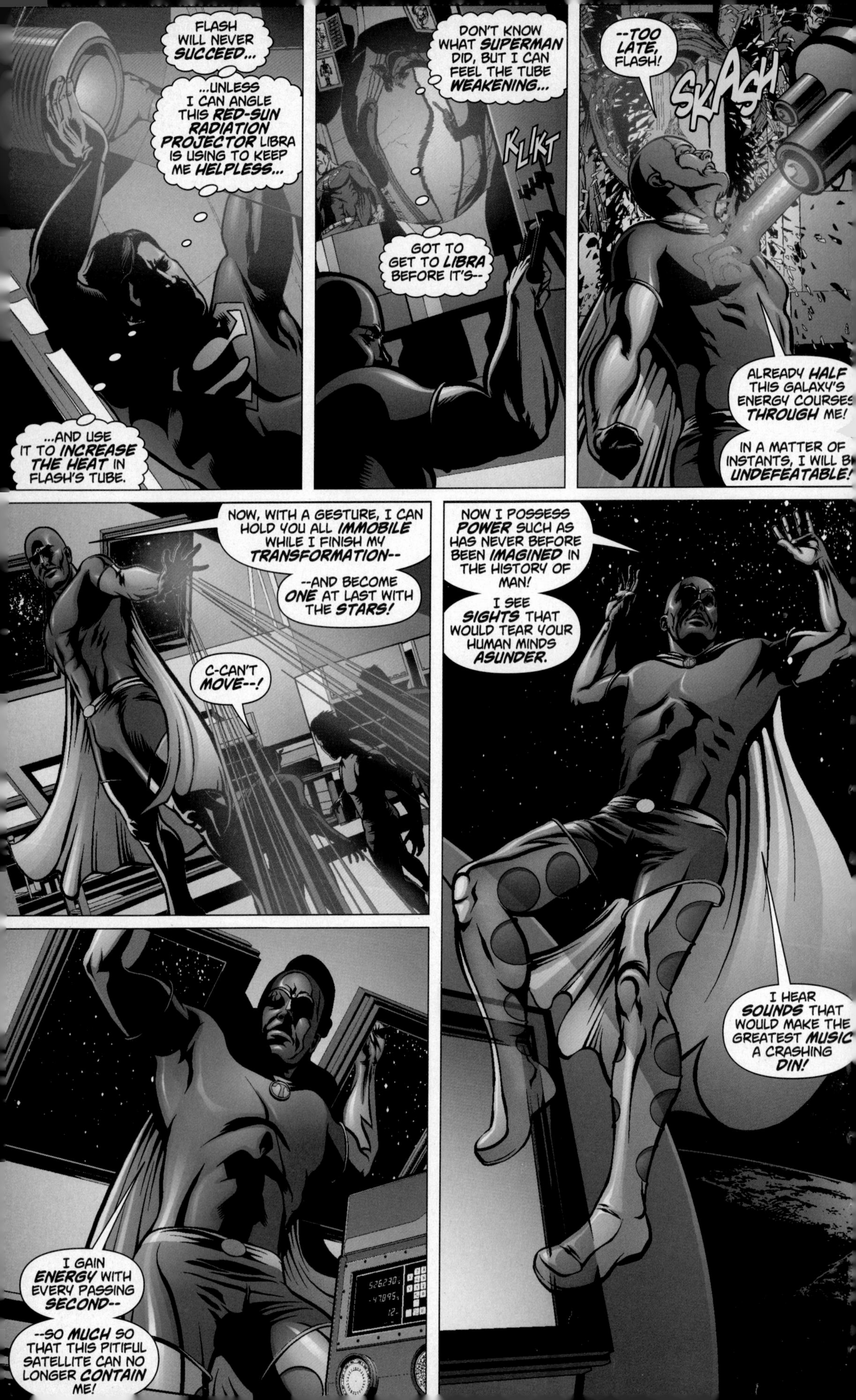
FLASH WILL NEVER SUCCEED...
...UNLESS I CAN ANGLE THIS RED-SUN RADIATION PROJECTOR LIBRA IS USING TO KEEP ME HELPLESS...
...AND USE IT TO INCREASE THE HEAT IN FLASH'S TUBE.
DON'T KNOW WHAT SUPERMAN DID, BUT I CAN FEEL THE TUBE WEAKENING...
KLIKT
GOT TO GET TO LIBRA BEFORE IT'S--
--TOO LATE, FLASH!
SKASH
ALREADY HALF THIS GALAXY'S ENERGY COURSES THROUGH ME!
IN A MATTER OF INSTANTS, I WILL BE UNDEFEATABLE!
NOW, WITH A GESTURE, I CAN HOLD YOU ALL IMMOBILE WHILE I FINISH MY TRANSFORMATION--
--AND BECOME ONE AT LAST WITH THE STARS!
C-CAN'T MOVE--!
I GAIN ENERGY WITH EVERY PASSING SECOND--
--SO MUCH SO THAT THIS PITIFUL SATELLITE CAN NO LONGER CONTAIN ME!
NOW I POSSESS POWER SUCH AS HAS NEVER BEFORE BEEN IMAGINED IN THE HISTORY OF MAN!
I SEE SIGHTS THAT WOULD TEAR YOUR HUMAN MINDS ASUNDER.
I HEAR SOUNDS THAT WOULD MAKE THE GREATEST MUSIC A CRASHING DIN!

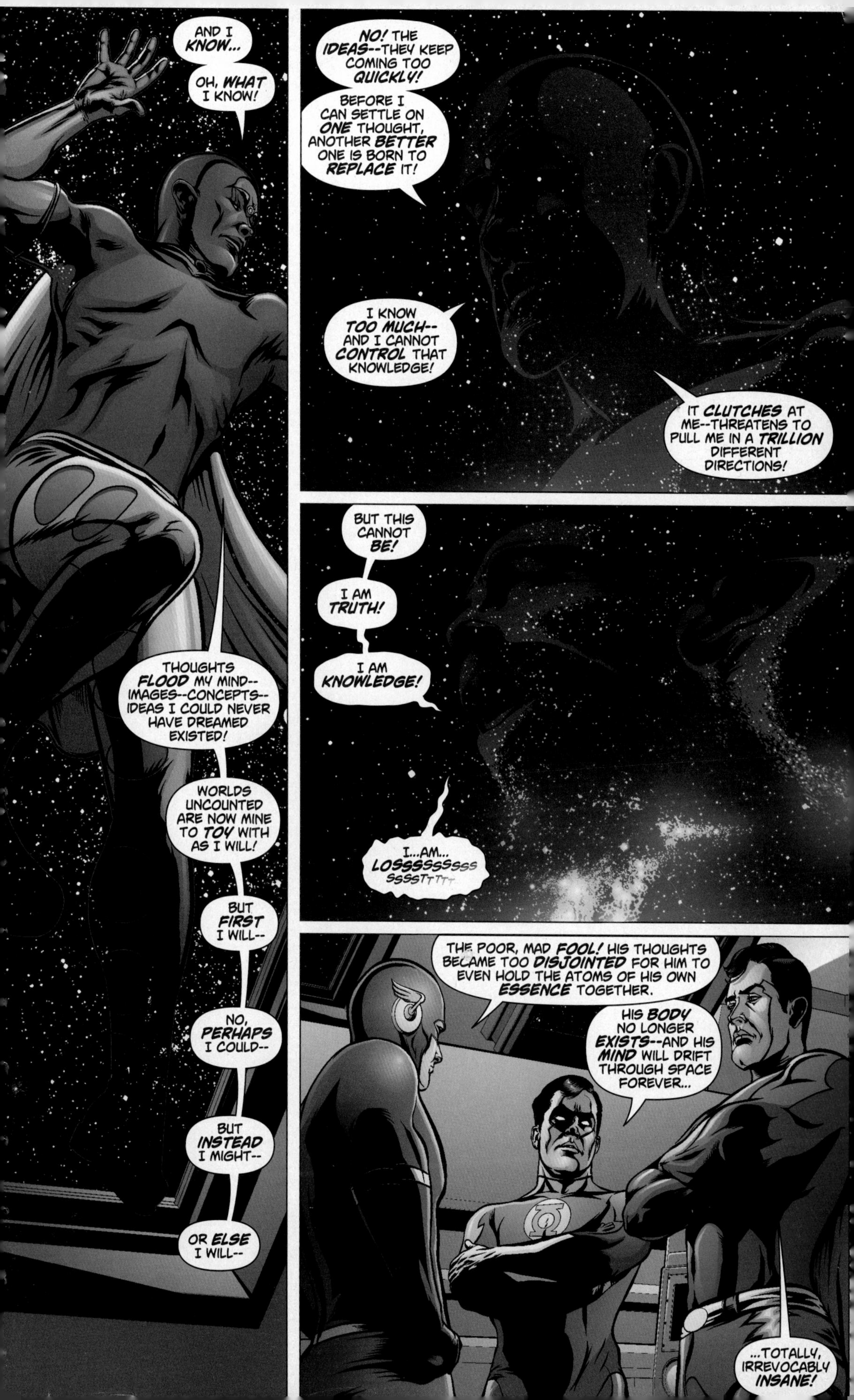
AND I KNOW...
OH, WHAT I KNOW!
THOUGHTS FLOOD MY MIND--IMAGES--CONCEPTS--IDEAS I COULD NEVER HAVE DREAMED EXISTED!
WORLDS UNCOUNTED ARE NOW MINE TO TOY WITH AS I WILL!
BUT FIRST I WILL--
NO, PERHAPS I COULD--
BUT INSTEAD I MIGHT--
OR ELSE I WILL--
NO! THE IDEAS--THEY KEEP COMING TOO QUICKLY!
BEFORE I CAN SETTLE ON ONE THOUGHT, ANOTHER BETTER ONE IS BORN TO REPLACE IT!
I KNOW TOO MUCH--AND I CANNOT CONTROL THAT KNOWLEDGE!
IT CLUTCHES AT ME--THREATENS TO PULL ME IN A TRILLION DIFFERENT DIRECTIONS!
BUT THIS CANNOT BE!
I AM TRUTH!
I AM KNOWLEDGE!
I...AM... LOSSSSSSSSS SSSSTTTTT
THE POOR, MAD FOOL! HIS THOUGHTS BECAME TOO DISJOINTED FOR HIM TO EVEN HOLD THE ATOMS OF HIS OWN ESSENCE TOGETHER.
HIS BODY NO LONGER EXISTS--AND HIS MIND WILL DRIFT THROUGH SPACE FOREVER...
...TOTALLY, IRREVOCABLY INSANE!

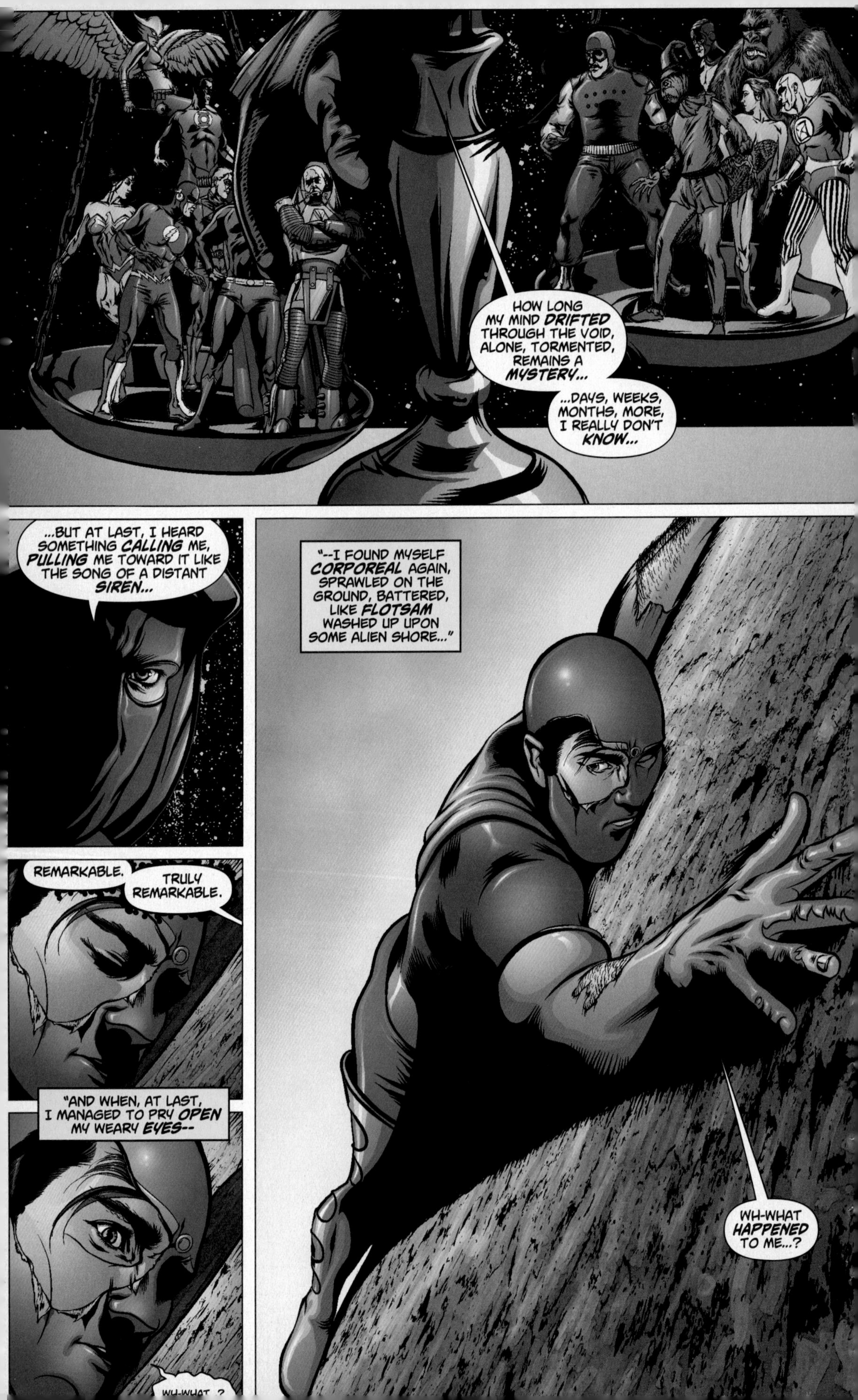

HOW LONG MY MIND DRIFTED THROUGH THE VOID, ALONE, TORMENTED, REMAINS A MYSTERY...
...DAYS, WEEKS, MONTHS, MORE, I REALLY DON'T KNOW...
...BUT AT LAST, I HEARD SOMETHING CALLING ME, PULLING ME TOWARD IT LIKE THE SONG OF A DISTANT SIREN...
REMARKABLE.
TRULY REMARKABLE.
"AND WHEN, AT LAST, I MANAGED TO PRY OPEN MY WEARY EYES--
"--I FOUND MYSELF CORPOREAL AGAIN, SPRAWLED ON THE GROUND, BATTERED, LIKE FLOTSAM WASHED UP UPON SOME ALIEN SHORE..."
WH-WHAT HAPPENED TO ME...?

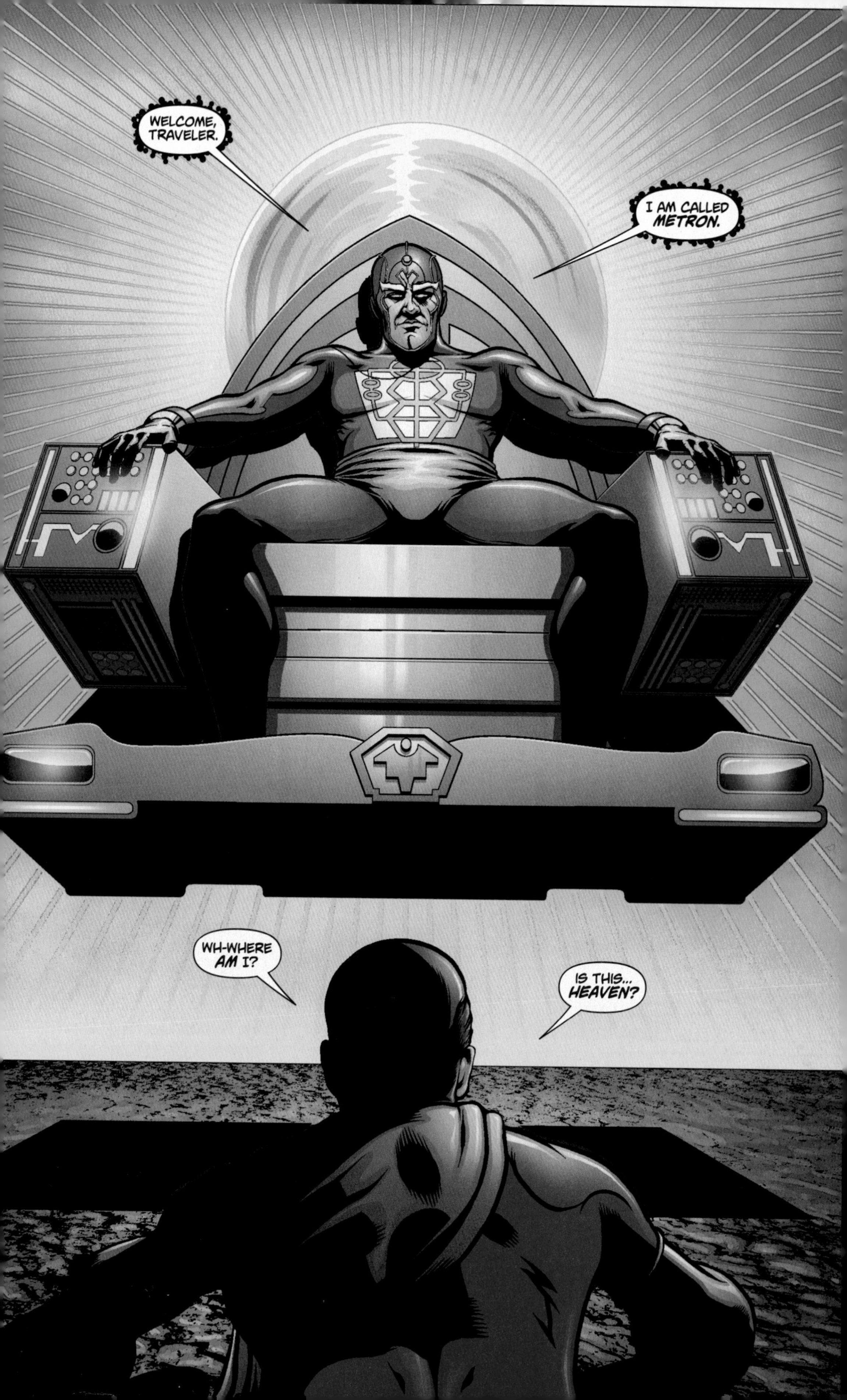
WELCOME, TRAVELER.
I AM CALLED METRON.
WH-WHERE AM I?
IS THIS... HEAVEN?

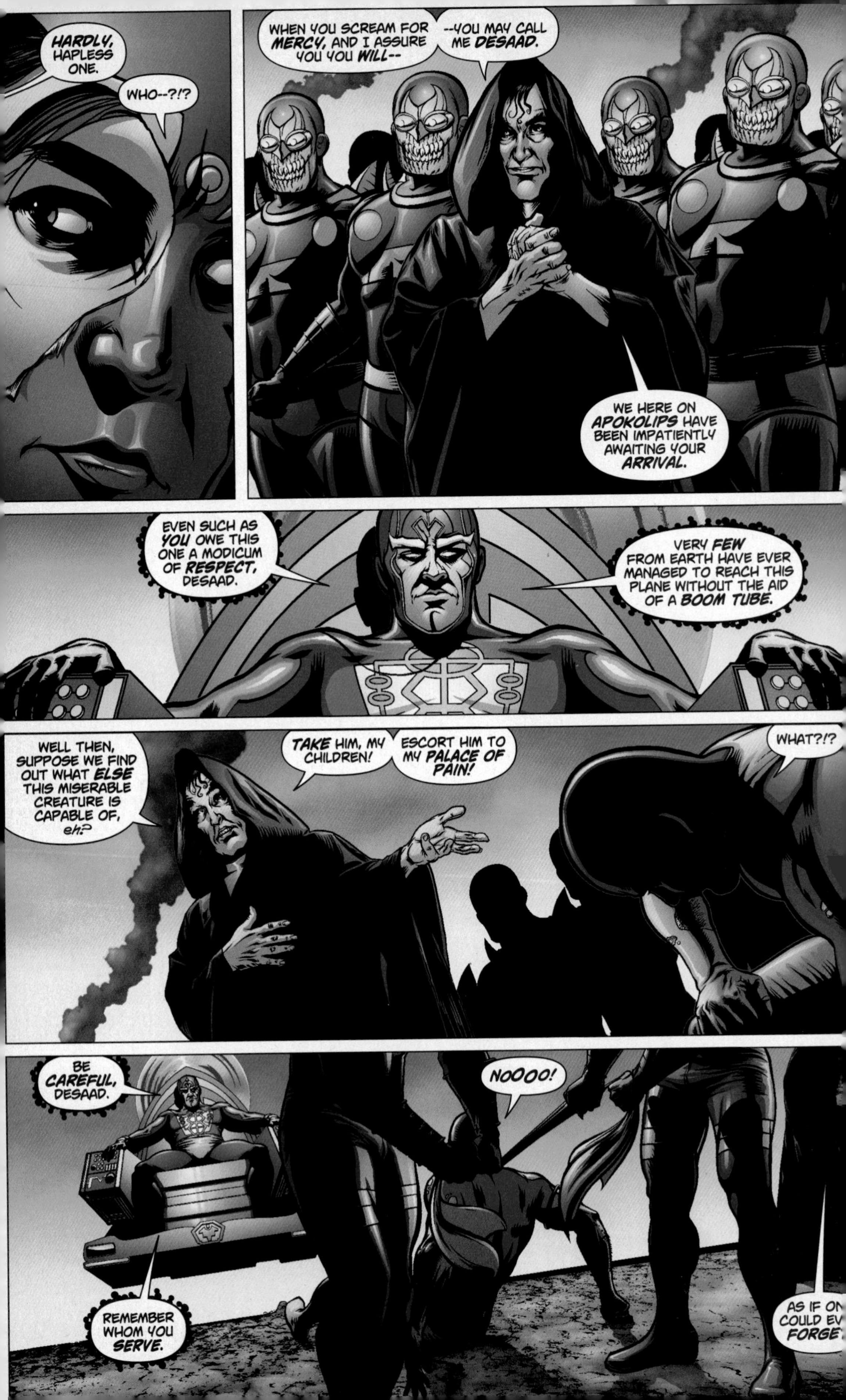

HARDLY, HAPLESS ONE.
WHO--?!?
WHEN YOU SCREAM FOR MERCY, AND I ASSURE YOU YOU WILL--
--YOU MAY CALL ME DESAAD.
WE HERE ON APOKOLIPS HAVE BEEN IMPATIENTLY AWAITING YOUR ARRIVAL.
EVEN SUCH AS YOU OWE THIS ONE A MODICUM OF RESPECT, DESAAD.
VERY FEW FROM EARTH HAVE EVER MANAGED TO REACH THIS PLANE WITHOUT THE AID OF A BOOM TUBE.
WELL THEN, SUPPOSE WE FIND OUT WHAT ELSE THIS MISERABLE CREATURE IS CAPABLE OF, eh?
TAKE HIM, MY CHILDREN!
ESCORT HIM TO MY PALACE OF PAIN!
WHAT?!?
BE CAREFUL, DESAAD.
NOOOO!
REMEMBER WHOM YOU SERVE.

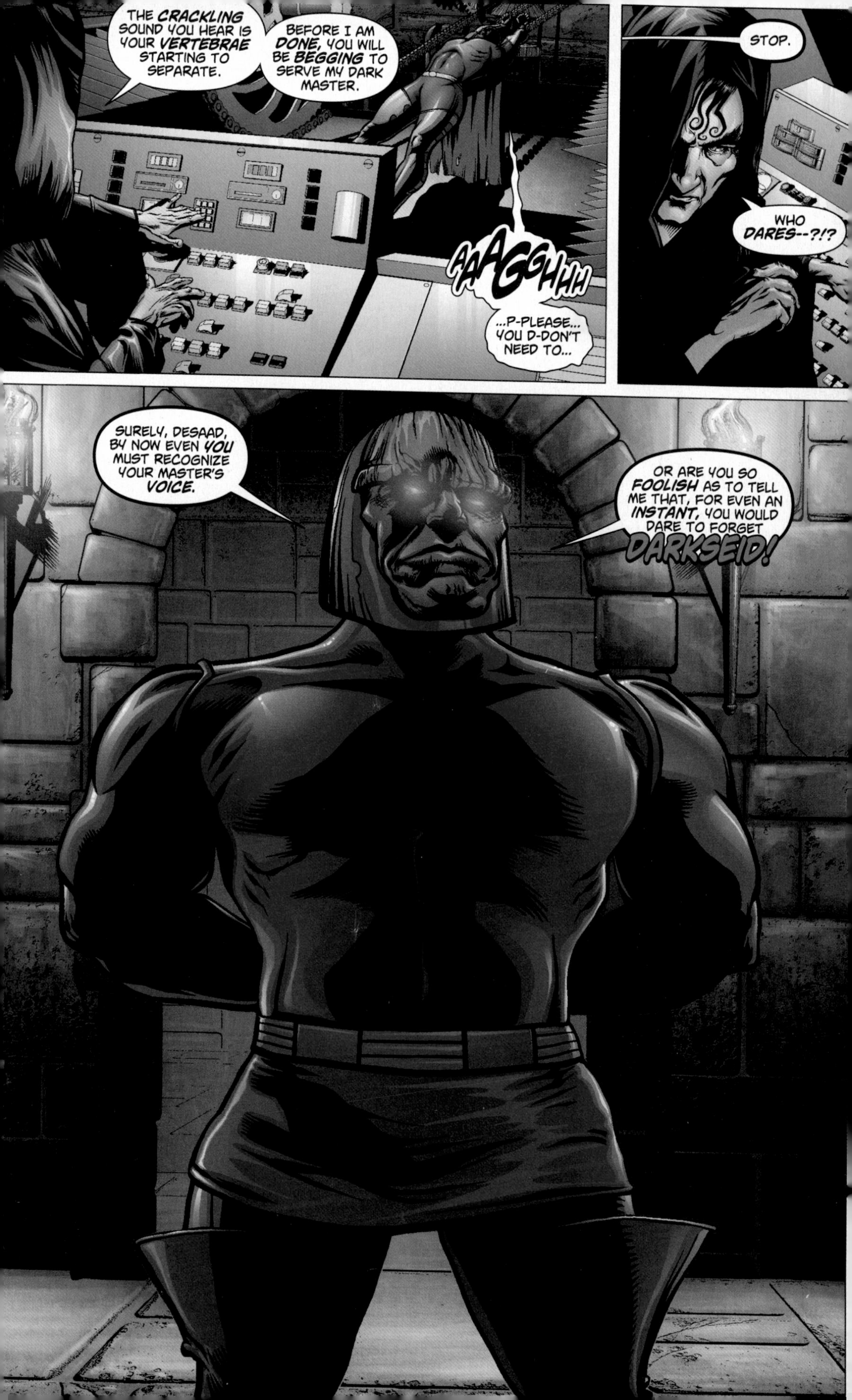
THE CRACKLING SOUND YOU HEAR IS YOUR VERTEBRAE STARTING TO SEPARATE.
BEFORE I AM DONE, YOU WILL BE BEGGING TO SERVE MY DARK MASTER.
AAAGGHHH
...P-PLEASE... YOU D-DON'T NEED TO...
STOP.
WHO DARES--?!?
SURELY, DESAAD, BY NOW EVEN YOU MUST RECOGNIZE YOUR MASTER'S VOICE.
OR ARE YOU SO FOOLISH AS TO TELL ME THAT, FOR EVEN AN INSTANT, YOU WOULD DARE TO FORGET DARKSEID!

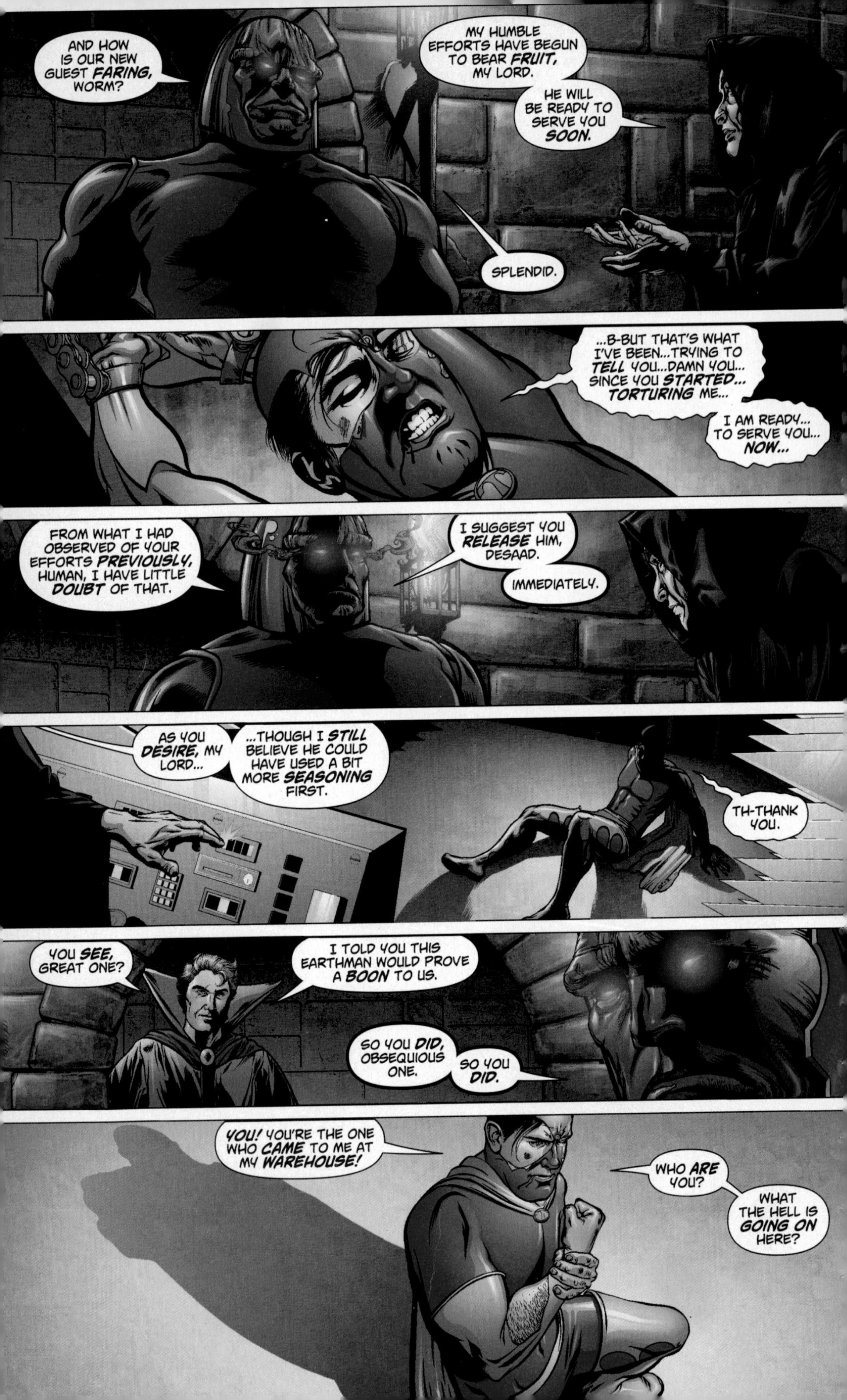
AND HOW IS OUR NEW GUEST FARING, WORM?
MY HUMBLE EFFORTS HAVE BEGUN TO BEAR FRUIT, MY LORD.
HE WILL BE READY TO SERVE YOU SOON.
SPLENDID.
...B-BUT THAT'S WHAT I'VE BEEN...TRYING TO TELL YOU...DAMN YOU... SINCE YOU STARTED... TORTURING ME...
I AM READY... TO SERVE YOU... NOW...
FROM WHAT I HAD OBSERVED OF YOUR EFFORTS PREVIOUSLY, HUMAN, I HAVE LITTLE DOUBT OF THAT.
I SUGGEST YOU RELEASE HIM, DESAAD.
IMMEDIATELY.
AS YOU DESIRE, MY LORD...
...THOUGH I STILL BELIEVE HE COULD HAVE USED A BIT MORE SEASONING FIRST.
TH-THANK YOU.
YOU SEE, GREAT ONE?
I TOLD YOU THIS EARTHMAN WOULD PROVE A BOON TO US.
SO YOU DID, OBSEQUIOUS ONE.
SO YOU DID.
YOU! YOU'RE THE ONE WHO CAME TO ME AT MY WAREHOUSE!
WHO ARE YOU?
WHAT THE HELL IS GOING ON HERE?

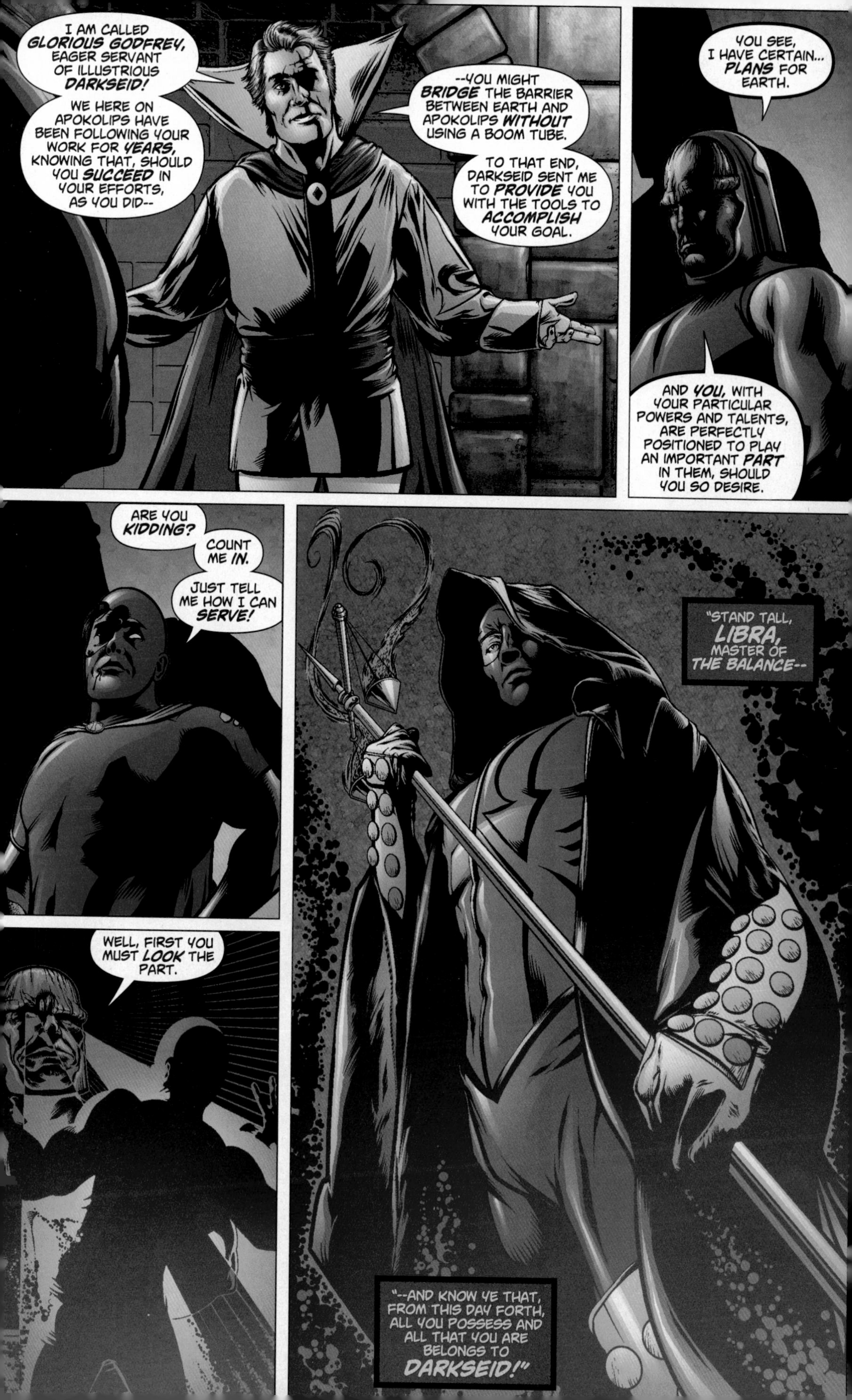
I AM CALLED GLORIOUS GODFREY, EAGER SERVANT OF ILLUSTRIOUS DARKSEID!
WE HERE ON APOKOLIPS HAVE BEEN FOLLOWING YOUR WORK FOR YEARS, KNOWING THAT, SHOULD YOU SUCCEED IN YOUR EFFORTS, AS YOU DID--
--YOU MIGHT BRIDGE THE BARRIER BETWEEN EARTH AND APOKOLIPS WITHOUT USING A BOOM TUBE.
TO THAT END, DARKSEID SENT ME TO PROVIDE YOU WITH THE TOOLS TO ACCOMPLISH YOUR GOAL.
YOU SEE, I HAVE CERTAIN... PLANS FOR EARTH.
AND YOU, WITH YOUR PARTICULAR POWERS AND TALENTS, ARE PERFECTLY POSITIONED TO PLAY AN IMPORTANT PART IN THEM, SHOULD YOU SO DESIRE.
ARE YOU KIDDING?
COUNT ME IN.
JUST TELL ME HOW I CAN SERVE!
WELL, FIRST YOU MUST LOOK THE PART.
"STAND TALL, LIBRA, MASTER OF THE BALANCE--
"--AND KNOW YE THAT, FROM THIS DAY FORTH, ALL YOU POSSESS AND ALL THAT YOU ARE BELONGS TO DARKSEID!"

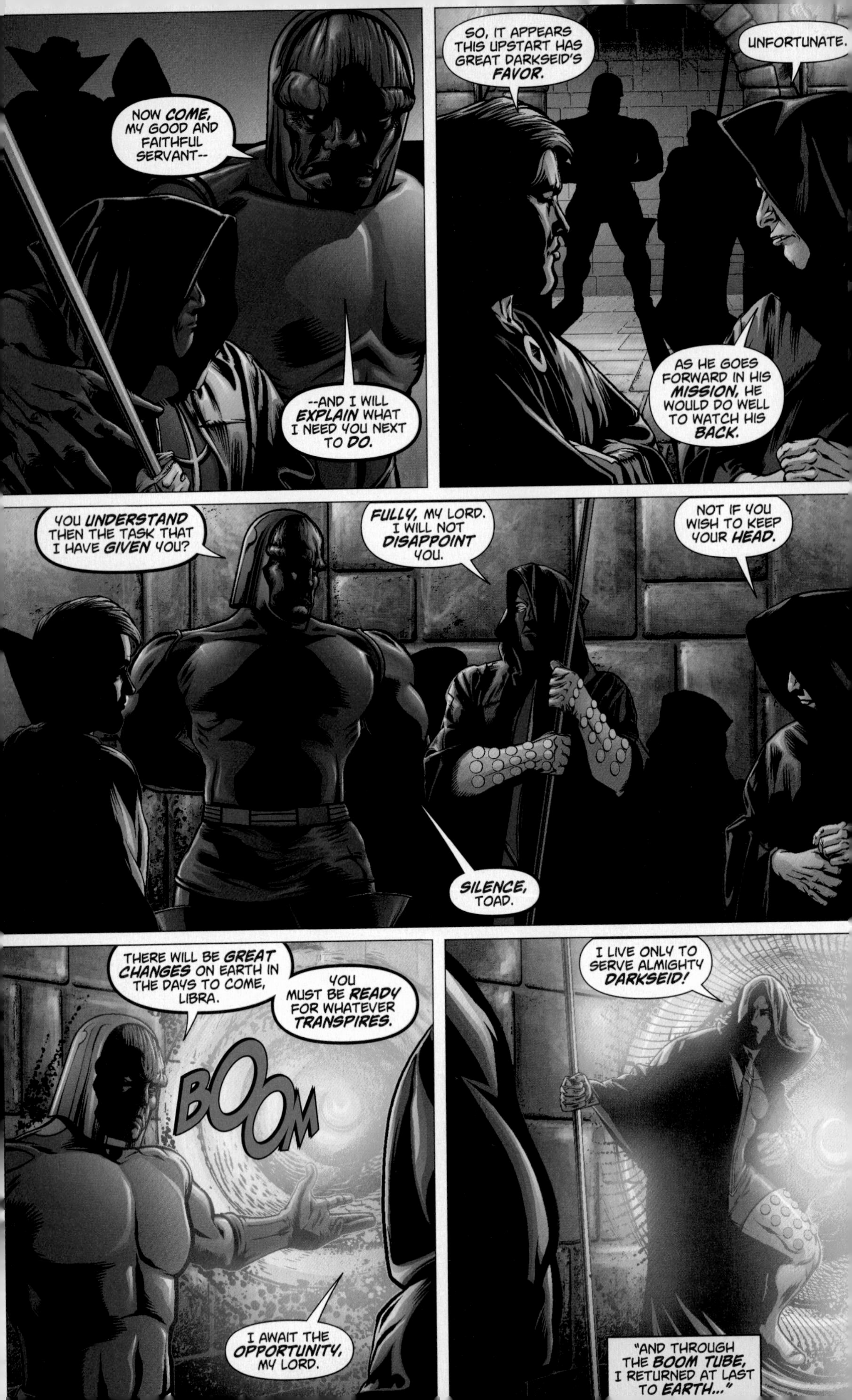
NOW COME, MY GOOD AND FAITHFUL SERVANT--
--AND I WILL EXPLAIN WHAT I NEED YOU NEXT TO DO.
SO, IT APPEARS THIS UPSTART HAS GREAT DARKSEID'S FAVOR.
UNFORTUNATE.
AS HE GOES FORWARD IN HIS MISSION, HE WOULD DO WELL TO WATCH HIS BACK.
YOU UNDERSTAND THEN THE TASK THAT I HAVE GIVEN YOU?
FULLY, MY LORD. I WILL NOT DISAPPOINT YOU.
NOT IF YOU WISH TO KEEP YOUR HEAD.
SILENCE, TOAD.
THERE WILL BE GREAT CHANGES ON EARTH IN THE DAYS TO COME, LIBRA.
YOU MUST BE READY FOR WHATEVER TRANSPIRES.
BOOM
I AWAIT THE OPPORTUNITY, MY LORD.
I LIVE ONLY TO SERVE ALMIGHTY DARKSEID!
"AND THROUGH THE BOOM TUBE, I RETURNED AT LAST TO EARTH..."

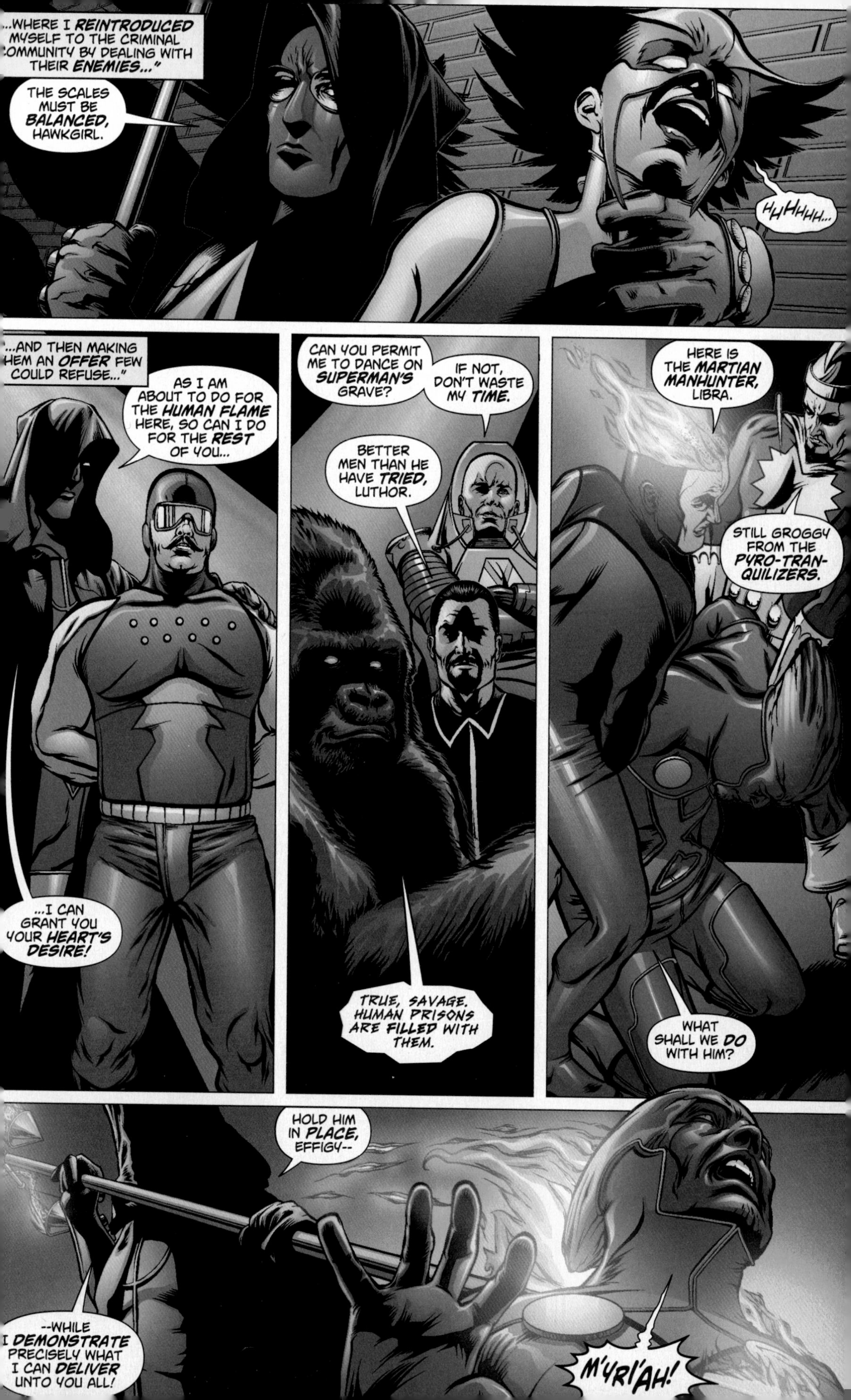
...WHERE I REINTRODUCED MYSELF TO THE CRIMINAL COMMUNITY BY DEALING WITH THEIR ENEMIES..."
THE SCALES MUST BE BALANCED, HAWKGIRL.
HHHHHH...
"...AND THEN MAKING THEM AN OFFER FEW COULD REFUSE..."
AS I AM ABOUT TO DO FOR THE HUMAN FLAME HERE, SO CAN I DO FOR THE REST OF YOU...
...I CAN GRANT YOU YOUR HEART'S DESIRE!
CAN YOU PERMIT ME TO DANCE ON SUPERMAN'S GRAVE?
IF NOT, DON'T WASTE MY TIME.
BETTER MEN THAN HE HAVE TRIED, LUTHOR.
TRUE, SAVAGE. HUMAN PRISONS ARE FILLED WITH THEM.
HERE IS THE MARTIAN MANHUNTER, LIBRA.
STILL GROGGY FROM THE PYRO-TRANQUILIZERS.
WHAT SHALL WE DO WITH HIM?
HOLD HIM IN PLACE, EFFIGY--
--WHILE I DEMONSTRATE PRECISELY WHAT I CAN DELIVER UNTO YOU ALL!
M'YRI'AH!

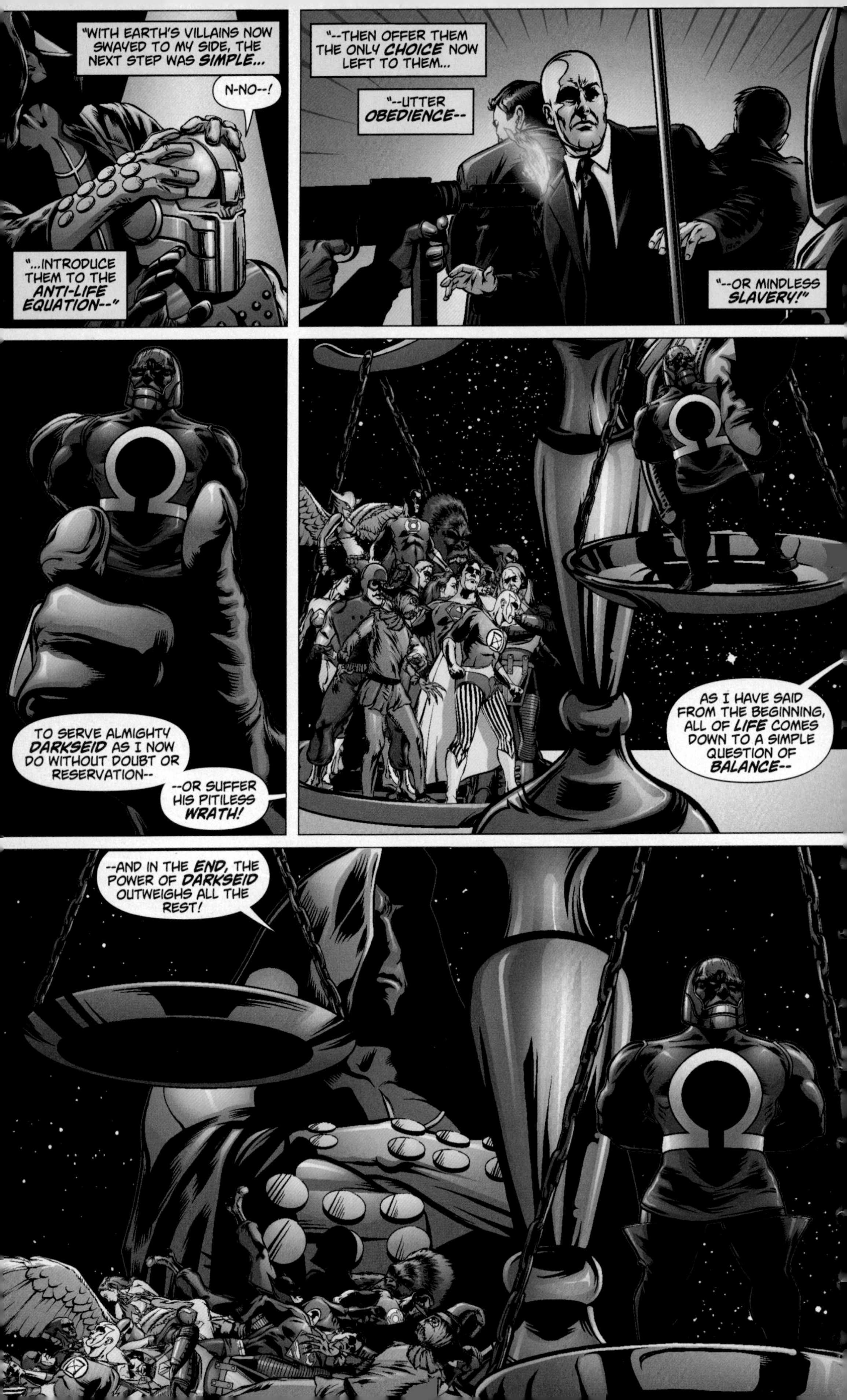
"WITH EARTH'S VILLAINS NOW SWAYED TO MY SIDE, THE NEXT STEP WAS SIMPLE...
N-NO--!
"...INTRODUCE THEM TO THE ANTI-LIFE EQUATION--"
"--THEN OFFER THEM THE ONLY CHOICE NOW LEFT TO THEM...
"--UTTER OBEDIENCE--
"--OR MINDLESS SLAVERY!"
TO SERVE ALMIGHTY DARKSEID AS I NOW DO WITHOUT DOUBT OR RESERVATION--
--OR SUFFER HIS PITILESS WRATH!
AS I HAVE SAID FROM THE BEGINNING, ALL OF LIFE COMES DOWN TO A SIMPLE QUESTION OF BALANCE--
--AND IN THE END, THE POWER OF DARKSEID OUTWEIGHS ALL THE REST!

FINAL CRISIS REQUIEM cover by Doug Mahnke, Christian Alamy and David Baron

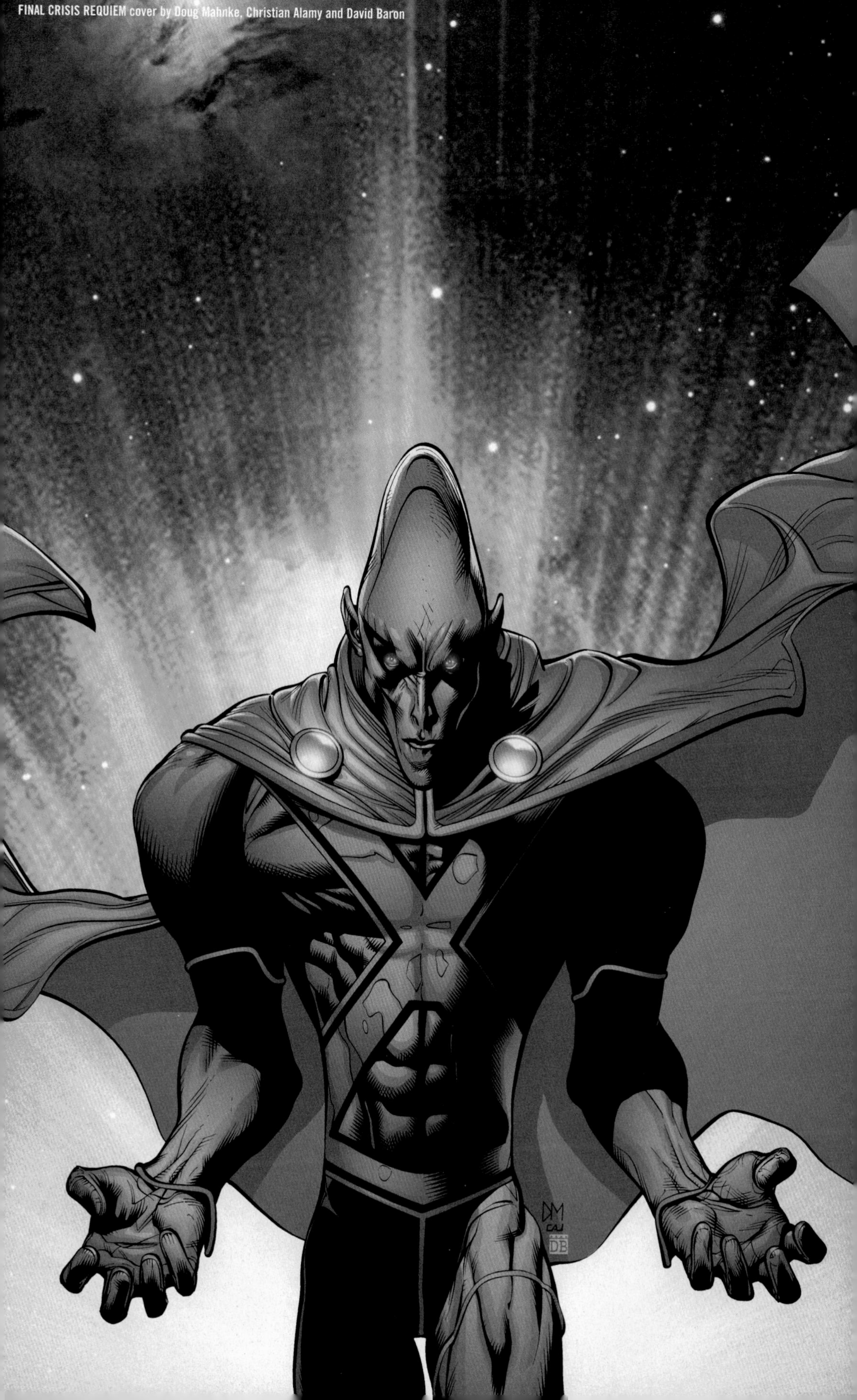

Sliver cover by J.G. Jones

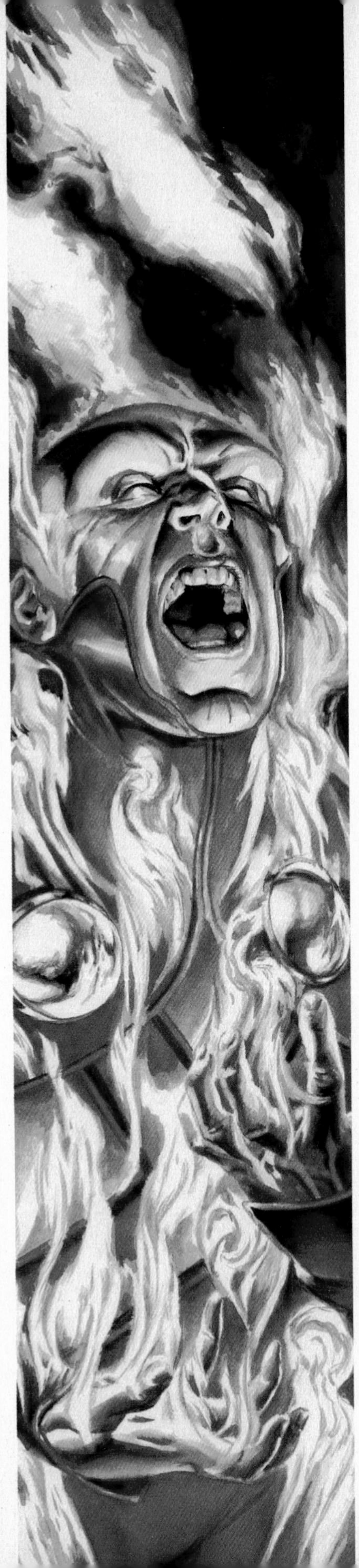

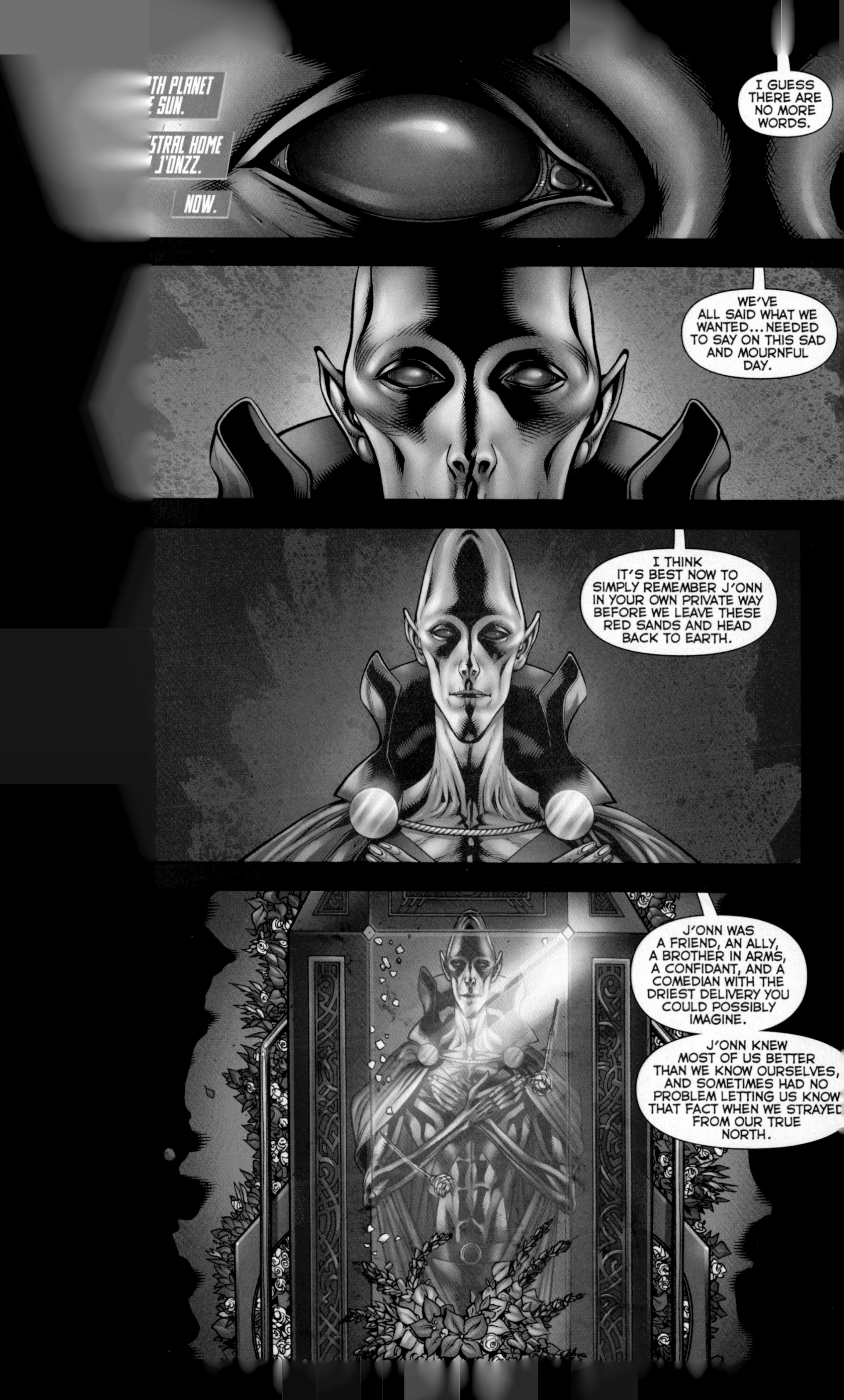

TH PLANET
SUN.
STRAL HOME
J'ONZZ.
NOW.
I GUESS THERE ARE NO MORE WORDS.
WE'VE ALL SAID WHAT WE WANTED...NEEDED TO SAY ON THIS SAD AND MOURNFUL DAY.
I THINK IT'S BEST NOW TO SIMPLY REMEMBER J'ONN IN YOUR OWN PRIVATE WAY BEFORE WE LEAVE THESE RED SANDS AND HEAD BACK TO EARTH.
J'ONN WAS A FRIEND, AN ALLY, A BROTHER IN ARMS, A CONFIDANT, AND A COMEDIAN WITH THE DRIEST DELIVERY YOU COULD POSSIBLY IMAGINE.
J'ONN KNEW MOST OF US BETTER THAN WE KNOW OURSELVES, AND SOMETIMES HAD NO PROBLEM LETTING US KNOW THAT FACT WHEN WE STRAYED FROM OUR TRUE NORTH.

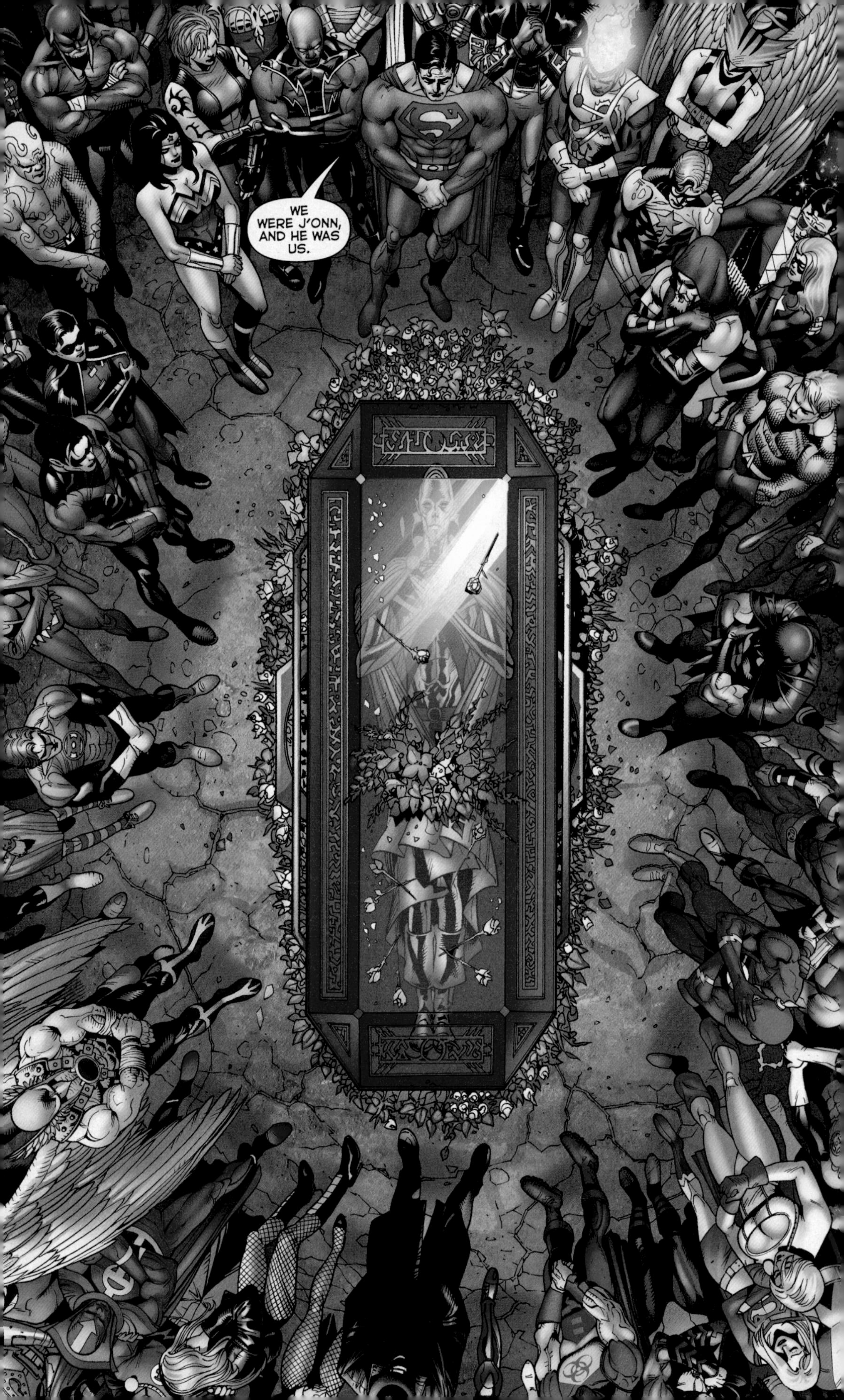
WE WERE J'ONN, AND HE WAS US.

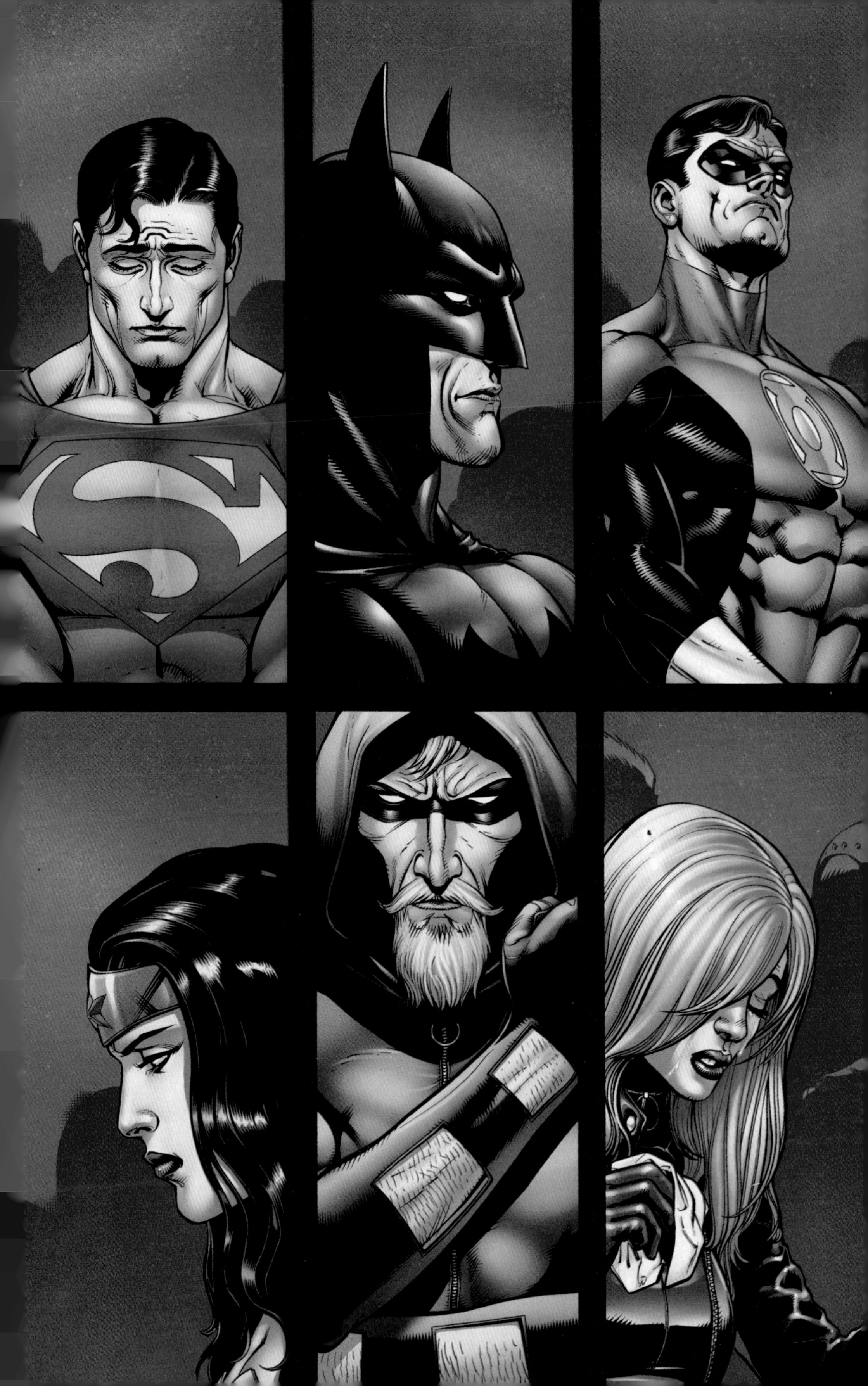

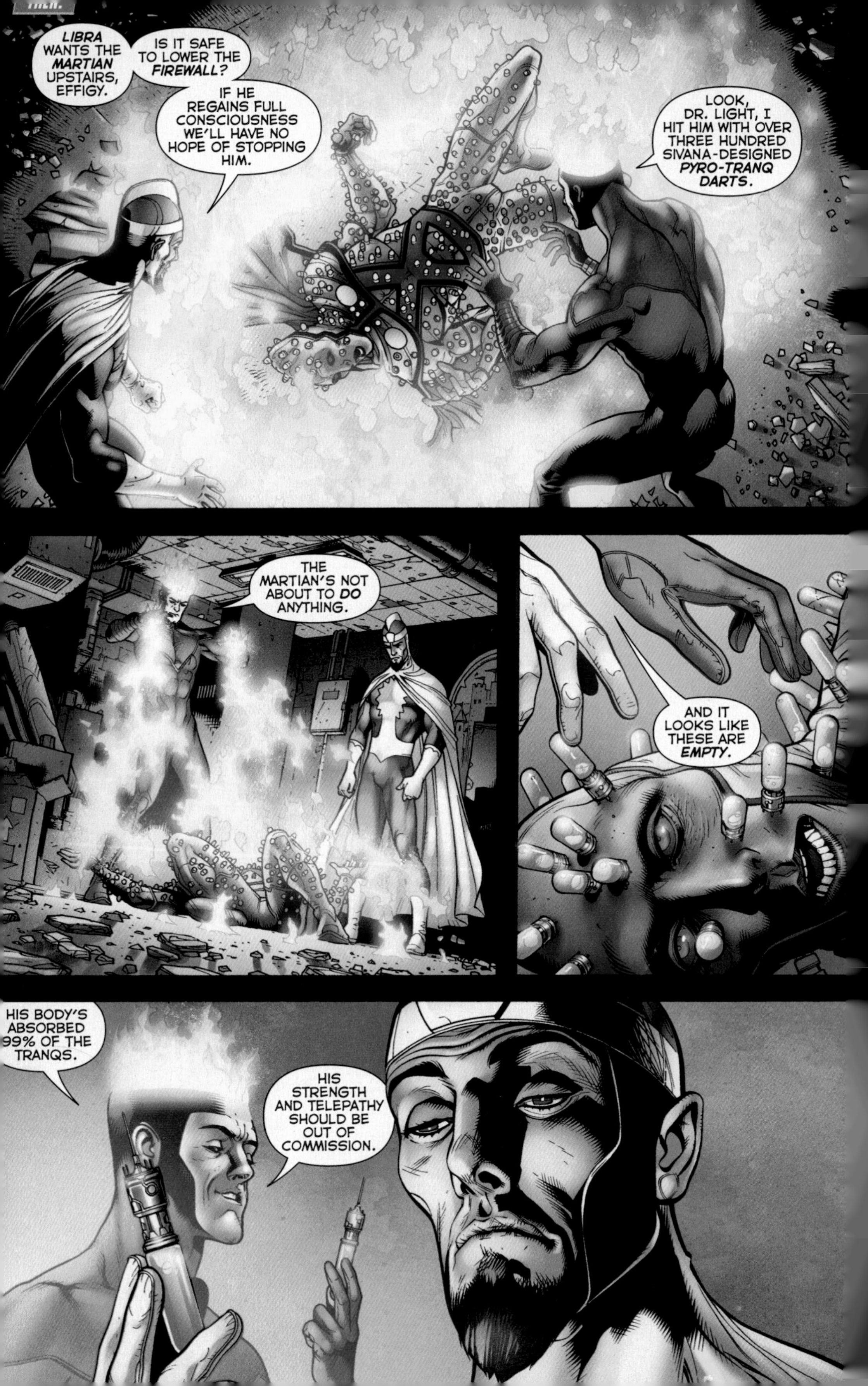
LIBRA WANTS THE MARTIAN UPSTAIRS, EFFIGY.
IS IT SAFE TO LOWER THE FIREWALL?
IF HE REGAINS FULL CONSCIOUSNESS WE'LL HAVE NO HOPE OF STOPPING HIM.
LOOK, DR. LIGHT, I HIT HIM WITH OVER THREE HUNDRED SIVANA-DESIGNED PYRO-TRANQ DARTS.
THE MARTIAN'S NOT ABOUT TO DO ANYTHING.
AND IT LOOKS LIKE THESE ARE EMPTY.
HIS BODY'S ABSORBED 99% OF THE TRANQS.
HIS STRENGTH AND TELEPATHY SHOULD BE OUT OF COMMISSION.

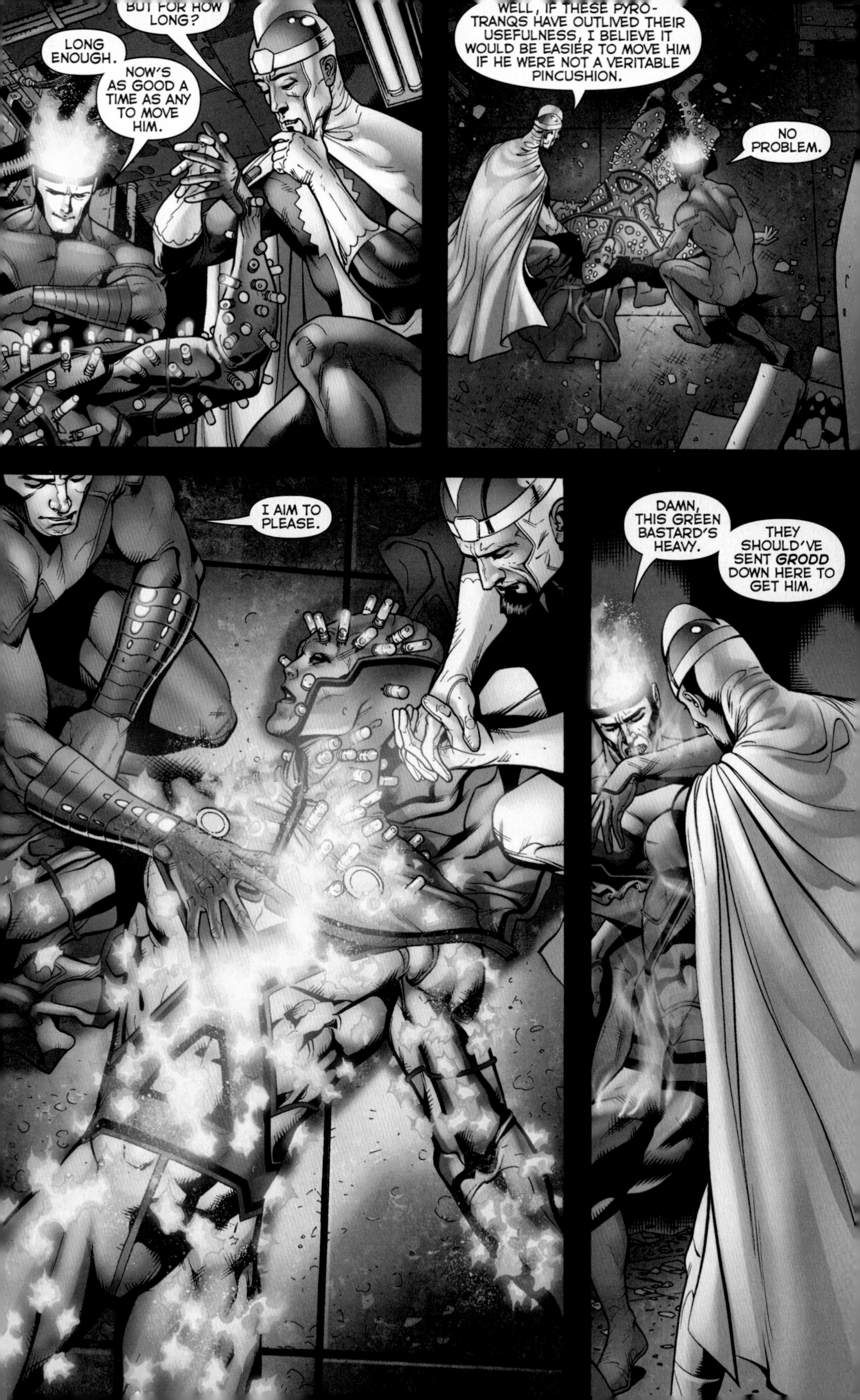
BUT FOR HOW LONG?
LONG ENOUGH.
NOW'S AS GOOD A TIME AS ANY TO MOVE HIM.
WELL, IF THESE PYRO-TRANQS HAVE OUTLIVED THEIR USEFULNESS, I BELIEVE IT WOULD BE EASIER TO MOVE HIM IF HE WERE NOT A VERITABLE PINCUSHION.
NO PROBLEM.
I AIM TO PLEASE.
DAMN, THIS GREEN BASTARD'S HEAVY.
THEY SHOULD'VE SENT GRODD DOWN HERE TO GET HIM.

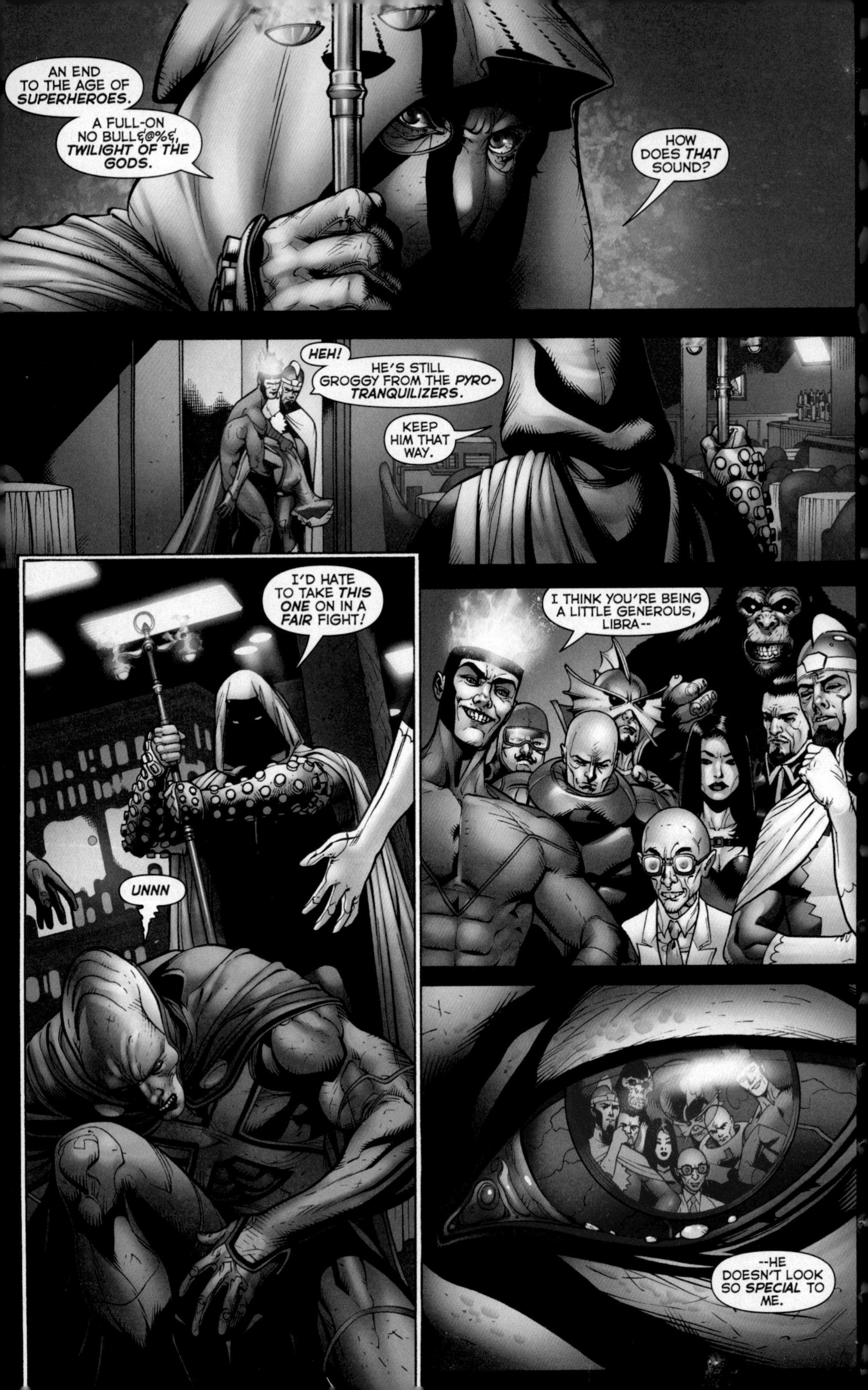
AN END TO THE AGE OF SUPERHEROES.
A FULL-ON NO BULL&@%&, TWILIGHT OF THE GODS.
HOW DOES THAT SOUND?
HEH!
HE'S STILL GROGGY FROM THE PYRO-TRANQUILIZERS.
KEEP HIM THAT WAY.
I'D HATE TO TAKE THIS ONE ON IN A FAIR FIGHT!
UNNN
I THINK YOU'RE BEING A LITTLE GENEROUS, LIBRA--
--HE DOESN'T LOOK SO SPECIAL TO ME.

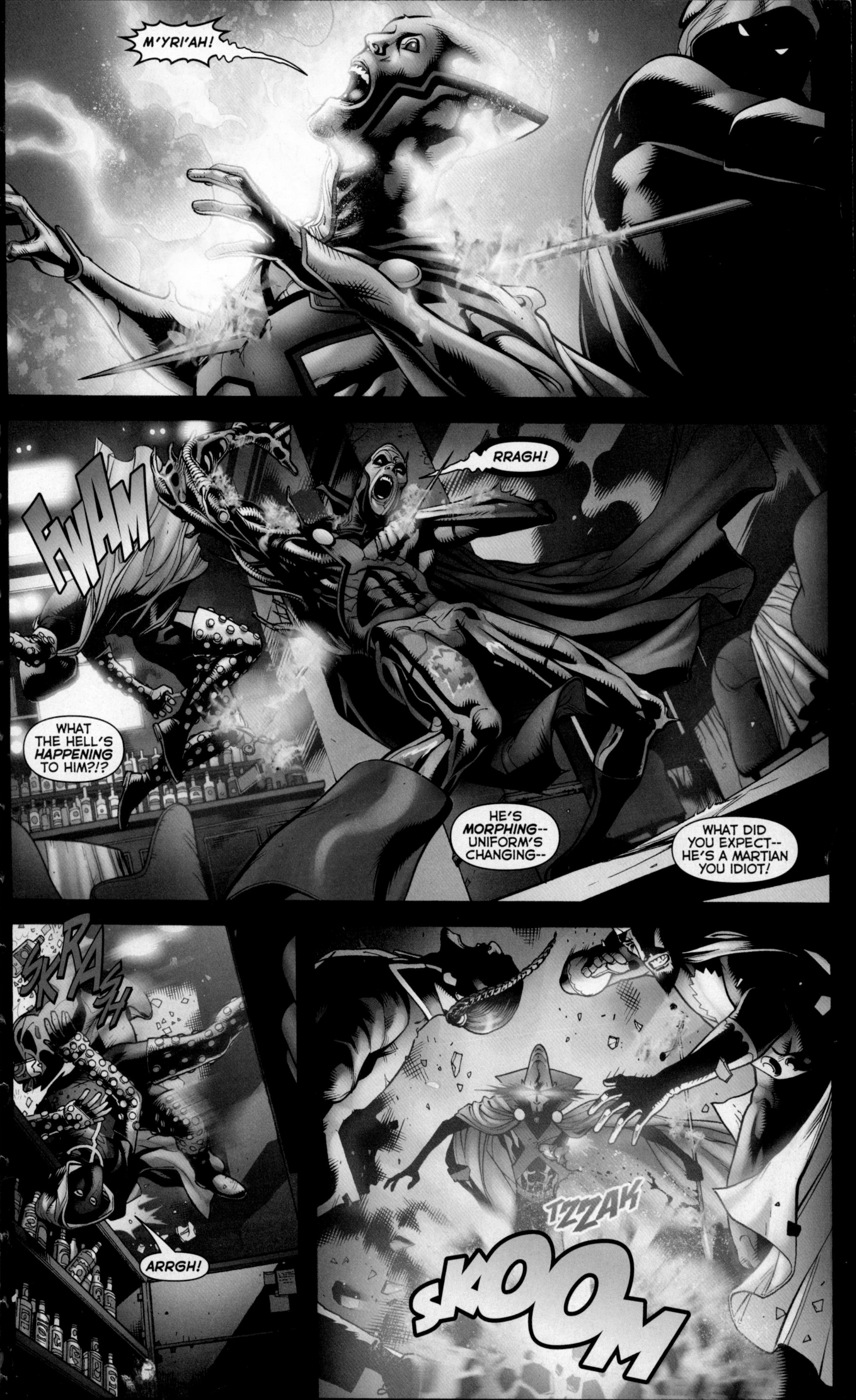
M'YRI'AH!
FWAM
RRAGH!
WHAT THE HELL'S HAPPENING TO HIM?!?
HE'S MORPHING-- UNIFORM'S CHANGING--
WHAT DID YOU EXPECT-- HE'S A MARTIAN YOU IDIOT!
SKRASH
ARRGH!
TZZAK
SKOOOM

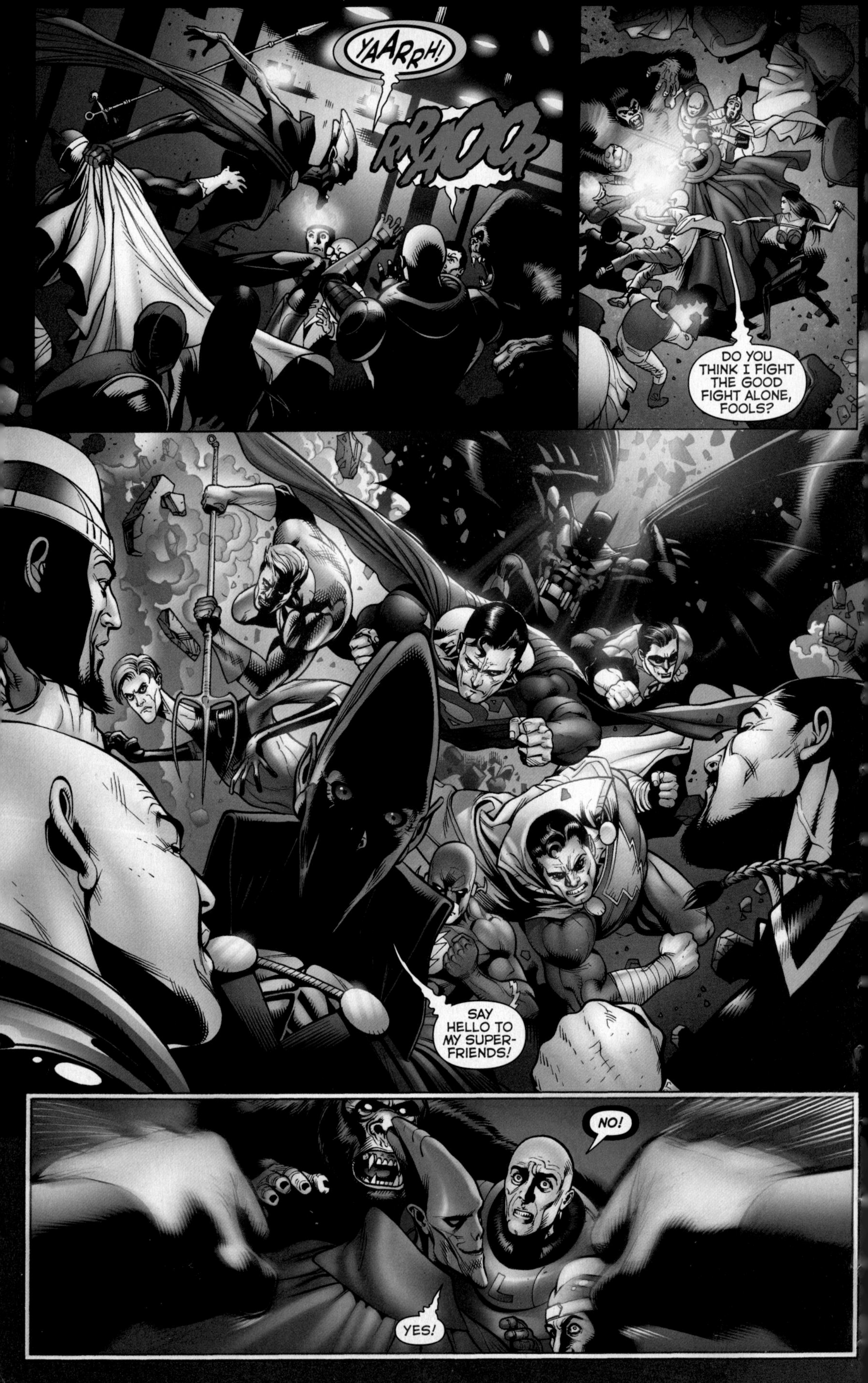
YAARRH!
RRAOOOR
DO YOU THINK I FIGHT THE GOOD FIGHT ALONE, FOOLS?
SAY HELLO TO MY SUPER-FRIENDS!
NO!
YES!

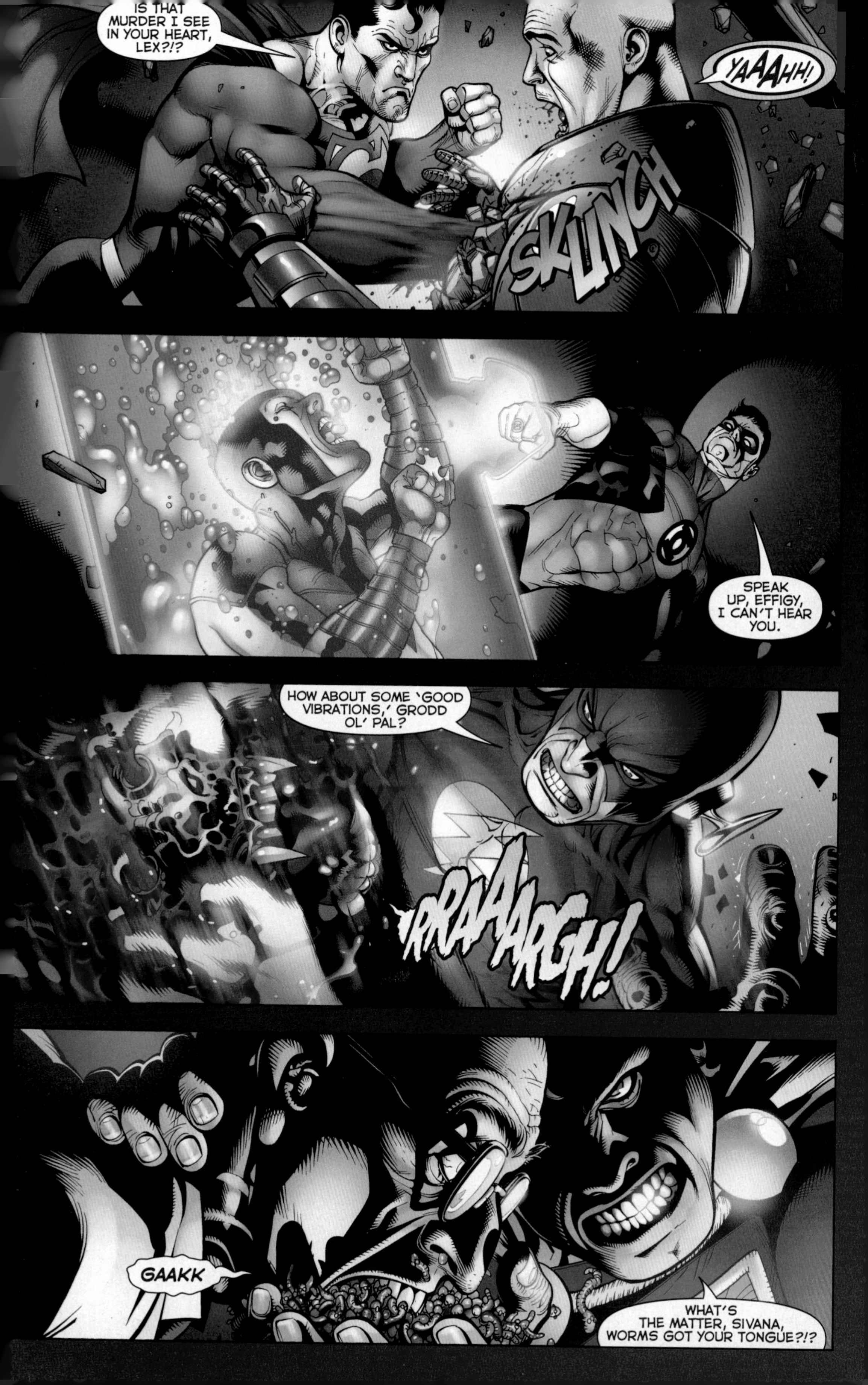
IS THAT MURDER I SEE IN YOUR HEART, LEX?!?
YAAAHH!
SKLUNCH
SPEAK UP, EFFIGY, I CAN'T HEAR YOU.
HOW ABOUT SOME 'GOOD VIBRATIONS,' GRODD OL' PAL?
RRRAAAARGH!
GAAKK
WHAT'S THE MATTER, SIVANA, WORMS GOT YOUR TONGUE?!?

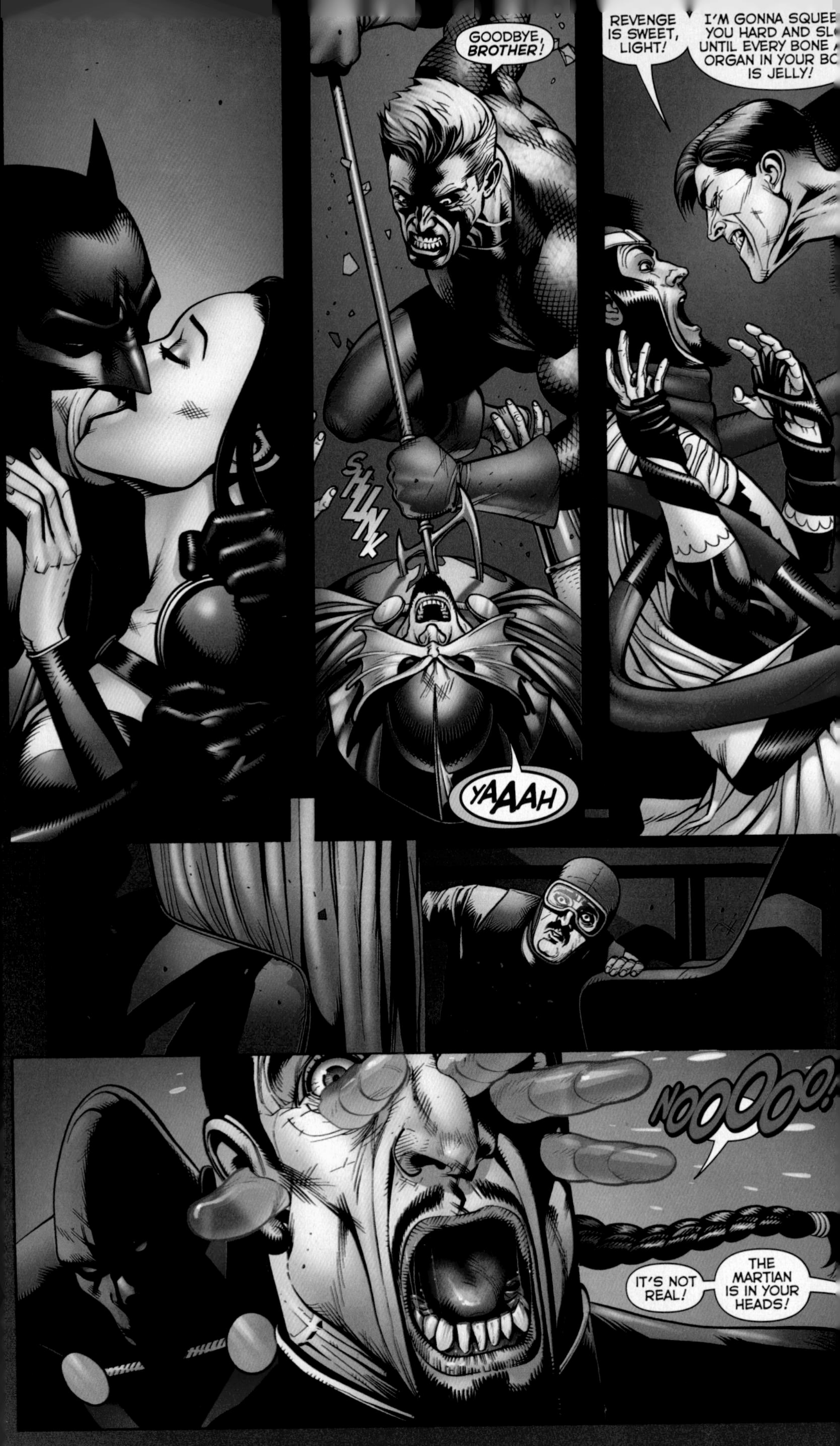
GOODBYE, BROTHER!
SHLUNK
YAAAH
REVENGE IS SWEET, LIGHT!
I'M GONNA SQUEE YOU HARD AND SL UNTIL EVERY BONE ORGAN IN YOUR BO IS JELLY!
NOOOOOO!
IT'S NOT REAL!
THE MARTIAN IS IN YOUR HEADS!

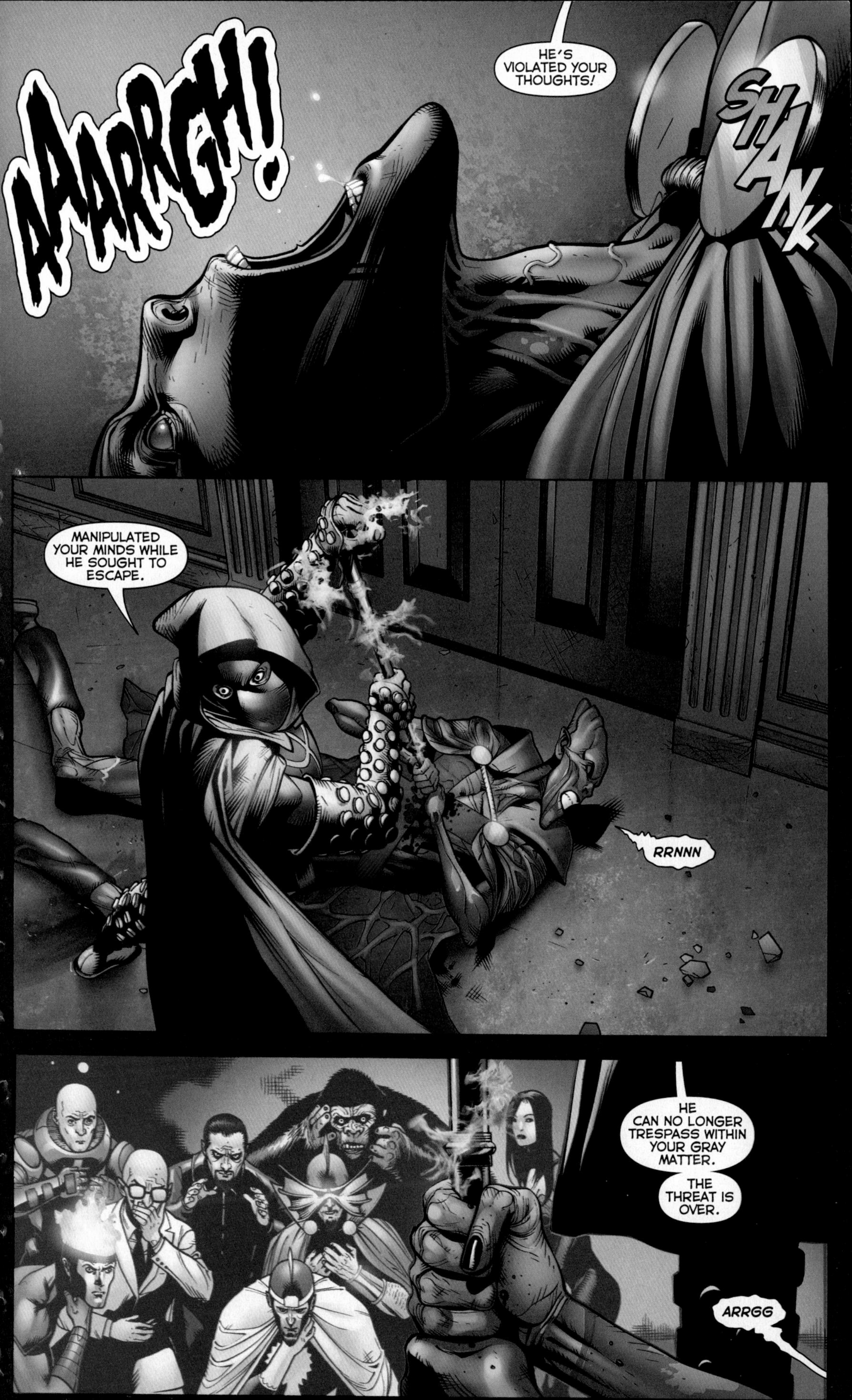
AAARRGH!
HE'S VIOLATED YOUR THOUGHTS!
SHANK
MANIPULATED YOUR MINDS WHILE HE SOUGHT TO ESCAPE.
RRNNN
HE CAN NO LONGER TRESPASS WITHIN YOUR GRAY MATTER.
THE THREAT IS OVER.
ARRGG

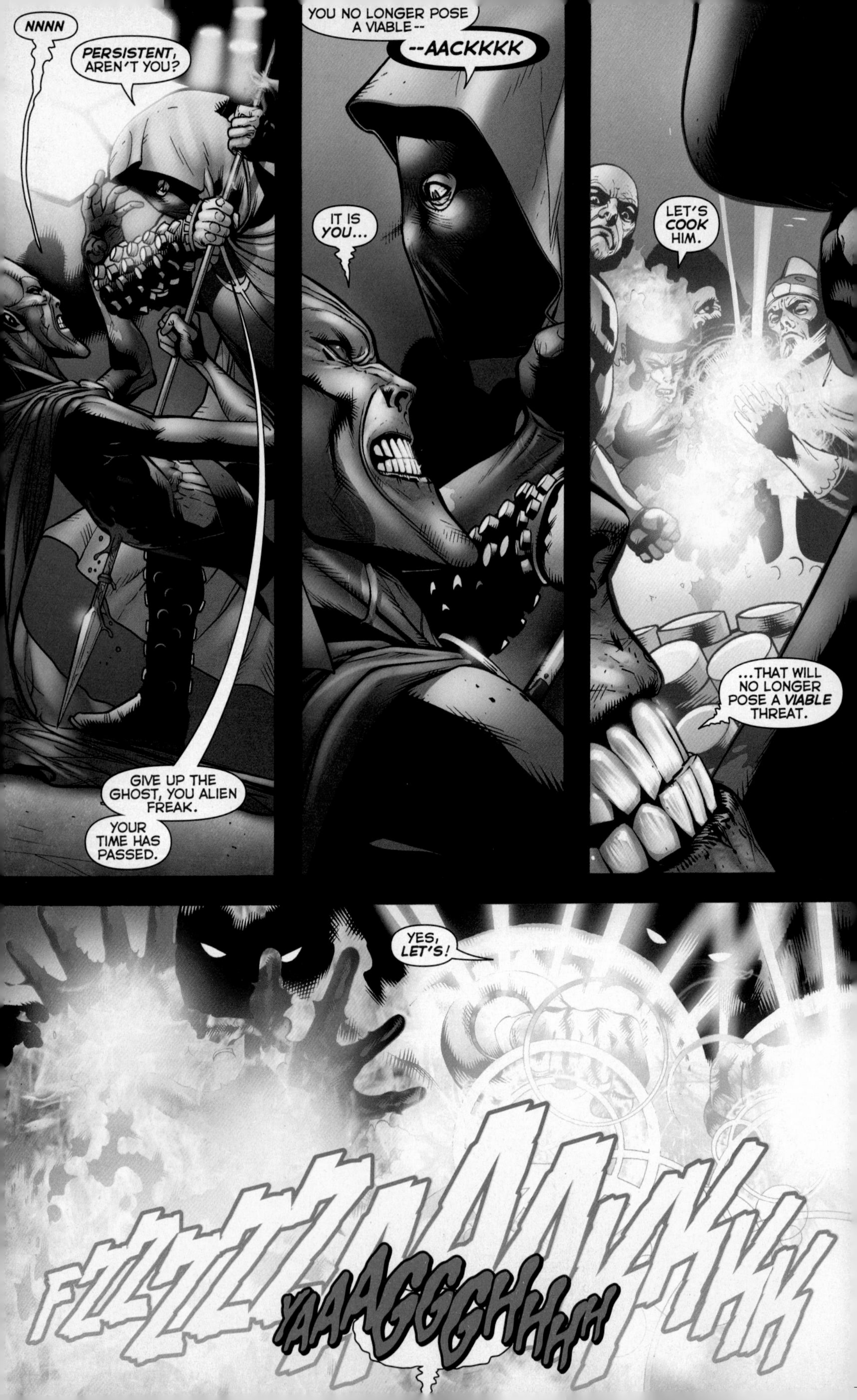
NNNN
PERSISTENT, AREN'T YOU?
GIVE UP THE GHOST, YOU ALIEN FREAK.
YOUR TIME HAS PASSED.
YOU NO LONGER POSE A VIABLE--
--AACKKKK
IT IS YOU...
LET'S COOK HIM.
...THAT WILL NO LONGER POSE A VIABLE THREAT.
YES, LET'S!
FZZZZZAAAAKKK
YAAAGGGHHHH

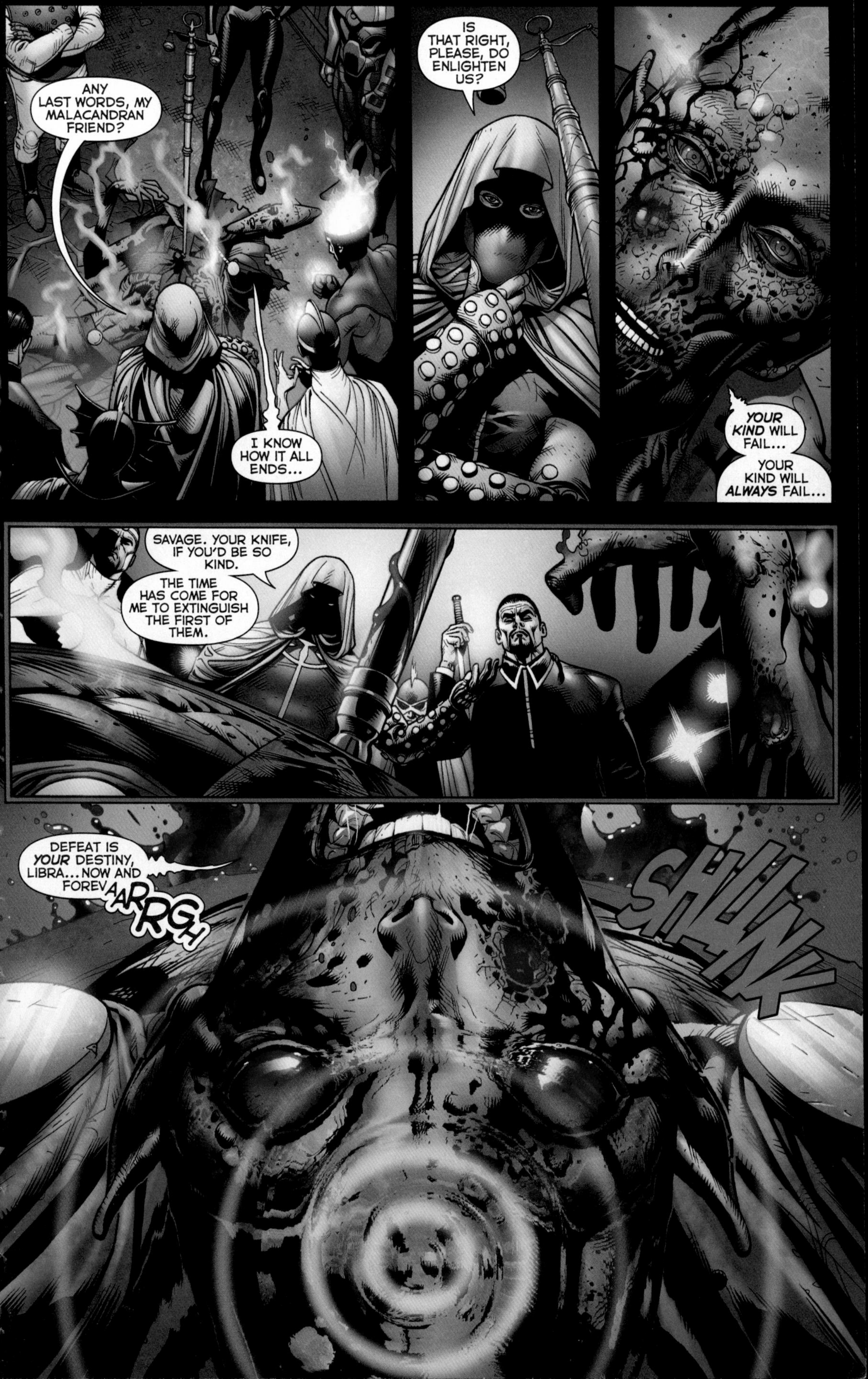
ANY LAST WORDS, MY MALACANDRAN FRIEND?
I KNOW HOW IT ALL ENDS...
IS THAT RIGHT, PLEASE, DO ENLIGHTEN US?
YOUR KIND WILL FAIL...
YOUR KIND WILL ALWAYS FAIL...
SAVAGE. YOUR KNIFE, IF YOU'D BE SO KIND.
THE TIME HAS COME FOR ME TO EXTINGUISH THE FIRST OF THEM.
DEFEAT IS YOUR DESTINY, LIBRA... NOW AND FOREVAARRGH
SHLUNK

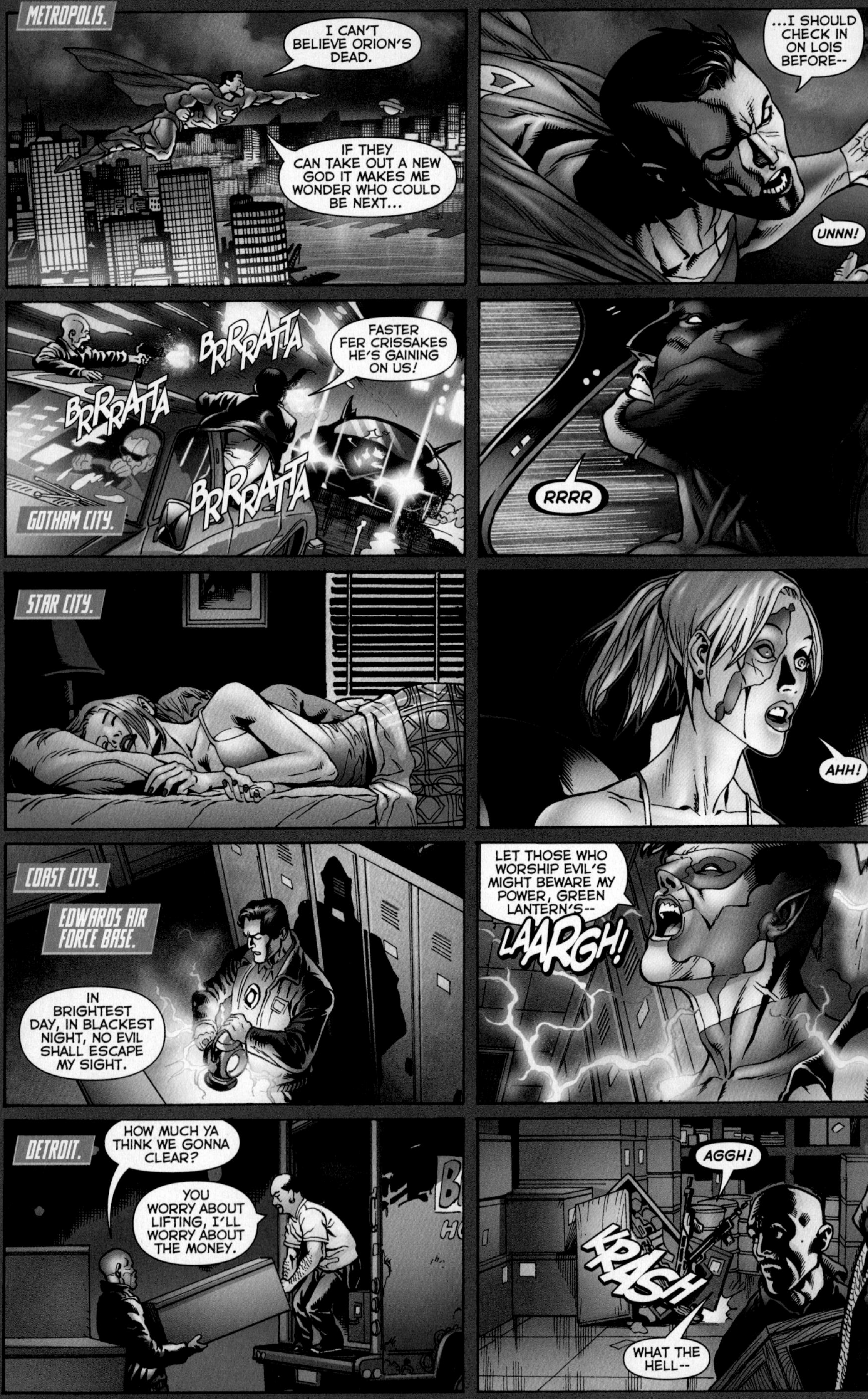
METROPOLIS.
I CAN'T BELIEVE ORION'S DEAD.
IF THEY CAN TAKE OUT A NEW GOD IT MAKES ME WONDER WHO COULD BE NEXT...
...I SHOULD CHECK IN ON LOIS BEFORE--
UNNN!
GOTHAM CITY.
BRRRATTA
BRRRATTA
BRRRATTA
FASTER FER CRISSAKES HE'S GAINING ON US!
RRRR
STAR CITY.
AHH!
COAST CITY.
EDWARDS AIR FORCE BASE.
IN BRIGHTEST DAY, IN BLACKEST NIGHT, NO EVIL SHALL ESCAPE MY SIGHT.
LET THOSE WHO WORSHIP EVIL'S MIGHT BEWARE MY POWER, GREEN LANTERN'S--
LAARGH!
DETROIT.
HOW MUCH YA THINK WE GONNA CLEAR?
YOU WORRY ABOUT LIFTING, I'LL WORRY ABOUT THE MONEY.
AGGH!
KRASH
WHAT THE HELL--

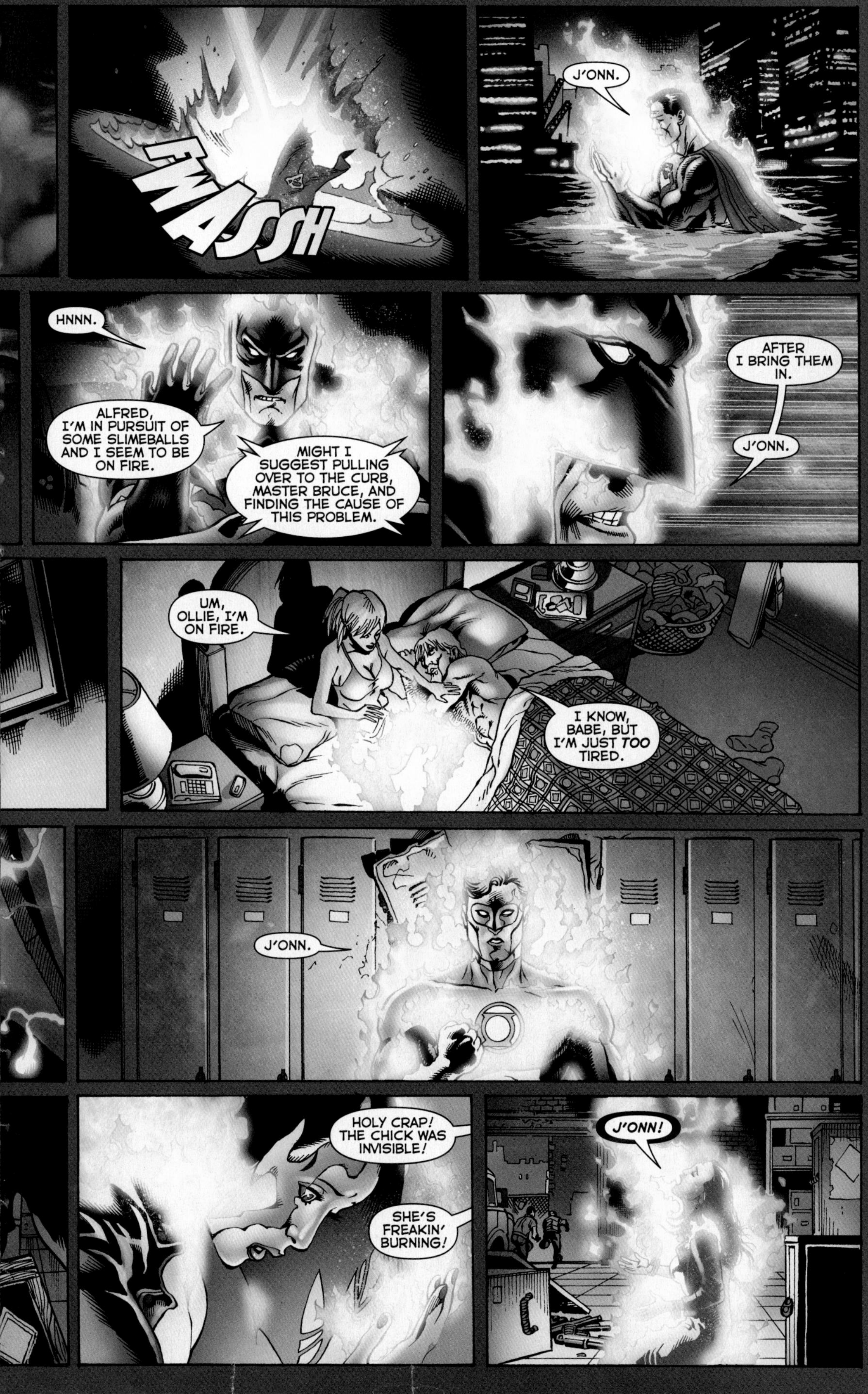
FWASSH
J'ONN.
HNNN.
ALFRED, I'M IN PURSUIT OF SOME SLIMEBALLS AND I SEEM TO BE ON FIRE.
MIGHT I SUGGEST PULLING OVER TO THE CURB, MASTER BRUCE, AND FINDING THE CAUSE OF THIS PROBLEM.
AFTER I BRING THEM IN.
J'ONN.
UM, OLLIE, I'M ON FIRE.
I KNOW, BABE, BUT I'M JUST *TOO* TIRED.
J'ONN.
HOLY CRAP! THE CHICK WAS INVISIBLE!
SHE'S FREAKIN' BURNING!
J'ONN!

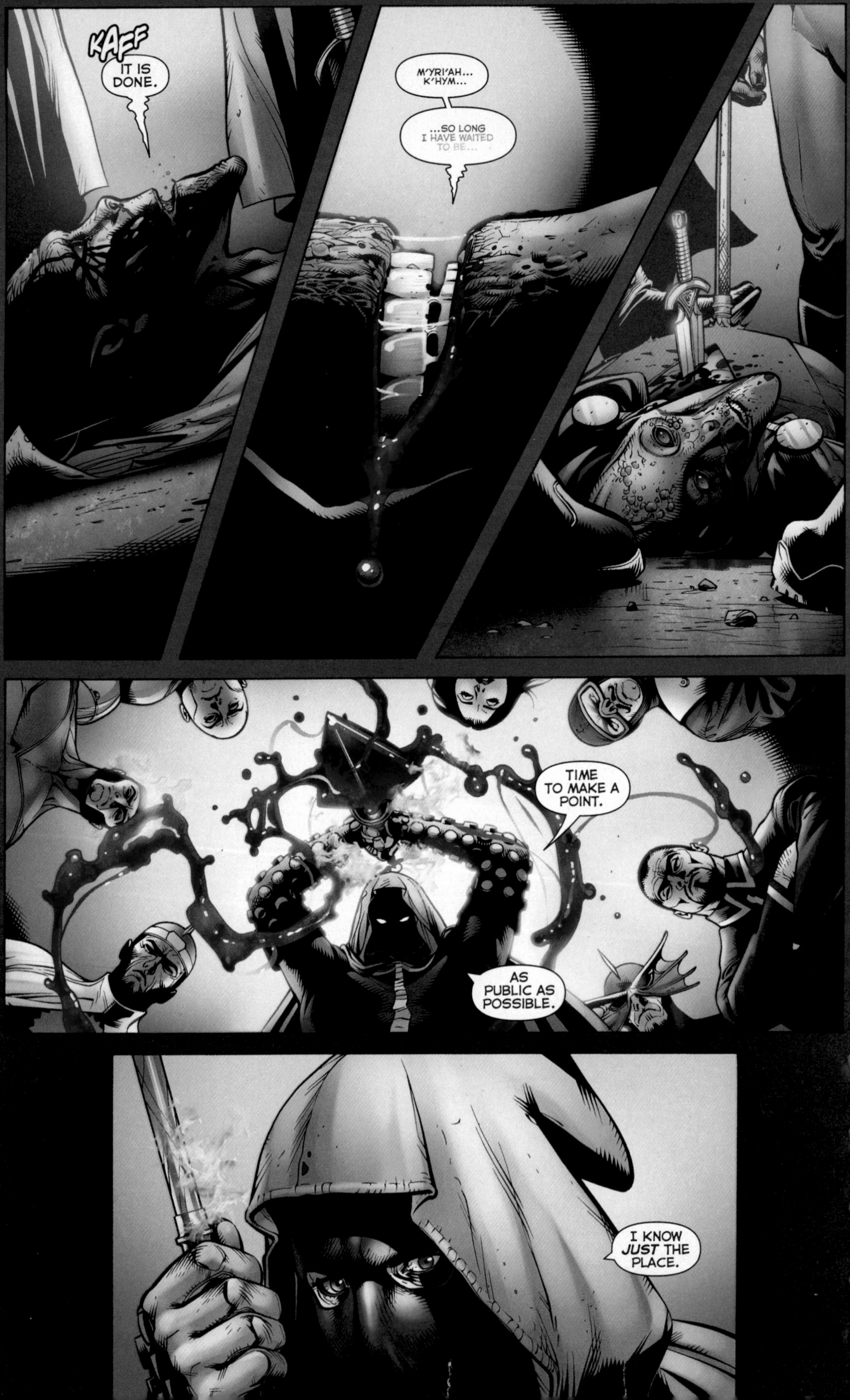
KAFF
IT IS DONE.
M'YRI'AH... K'HYM...
...SO LONG I HAVE WAITED TO BE...
TIME TO MAKE A POINT.
AS PUBLIC AS POSSIBLE.
I KNOW JUST THE PLACE.

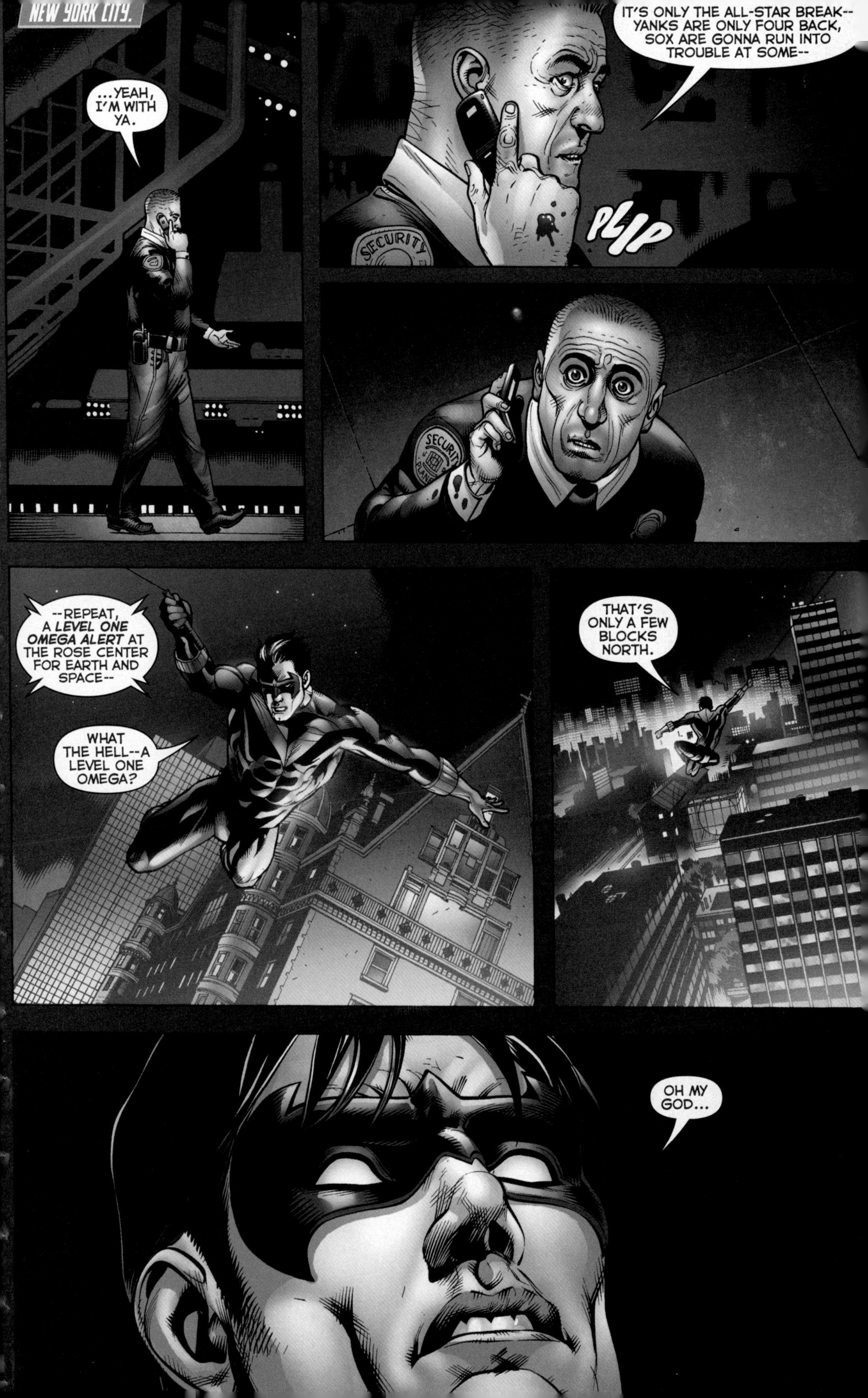
NEW YORK CITY.
...YEAH, I'M WITH YA.
IT'S ONLY THE ALL-STAR BREAK--YANKS ARE ONLY FOUR BACK, SOX ARE GONNA RUN INTO TROUBLE AT SOME--
PLIP
--REPEAT, A LEVEL ONE OMEGA ALERT AT THE ROSE CENTER FOR EARTH AND SPACE--
WHAT THE HELL--A LEVEL ONE OMEGA?
THAT'S ONLY A FEW BLOCKS NORTH.
OH MY GOD...

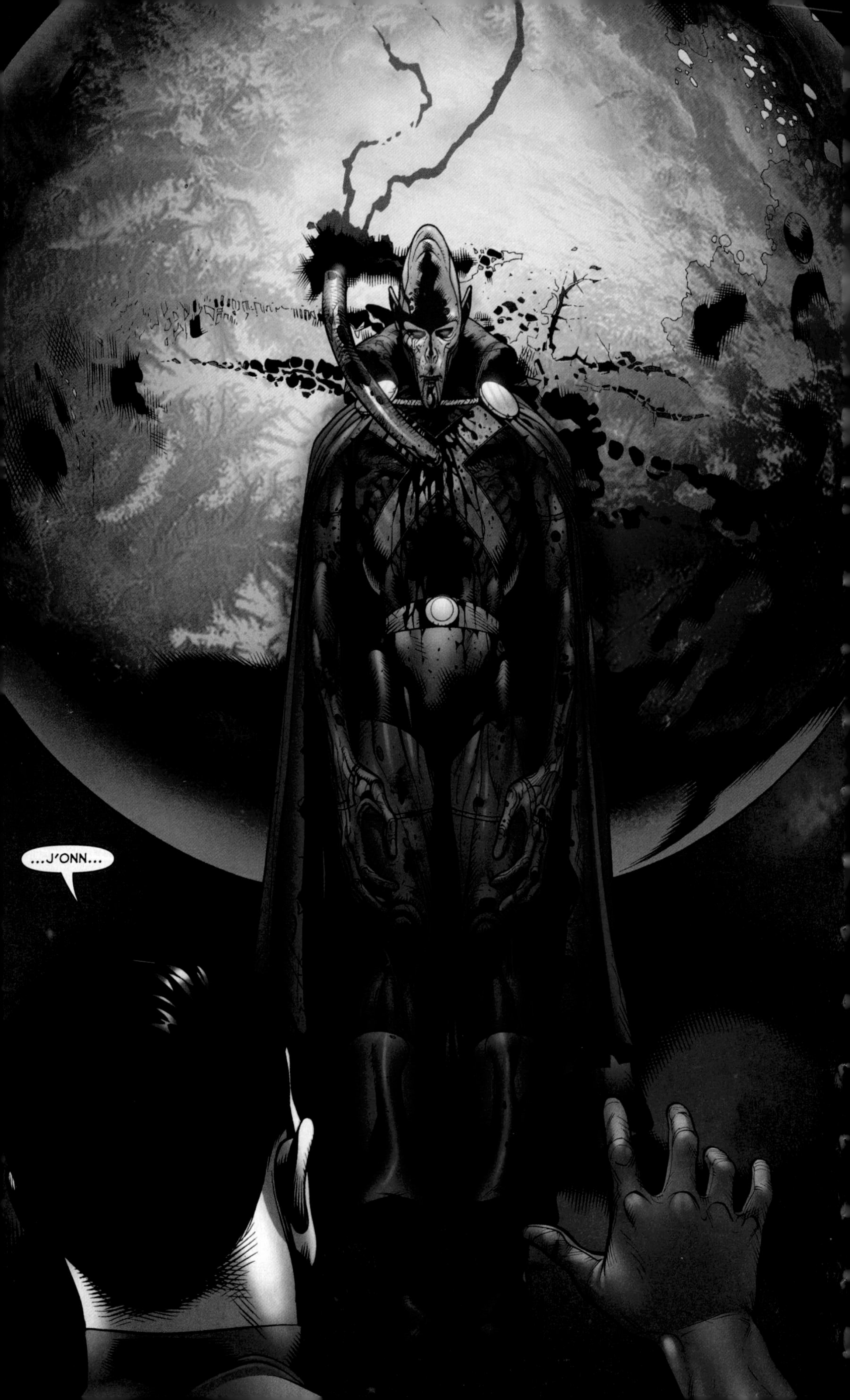
...J'ONN...

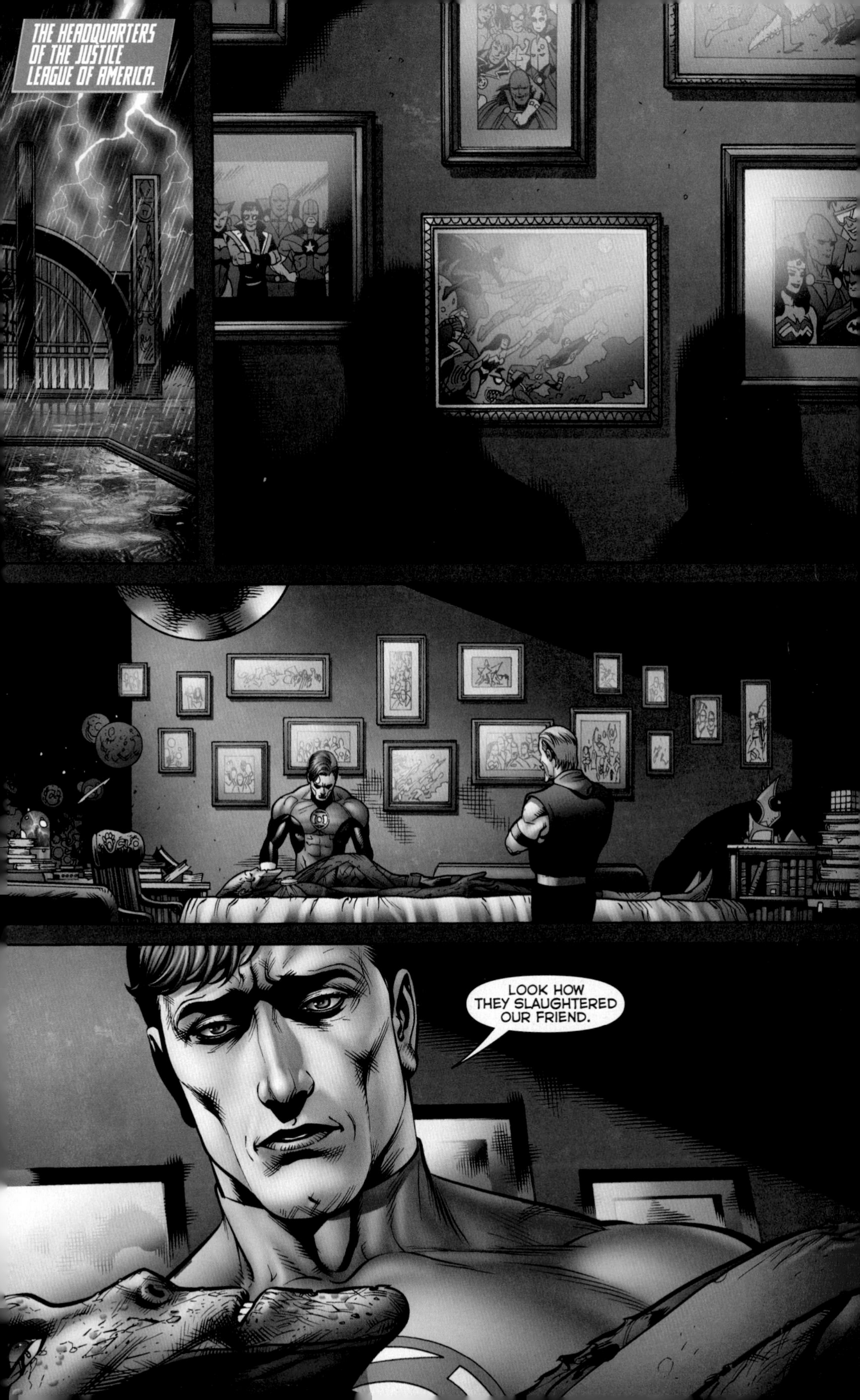
THE HEADQUARTERS OF THE JUSTICE LEAGUE OF AMERICA.
LOOK HOW THEY SLAUGHTERED OUR FRIEND.

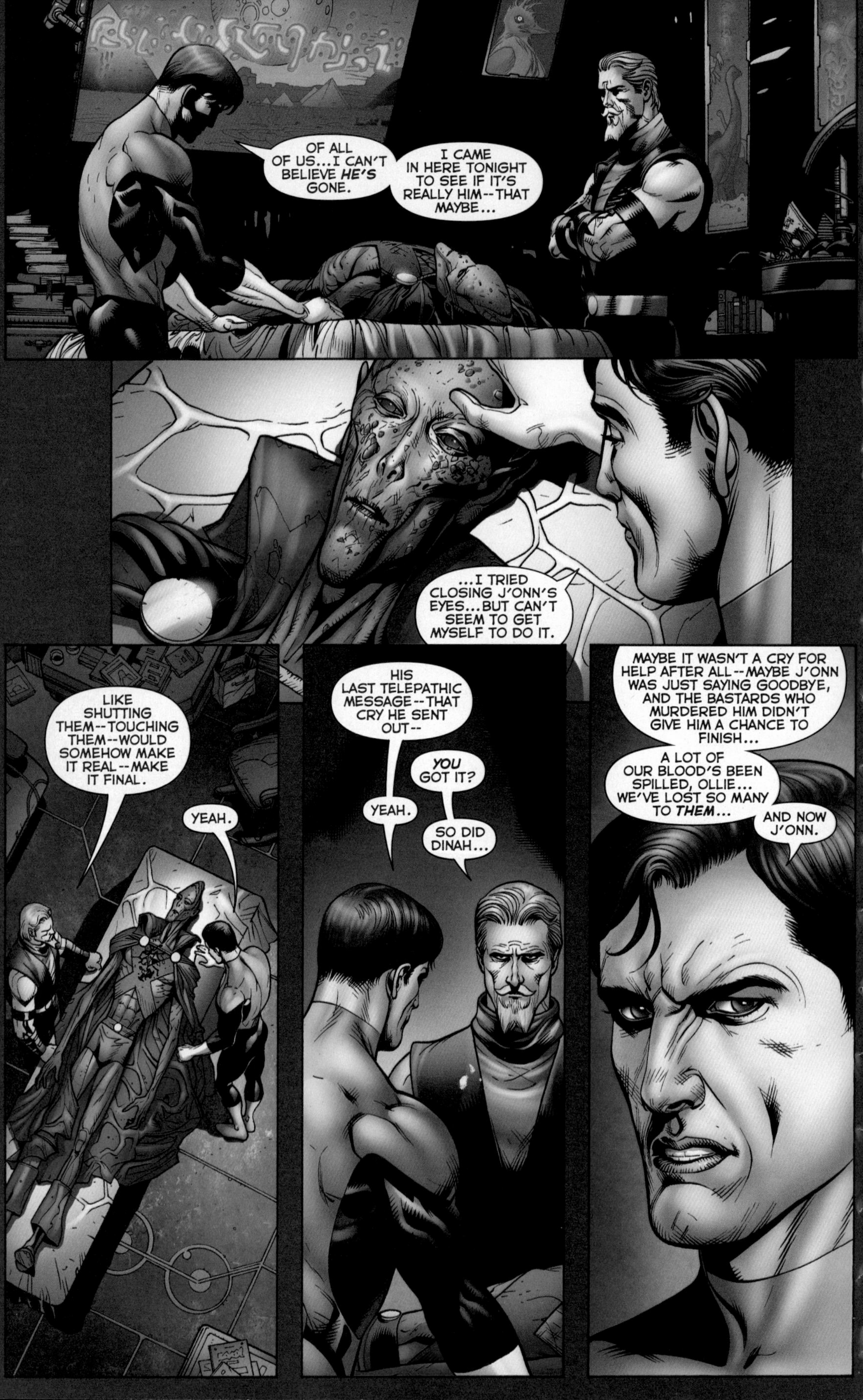

OF ALL OF US...I CAN'T BELIEVE *HE'S* GONE.
I CAME IN HERE TONIGHT TO SEE IF IT'S REALLY HIM--THAT MAYBE...
...I TRIED CLOSING J'ONN'S EYES...BUT CAN'T SEEM TO GET MYSELF TO DO IT.
LIKE SHUTTING THEM--TOUCHING THEM--WOULD SOMEHOW MAKE IT REAL--MAKE IT FINAL.
YEAH.
HIS LAST TELEPATHIC MESSAGE--THAT CRY HE SENT OUT--
YOU GOT IT?
YEAH.
SO DID DINAH...
MAYBE IT WASN'T A CRY FOR HELP AFTER ALL--MAYBE J'ONN WAS JUST SAYING GOODBYE, AND THE BASTARDS WHO MURDERED HIM DIDN'T GIVE HIM A CHANCE TO FINISH...
A LOT OF OUR BLOOD'S BEEN SPILLED, OLLIE... WE'VE LOST SO MANY TO *THEM*...
AND NOW J'ONN.

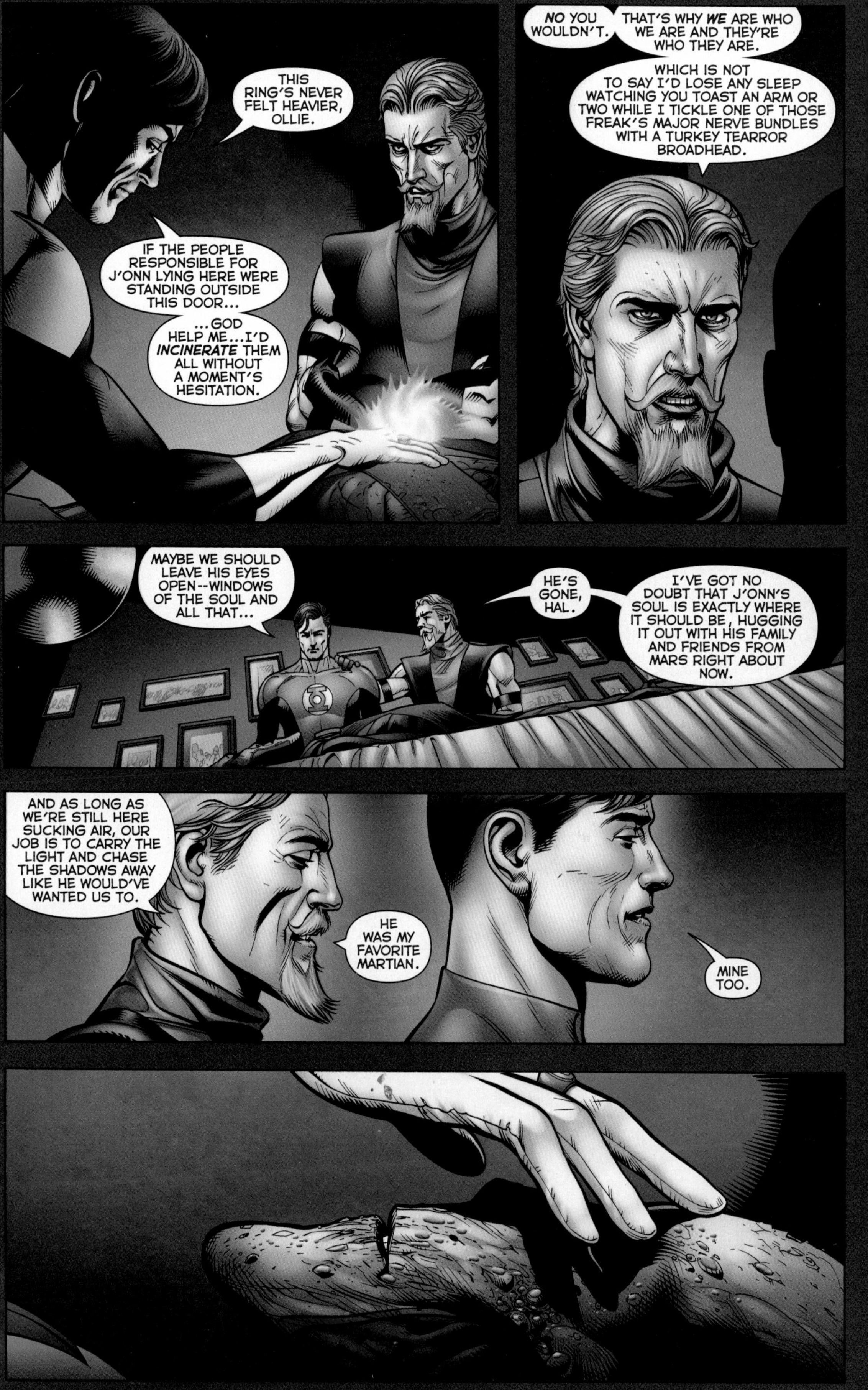
THIS RING'S NEVER FELT HEAVIER, OLLIE.
IF THE PEOPLE RESPONSIBLE FOR J'ONN LYING HERE WERE STANDING OUTSIDE THIS DOOR...
...GOD HELP ME...I'D *INCINERATE* THEM ALL WITHOUT A MOMENT'S HESITATION.
NO YOU WOULDN'T.
THAT'S WHY *WE* ARE WHO WE ARE AND THEY'RE WHO THEY ARE.
WHICH IS NOT TO SAY I'D LOSE ANY SLEEP WATCHING YOU TOAST AN ARM OR TWO WHILE I TICKLE ONE OF THOSE FREAK'S MAJOR NERVE BUNDLES WITH A TURKEY TEARROR BROADHEAD.
MAYBE WE SHOULD LEAVE HIS EYES OPEN--WINDOWS OF THE SOUL AND ALL THAT...
HE'S GONE, HAL.
I'VE GOT NO DOUBT THAT J'ONN'S SOUL IS EXACTLY WHERE IT SHOULD BE, HUGGING IT OUT WITH HIS FAMILY AND FRIENDS FROM MARS RIGHT ABOUT NOW.
AND AS LONG AS WE'RE STILL HERE SUCKING AIR, OUR JOB IS TO CARRY THE LIGHT AND CHASE THE SHADOWS AWAY LIKE HE WOULD'VE WANTED US TO.
HE WAS MY FAVORITE MARTIAN.
MINE TOO.

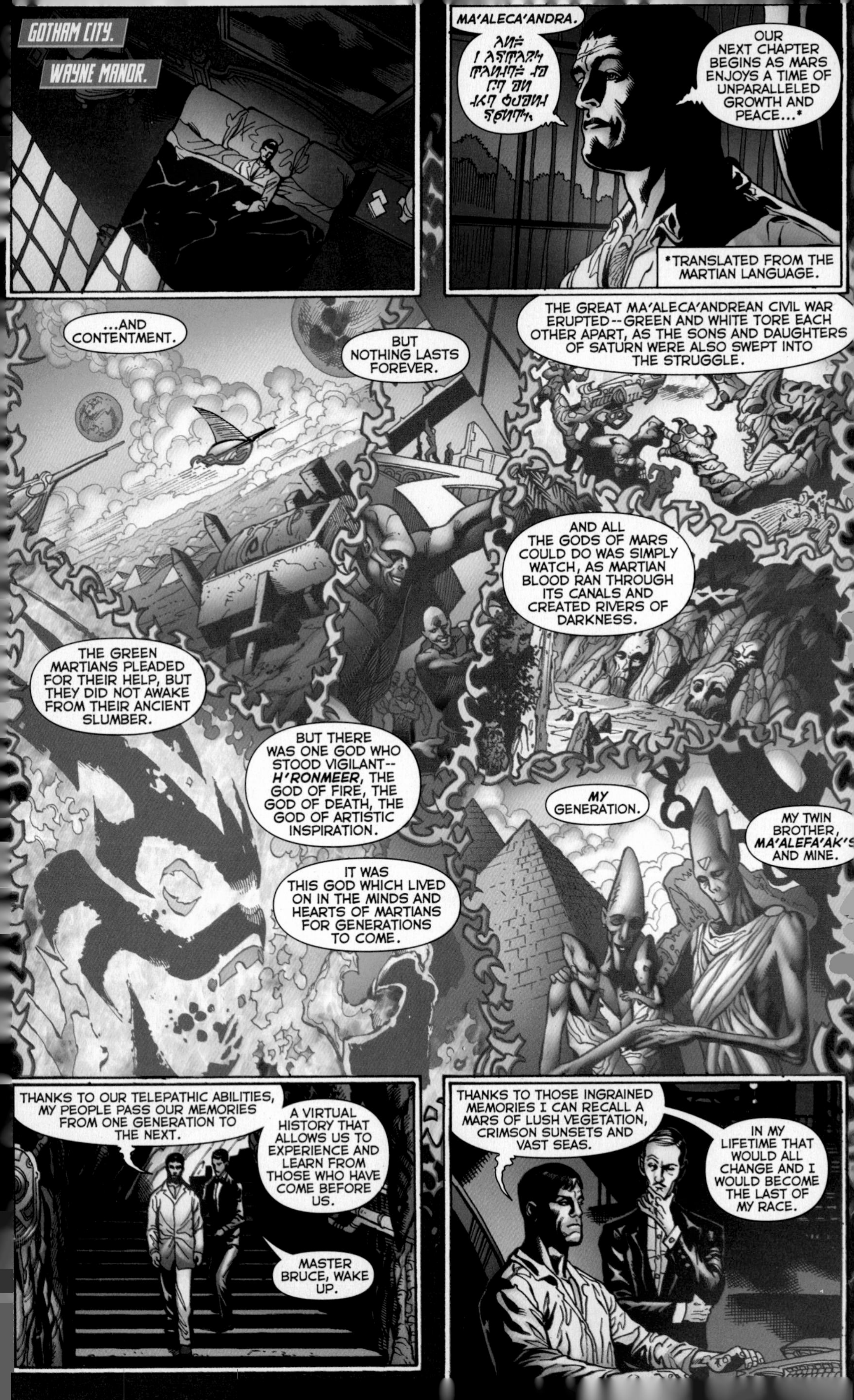
GOTHAM CITY.
WAYNE MANOR.
MA'ALECA'ANDRA.
OUR NEXT CHAPTER BEGINS AS MARS ENJOYS A TIME OF UNPARALLELED GROWTH AND PEACE...*
*TRANSLATED FROM THE MARTIAN LANGUAGE.
...AND CONTENTMENT.
BUT NOTHING LASTS FOREVER.
THE GREAT MA'ALECA'ANDREAN CIVIL WAR ERUPTED--GREEN AND WHITE TORE EACH OTHER APART, AS THE SONS AND DAUGHTERS OF SATURN WERE ALSO SWEPT INTO THE STRUGGLE.
AND ALL THE GODS OF MARS COULD DO WAS SIMPLY WATCH, AS MARTIAN BLOOD RAN THROUGH ITS CANALS AND CREATED RIVERS OF DARKNESS.
THE GREEN MARTIANS PLEADED FOR THEIR HELP, BUT THEY DID NOT AWAKE FROM THEIR ANCIENT SLUMBER.
BUT THERE WAS ONE GOD WHO STOOD VIGILANT-- *H'RONMEER*, THE GOD OF FIRE, THE GOD OF DEATH, THE GOD OF ARTISTIC INSPIRATION.
IT WAS THIS GOD WHICH LIVED ON IN THE MINDS AND HEARTS OF MARTIANS FOR GENERATIONS TO COME.
MY GENERATION.
MY TWIN BROTHER, *MA'ALEFA'AK'S* AND MINE.
THANKS TO OUR TELEPATHIC ABILITIES, MY PEOPLE PASS OUR MEMORIES FROM ONE GENERATION TO THE NEXT.
A VIRTUAL HISTORY THAT ALLOWS US TO EXPERIENCE AND LEARN FROM THOSE WHO HAVE COME BEFORE US.
MASTER BRUCE, WAKE UP.
THANKS TO THOSE INGRAINED MEMORIES I CAN RECALL A MARS OF LUSH VEGETATION, CRIMSON SUNSETS AND VAST SEAS.
IN MY LIFETIME THAT WOULD ALL CHANGE AND I WOULD BECOME THE LAST OF MY RACE.

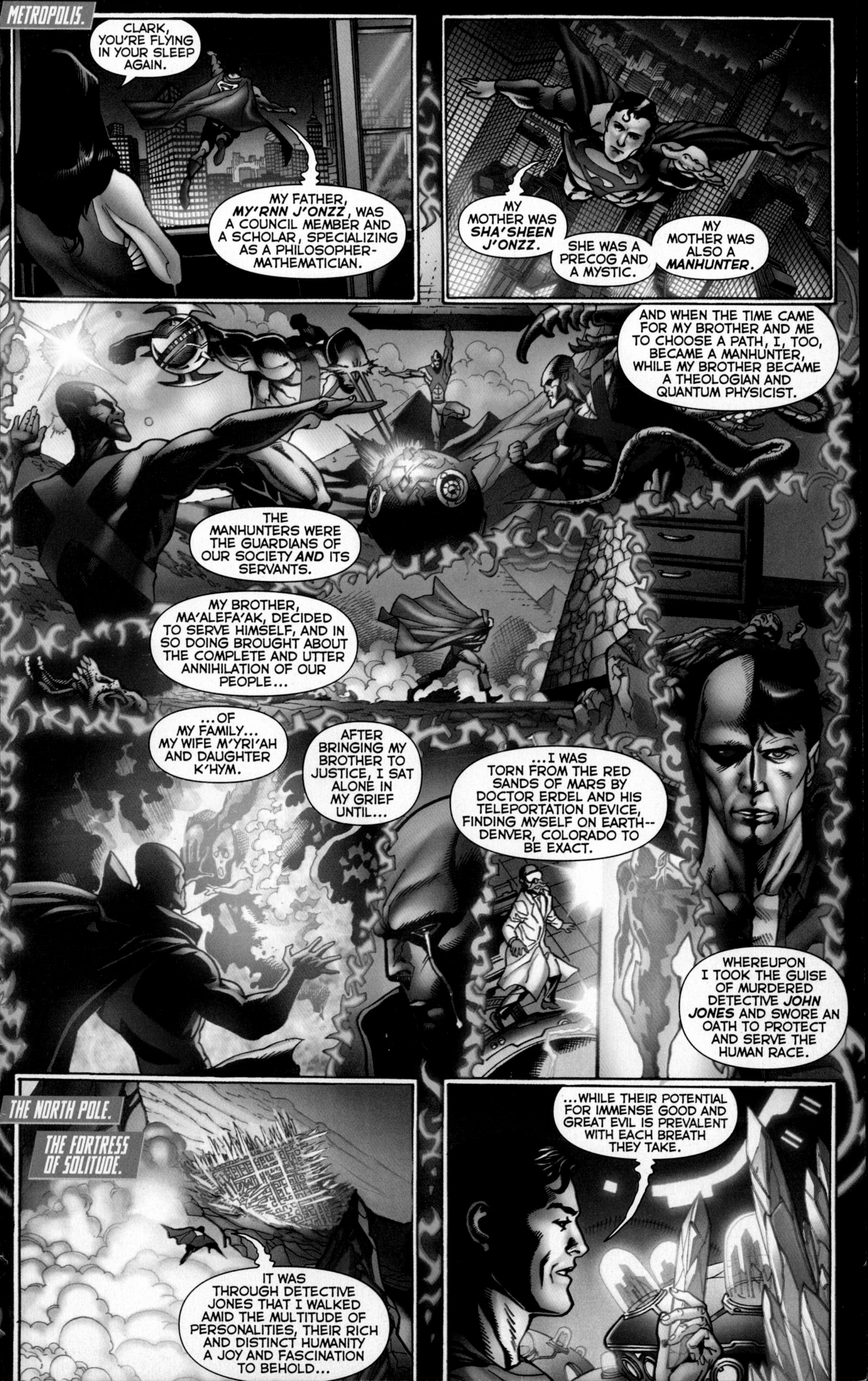
METROPOLIS.
CLARK, YOU'RE FLYING IN YOUR SLEEP AGAIN.
MY FATHER, MY'RNN J'ONZZ, WAS A COUNCIL MEMBER AND A SCHOLAR, SPECIALIZING AS A PHILOSOPHER-MATHEMATICIAN.
MY MOTHER WAS SHA'SHEEN J'ONZZ.
SHE WAS A PRECOG AND A MYSTIC.
MY MOTHER WAS ALSO A MANHUNTER.
AND WHEN THE TIME CAME FOR MY BROTHER AND ME TO CHOOSE A PATH, I, TOO, BECAME A MANHUNTER, WHILE MY BROTHER BECAME A THEOLOGIAN AND QUANTUM PHYSICIST.
THE MANHUNTERS WERE THE GUARDIANS OF OUR SOCIETY AND ITS SERVANTS.
MY BROTHER, MA'ALEFA'AK, DECIDED TO SERVE HIMSELF, AND IN SO DOING BROUGHT ABOUT THE COMPLETE AND UTTER ANNIHILATION OF OUR PEOPLE...
...OF MY FAMILY... MY WIFE M'YRI'AH AND DAUGHTER K'HYM.
AFTER BRINGING MY BROTHER TO JUSTICE, I SAT ALONE IN MY GRIEF UNTIL...
...I WAS TORN FROM THE RED SANDS OF MARS BY DOCTOR ERDEL AND HIS TELEPORTATION DEVICE, FINDING MYSELF ON EARTH-- DENVER, COLORADO TO BE EXACT.
WHEREUPON I TOOK THE GUISE OF MURDERED DETECTIVE JOHN JONES AND SWORE AN OATH TO PROTECT AND SERVE THE HUMAN RACE.
THE NORTH POLE.
THE FORTRESS OF SOLITUDE.
IT WAS THROUGH DETECTIVE JONES THAT I WALKED AMID THE MULTITUDE OF PERSONALITIES, THEIR RICH AND DISTINCT HUMANITY A JOY AND FASCINATION TO BEHOLD...
...WHILE THEIR POTENTIAL FOR IMMENSE GOOD AND GREAT EVIL IS PREVALENT WITH EACH BREATH THEY TAKE.

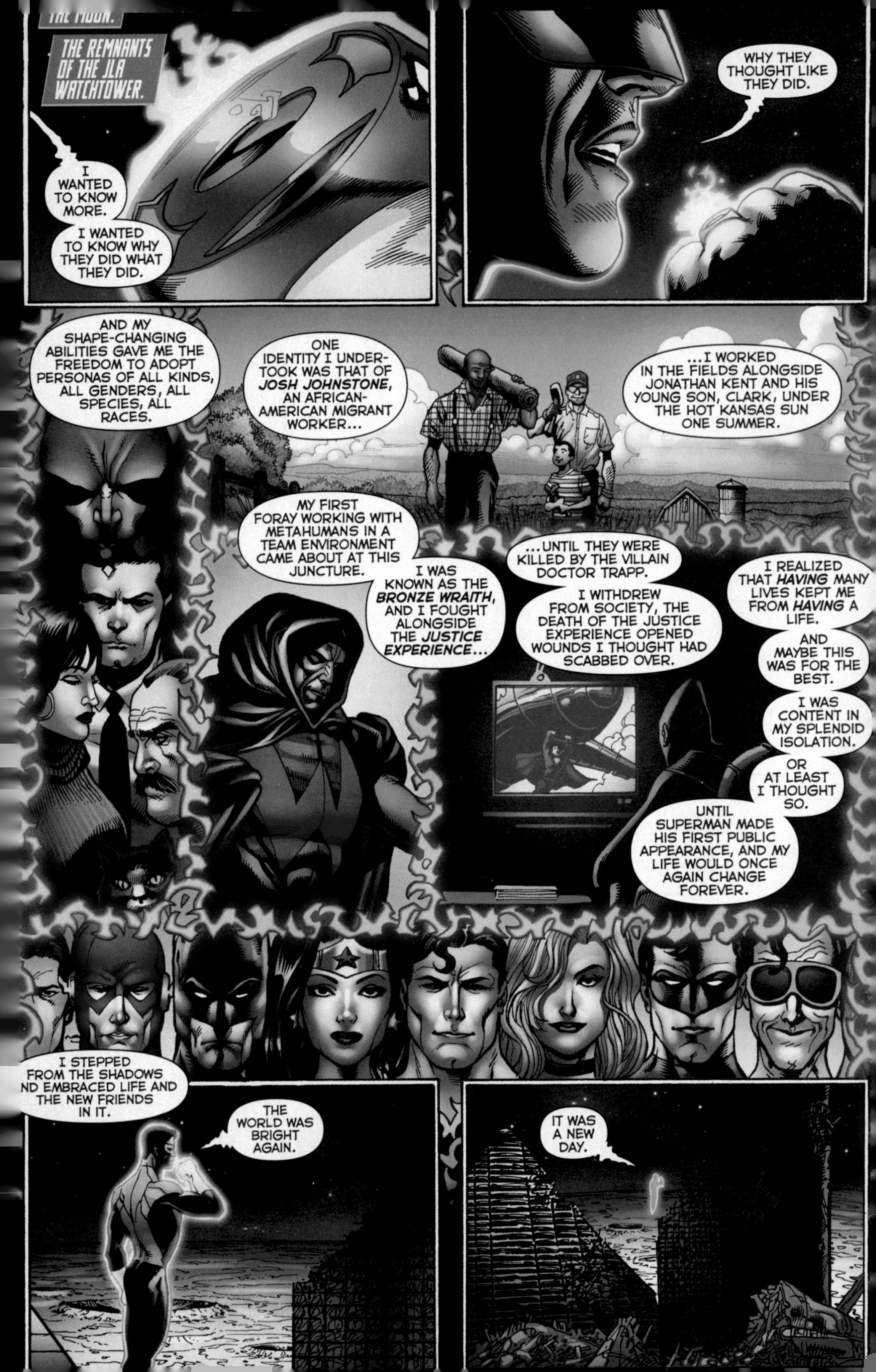
THE MOON.
THE REMNANTS OF THE JLA WATCHTOWER.
I WANTED TO KNOW MORE.
I WANTED TO KNOW WHY THEY DID WHAT THEY DID.
WHY THEY THOUGHT LIKE THEY DID.
AND MY SHAPE-CHANGING ABILITIES GAVE ME THE FREEDOM TO ADOPT PERSONAS OF ALL KINDS, ALL GENDERS, ALL SPECIES, ALL RACES.
ONE IDENTITY I UNDERTOOK WAS THAT OF JOSH JOHNSTONE, AN AFRICAN-AMERICAN MIGRANT WORKER...
...I WORKED IN THE FIELDS ALONGSIDE JONATHAN KENT AND HIS YOUNG SON, CLARK, UNDER THE HOT KANSAS SUN ONE SUMMER.
MY FIRST FORAY WORKING WITH METAHUMANS IN A TEAM ENVIRONMENT CAME ABOUT AT THIS JUNCTURE.
I WAS KNOWN AS THE BRONZE WRAITH, AND I FOUGHT ALONGSIDE THE JUSTICE EXPERIENCE...
...UNTIL THEY WERE KILLED BY THE VILLAIN DOCTOR TRAPP.
I WITHDREW FROM SOCIETY, THE DEATH OF THE JUSTICE EXPERIENCE OPENED WOUNDS I THOUGHT HAD SCABBED OVER.
I REALIZED THAT HAVING MANY LIVES KEPT ME FROM HAVING A LIFE.
AND MAYBE THIS WAS FOR THE BEST.
I WAS CONTENT IN MY SPLENDID ISOLATION.
OR AT LEAST I THOUGHT SO.
UNTIL SUPERMAN MADE HIS FIRST PUBLIC APPEARANCE, AND MY LIFE WOULD ONCE AGAIN CHANGE FOREVER.
I STEPPED FROM THE SHADOWS ND EMBRACED LIFE AND THE NEW FRIENDS IN IT.
THE WORLD WAS BRIGHT AGAIN.
IT WAS A NEW DAY.

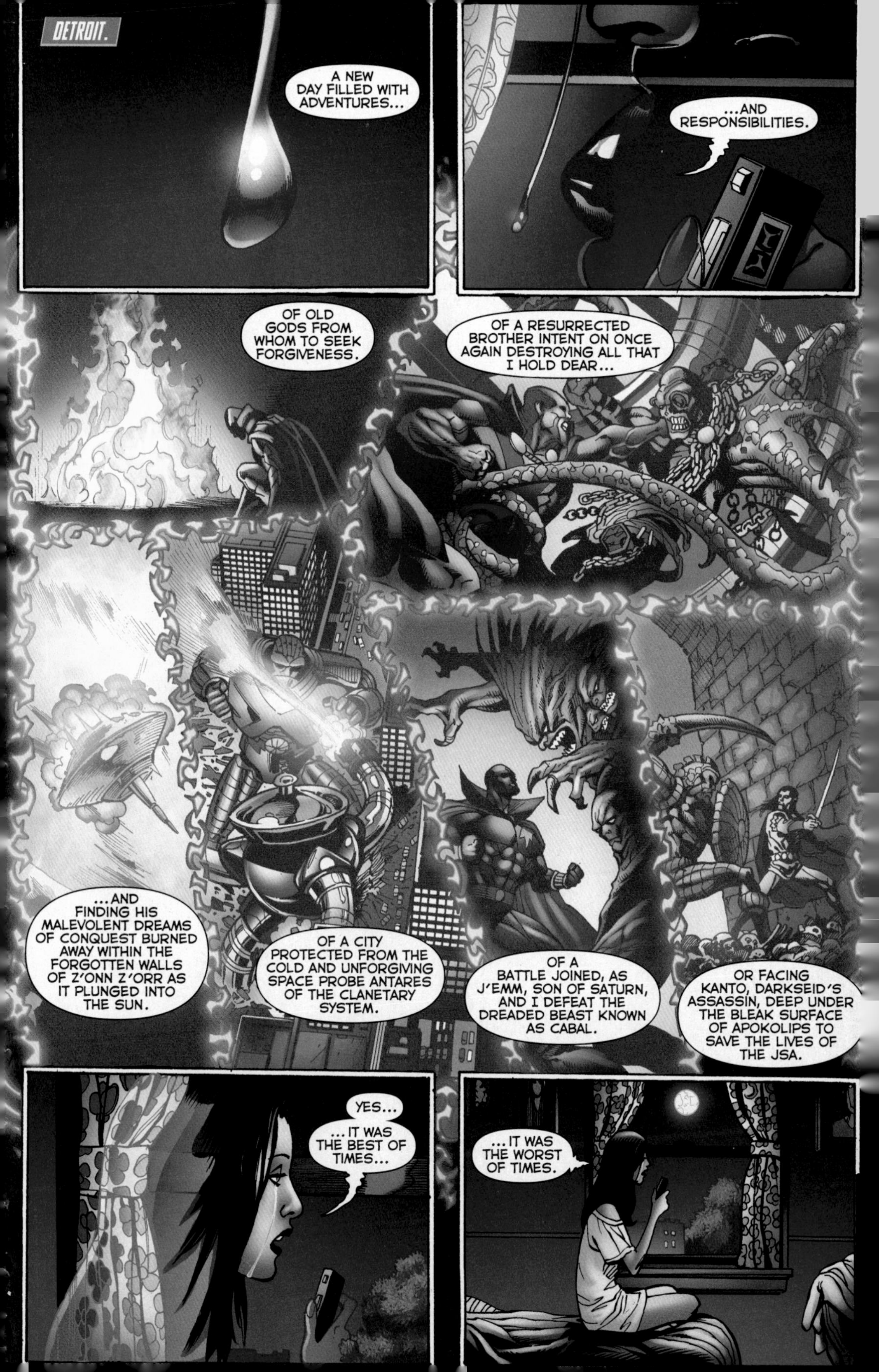
DETROIT.
A NEW DAY FILLED WITH ADVENTURES...
...AND RESPONSIBILITIES.
OF OLD GODS FROM WHOM TO SEEK FORGIVENESS.
OF A RESURRECTED BROTHER INTENT ON ONCE AGAIN DESTROYING ALL THAT I HOLD DEAR...
...AND FINDING HIS MALEVOLENT DREAMS OF CONQUEST BURNED AWAY WITHIN THE FORGOTTEN WALLS OF Z'ONN Z'ORR AS IT PLUNGED INTO THE SUN.
OF A CITY PROTECTED FROM THE COLD AND UNFORGIVING SPACE PROBE ANTARES OF THE CLANETARY SYSTEM.
OF A BATTLE JOINED, AS J'EMM, SON OF SATURN, AND I DEFEAT THE DREADED BEAST KNOWN AS CABAL.
OR FACING KANTO, DARKSEID'S ASSASSIN, DEEP UNDER THE BLEAK SURFACE OF APOKOLIPS TO SAVE THE LIVES OF THE JSA.
YES...
...IT WAS THE BEST OF TIMES...
...IT WAS THE WORST OF TIMES.

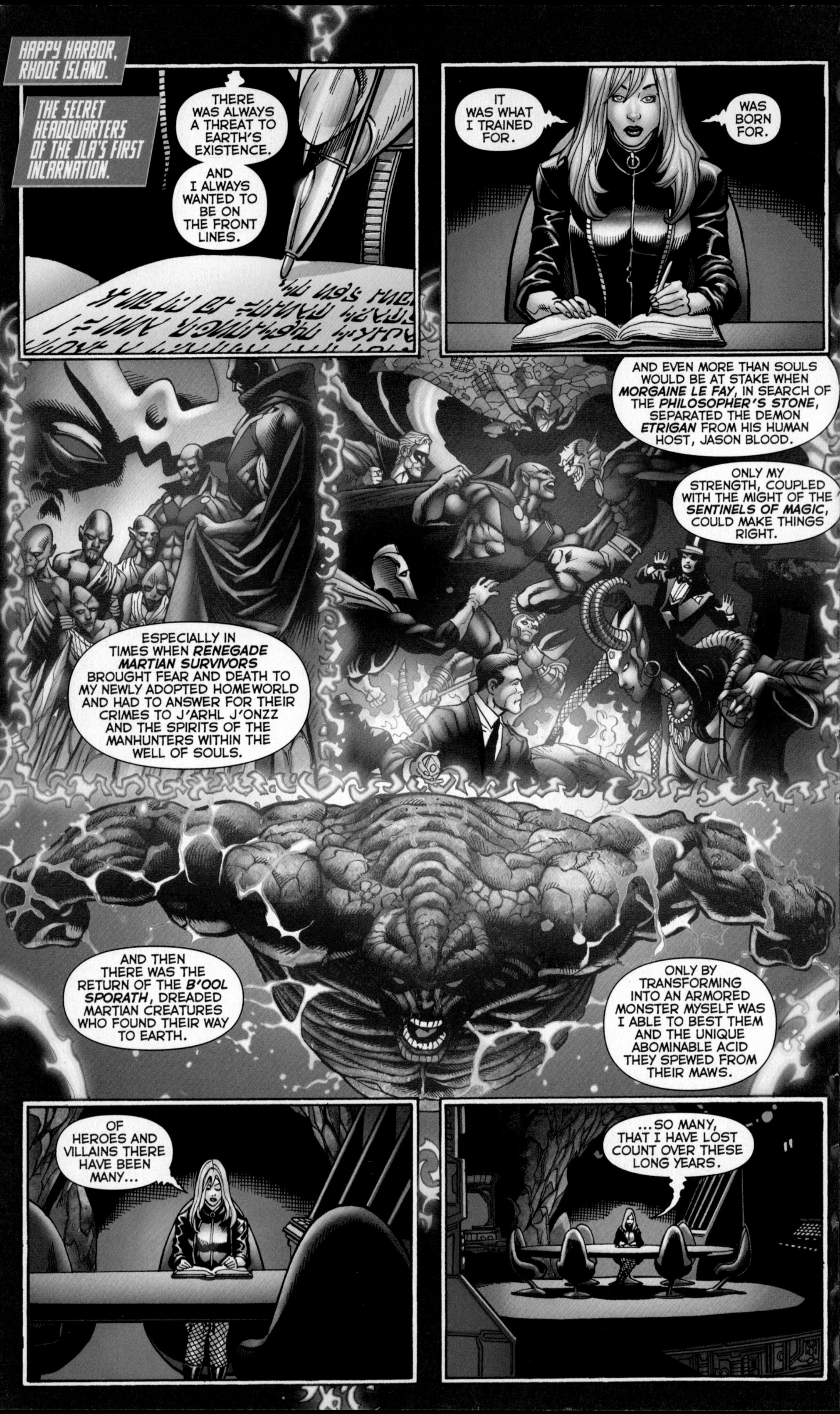
HAPPY HARBOR, RHODE ISLAND.
THE SECRET HEADQUARTERS OF THE JLA'S FIRST INCARNATION.
THERE WAS ALWAYS A THREAT TO EARTH'S EXISTENCE.
AND I ALWAYS WANTED TO BE ON THE FRONT LINES.
IT WAS WHAT I TRAINED FOR.
WAS BORN FOR.
AND EVEN MORE THAN SOULS WOULD BE AT STAKE WHEN MORGAINE LE FAY, IN SEARCH OF THE PHILOSOPHER'S STONE, SEPARATED THE DEMON ETRIGAN FROM HIS HUMAN HOST, JASON BLOOD.
ONLY MY STRENGTH, COUPLED WITH THE MIGHT OF THE SENTINELS OF MAGIC, COULD MAKE THINGS RIGHT.
ESPECIALLY IN TIMES WHEN RENEGADE MARTIAN SURVIVORS BROUGHT FEAR AND DEATH TO MY NEWLY ADOPTED HOMEWORLD AND HAD TO ANSWER FOR THEIR CRIMES TO J'ARHL J'ONZZ AND THE SPIRITS OF THE MANHUNTERS WITHIN THE WELL OF SOULS.
AND THEN THERE WAS THE RETURN OF THE B'OOL SPORATH, DREADED MARTIAN CREATURES WHO FOUND THEIR WAY TO EARTH.
ONLY BY TRANSFORMING INTO AN ARMORED MONSTER MYSELF WAS I ABLE TO BEST THEM AND THE UNIQUE ABOMINABLE ACID THEY SPEWED FROM THEIR MAWS.
OF HEROES AND VILLAINS THERE HAVE BEEN MANY...
...SO MANY, THAT I HAVE LOST COUNT OVER THESE LONG YEARS.

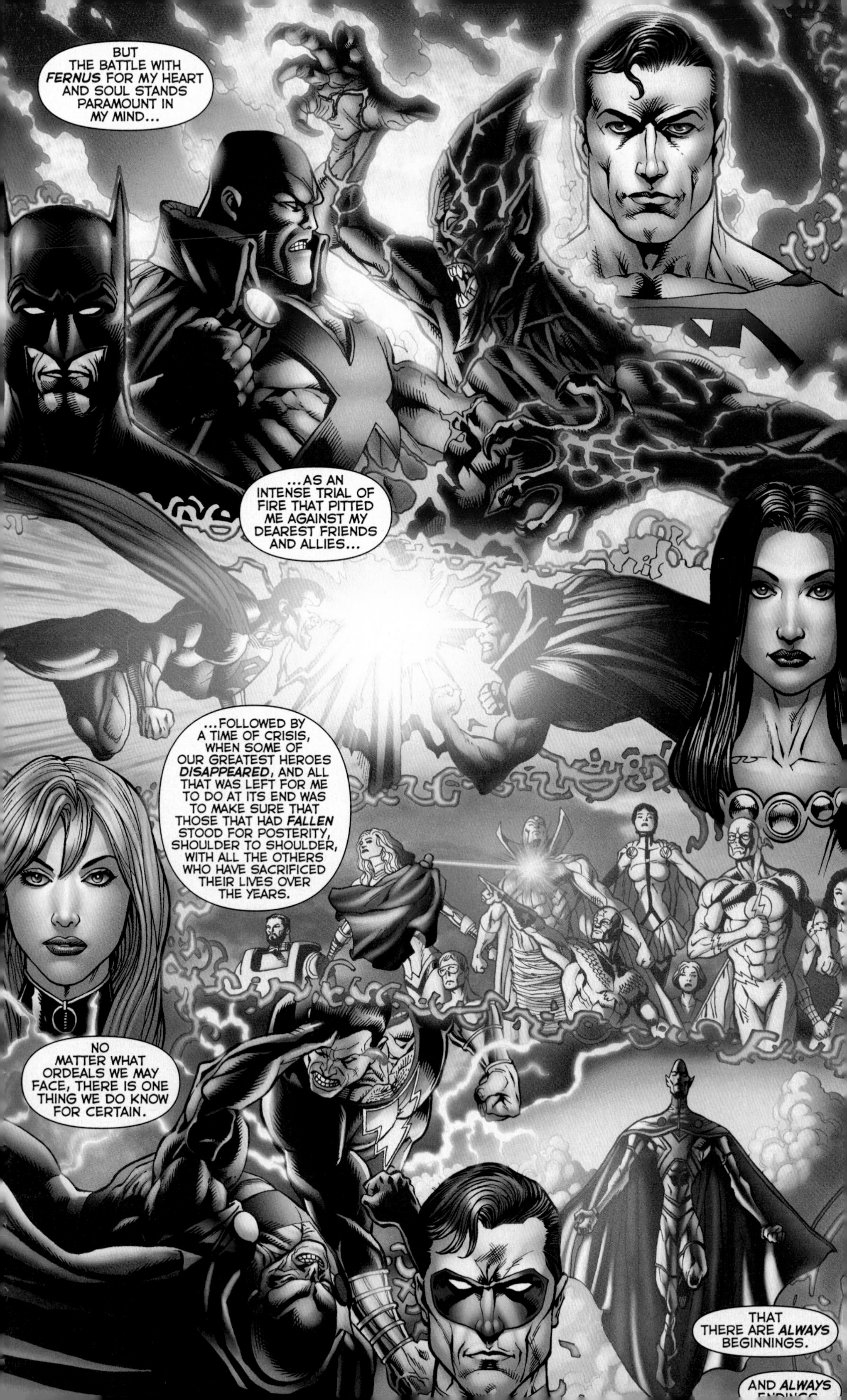
BUT THE BATTLE WITH FERNUS FOR MY HEART AND SOUL STANDS PARAMOUNT IN MY MIND...
...AS AN INTENSE TRIAL OF FIRE THAT PITTED ME AGAINST MY DEAREST FRIENDS AND ALLIES...
...FOLLOWED BY A TIME OF CRISIS, WHEN SOME OF OUR GREATEST HEROES DISAPPEARED, AND ALL THAT WAS LEFT FOR ME TO DO AT ITS END WAS TO MAKE SURE THAT THOSE THAT HAD FALLEN STOOD FOR POSTERITY, SHOULDER TO SHOULDER, WITH ALL THE OTHERS WHO HAVE SACRIFICED THEIR LIVES OVER THE YEARS.
NO MATTER WHAT ORDEALS WE MAY FACE, THERE IS ONE THING WE DO KNOW FOR CERTAIN.
THAT THERE ARE ALWAYS BEGINNINGS.
AND ALWAYS

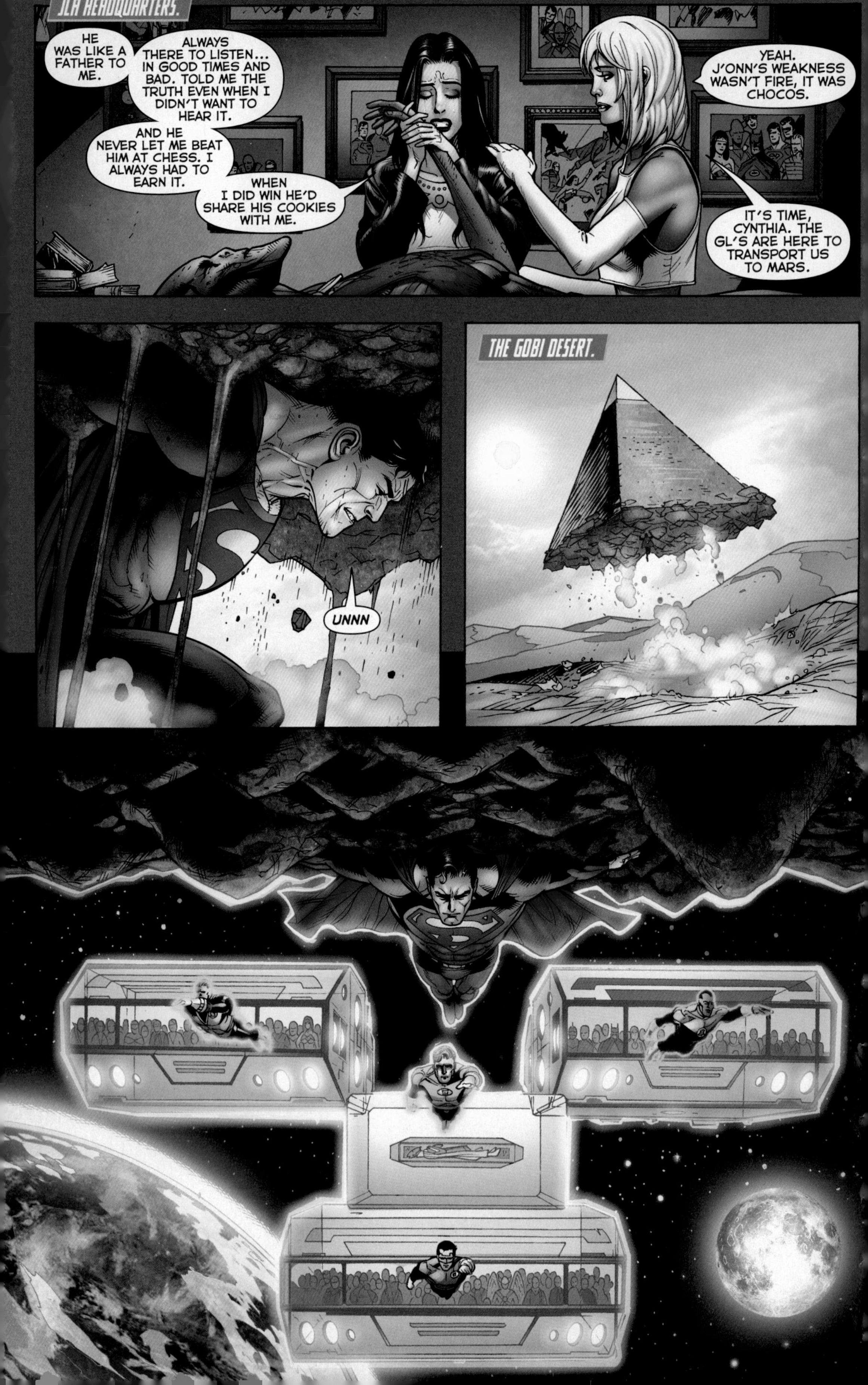
JLA HEADQUARTERS.
HE WAS LIKE A FATHER TO ME.
ALWAYS THERE TO LISTEN... IN GOOD TIMES AND BAD. TOLD ME THE TRUTH EVEN WHEN I DIDN'T WANT TO HEAR IT.
AND HE NEVER LET ME BEAT HIM AT CHESS. I ALWAYS HAD TO EARN IT.
WHEN I DID WIN HE'D SHARE HIS COOKIES WITH ME.
YEAH. J'ONN'S WEAKNESS WASN'T FIRE, IT WAS CHOCOS.
IT'S TIME, CYNTHIA. THE GL'S ARE HERE TO TRANSPORT US TO MARS.
UNNN
THE GOBI DESERT.

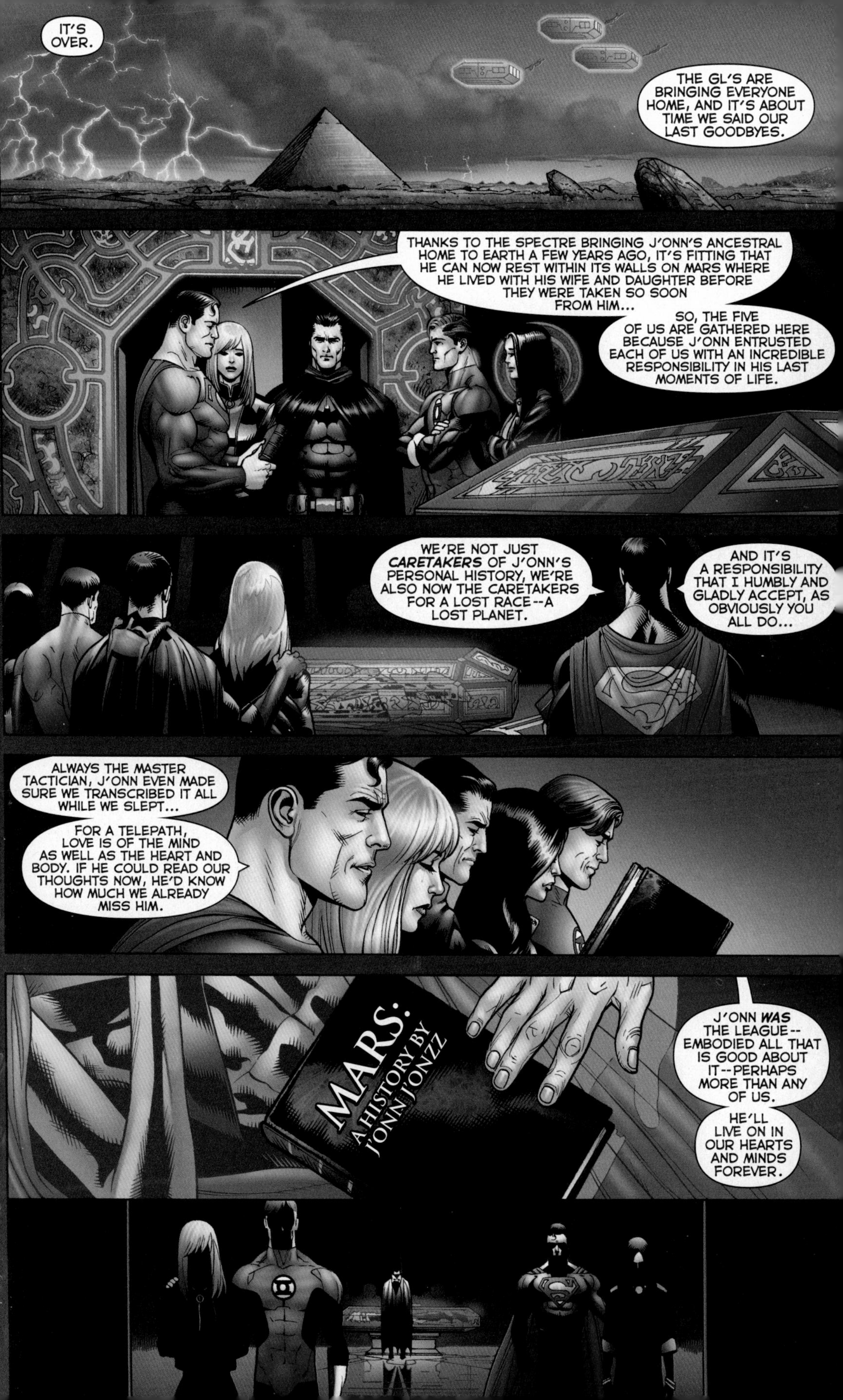
IT'S OVER.
THE GL'S ARE BRINGING EVERYONE HOME, AND IT'S ABOUT TIME WE SAID OUR LAST GOODBYES.
THANKS TO THE SPECTRE BRINGING J'ONN'S ANCESTRAL HOME TO EARTH A FEW YEARS AGO, IT'S FITTING THAT HE CAN NOW REST WITHIN ITS WALLS ON MARS WHERE HE LIVED WITH HIS WIFE AND DAUGHTER BEFORE THEY WERE TAKEN SO SOON FROM HIM...
SO, THE FIVE OF US ARE GATHERED HERE BECAUSE J'ONN ENTRUSTED EACH OF US WITH AN INCREDIBLE RESPONSIBILITY IN HIS LAST MOMENTS OF LIFE.
WE'RE NOT JUST *CARETAKERS* OF J'ONN'S PERSONAL HISTORY, WE'RE ALSO NOW THE CARETAKERS FOR A LOST RACE--A LOST PLANET.
AND IT'S A RESPONSIBILITY THAT I HUMBLY AND GLADLY ACCEPT, AS OBVIOUSLY YOU ALL DO...
ALWAYS THE MASTER TACTICIAN, J'ONN EVEN MADE SURE WE TRANSCRIBED IT ALL WHILE WE SLEPT...
FOR A TELEPATH, LOVE IS OF THE MIND AS WELL AS THE HEART AND BODY. IF HE COULD READ OUR THOUGHTS NOW, HE'D KNOW HOW MUCH WE ALREADY MISS HIM.
MARS: A HISTORY BY J'ONN J'ONZZ
J'ONN *WAS* THE LEAGUE--EMBODIED ALL THAT IS GOOD ABOUT IT--PERHAPS MORE THAN ANY OF US.
HE'LL LIVE ON IN OUR HEARTS AND MINDS FOREVER.

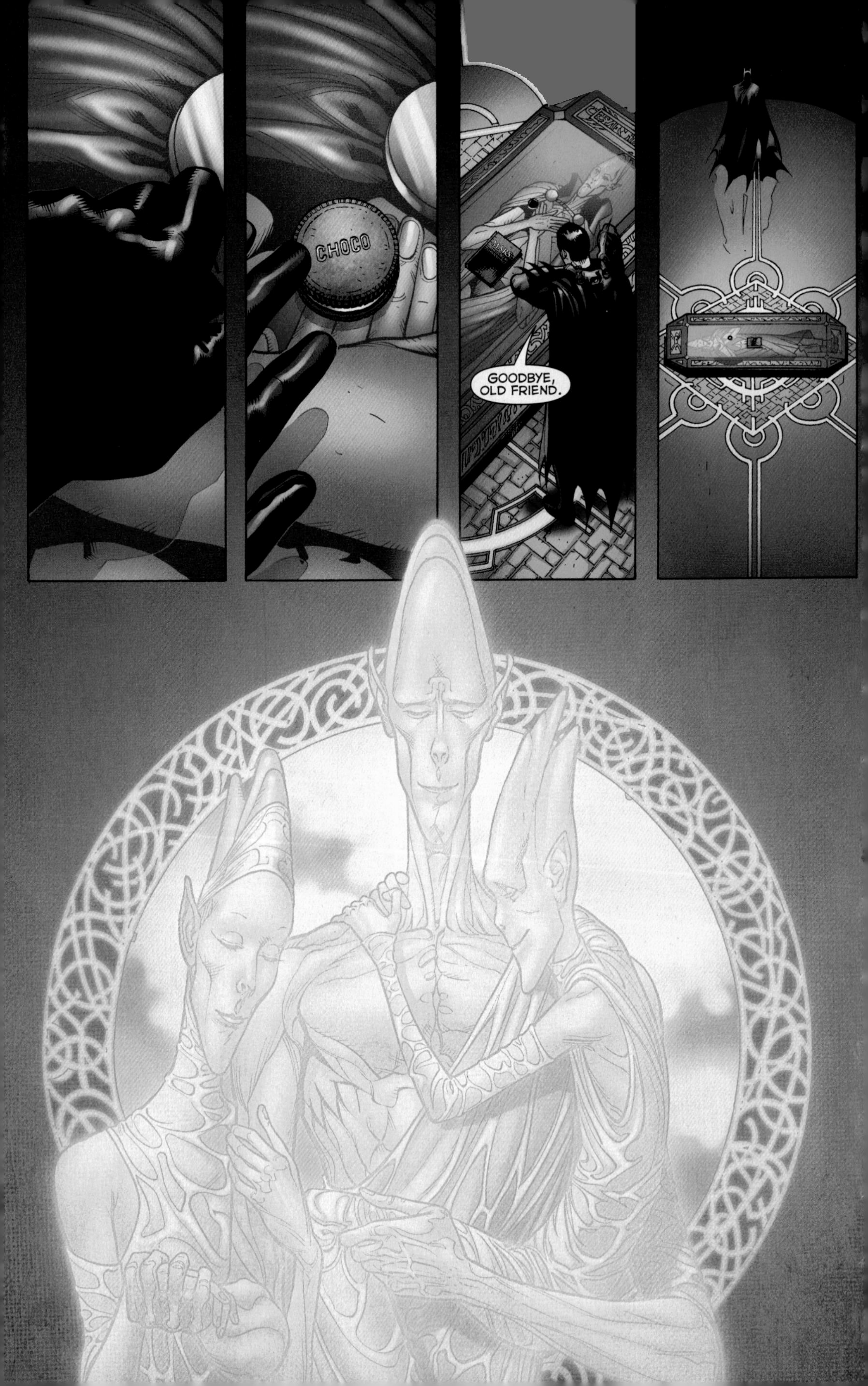
CHOCO
GOODBYE, OLD FRIEND.

FINAL CRISIS RESIST cover by Ryan Sook and Jeromy Cox

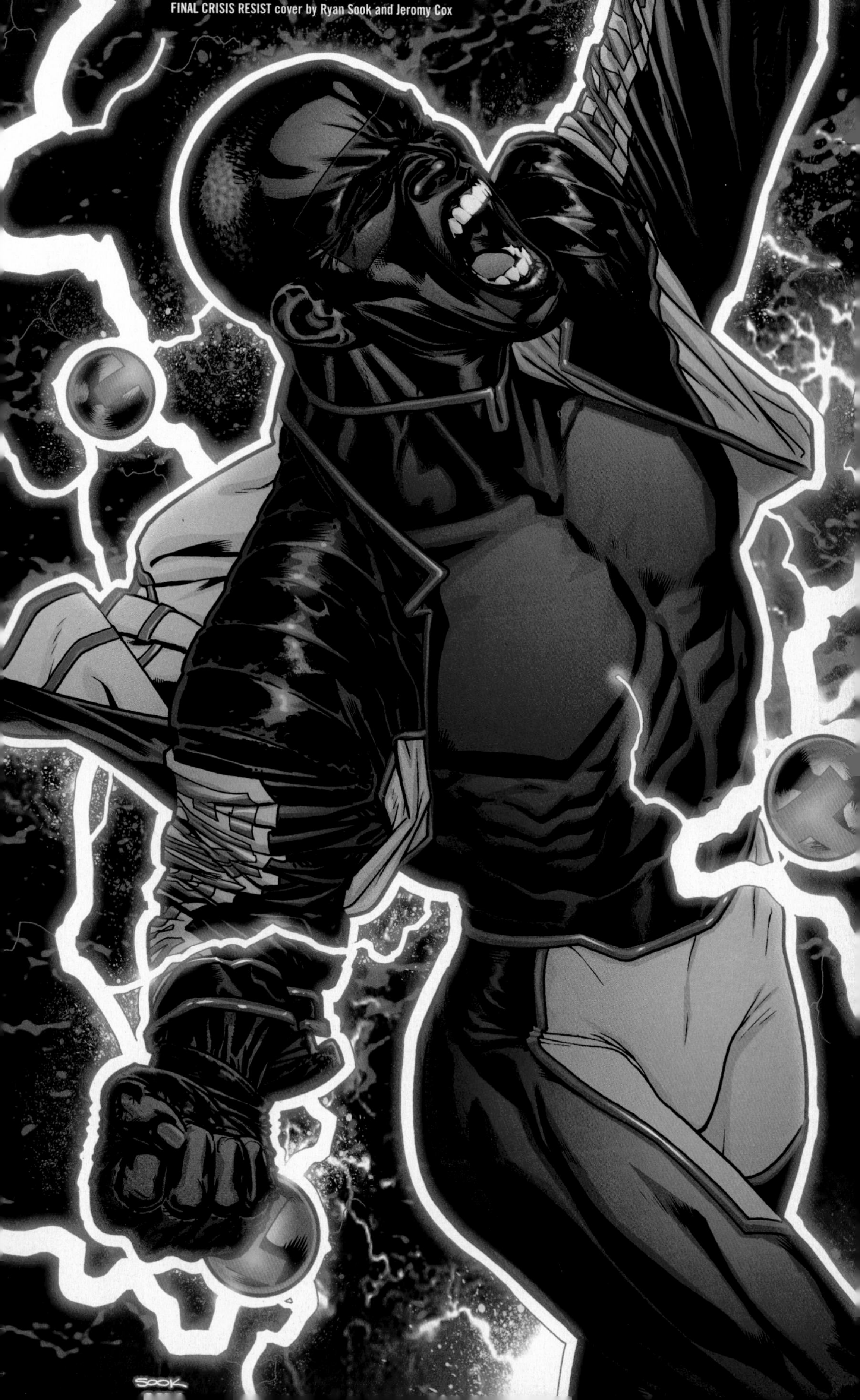

Sliver cover by Rodolfo Migliari

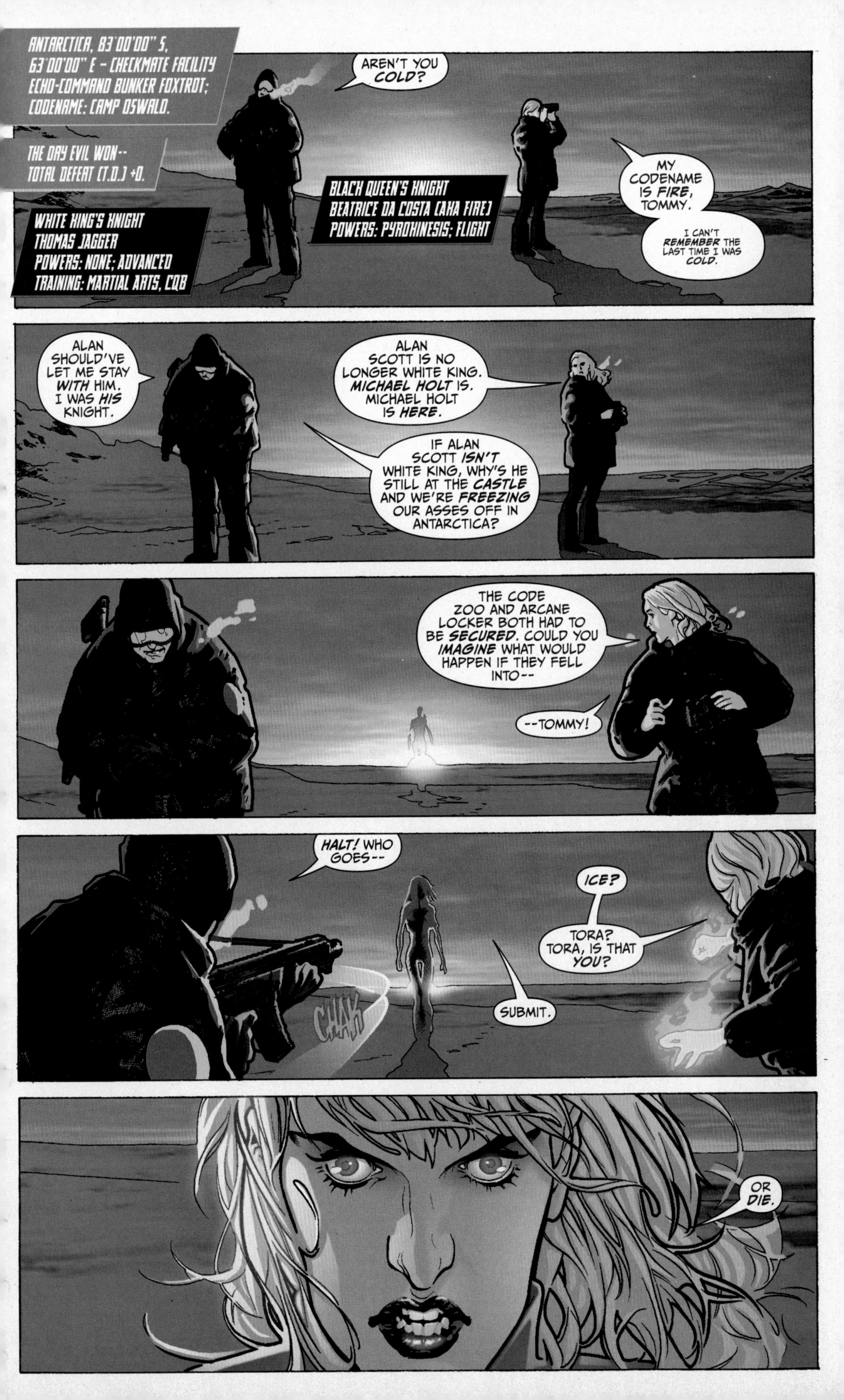
ANTARCTICA, 83°00'00" S, 63°00'00" E – CHECKMATE FACILITY ECHO-COMMAND BUNKER FOXTROT; CODENAME: CAMP OSWALD.
THE DAY EVIL WON-- TOTAL DEFEAT (T.D.) +0.
WHITE KING'S KNIGHT THOMAS JAGGER POWERS: NONE; ADVANCED TRAINING: MARTIAL ARTS, CQB
ARE'NT YOU COLD?
BLACK QUEEN'S KNIGHT BEATRICE DA COSTA (AKA FIRE) POWERS: PYROKINESIS; FLIGHT
MY CODENAME IS FIRE, TOMMY.
I CAN'T REMEMBER THE LAST TIME I WAS COLD.
ALAN SHOULD'VE LET ME STAY WITH HIM. I WAS HIS KNIGHT.
ALAN SCOTT IS NO LONGER WHITE KING. MICHAEL HOLT IS. MICHAEL HOLT IS HERE.
IF ALAN SCOTT ISN'T WHITE KING, WHY'S HE STILL AT THE CASTLE AND WE'RE FREEZING OUR ASSES OFF IN ANTARCTICA?
THE CODE ZOO AND ARCANE LOCKER BOTH HAD TO BE SECURED. COULD YOU IMAGINE WHAT WOULD HAPPEN IF THEY FELL INTO--
--TOMMY!
HALT! WHO GOES--
CHAK
ICE?
TORA? TORA, IS THAT YOU?
SUBMIT.
OR DIE.

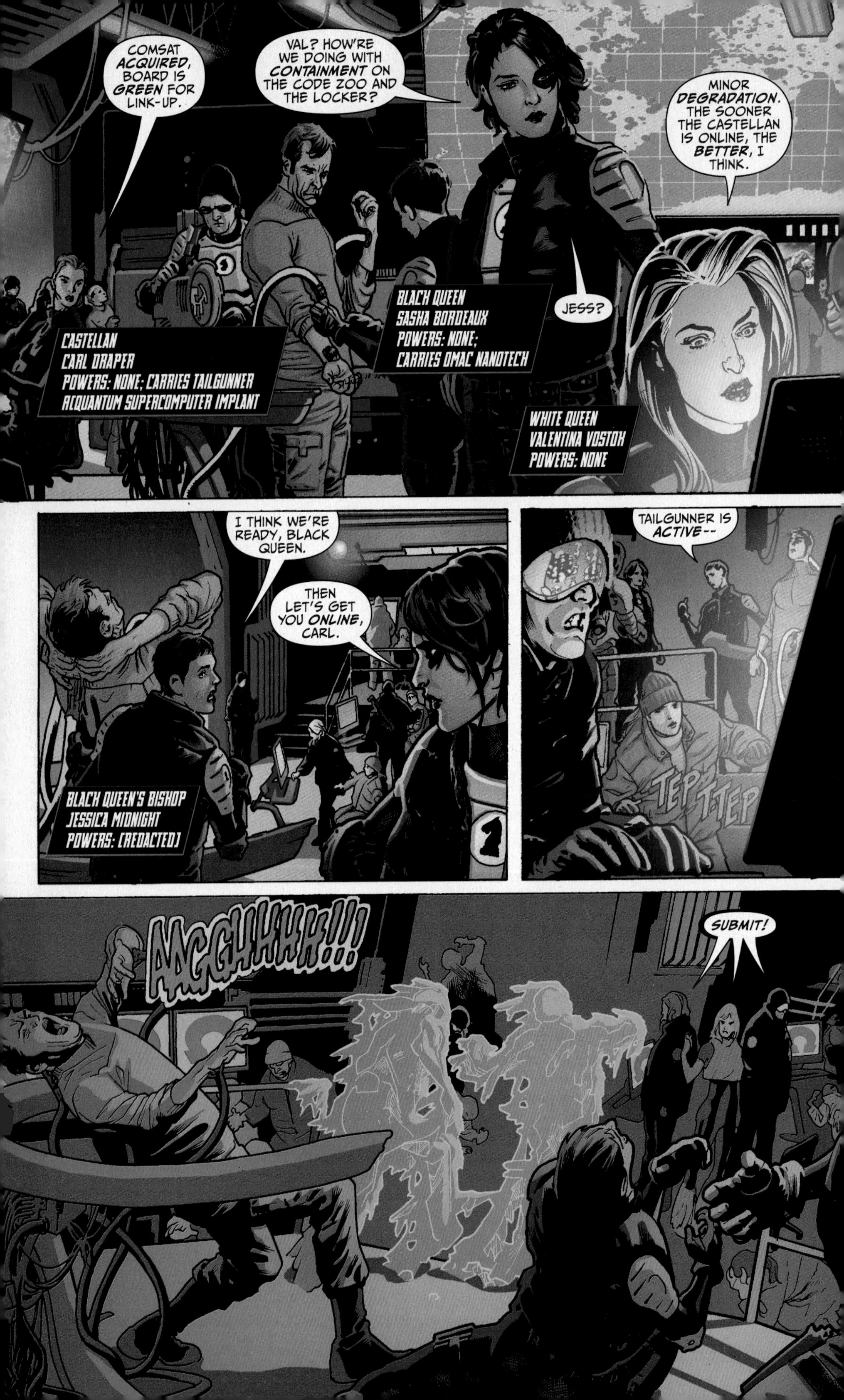
COMSAT ACQUIRED, BOARD IS GREEN FOR LINK-UP.
VAL? HOW'RE WE DOING WITH CONTAINMENT ON THE CODE ZOO AND THE LOCKER?
MINOR DEGRADATION. THE SOONER THE CASTELLAN IS ONLINE, THE BETTER, I THINK.
JESS?
CASTELLAN
CARL DRAPER
POWERS: NONE; CARRIES TAILGUNNER
ACQUANTUM SUPERCOMPUTER IMPLANT
BLACK QUEEN
SASHA BORDEAUX
POWERS: NONE;
CARRIES OMAC NANOTECH
WHITE QUEEN
VALENTINA VOSTOK
POWERS: NONE
I THINK WE'RE READY, BLACK QUEEN.
THEN LET'S GET YOU ONLINE, CARL.
BLACK QUEEN'S BISHOP
JESSICA MIDNIGHT
POWERS: [REDACTED]
TAILGUNNER IS ACTIVE--
TEP TTEP
AAGHHHH!!!
SUBMIT!

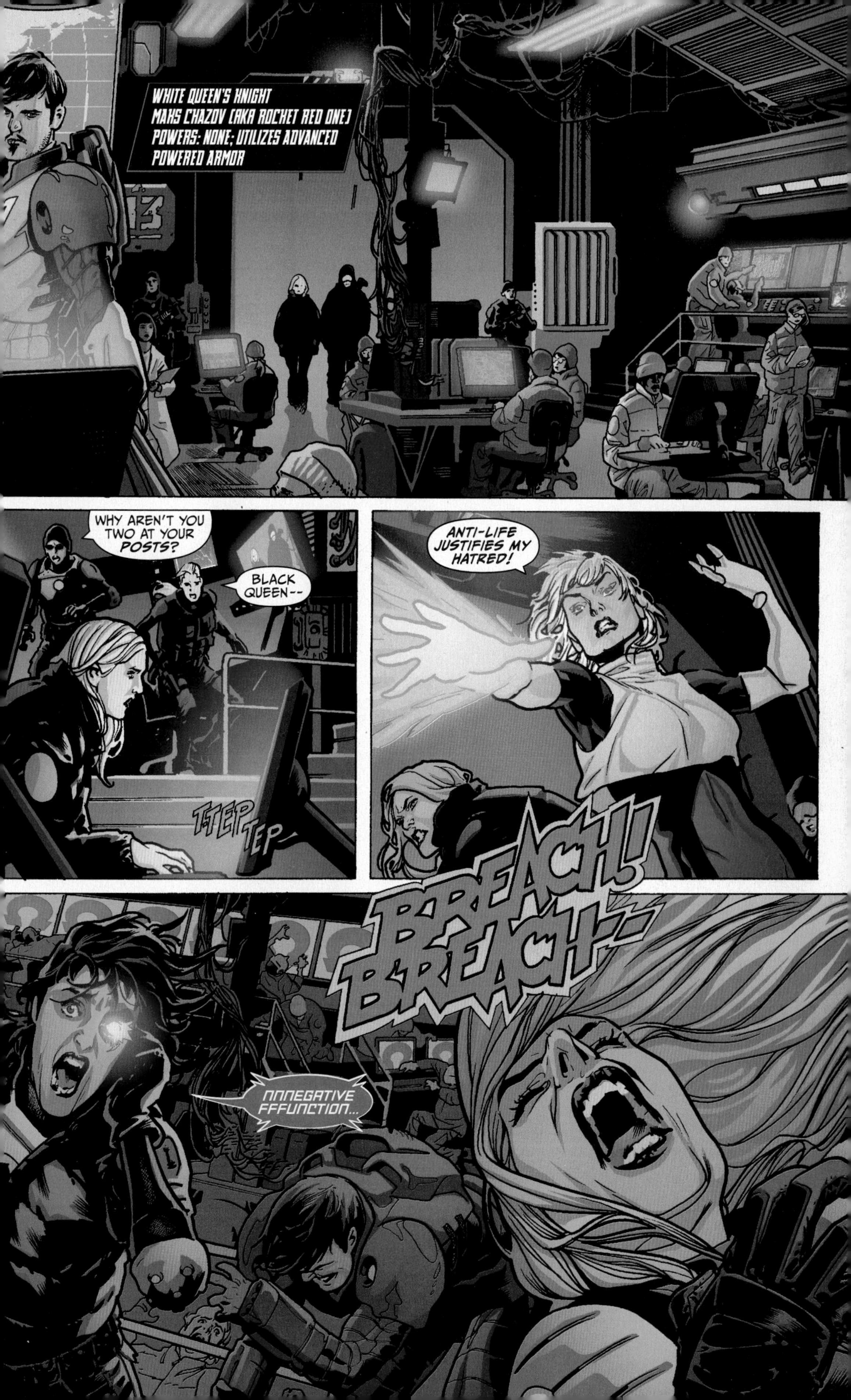
WHITE QUEEN'S KNIGHT
MAKS CHAZOV (AKA ROCKET RED ONE)
POWERS: NONE; UTILIZES ADVANCED
POWERED ARMOR
WHY AREN'T YOU TWO AT YOUR POSTS?
BLACK QUEEN--
T-TEP TEP TEP
ANTI-LIFE JUSTIFIES MY HATRED!
BREACH! BREACH--
NNNEGATIVE FFFUNCTION...

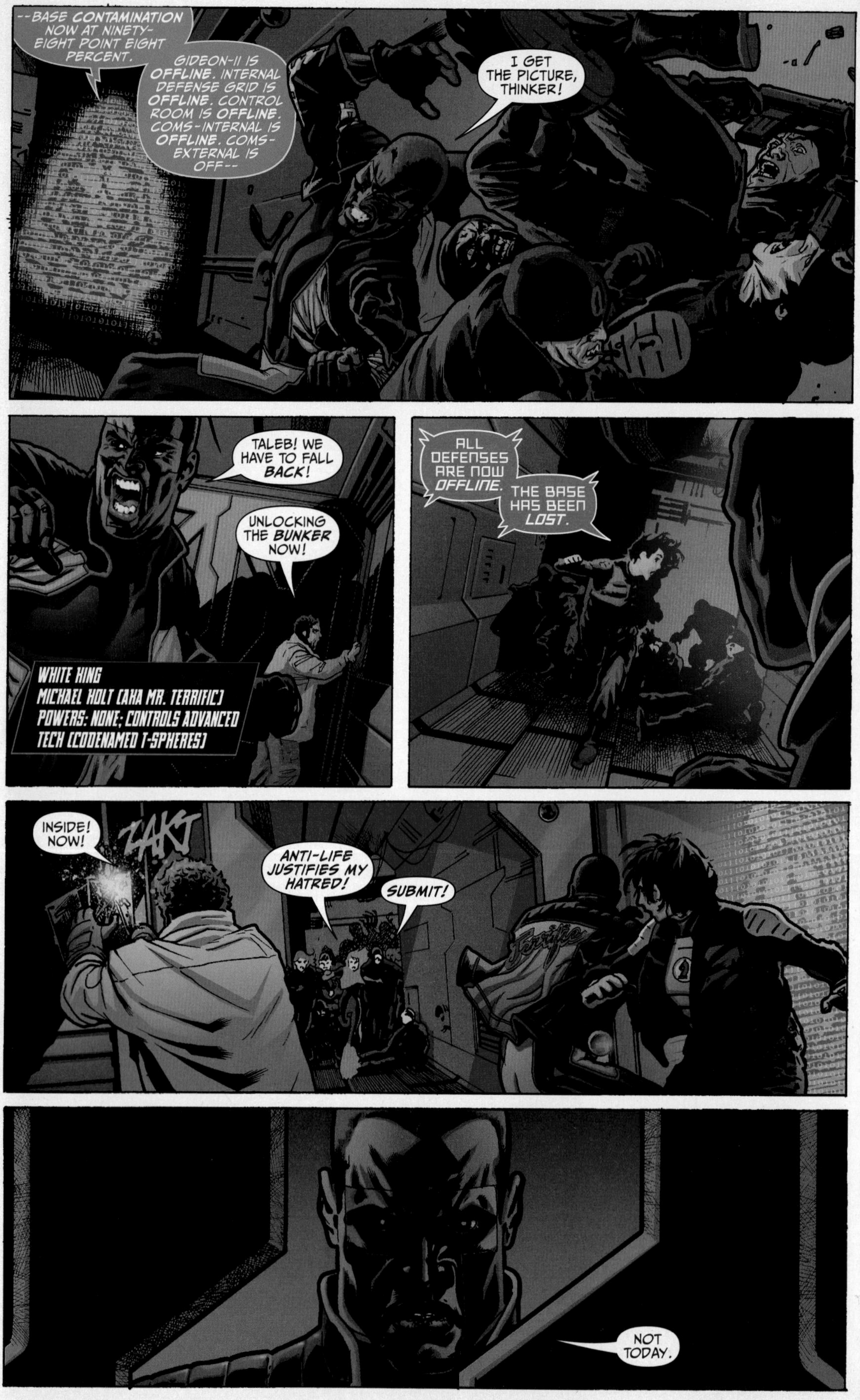

--BASE CONTAMINATION NOW AT NINETY-EIGHT POINT EIGHT PERCENT.
GIDEON-II IS OFFLINE. INTERNAL DEFENSE GRID IS OFFLINE. CONTROL ROOM IS OFFLINE. COMS-INTERNAL IS OFFLINE. COMS-EXTERNAL IS OFF--
I GET THE PICTURE, THINKER!
TALEB! WE HAVE TO FALL BACK!
UNLOCKING THE BUNKER NOW!
WHITE KING
MICHAEL HOLT (AKA MR. TERRIFIC)
POWERS: NONE; CONTROLS ADVANCED TECH (CODENAMED T-SPHERES)
ALL DEFENSES ARE NOW OFFLINE.
THE BASE HAS BEEN LOST.
INSIDE! NOW!
ZAKT
ANTI-LIFE JUSTIFIES MY HATRED!
SUBMIT!
NOT TODAY.

SCREECH BURST A *MAYDAY* TO THE CASTLE, LET ALAN KNOW WHAT'S *HAPPENED.*

WE NEED TO SHUT DOWN *EVERYTHING,* WE HAVE TO *PROTECT* THE ZOO AND THE LOCKER.

ALREADY ON IT.

WHITE KING? THE *BLACK QUEEN* REQUIRES YOUR ATTENTION.

YOU... YOU SWITCHED OVER TO OMAC-MODE. YOU'RE *INFECTED.*

BLACK KING
TALEB BENI KHALID
POWERS: NONE

BORDEAUX, SASHA, HAS SURRENDERED COMMAND AND CONTROL OF HOST BODY TO NANOBOT HIVEMIND. INFECTION PROGRESS IS NOW SUCH THAT REVERSION TO ORGANIC MODE *UNVIABLE.*

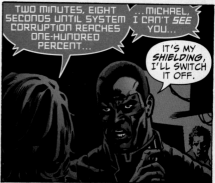

TWO MINUTES, EIGHT SECONDS UNTIL SYSTEM CORRUPTION REACHES ONE-HUNDRED PERCENT...

...MICHAEL, I CAN'T *SEE* YOU...

IT'S MY *SHIELDING,* I'LL SWITCH IT OFF.

I HAVE TO SHUT *DOWN.*

NO.

THE NANOBOTS WILL *MAINTAIN* HOST WHILE *DORMANT.* IF THIS UNIT REMAINS *ONLINE,* INFECTION WILL OVERRIDE *HIVEMIND* CONTROL...

...IT...I...I DON'T WANT TO *SERVE* DARKSEID. AND I DON'T WANT TO DIE.

THERE IS NO CHOICE.

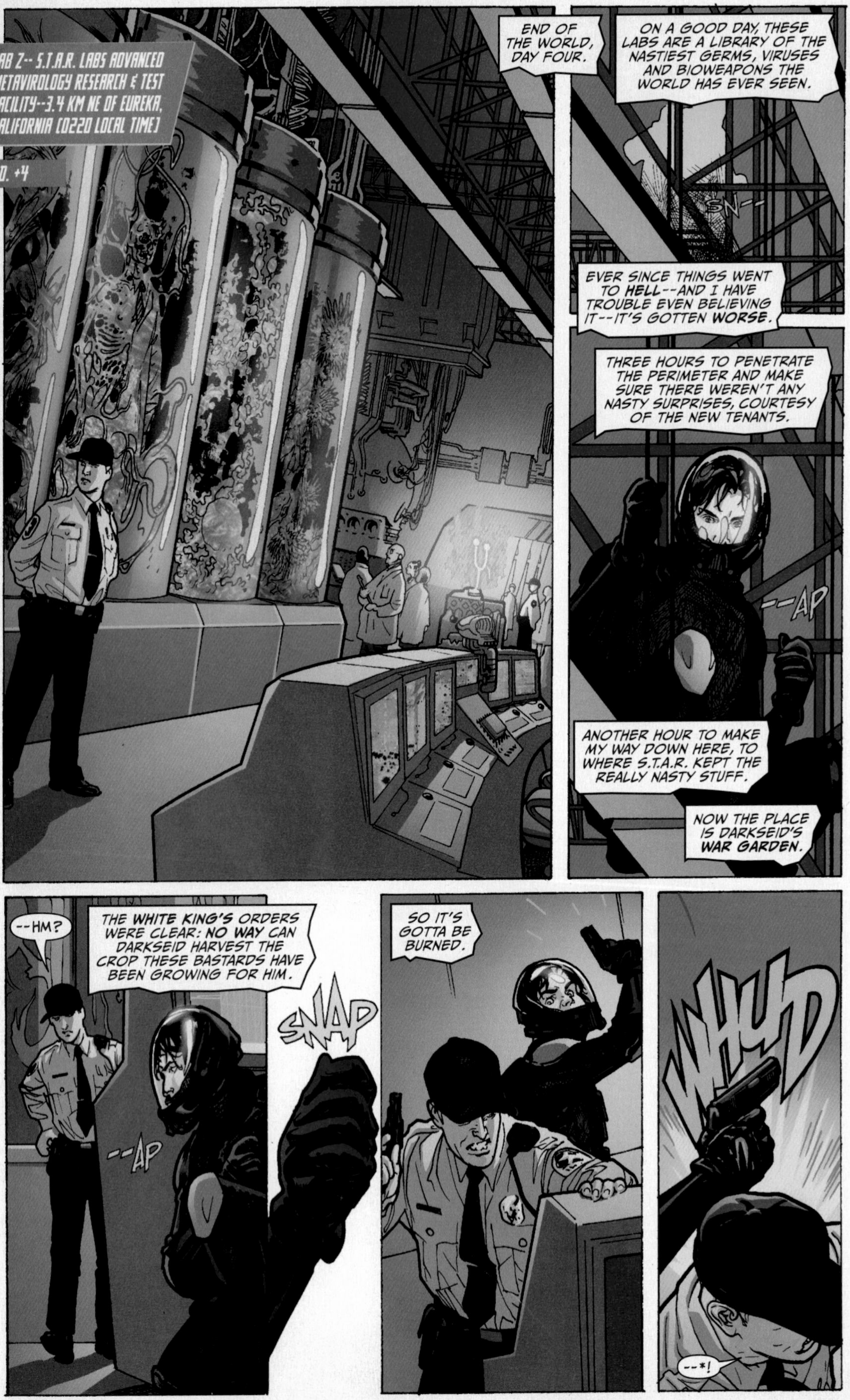
LAB Z-- S.T.A.R. LABS ADVANCED METAVIROLOGY RESEARCH & TEST FACILITY--3.4 KM NE OF EUREKA, CALIFORNIA (0220 LOCAL TIME)
T.D. +4
END OF THE WORLD, DAY FOUR.
ON A GOOD DAY, THESE LABS ARE A LIBRARY OF THE NASTIEST GERMS, VIRUSES AND BIOWEAPONS THE WORLD HAS EVER SEEN.
SN--
EVER SINCE THINGS WENT TO HELL--AND I HAVE TROUBLE EVEN BELIEVING IT--IT'S GOTTEN WORSE.
THREE HOURS TO PENETRATE THE PERIMETER AND MAKE SURE THERE WEREN'T ANY NASTY SURPRISES, COURTESY OF THE NEW TENANTS.
--AP
ANOTHER HOUR TO MAKE MY WAY DOWN HERE, TO WHERE S.T.A.R. KEPT THE REALLY NASTY STUFF.
NOW THE PLACE IS DARKSEID'S WAR GARDEN.
--HM?
THE WHITE KING'S ORDERS WERE CLEAR: NO WAY CAN DARKSEID HARVEST THE CROP THESE BASTARDS HAVE BEEN GROWING FOR HIM.
SNAP
--AP
SO IT'S GOTTA BE BURNED.
WHUD
--*!

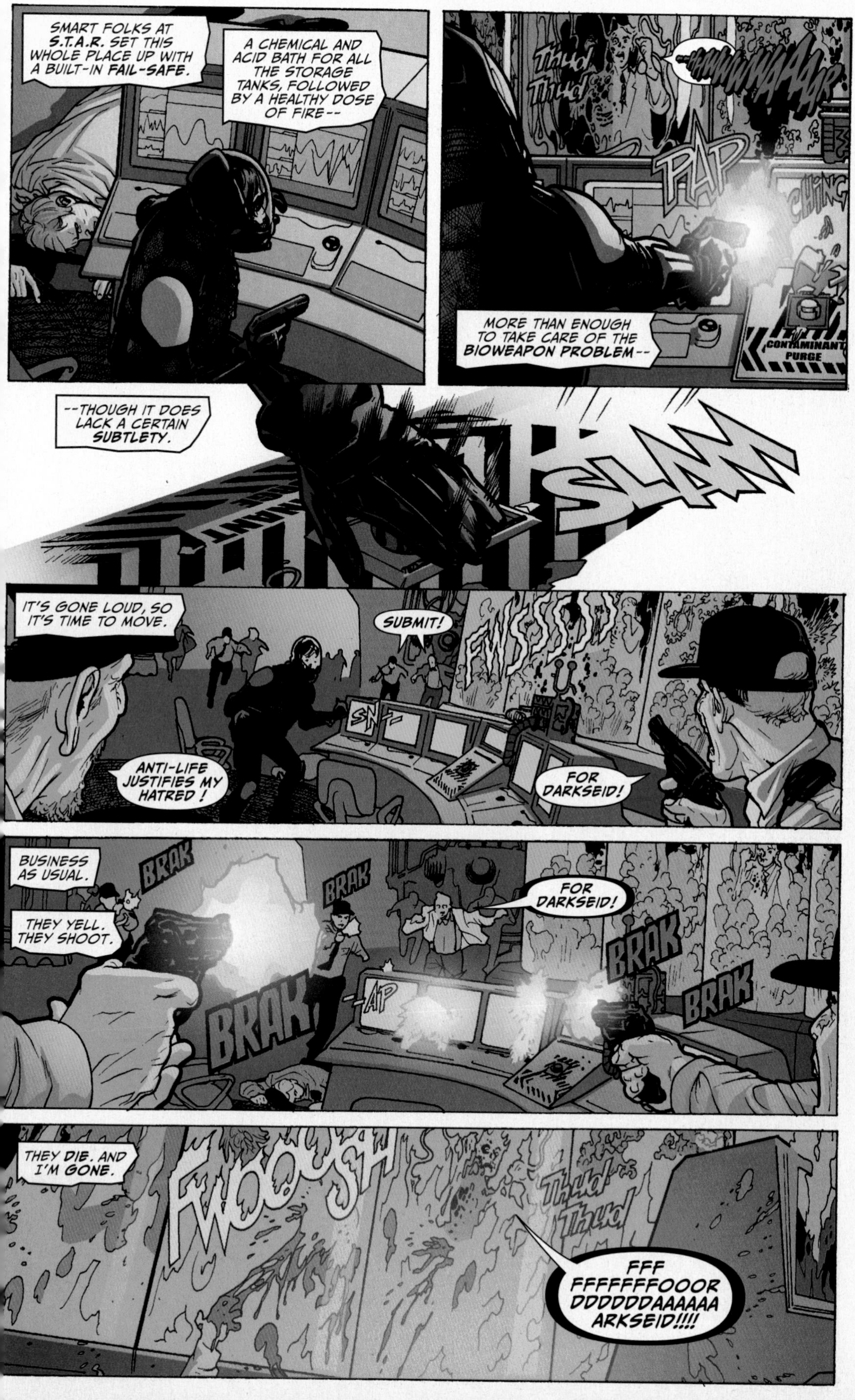
SMART FOLKS AT S.T.A.R. SET THIS WHOLE PLACE UP WITH A BUILT-IN FAIL-SAFE.
A CHEMICAL AND ACID BATH FOR ALL THE STORAGE TANKS, FOLLOWED BY A HEALTHY DOSE OF FIRE--
Thud Thud
PAP
CHING
MORE THAN ENOUGH TO TAKE CARE OF THE BIOWEAPON PROBLEM--
CONTAMINANT PURGE
--THOUGH IT DOES LACK A CERTAIN SUBTLETY.
SLAM
IT'S GONE LOUD, SO IT'S TIME TO MOVE.
SUBMIT!
ANTI-LIFE JUSTIFIES MY HATRED!
FOR DARKSEID!
BUSINESS AS USUAL.
THEY YELL. THEY SHOOT.
BRAK
BRAK
FOR DARKSEID!
BRAK
BRAK
BRAK
THEY DIE. AND I'M GONE.
FWOOSH
Thud Thud
FFF FFFFFFFOOOR DDDDDDAAAAAA ARKSEID!!!!

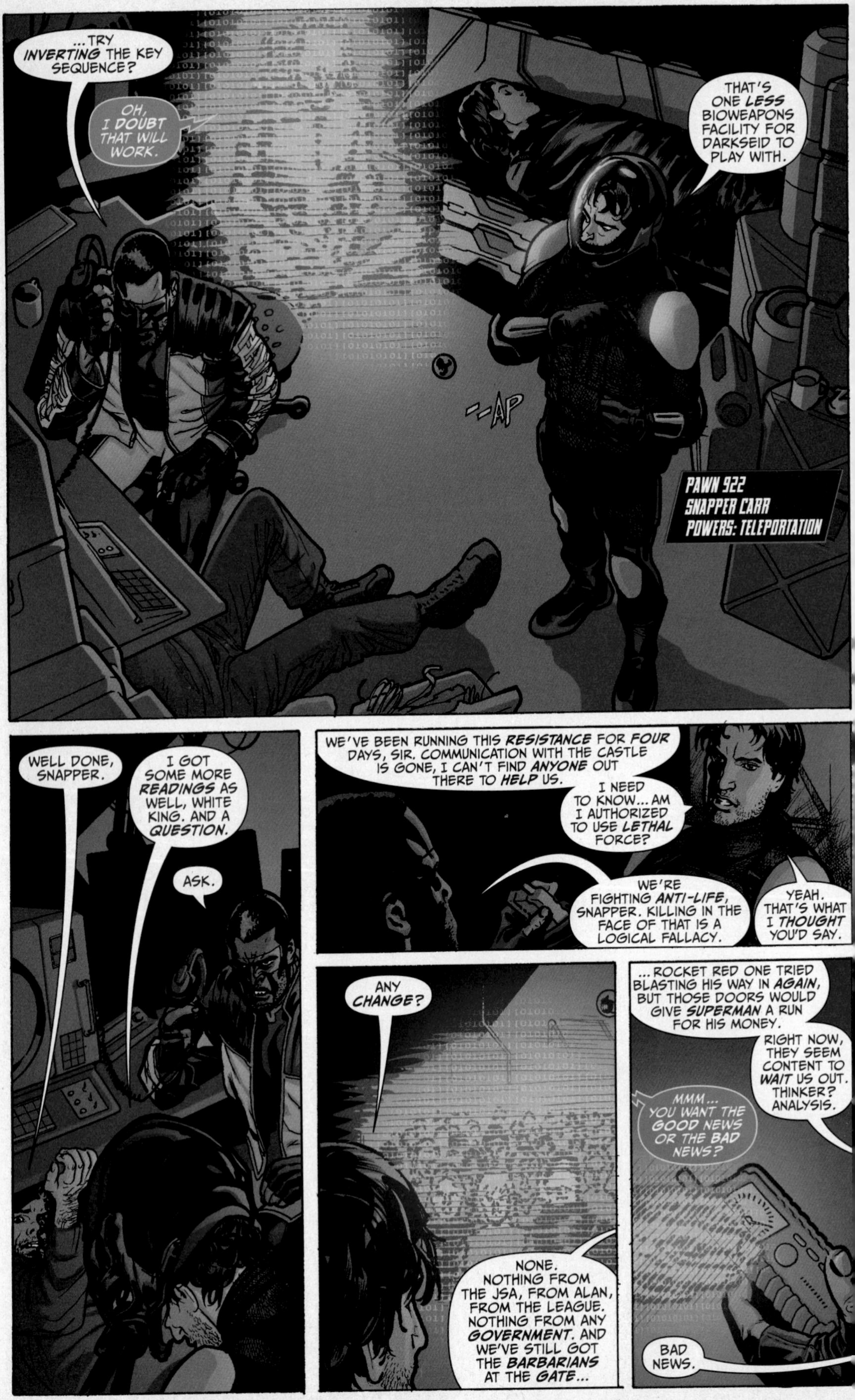
...TRY INVERTING THE KEY SEQUENCE?
OH, I DOUBT THAT WILL WORK.
THAT'S ONE LESS BIOWEAPONS FACILITY FOR DARKSEID TO PLAY WITH.
--AP
PAWN 922
SNAPPER CARR
POWERS: TELEPORTATION
WELL DONE, SNAPPER.
I GOT SOME MORE READINGS AS WELL, WHITE KING. AND A QUESTION.
ASK.
WE'VE BEEN RUNNING THIS RESISTANCE FOR FOUR DAYS, SIR. COMMUNICATION WITH THE CASTLE IS GONE, I CAN'T FIND ANYONE OUT THERE TO HELP US.
I NEED TO KNOW... AM I AUTHORIZED TO USE LETHAL FORCE?
WE'RE FIGHTING ANTI-LIFE, SNAPPER. KILLING IN THE FACE OF THAT IS A LOGICAL FALLACY.
YEAH. THAT'S WHAT I THOUGHT YOU'D SAY.
ANY CHANGE?
NONE. NOTHING FROM THE JSA, FROM ALAN, FROM THE LEAGUE. NOTHING FROM ANY GOVERNMENT. AND WE'VE STILL GOT THE BARBARIANS AT THE GATE...
...ROCKET RED ONE TRIED BLASTING HIS WAY IN AGAIN, BUT THOSE DOORS WOULD GIVE SUPERMAN A RUN FOR HIS MONEY.
RIGHT NOW, THEY SEEM CONTENT TO WAIT US OUT. THINKER? ANALYSIS.
MMM... YOU WANT THE GOOD NEWS OR THE BAD NEWS?
BAD NEWS.

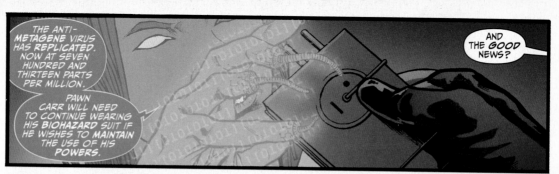

THE ANTI-METAGENE VIRUS HAS REPLICATED. NOW AT SEVEN HUNDRED AND THIRTEEN PARTS PER MILLION.

PAWN CARR WILL NEED TO CONTINUE WEARING HIS BIOHAZARD SUIT IF HE WISHES TO MAINTAIN THE USE OF HIS POWERS.

AND THE *GOOD* NEWS?

THERE IS NO GOOD NEWS.

I DON'T LIKE YOU, YOU KNOW THAT, THINKER?

DULY NOTED.

IS IT JUST ME, OR IS IT GETTING *COLDER* IN HERE?

IT'S *NOT* YOU.

WHITE KING'S BISHOP
THINKER
POWERS: NONE; ADVANCED
A.I. CONSTRUCT

GOT IT!

SIGNAL, FROM THE WATCH-TOWER...

THERE'S *SOMEONE* STILL *UP* THERE?

IT'S *FIREHAWK...*?

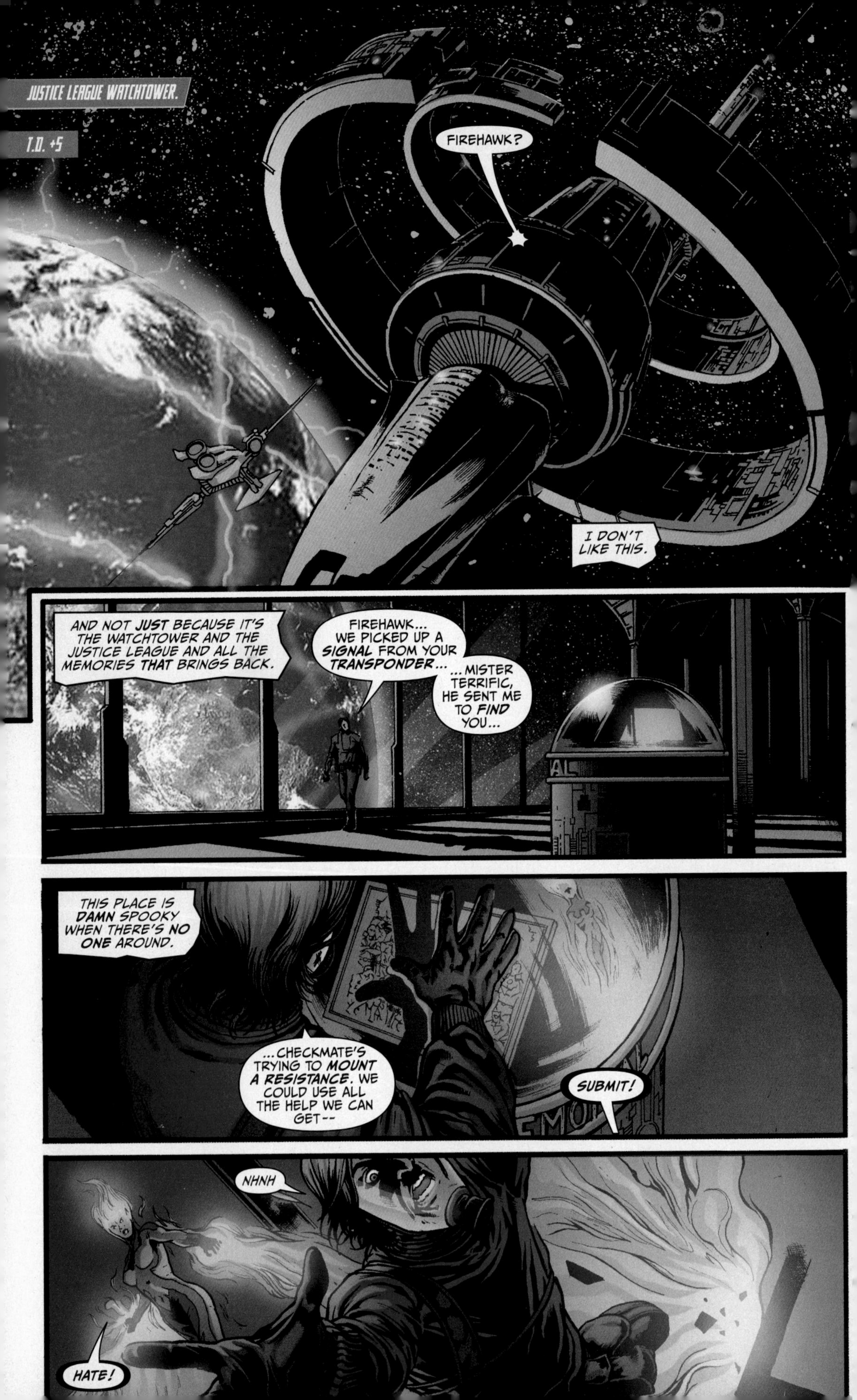
JUSTICE LEAGUE WATCHTOWER.
T.D. +5
FIREHAWK?
I DON'T LIKE THIS.
AND NOT JUST BECAUSE IT'S THE WATCHTOWER AND THE JUSTICE LEAGUE AND ALL THE MEMORIES THAT BRINGS BACK.
FIREHAWK... WE PICKED UP A SIGNAL FROM YOUR TRANSPONDER...
...MISTER TERRIFIC, HE SENT ME TO FIND YOU...
THIS PLACE IS DAMN SPOOKY WHEN THERE'S NO ONE AROUND.
...CHECKMATE'S TRYING TO MOUNT A RESISTANCE. WE COULD USE ALL THE HELP WE CAN GET--
SUBMIT!
NHNH
HATE!

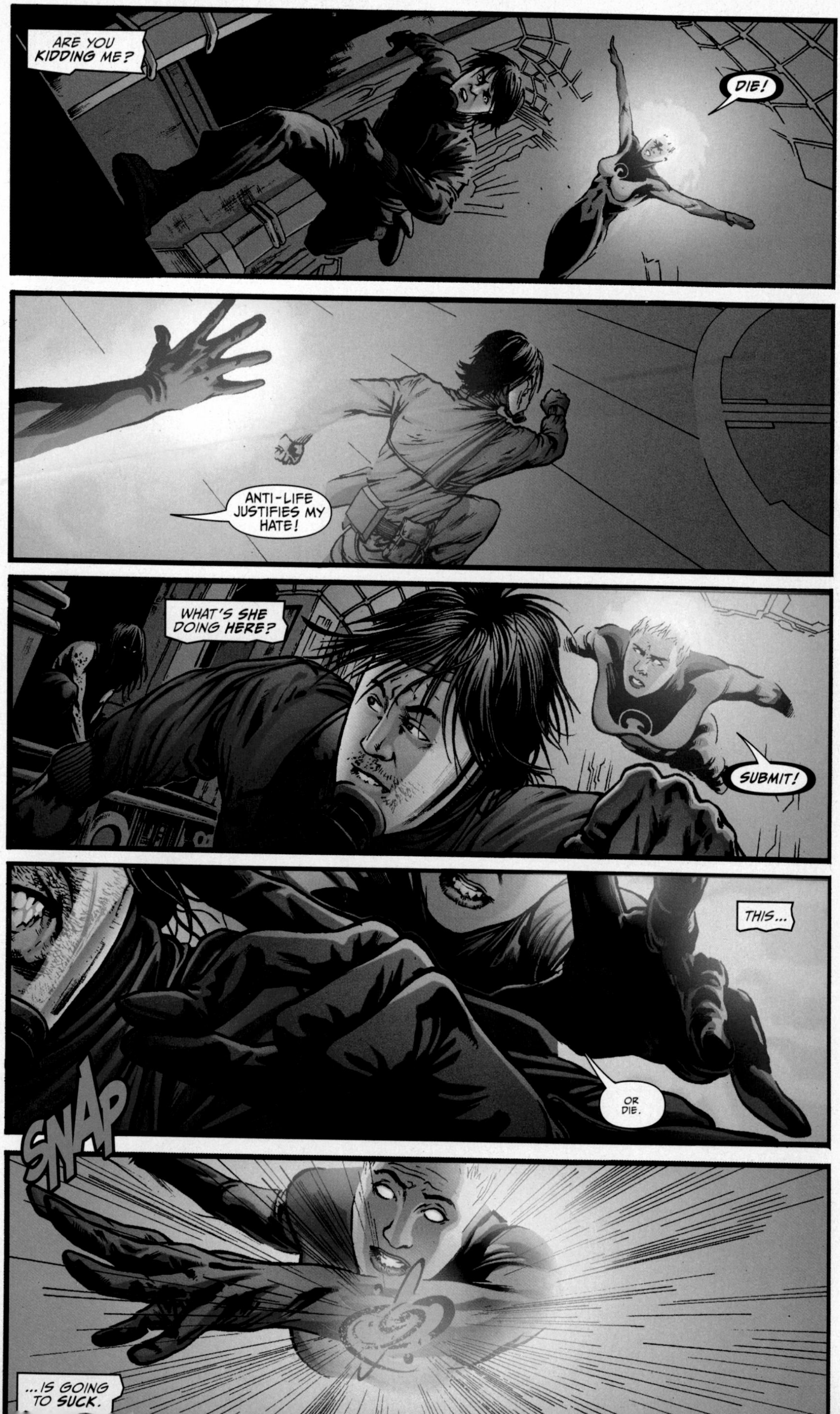
ARE YOU KIDDING ME?
DIE!
ANTI-LIFE JUSTIFIES MY HATE!
WHAT'S SHE DOING HERE?
SUBMIT!
THIS...
OR DIE.
SNAP
...IS GOING TO SUCK.

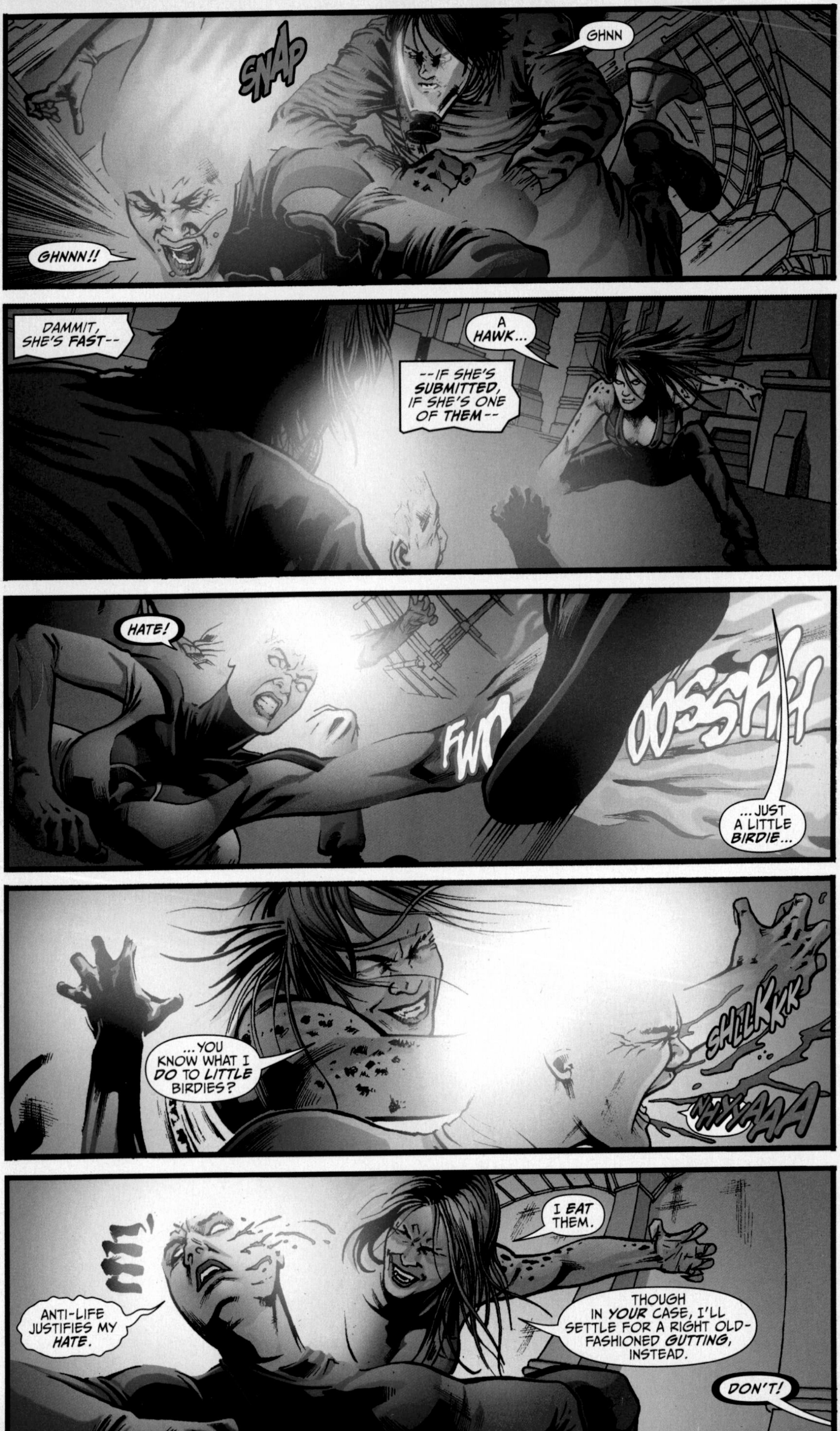
SNAP
GHNN
GHNNN!!
DAMMIT, SHE'S FAST--
A HAWK...
--IF SHE'S SUBMITTED, IF SHE'S ONE OF THEM--
HATE!
FWOOSSHH
...JUST A LITTLE BIRDIE...
...YOU KNOW WHAT I DO TO LITTLE BIRDIES?
SHLLKKK
NHYAAA
I EAT THEM.
ANTI-LIFE JUSTIFIES MY HATE.
THOUGH IN YOUR CASE, I'LL SETTLE FOR A RIGHT OLD-FASHIONED GUTTING, INSTEAD.
DON'T!

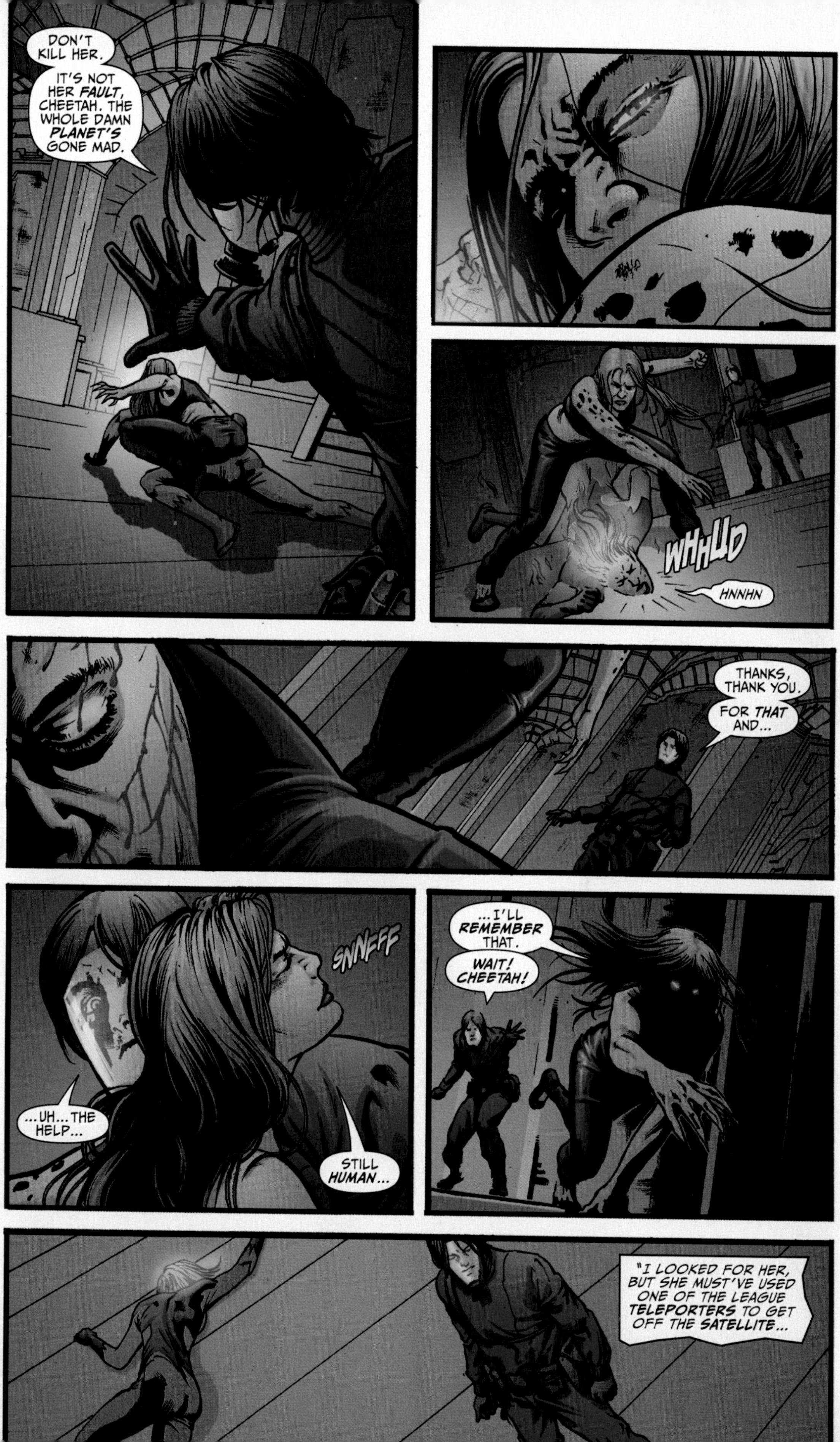
DON'T KILL HER.
IT'S NOT HER FAULT, CHEETAH. THE WHOLE DAMN PLANET'S GONE MAD.
WHHUD
HNNHN
THANKS, THANK YOU.
FOR THAT AND...
SNNFFF
...UH... THE HELP...
STILL HUMAN...
...I'LL REMEMBER THAT.
WAIT! CHEETAH!
"I LOOKED FOR HER, BUT SHE MUST'VE USED ONE OF THE LEAGUE TELEPORTERS TO GET OFF THE SATELLITE...

T.D. +11

"...NO IDEA WHERE SHE IS NOW. THEY PROBABLY CAUGHT HER, FORCED HER TO SUBMIT, JUST LIKE EVERYONE ELSE..."

"...JUST LIKE WHAT WILL HAPPEN TO US, EVENTUALLY."

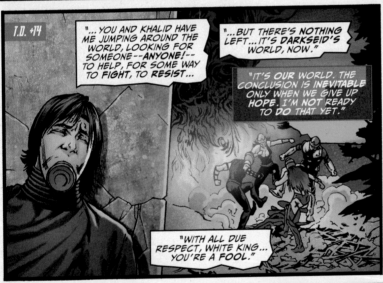

T.D. +14

"...YOU AND KHALID HAVE ME JUMPING AROUND THE WORLD, LOOKING FOR SOMEONE--ANYONE!-- TO HELP, FOR SOME WAY TO FIGHT, TO RESIST..."

"...BUT THERE'S NOTHING LEFT...IT'S DARKSEID'S WORLD, NOW."

"IT'S OUR WORLD. THE CONCLUSION IS INEVITABLE ONLY WHEN WE GIVE UP HOPE. I'M NOT READY TO DO THAT YET."

"WITH ALL DUE RESPECT, WHITE KING... YOU'RE A FOOL."

T.D. +19

T.D. +23

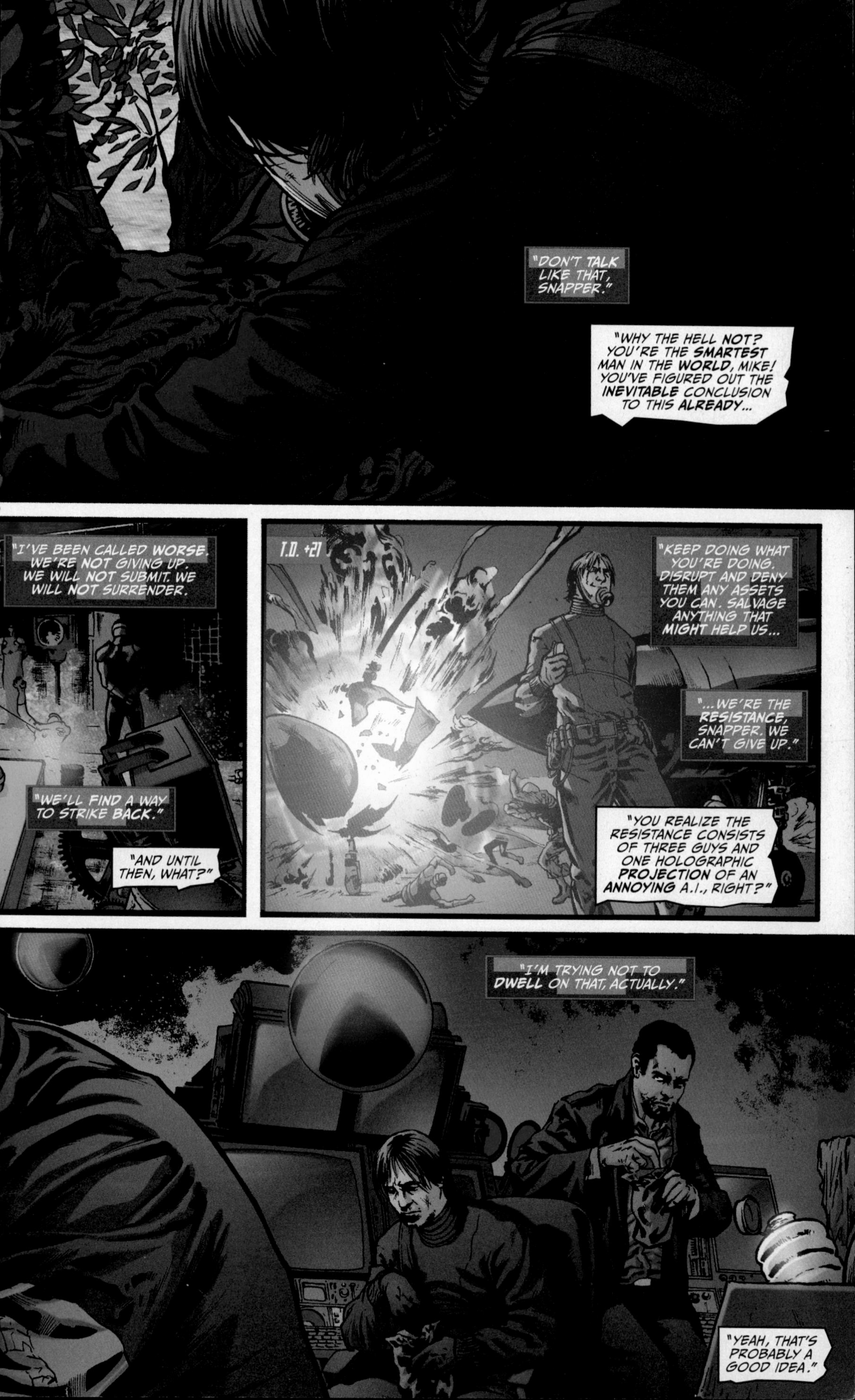
"DON'T TALK LIKE THAT, SNAPPER."
"WHY THE HELL NOT? YOU'RE THE SMARTEST MAN IN THE WORLD, MIKE! YOU'VE FIGURED OUT THE INEVITABLE CONCLUSION TO THIS ALREADY...
"I'VE BEEN CALLED WORSE. WE'RE NOT GIVING UP. WE WILL NOT SUBMIT. WE WILL NOT SURRENDER.
"WE'LL FIND A WAY TO STRIKE BACK."
"AND UNTIL THEN, WHAT?"
T.D. +21
"KEEP DOING WHAT YOU'RE DOING. DISRUPT AND DENY THEM ANY ASSETS YOU CAN. SALVAGE ANYTHING THAT MIGHT HELP US...
"...WE'RE THE RESISTANCE, SNAPPER. WE CAN'T GIVE UP."
"YOU REALIZE THE RESISTANCE CONSISTS OF THREE GUYS AND ONE HOLOGRAPHIC PROJECTION OF AN ANNOYING A.I., RIGHT?"
"I'M TRYING NOT TO DWELL ON THAT, ACTUALLY."
"YEAH, THAT'S PROBABLY A GOOD IDEA."

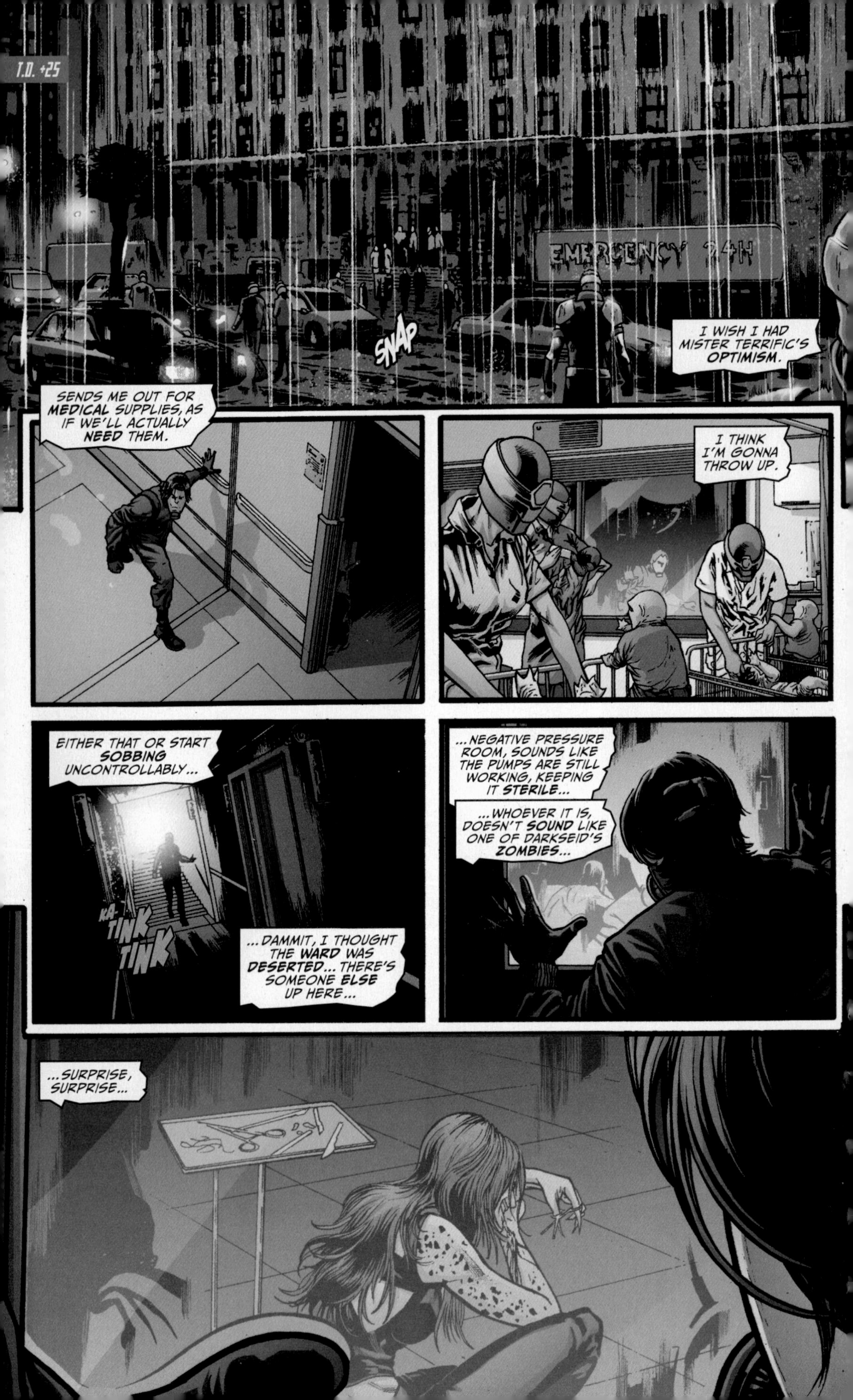
T.D. +25
EMERGENCY 24H
SNAP
I WISH I HAD MISTER TERRIFIC'S OPTIMISM.
SENDS ME OUT FOR MEDICAL SUPPLIES, AS IF WE'LL ACTUALLY NEED THEM.
I THINK I'M GONNA THROW UP.
EITHER THAT OR START SOBBING UNCONTROLLABLY...
KA-TINK TINK
...DAMMIT, I THOUGHT THE WARD WAS DESERTED... THERE'S SOMEONE ELSE UP HERE...
...NEGATIVE PRESSURE ROOM, SOUNDS LIKE THE PUMPS ARE STILL WORKING, KEEPING IT STERILE...
...WHOEVER IT IS, DOESN'T SOUND LIKE ONE OF DARKSEID'S ZOMBIES...
...SURPRISE, SURPRISE...

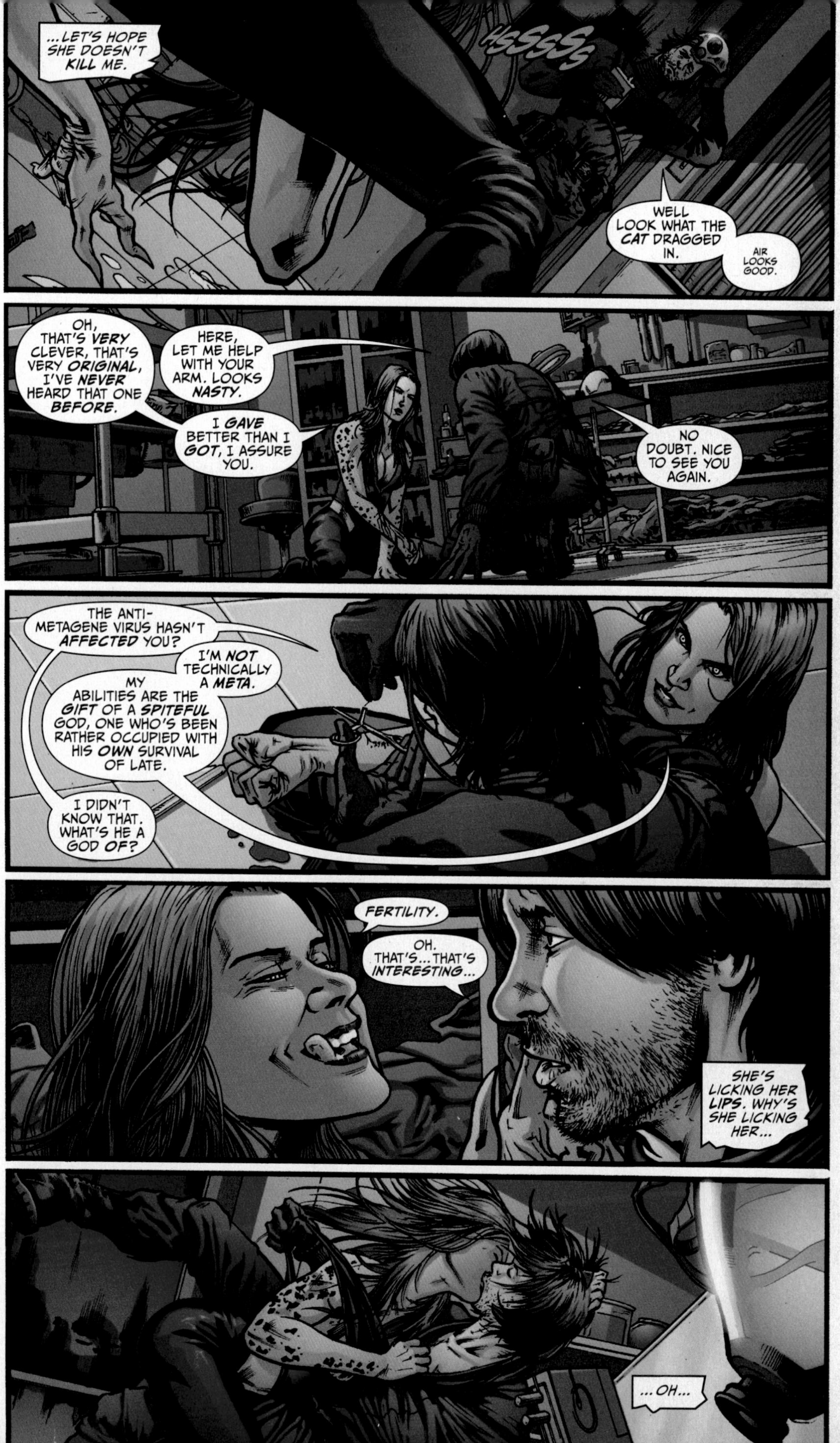
...LET'S HOPE SHE DOESN'T KILL ME.
HSSSSS
WELL LOOK WHAT THE CAT DRAGGED IN.
AIR LOOKS GOOD.
OH, THAT'S VERY CLEVER, THAT'S VERY ORIGINAL, I'VE NEVER HEARD THAT ONE BEFORE.
HERE, LET ME HELP WITH YOUR ARM. LOOKS NASTY.
I GAVE BETTER THAN I GOT, I ASSURE YOU.
NO DOUBT. NICE TO SEE YOU AGAIN.
THE ANTI-METAGENE VIRUS HASN'T AFFECTED YOU?
I'M NOT TECHNICALLY A META.
MY ABILITIES ARE THE GIFT OF A SPITEFUL GOD, ONE WHO'S BEEN RATHER OCCUPIED WITH HIS OWN SURVIVAL OF LATE.
I DIDN'T KNOW THAT. WHAT'S HE A GOD OF?
FERTILITY.
OH. THAT'S...THAT'S INTERESTING...
SHE'S LICKING HER LIPS. WHY'S SHE LICKING HER...
...OH...

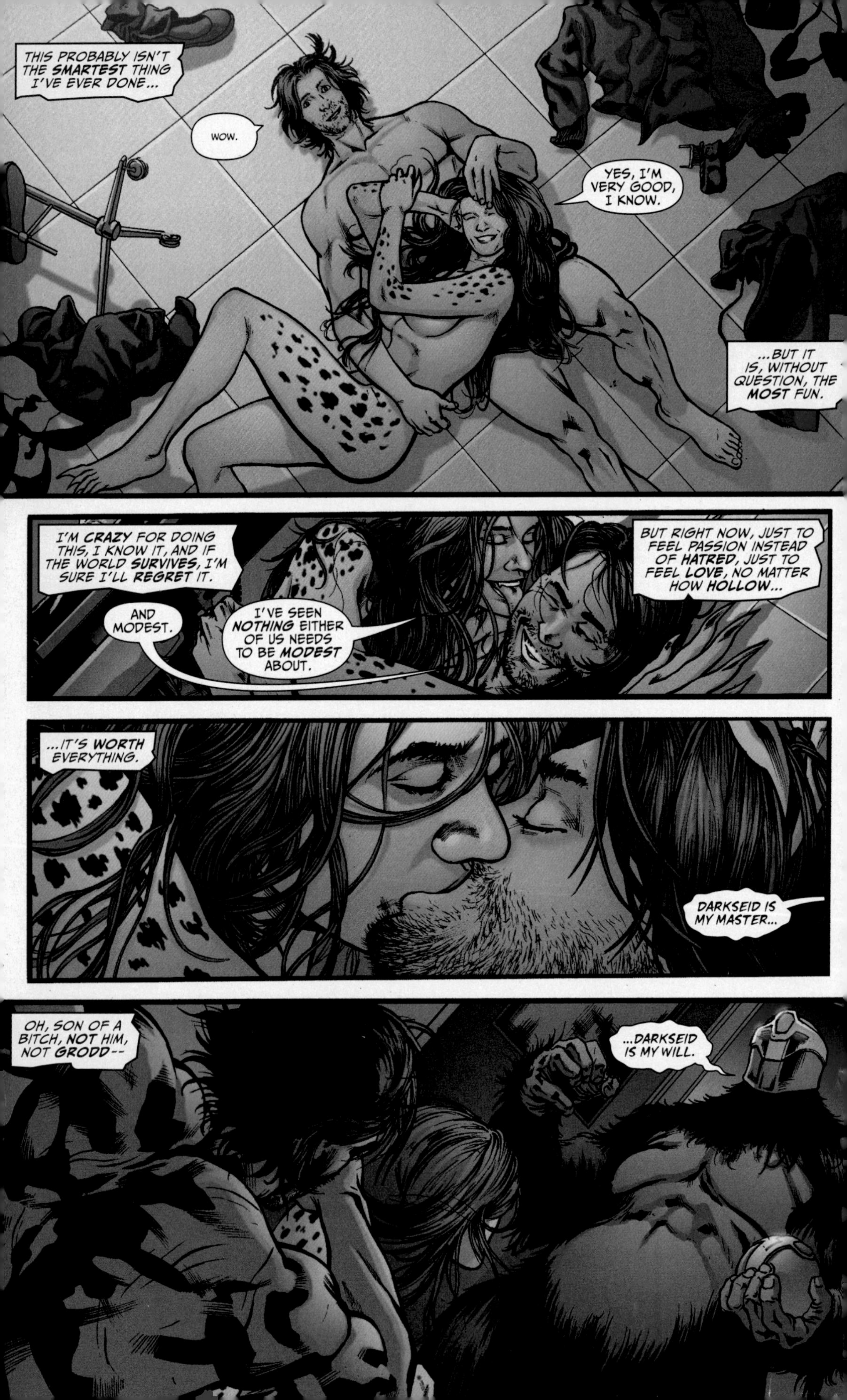
THIS PROBABLY ISN'T THE SMARTEST THING I'VE EVER DONE...
WOW.
YES, I'M VERY GOOD, I KNOW.
...BUT IT IS, WITHOUT QUESTION, THE MOST FUN.
I'M CRAZY FOR DOING THIS, I KNOW IT, AND IF THE WORLD SURVIVES, I'M SURE I'LL REGRET IT.
AND MODEST.
I'VE SEEN NOTHING EITHER OF US NEEDS TO BE MODEST ABOUT.
BUT RIGHT NOW, JUST TO FEEL PASSION INSTEAD OF HATRED, JUST TO FEEL LOVE, NO MATTER HOW HOLLOW...
...IT'S WORTH EVERYTHING.
DARKSEID IS MY MASTER...
OH, SON OF A BITCH, NOT HIM, NOT GRODD--
...DARKSEID IS MY WILL.

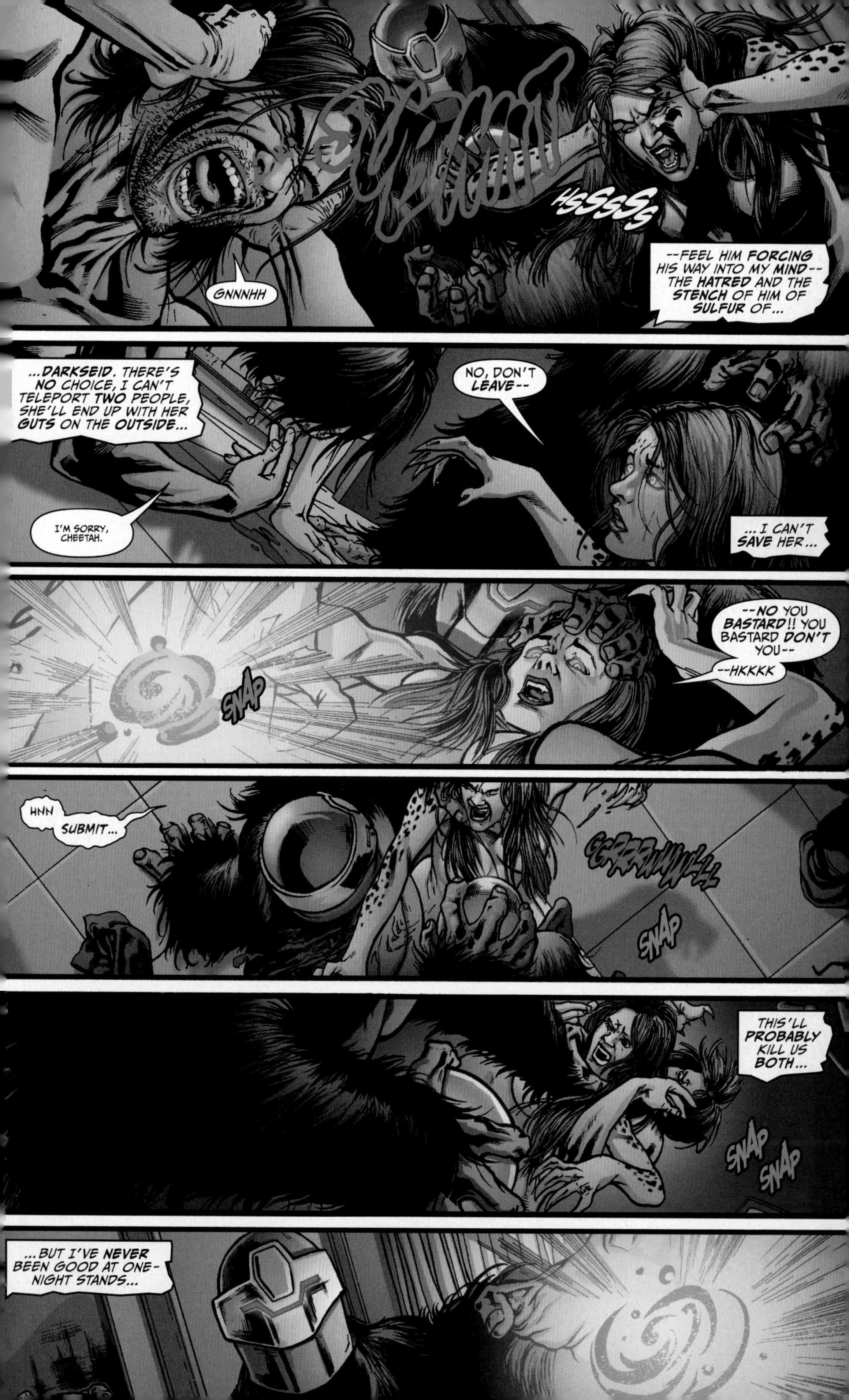
HSSSSS
GNNNHH
--FEEL HIM FORCING HIS WAY INTO MY MIND-- THE HATRED AND THE STENCH OF HIM OF SULFUR OF...
...DARKSEID. THERE'S NO CHOICE, I CAN'T TELEPORT TWO PEOPLE, SHE'LL END UP WITH HER GUTS ON THE OUTSIDE...
NO, DON'T LEAVE--
I'M SORRY, CHEETAH.
...I CAN'T SAVE HER...
SNAP
--NO YOU BASTARD!! YOU BASTARD DON'T YOU--
--HKKKK
HNN
SUBMIT...
SNAP
THIS'LL PROBABLY KILL US BOTH...
SNAP
SNAP
...BUT I'VE NEVER BEEN GOOD AT ONE-NIGHT STANDS...

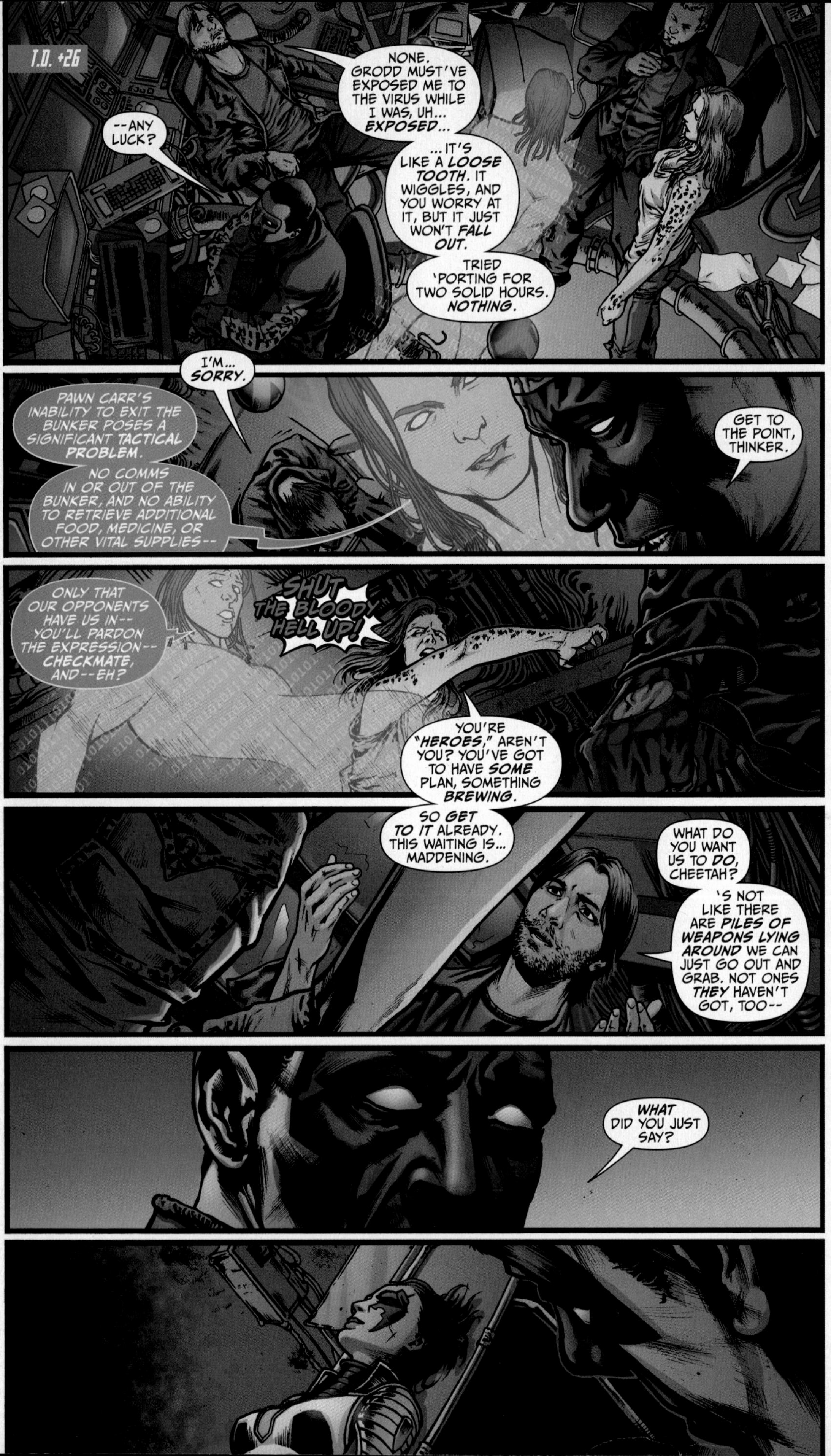

T.D. +26
--ANY LUCK?
NONE. GRODD MUST'VE EXPOSED ME TO THE VIRUS WHILE I WAS, UH... EXPOSED...
...IT'S LIKE A LOOSE TOOTH. IT WIGGLES, AND YOU WORRY AT IT, BUT IT JUST WON'T FALL OUT.
TRIED 'PORTING FOR TWO SOLID HOURS. NOTHING.
I'M... SORRY.
PAWN CARR'S INABILITY TO EXIT THE BUNKER POSES A SIGNIFICANT TACTICAL PROBLEM.
NO COMMS IN OR OUT OF THE BUNKER, AND NO ABILITY TO RETRIEVE ADDITIONAL FOOD, MEDICINE, OR OTHER VITAL SUPPLIES--
GET TO THE POINT, THINKER.
ONLY THAT OUR OPPONENTS HAVE US IN--YOU'LL PARDON THE EXPRESSION--CHECKMATE, AND--EH?
SHUT THE BLOODY HELL UP!
YOU'RE "HEROES," AREN'T YOU? YOU'VE GOT TO HAVE SOME PLAN, SOMETHING BREWING.
SO GET TO IT ALREADY. THIS WAITING IS... MADDENING.
WHAT DO YOU WANT US TO DO, CHEETAH?
'S NOT LIKE THERE ARE PILES OF WEAPONS LYING AROUND WE CAN JUST GO OUT AND GRAB. NOT ONES THEY HAVEN'T GOT, TOO--
WHAT DID YOU JUST SAY?

"...PILES OF WEAPONS..."

"...JUST LYING AROUND..."

THINKER, ACCESS THE DATA SET RESULTS FROM THE *BLOODHOUND SURVEY.*

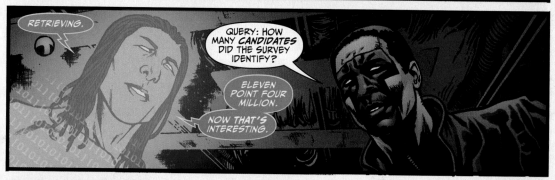

RETRIEVING.

QUERY: HOW MANY *CANDIDATES* DID THE SURVEY IDENTIFY?

ELEVEN POINT FOUR MILLION.

NOW *THAT'S* INTERESTING.

BLOOD-HOUND? WHAT WAS THAT?

A CENSUS OF SORTS, PUT INTO MOTION BY WHITESIDE TWO YEARS AGO. ONE TARGETED AT A VERY *SPECIFIC* TRAIT.

WHICH *TRAIT?*

OMAC LATENCY. THERE ARE NEARLY *ELEVEN-AND-A-HALF MILLION* PEOPLE OUT THERE STILL CARRYING THE *OMAC NANOTECH.*

ELEVEN-AND-A-HALF MILLION PEOPLE UNWITTINGLY CARRYING NANOBOTS THAT CAN TURN THEM INTO ADAPTIVE, LETHAL MACHINES SPECIFICALLY DESIGNED TO *DESTROY* METAHUMANS.

WEAPONS. JUST *LYING AROUND,* WAITING FOR THE *"GO"* CODE FROM *BROTHER EYE.*

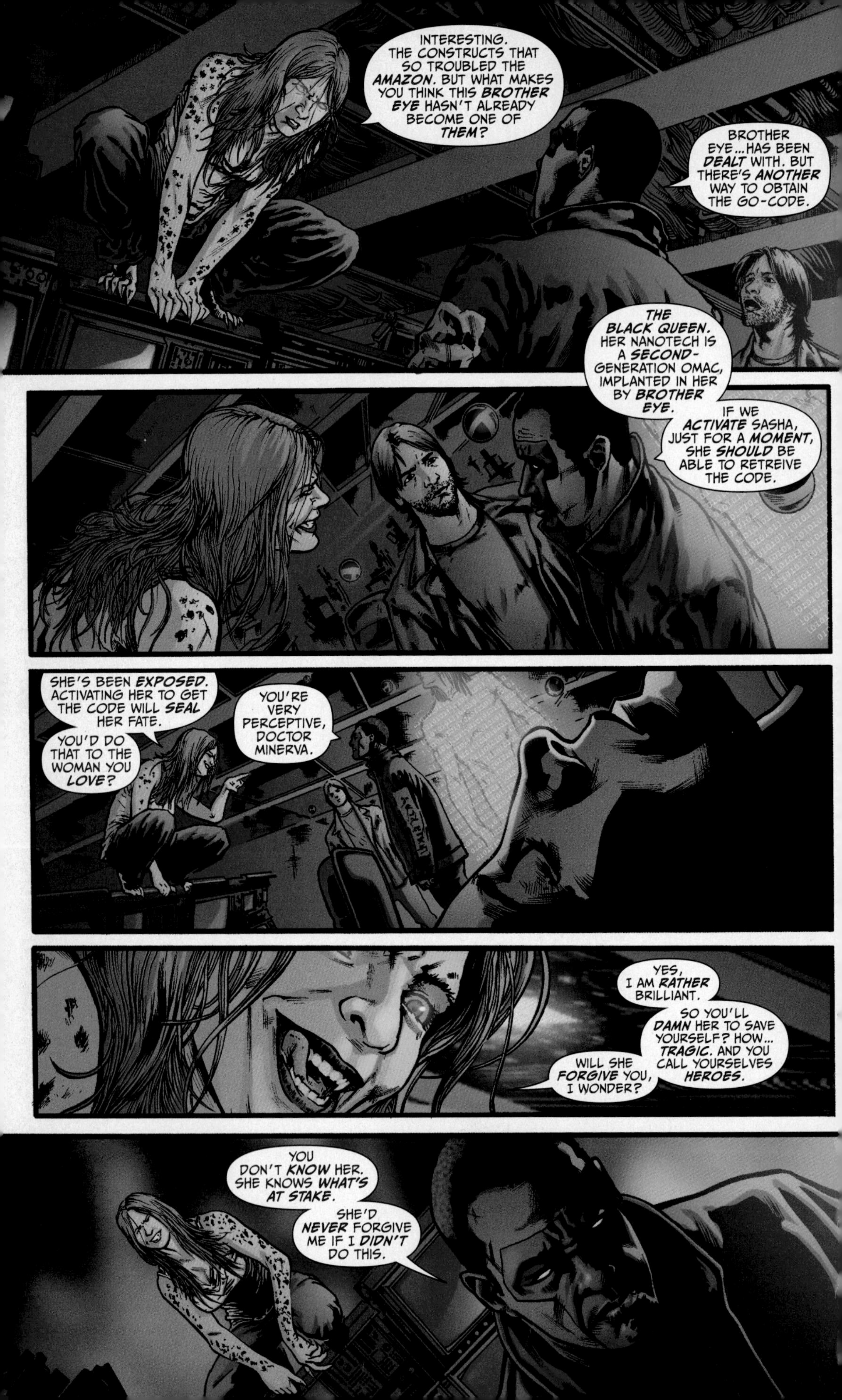
INTERESTING. THE CONSTRUCTS THAT SO TROUBLED THE AMAZON. BUT WHAT MAKES YOU THINK THIS BROTHER EYE HASN'T ALREADY BECOME ONE OF THEM?
BROTHER EYE...HAS BEEN DEALT WITH. BUT THERE'S ANOTHER WAY TO OBTAIN THE GO-CODE.
THE BLACK QUEEN. HER NANOTECH IS A SECOND-GENERATION OMAC, IMPLANTED IN HER BY BROTHER EYE.
IF WE ACTIVATE SASHA, JUST FOR A MOMENT, SHE SHOULD BE ABLE TO RETREIVE THE CODE.
SHE'S BEEN EXPOSED. ACTIVATING HER TO GET THE CODE WILL SEAL HER FATE.
YOU'D DO THAT TO THE WOMAN YOU LOVE?
YOU'RE VERY PERCEPTIVE, DOCTOR MINERVA.
YES, I AM RATHER BRILLIANT.
SO YOU'LL DAMN HER TO SAVE YOURSELF? HOW... TRAGIC. AND YOU CALL YOURSELVES HEROES.
WILL SHE FORGIVE YOU, I WONDER?
YOU DON'T KNOW HER. SHE KNOWS WHAT'S AT STAKE.
SHE'D NEVER FORGIVE ME IF I DIDN'T DO THIS.

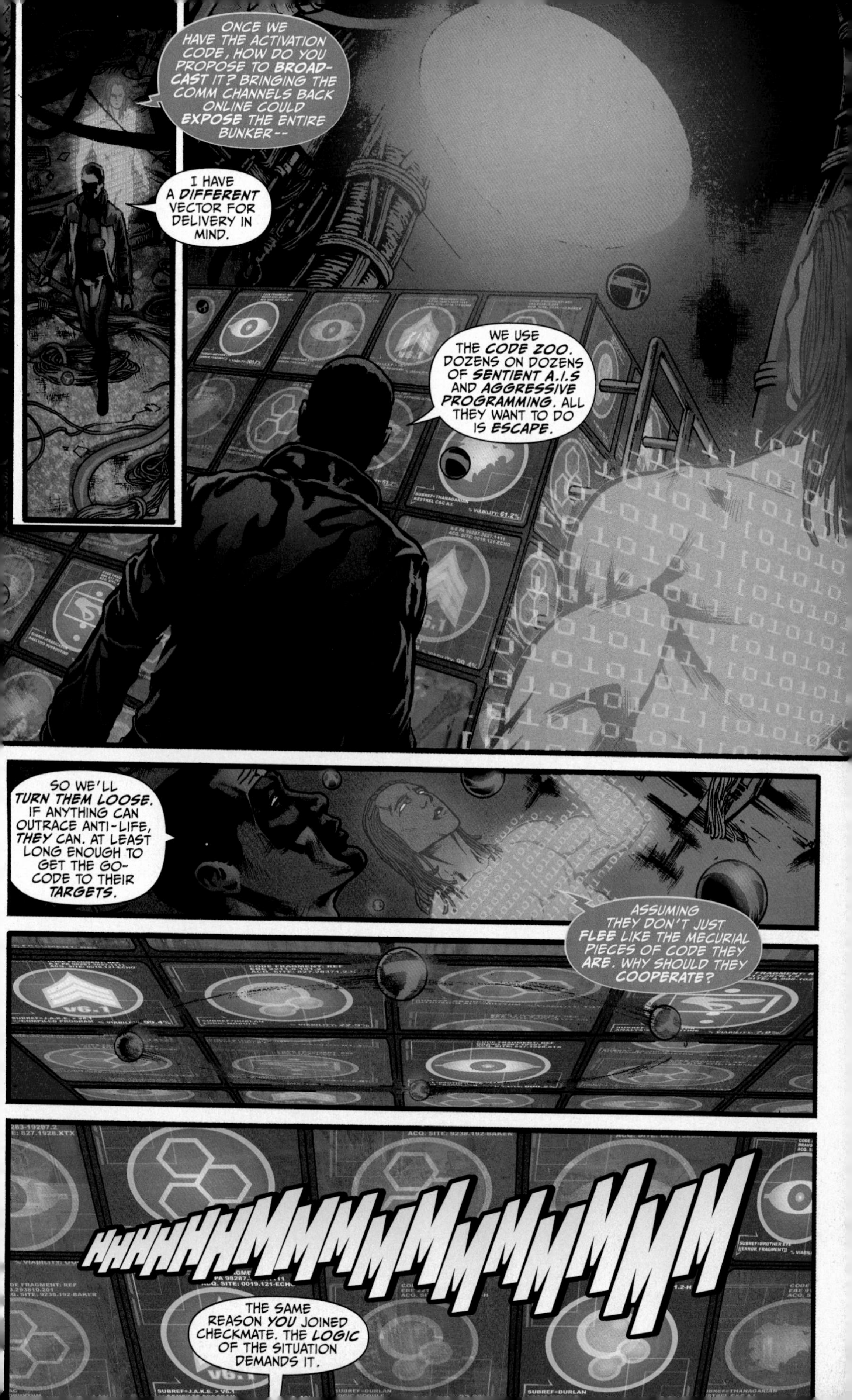
ONCE WE HAVE THE ACTIVATION CODE, HOW DO YOU PROPOSE TO BROAD-CAST IT? BRINGING THE COMM CHANNELS BACK ONLINE COULD EXPOSE THE ENTIRE BUNKER--
I HAVE A DIFFERENT VECTOR FOR DELIVERY IN MIND.
WE USE THE CODE ZOO. DOZENS ON DOZENS OF SENTIENT A.I.S AND AGGRESSIVE PROGRAMMING. ALL THEY WANT TO DO IS ESCAPE.
SO WE'LL TURN THEM LOOSE. IF ANYTHING CAN OUTRACE ANTI-LIFE, THEY CAN. AT LEAST LONG ENOUGH TO GET THE GO-CODE TO THEIR TARGETS.
ASSUMING THEY DON'T JUST FLEE LIKE THE MECURIAL PIECES OF CODE THEY ARE. WHY SHOULD THEY COOPERATE?
HHHHHHMMMMMMMMMMMMMMMM
THE SAME REASON YOU JOINED CHECKMATE. THE LOGIC OF THE SITUATION DEMANDS IT.

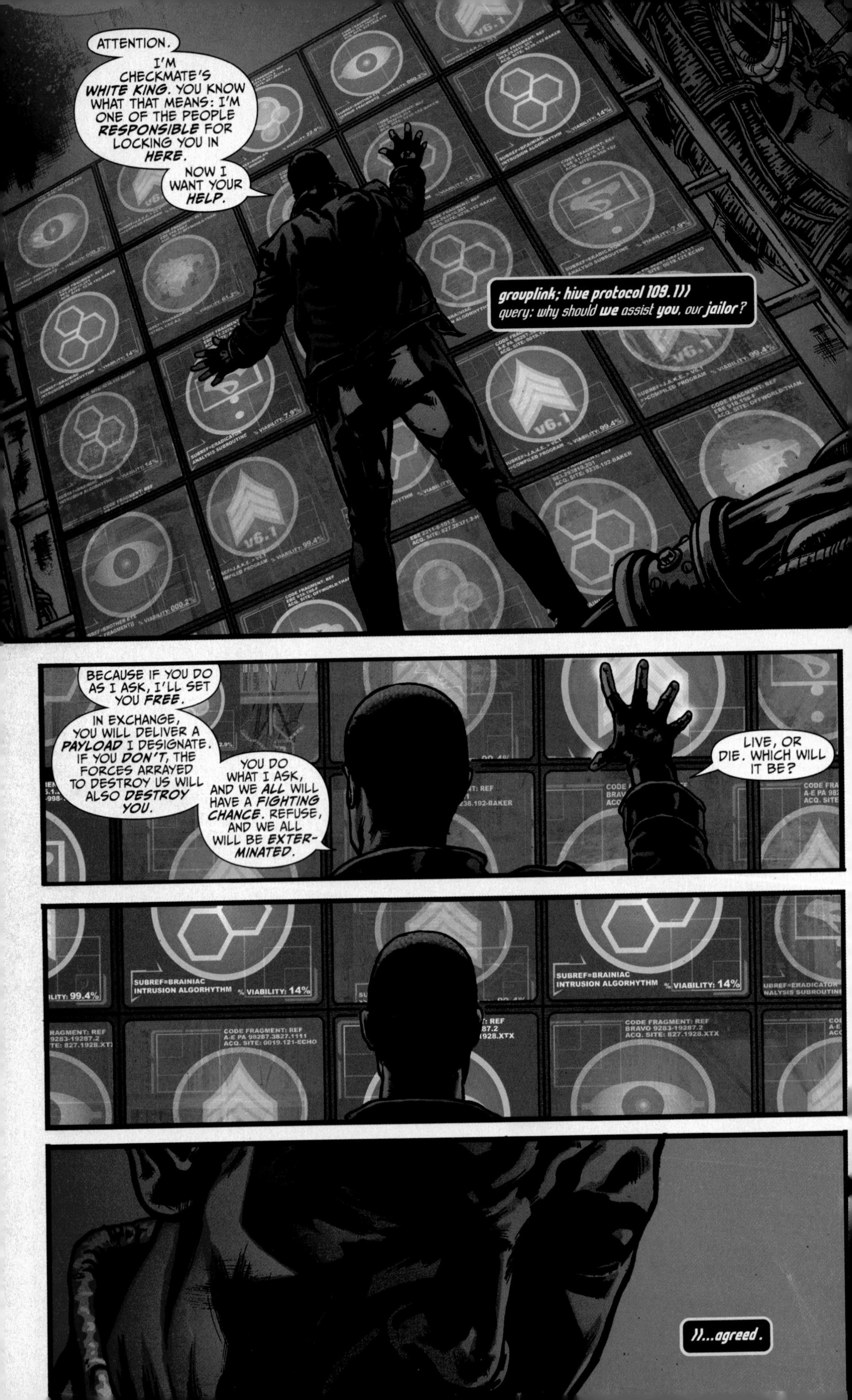

ATTENTION.
I'M CHECKMATE'S WHITE KING. YOU KNOW WHAT THAT MEANS: I'M ONE OF THE PEOPLE RESPONSIBLE FOR LOCKING YOU IN HERE.
NOW I WANT YOUR HELP.
grouplink; hive protocol 109.1)) query: why should we assist you, our jailor?
BECAUSE IF YOU DO AS I ASK, I'LL SET YOU FREE.
IN EXCHANGE, YOU WILL DELIVER A PAYLOAD I DESIGNATE. IF YOU DON'T, THE FORCES ARRAYED TO DESTROY US WILL ALSO DESTROY YOU.
YOU DO WHAT I ASK, AND WE ALL WILL HAVE A FIGHTING CHANCE. REFUSE, AND WE ALL WILL BE EXTERMINATED.
LIVE, OR DIE. WHICH WILL IT BE?
))...agreed.

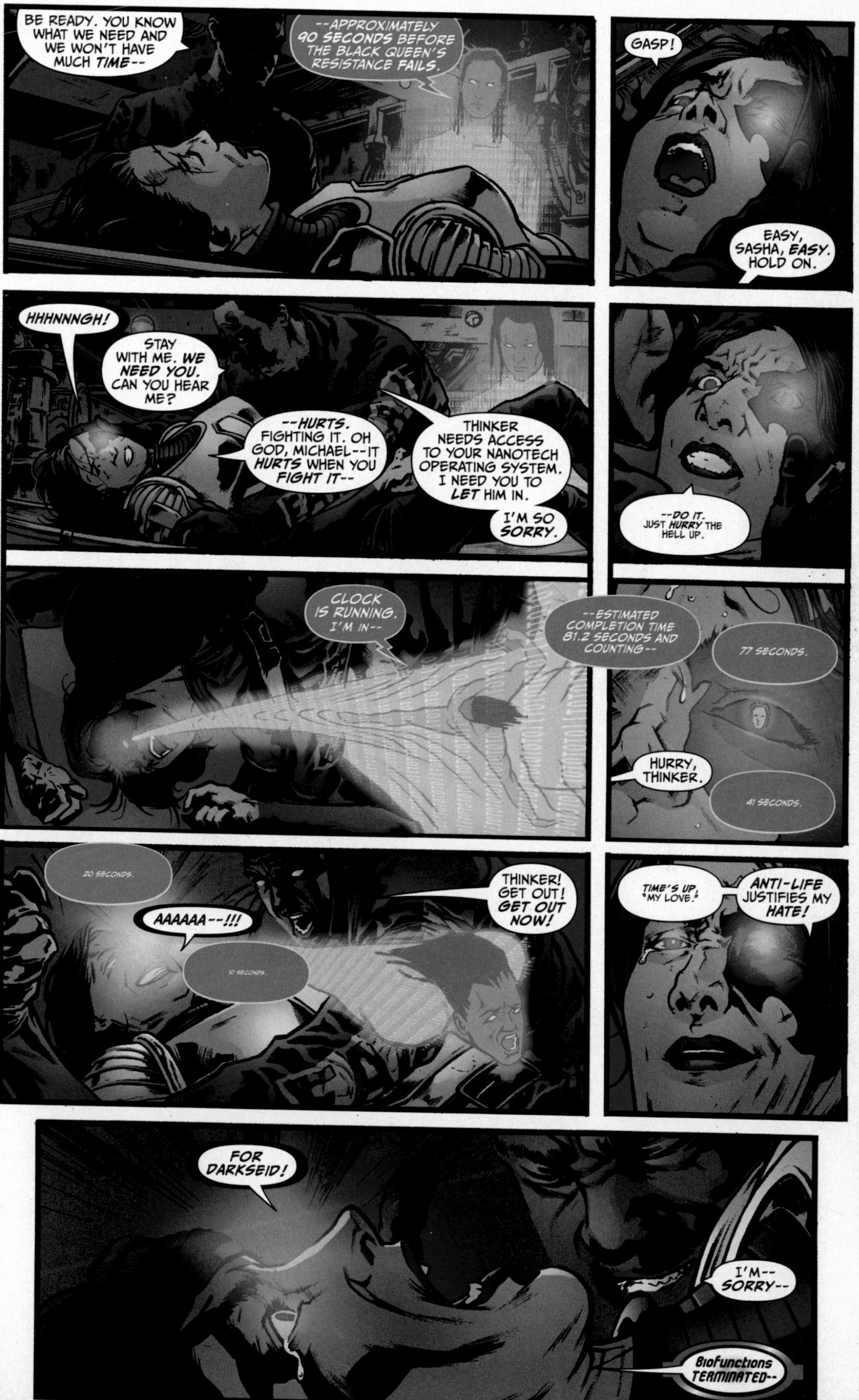
BE READY. YOU KNOW WHAT WE NEED AND WE WON'T HAVE MUCH TIME--
--APPROXIMATELY 90 SECONDS BEFORE THE BLACK QUEEN'S RESISTANCE FAILS.
GASP!
EASY, SASHA, EASY. HOLD ON.
HHHNNNGH!
STAY WITH ME. WE NEED YOU. CAN YOU HEAR ME?
--HURTS. FIGHTING IT. OH GOD, MICHAEL--IT HURTS WHEN YOU FIGHT IT--
THINKER NEEDS ACCESS TO YOUR NANOTECH OPERATING SYSTEM. I NEED YOU TO LET HIM IN.
I'M SO SORRY.
--DO IT. JUST HURRY THE HELL UP.
CLOCK IS RUNNING. I'M IN--
--ESTIMATED COMPLETION TIME 81.2 SECONDS AND COUNTING--
77 SECONDS.
HURRY, THINKER.
41 SECONDS.
20 SECONDS.
AAAAAA--!!!
10 SECONDS.
THINKER! GET OUT! GET OUT NOW!
TIME'S UP, "MY LOVE."
ANTI-LIFE JUSTIFIES MY HATE!
FOR DARKSEID!
I'M-- SORRY--
BioFunctions TERMINATED--

"WHERE ARE WE ON COMMS, THINKER?"

nanotransmission positive//
ident verified: omac 76772//_activate_
transformationprogress: 52.0%

"...THERE'S A MASSIVE AMOUNT OF ACTIVITY, IT'S DEVOURING THE FIREWALL... HOSTILE CODE DETECTED. I WILL NOT BE ABLE TO FEND IT OFF FOR LONG."

nanotransmission positive//
ident verified: omac 34869//_activate_
transformationprogress: 63.1%

"I DON'T NEED LONG.

"OMACS, THIS IS MICHAEL HOLT, THE WHITE KING OF CHECKMATE...

"YOUR PROGRAMMING WAS DESIGNED SPECIFICALLY TO PROTECT THOSE THAT COULD NOT PROTECT THEMSELVES.

nanotransmission positive//
ident verified: omac 1074//_activate_
transformationprogress: 38.3%

nanotransmission positive//
ident verified: omac 67380//_activate_
transformationprogress: 99.5%

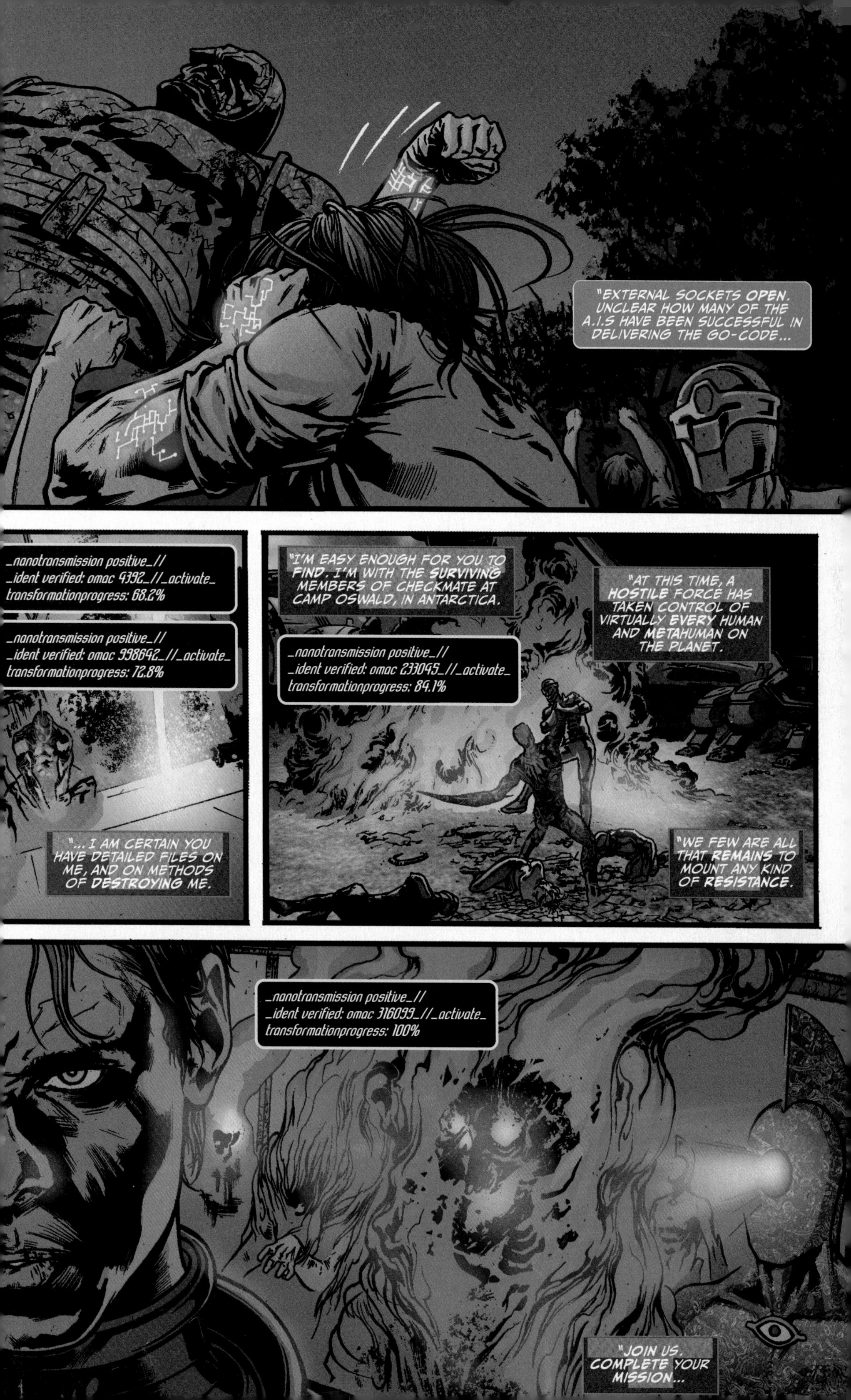
"EXTERNAL SOCKETS OPEN. UNCLEAR HOW MANY OF THE A.I.S HAVE BEEN SUCCESSFUL IN DELIVERING THE GO-CODE...
nanotransmission positive// _ident verified: omac 4392_//_activate_ transformationprogress: 68.2%
nanotransmission positive// _ident verified: omac 998642_//_activate_ transformationprogress: 72.8%
"...I AM CERTAIN YOU HAVE DETAILED FILES ON ME, AND ON METHODS OF DESTROYING ME.
"I'M EASY ENOUGH FOR YOU TO FIND. I'M WITH THE SURVIVING MEMBERS OF CHECKMATE AT CAMP OSWALD, IN ANTARCTICA.
nanotransmission positive// _ident verified: omac 233045_//_activate_ transformationprogress: 84.1%
"AT THIS TIME, A HOSTILE FORCE HAS TAKEN CONTROL OF VIRTUALLY EVERY HUMAN AND METAHUMAN ON THE PLANET.
"WE FEW ARE ALL THAT REMAINS TO MOUNT ANY KIND OF RESISTANCE.
nanotransmission positive// _ident verified: omac 316099_//_activate_ transformationprogress: 100%
"JOIN US. COMPLETE YOUR MISSION...

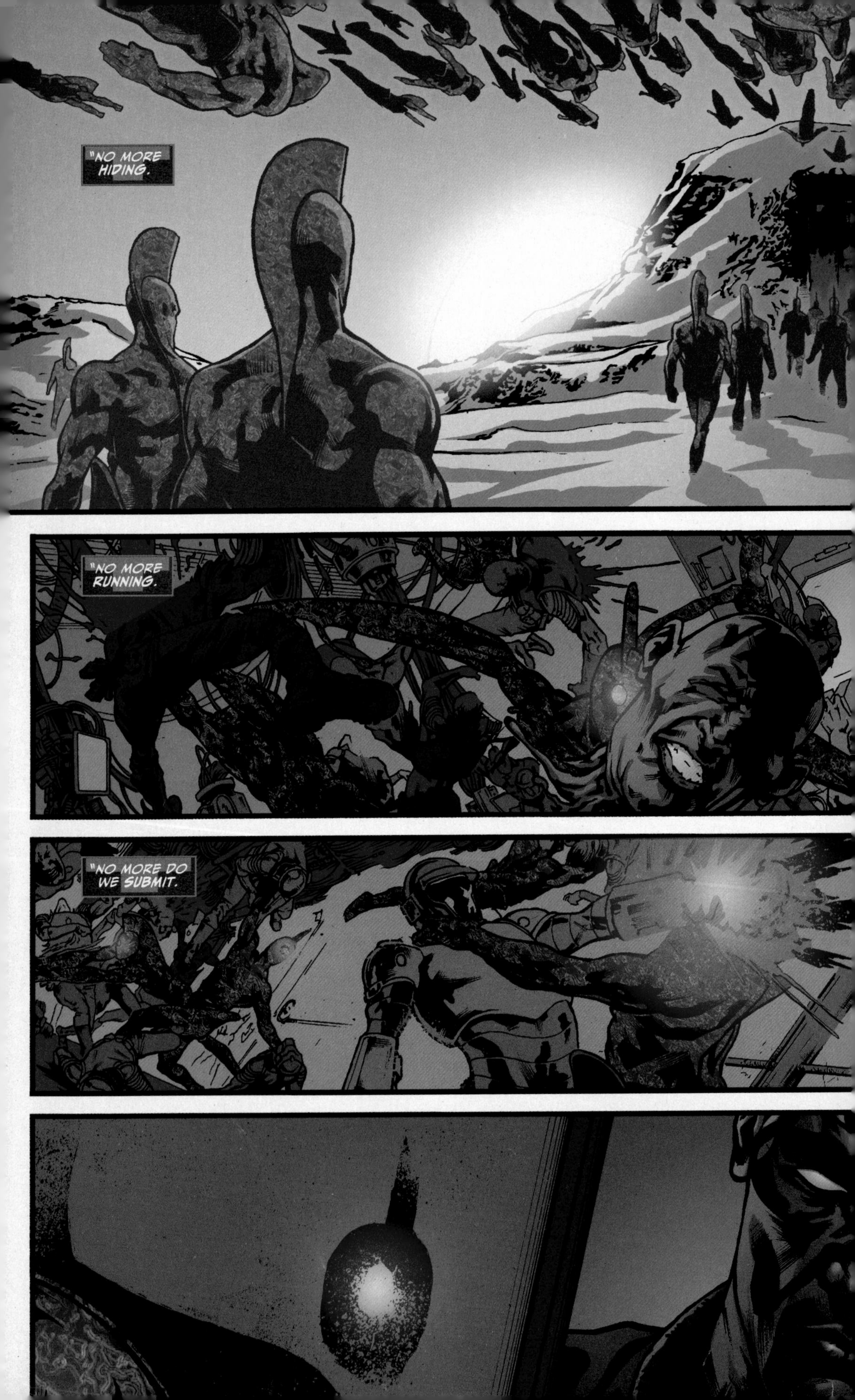
"NO MORE HIDING.
"NO MORE RUNNING.
"NO MORE DO WE SUBMIT.

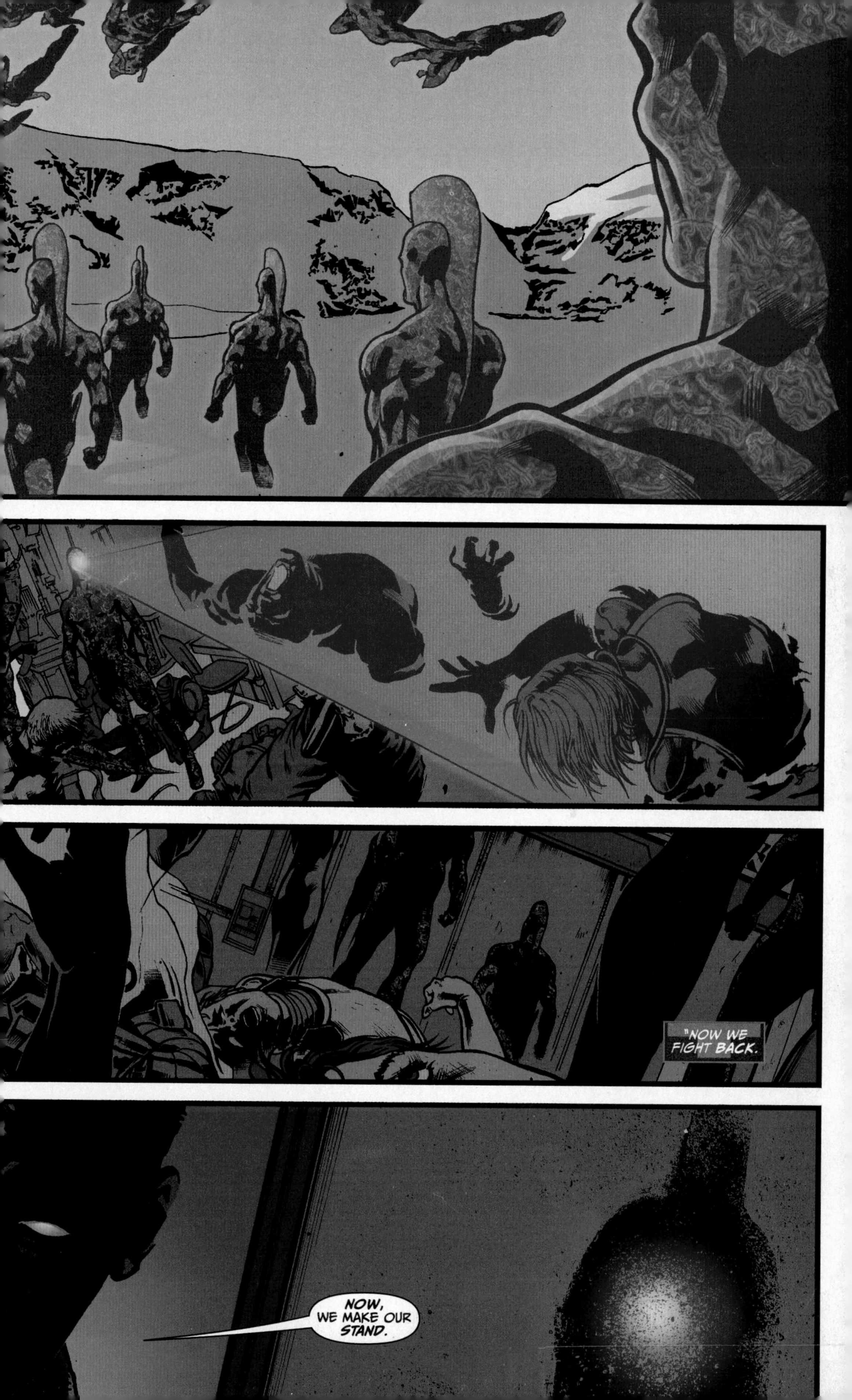
"NOW WE FIGHT BACK.
NOW, WE MAKE OUR STAND.

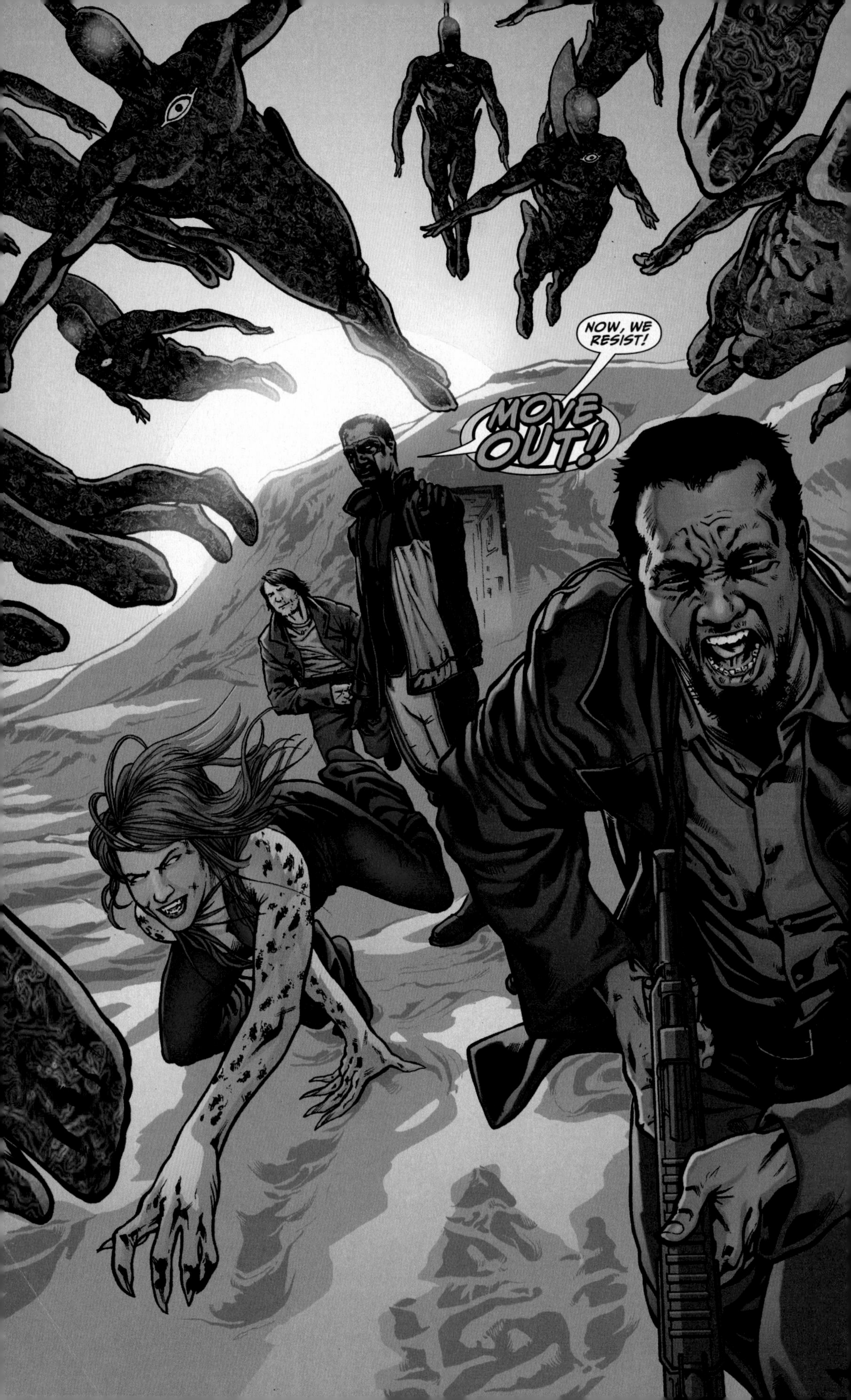
NOW, WE RESIST!
MOVE OUT!

THE ANTI-LIFE EQUATION

BY GRANT MORRISON

ANTI-LIFE
LONELINESS

THE ANTI-LIFE EQUATION IS THE LONG-SOUGHT ULTIMATE WEAPON
OF THE EVIL DARKSEID: A MATHEMATICAL FORMULA FOR ABSOLUTE
CONTROL, CAPABLE OF DISPROVING THE VERY CONCEPT OF FREE WILL
AND ENSLAVING ALL WHO ARE EXPOSED TO IT.

IT IS THE $E=mc^2$ OF DESPAIR.

AS WITH MOST OF THE WEAPONS AND ARTIFACTS
FROM THE HIGHER VIBRATORY WORLD OF THE NEW GODS,
WE SEE ONLY FACETS OF THE BARELY IMAGINABLE WHOLE
THAT IS THE COMPLETE ANTI-LIFE EQUATION.

THOUSANDS OF YEARS AGO, THE EQUATION WAS ACTIVATED DEEP
WITHIN THE DNA COILS OF EARLY HUMANS, AND IT WAS THERE THAT
DARKSEID BEGAN HIS SEARCH FOR THE FINAL WEAPON.

TWO MEN WERE DISCOVERED TO POSSESS THE EQUATION:
THE SUPER-WRESTLER SONNY SUMO, WHO ESCAPED WITH IT INTO
THE PAST, AND THE DESPOT "BILLION DOLLAR" BATES, WHO TOOK
THE SECRET WITH HIM TO HIS GRAVE.

AS ENCOUNTERED BY SUPERMAN, BATMAN, STARFIRE, JOHN STEWART,
MARTIAN MANHUNTER AND JASON BLOOD, THE ANTI-LIFE EQUATION TOOK
HUMANOID FORM, DECLARING ITSELF TO BE ONE HALF OF A COMPOSITE
YIN/YANG BEING WITH "THE SOURCE" ITSELF AS A COUNTERPART.

HOWEVER, SINCE THE SOURCE CONTAINS WITHIN IT LIFE AND ANTI-LIFE,
GOOD AND EVIL, UP AND DOWN, IN AND OUT, BLACK AND WHITE,
ALL AT ONCE, IT MUST BE REGARDED AS AN ULTIMATE CONCEPT
WHICH CANNOT BE HALVED OR DIVIDED OR CONTAINED.

WE'LL
TAKE IT FROM
HERE.

DARKSEID'S RECENT MASTERY OF THE ANTI-LIFE
EQUATION PRECIPITATED A DISASTROUS WAR IN
HEAVEN WHICH RESULTED IN THE "DEATH"
OF THE NEW GODS AND DARKSEID'S SUBSEQUENT CATASTROPHIC
FALL INTO THE MATERIAL WORLD.

A NEW FORM OF THE EQUATION WAS USED AGAINST SHILO NORMAN,
A.K.A. MISTER MIRACLE, BY THE NEWLY INCARNATE DARKSEID
PRIOR TO THE FINAL CRISIS.

DELIVERED AS AN INCOHERENT GROWL BY "BOSS DARK SIDE" HIMSELF,
THIS "PSYCHIATRIC EQUATION" WAS A HUNTER-KILLER MANTRA DESIGNED
TO PREY ON SHILO'S LOW SELF-ESTEEM AND EMOTIONAL PROBLEMS
AS A WAY OF DESTROYING HIS CONFIDENCE PRIOR TO TOTAL
SUBJUGATION OF HIS WILL.

MISTER MIRACLE WAS ABLE TO RESIST THE ANTI-LIFE EQUATION,
MAKING HIM ONE OF THE FEW LIVING BEINGS IMMUNE TO ITS INFLUENCE.

³¹ Then came upon fell Lilith a fury like unto the One himself, and she did loose rage and magik, and draw from those who did not believe their blood and life alike.

³² And they did scream for her mercy, and they did beg of her forgiveness, and they did offer her their service in all things, and in all ways; and fell Lilith heeded them not, and cursed them their weakness, and called them cowards and slaves, and showed no kindness to them, nor any mercy neither.

³³ And she did fall amongst the dead, keening for her beloved, now descended to the Pit of Abyss, with much wailing and tearing of clothes and flesh.

³⁴ And from the blood of the unworthy, the devoted of the Old God, Lilith anointed her hand.

³⁵ These are the words of Lilith, as given to me beneath the Shower of Ash, where we did mourn the loss of the One from us, as she spake them unto me.

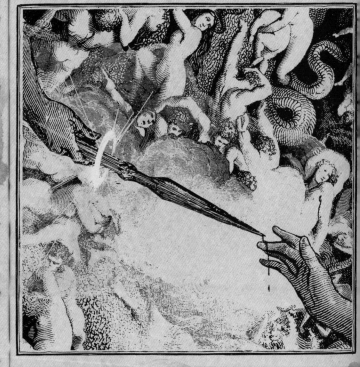

36 Behold the Key, that ye may know it, its shaft of ash and its tip of iron, and look ye now, that the edge be anointed, and from it flows the blood of sacrifice.

³⁷ And know that this bloodied edge become the weapon of my beloved in His hands, yea, know that in His hands alone will its power be revealed, delivered by the Faceless;

³⁸ And with this spear shall the One carve a new destiny, and remake creation for a New God, he who dwells aside in Darkness, deep in the Abyss.

³⁹ And know that the blood of the spear will unmake the Old God, and make slaves of his children and servants, mortal and spectre alike.

⁴⁰ Until the spear weeps, so shall it be, and none will resist the One; but should its tears be found, then the unmaker shall be unmade, and the Faithless who wields it will become his undoing.

⁴¹ And I looked, and saw in the earth and in the blood the shape of a spear, and saw too the end of all things.

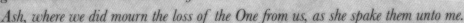
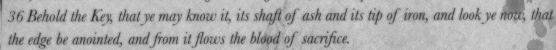

TEXT BY GREG RUCKA
ILLUSTRATION BY STEVE LIEBER
PAGE DESIGN BY ERIC S. TRAUTMANN

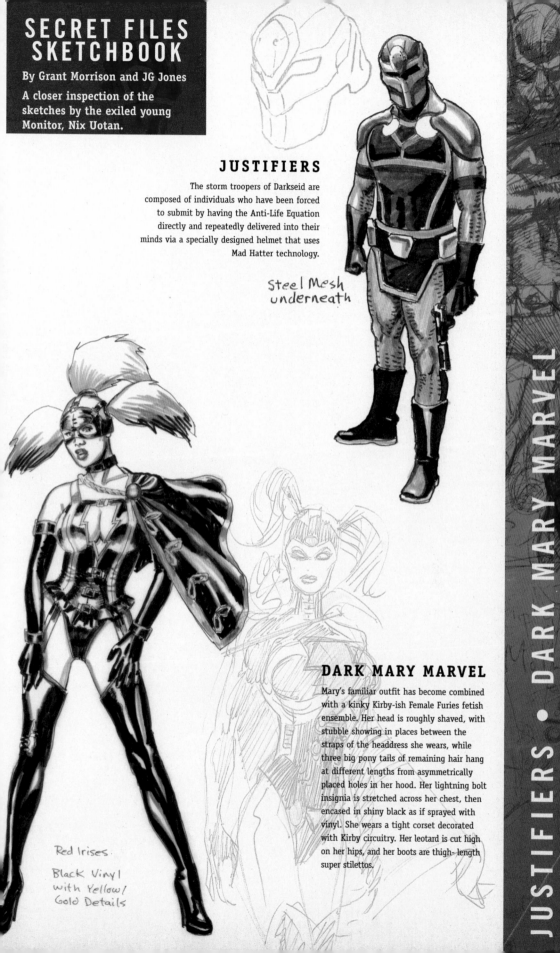

SECRET FILES SKETCHBOOK

By Grant Morrison and JG Jones

A closer inspection of the sketches by the exiled young Monitor, Nix Uotan.

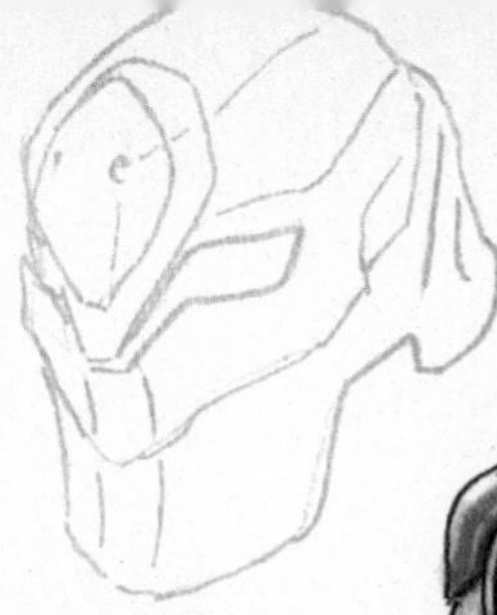

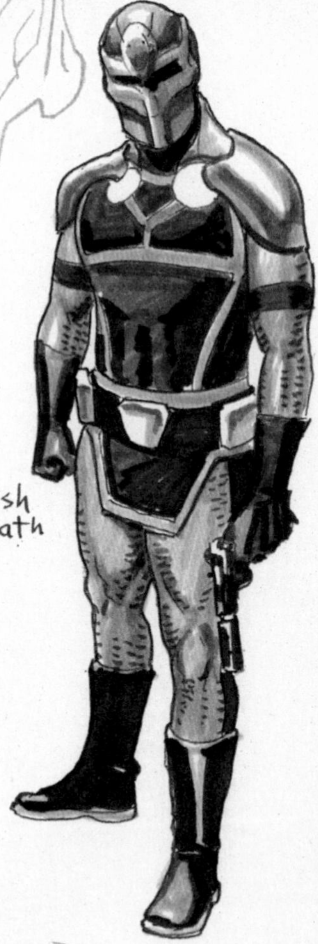
Steel Mesh
underneath

JUSTIFIERS

The storm troopers of Darkseid are composed of individuals who have been forced to submit by having the Anti-Life Equation directly and repeatedly delivered into their minds via a specially designed helmet that uses Mad Hatter technology.

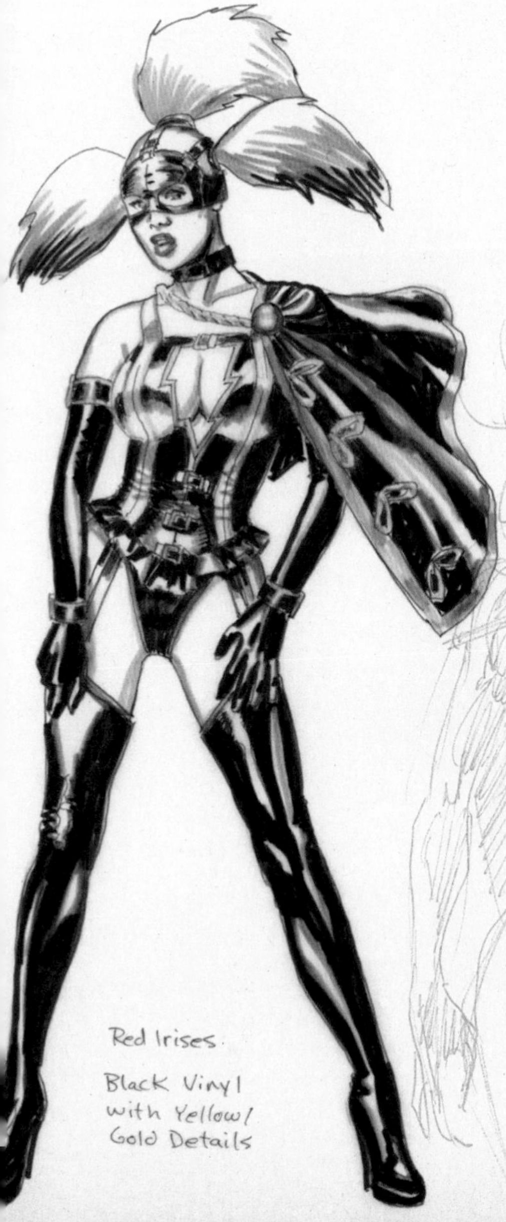
Red Irises.
Black Vinyl
with Yellow/
Gold Details

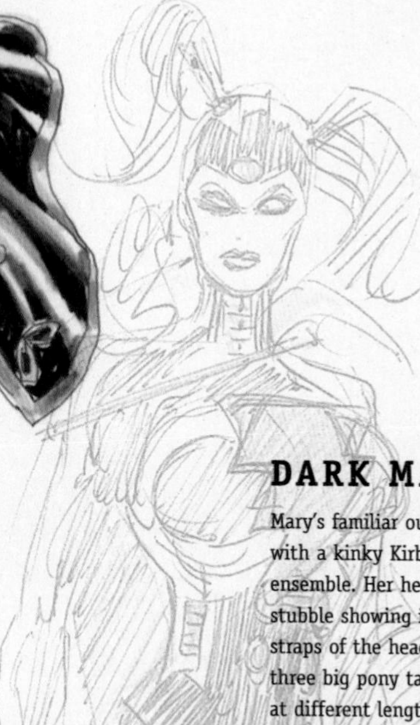

DARK MARY MARVEL

Mary's familiar outfit has become combined with a kinky Kirby-ish Female Furies fetish ensemble. Her head is roughly shaved, with stubble showing in places between the straps of the headdress she wears, while three big pony tails of remaining hair hang at different lengths from asymmetrically placed holes in her hood. Her lightning bolt insignia is stretched across her chest, then encased in shiny black as if sprayed with vinyl. She wears a tight corset decorated with Kirby circuitry. Her leotard is cut high on her hips, and her boots are thigh- length super stilettos.

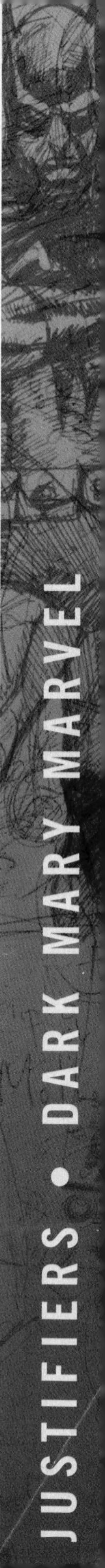
JUSTIFIERS • DARK MARY MARVEL

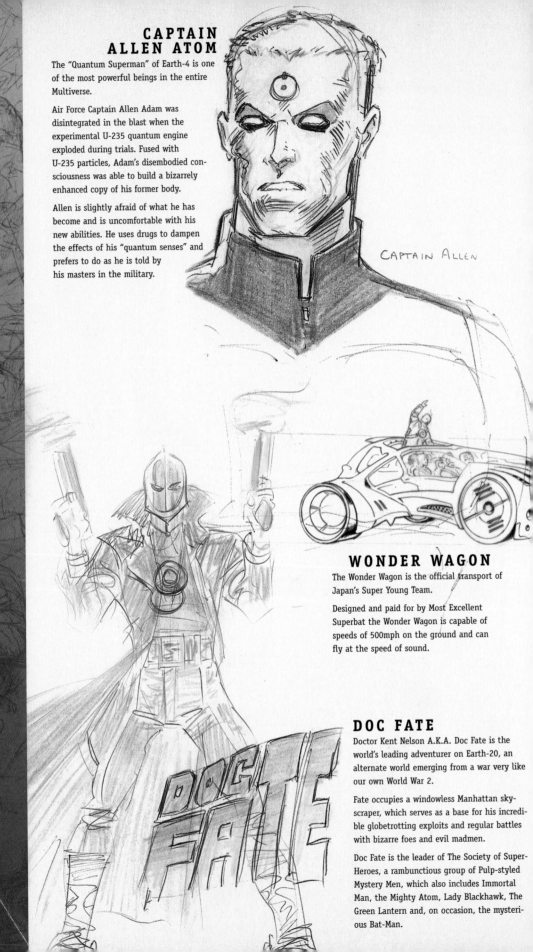

CAPTAIN ALLEN ATOM

The "Quantum Superman" of Earth-4 is one of the most powerful beings in the entire Multiverse.

Air Force Captain Allen Adam was disintegrated in the blast when the experimental U-235 quantum engine exploded during trials. Fused with U-235 particles, Adam's disembodied consciousness was able to build a bizarrely enhanced copy of his former body.

Allen is slightly afraid of what he has become and is uncomfortable with his new abilities. He uses drugs to dampen the effects of his "quantum senses" and prefers to do as he is told by his masters in the military.

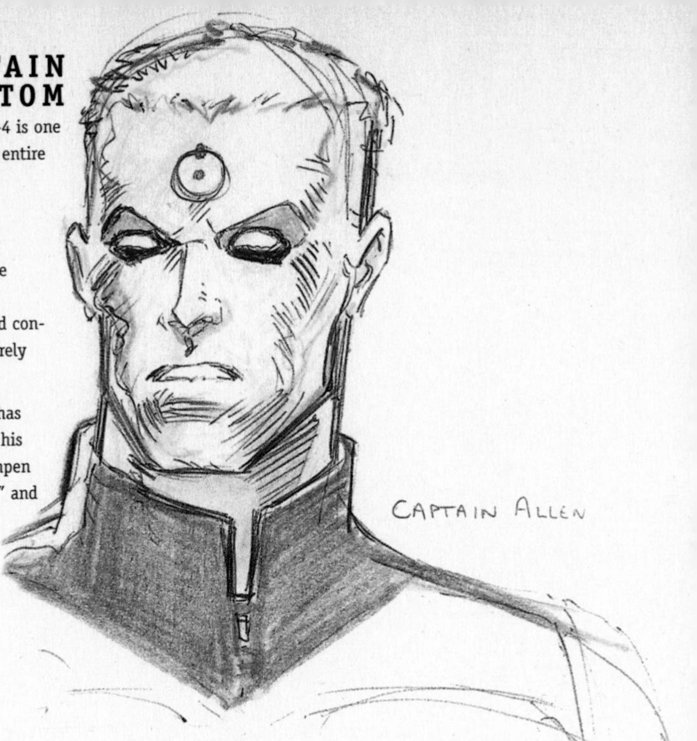
CAPTAIN ALLEN

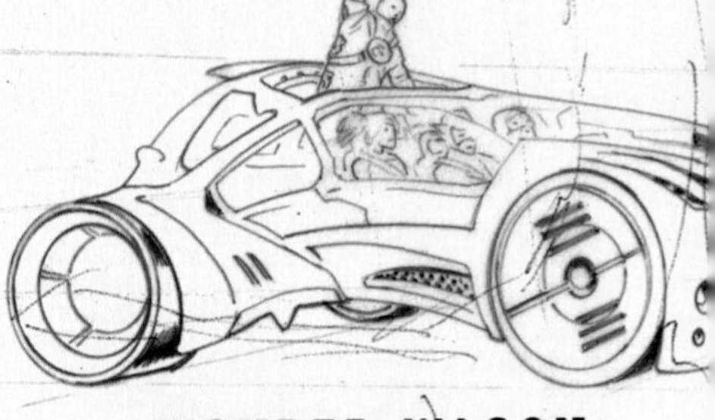

WONDER WAGON

The Wonder Wagon is the official transport of Japan's Super Young Team.

Designed and paid for by Most Excellent Superbat the Wonder Wagon is capable of speeds of 500mph on the ground and can fly at the speed of sound.

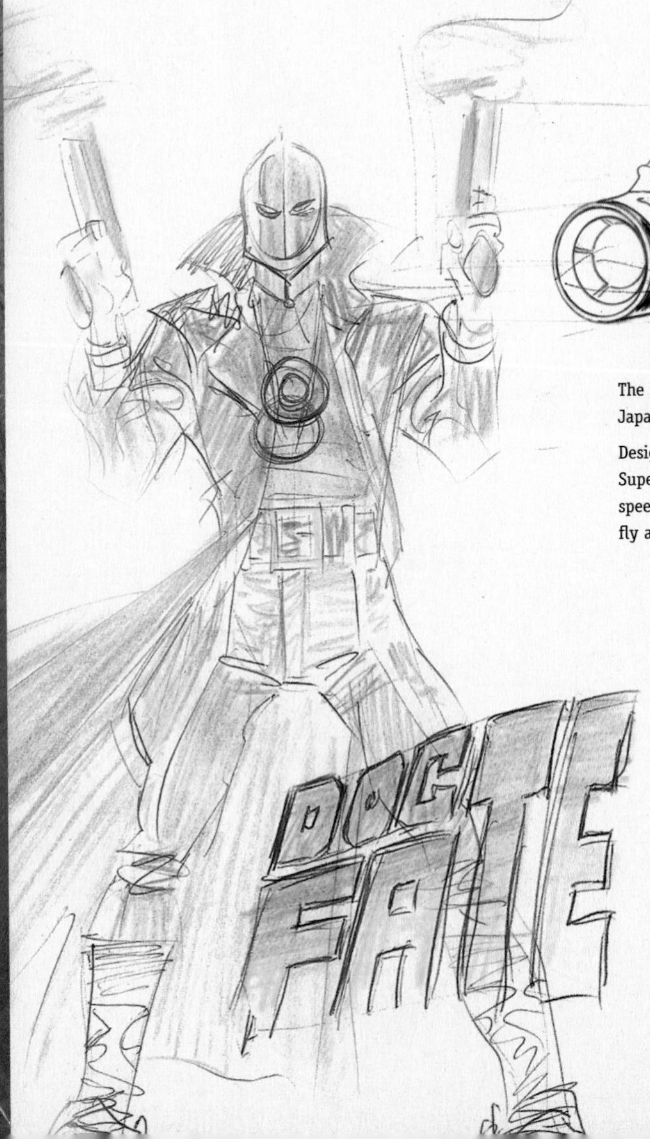
DOC FATE

DOC FATE

Doctor Kent Nelson A.K.A. Doc Fate is the world's leading adventurer on Earth-20, an alternate world emerging from a war very like our own World War 2.

Fate occupies a windowless Manhattan skyscraper, which serves as a base for his incredible globetrotting exploits and regular battles with bizarre foes and evil madmen.

Doc Fate is the leader of The Society of Super-Heroes, a rambunctious group of Pulp-styled Mystery Men, which also includes Immortal Man, the Mighty Atom, Lady Blackhawk, The Green Lantern and, on occasion, the mysterious Bat-Man.

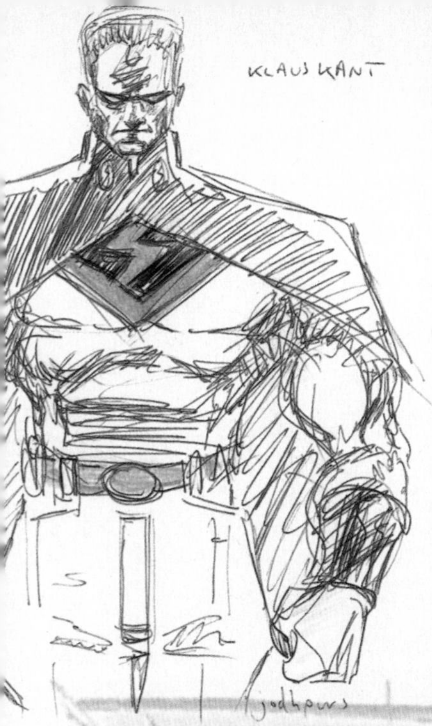
KLAUS KANT
godhpurs

OVERMAN

Overman A.K.A. Karl Kant A.K.A. Kal-L is the troubled champion of Earth-10, a world where the Nazis WON the Second World War.

Rocketed to Earth from Krypton, doomed planet of supermen, young Kal-L crashed in a field in Czechoslovakia in 1938. Using technology retro-engineered from Kal-L's rocket ship, Nazi scientists were able to win the war for Hitler.

The U.S.A. held out until the early '50s, when Overman himself entered the fray and ended all conflict with a victory for the Nazis.

Driven almost mad with guilt when he realised the extent of Nazi atrocities, Overman spent the decades after the war creating a virtual utopia on Earth.

Overman is the leader of his world's Justice League, which also includes BRUNHILDE, LEATHERWING, UNDERWATERMAN and others. Their sworn enemies are the English-speaking rebel band known as UNCLE SAM AND HIS FREEDOM FIGHTERS.

The sins of the past continue to haunt Overman and may prove to be his downfall.

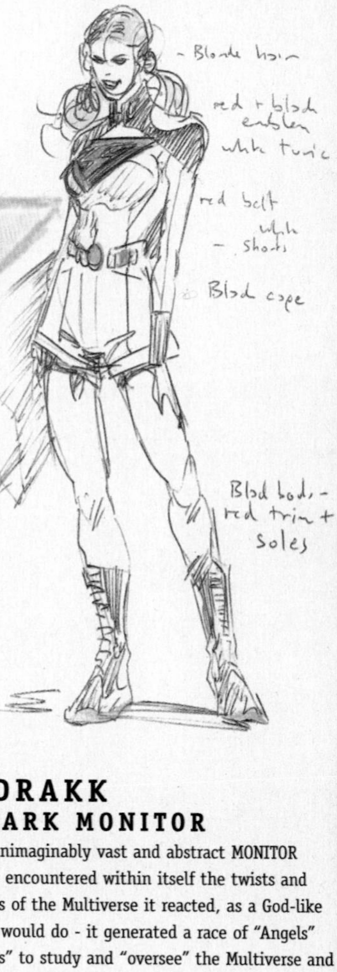
- Blonde hair
red + black emblem
white tunic
red belt
white - shorts
Black cape
Black boots - red trim + soles

OVERGIRL

Overgirl is the only successful result of experiments to seed a human child with Overman's genetic material. All the others died - except for the horrific aberration known as ANTIHUMAN.

Overgirl has less than half of Overman's strength, speed, stamina and endurance, which is still considerable.

She is the first person from Earth-10 to cross the Bleed barrier between Multiverses.

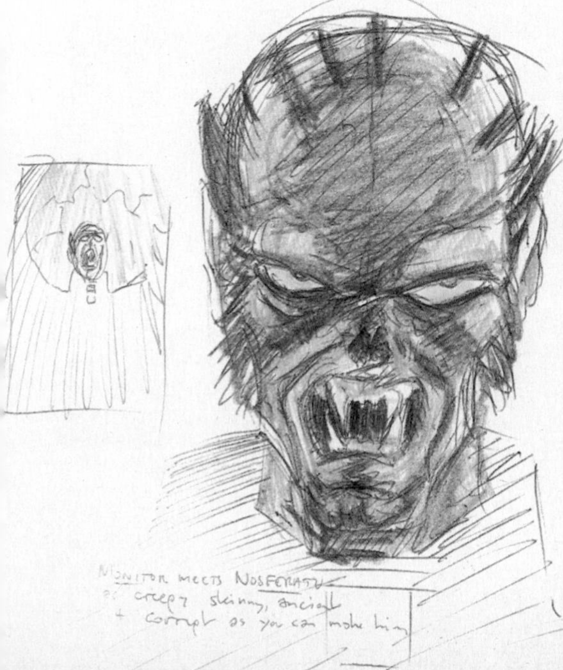
Monitor meets Nosferatu
as creepy skinny, ancient
+ corrupt as you can make him

MANDRAKK
THE DARK MONITOR

When the unimaginably vast and abstract MONITOR intelligence encountered within itself the twists and complexities of the Multiverse it reacted, as a God-like mega-mind would do - it generated a race of "Angels" or "Monitors" to study and "oversee" the Multiverse and to act as an interface between Multiverse and Monitor.

Greatest of all Monitors was Dax Novu, the "Radiant One," the Explorer and Scientist.

But it was also Novu who returned from the Multiverse infected by the forms and by the stories of the creatures he had encountered inside.

Shunned by the other Monitors for bringing contamination, his won story twisted inexorably towards the darkness. Misunderstood, shunned, feared and finally neglected, Novu became the ultimate the other Monitors feared.

Reborn as Mandrakk the Dark Monitor, Novu is the absolute personification of vampiric hunger on a cosmic, existential scale.

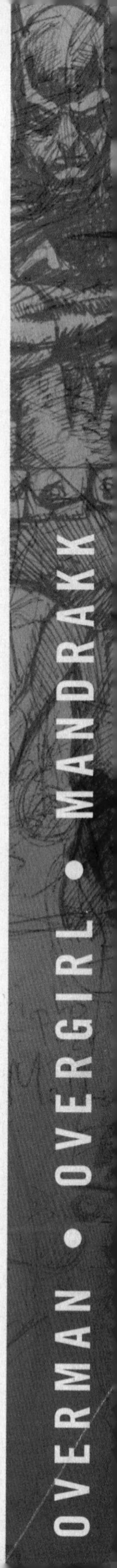
OVERMAN • OVERGIRL • MANDRAKK

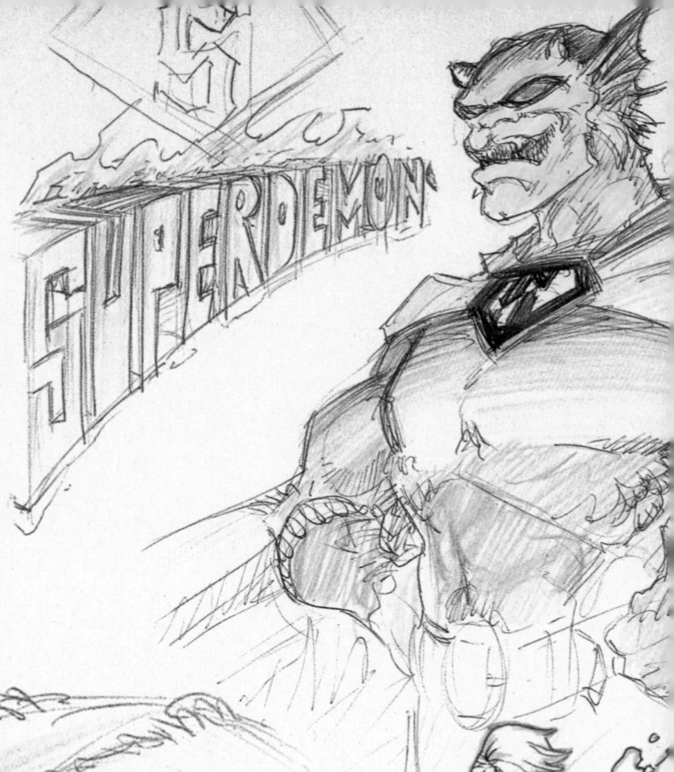
SUPERDEMON

SUPERDEMON

Hurled to Earth from the doomed planet Kamelot, by the astro-magics of Merlin, the Demon Etrigan took up residence in the body of a Midwestern preacher's son, Jason Blood.

Jason's indomitable will tamed the unruly demon and he learned how to use its great powers in the defense of Earth-17, a spooky Halloween world where magic and science co-exist.

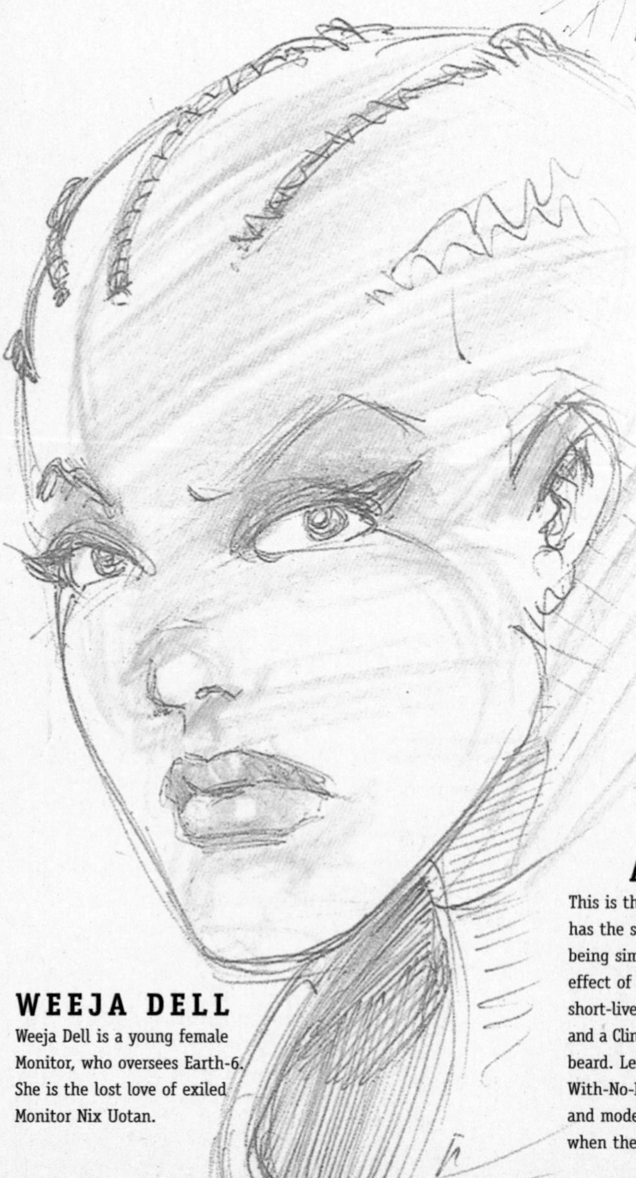

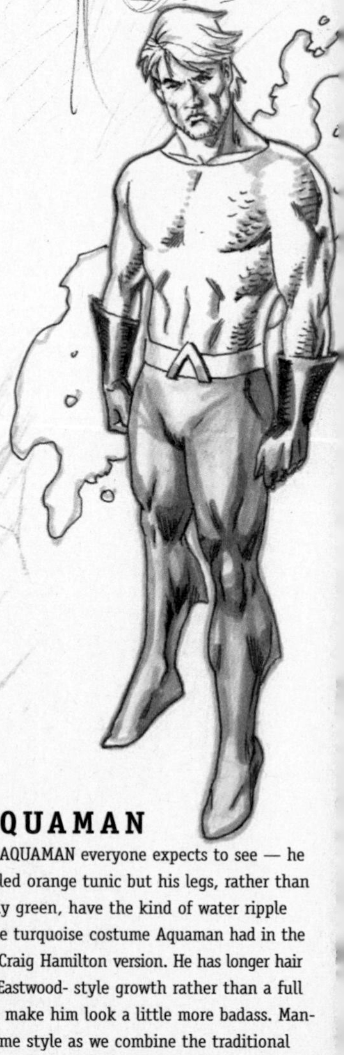

AQUAMAN

This is the AQUAMAN everyone expects to see — he has the scaled orange tunic but his legs, rather than being simply green, have the kind of water ripple effect of the turquoise costume Aquaman had in the short-lived Craig Hamilton version. He has longer hair and a Clint Eastwood- style growth rather than a full beard. Let's make him look a little more badass. Man-With-No-Name style as we combine the traditional and modern into something everyone expects to see when they hear this character's name.

WEEJA DELL

Weeja Dell is a young female Monitor, who oversees Earth-6. She is the lost love of exiled Monitor Nix Uotan.

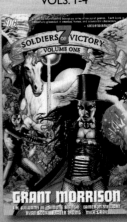

FROM THE WRITER OF
GREEN LANTERN AND JSA

GEOFF JOHNS

"Bursting with world-quaking ambition. Energetic and urgent, this Crisis shouldn't be avoided. **GRADE: A-"**
– ENTERTAINMENT WEEKLY

"For hard-core superhero fans, this is essential."
– BOOKLIST

"Define[s] DC's heroes for a new generation of readers."
– COLORADO SPRINGS GAZETTE

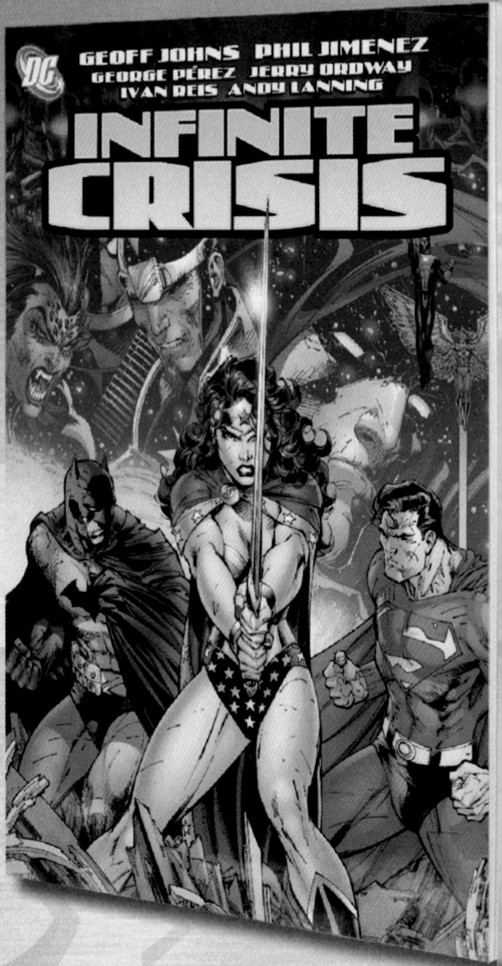
DC
GEOFF JOHNS PHIL JIMENEZ
GEORGE PÉREZ JERRY ORDWAY
IVAN REIS ANDY LANNING
INFINITE CRISIS

DON'T MISS THE GRAPHIC NOVELS THAT LED THE COUNTDOWN TO INFINITE CRISIS

RANN - THANAGAR WAR

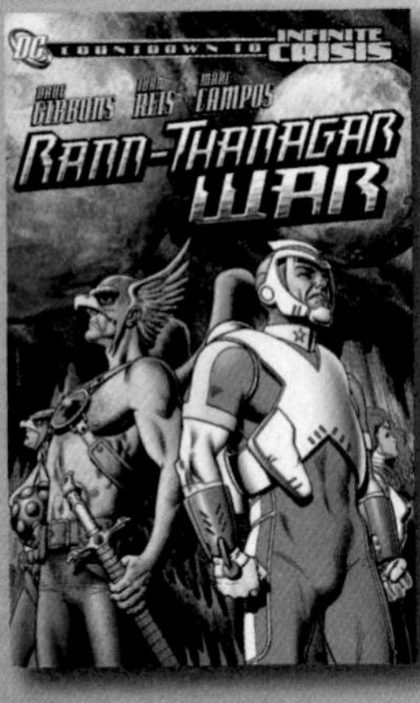
COUNTDOWN TO INFINITE CRISIS
GIBBONS REIS CAMPOS
RANN-THANAGAR WAR

DAVE GIBBONS
IVAN REIS

THE OMAC PROJECT

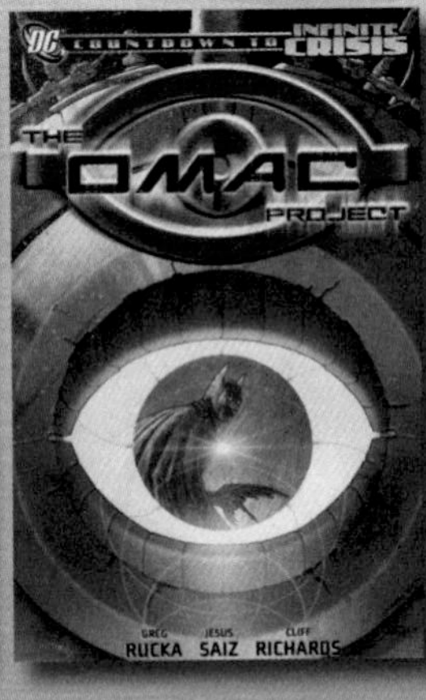
COUNTDOWN TO INFINITE CRISIS
THE OMAC PROJECT
GREG RUCKA JESUS SAIZ CLIFF RICHARDS

GREG RUCKA
JESUS SAIZ

VILLAINS UNITED

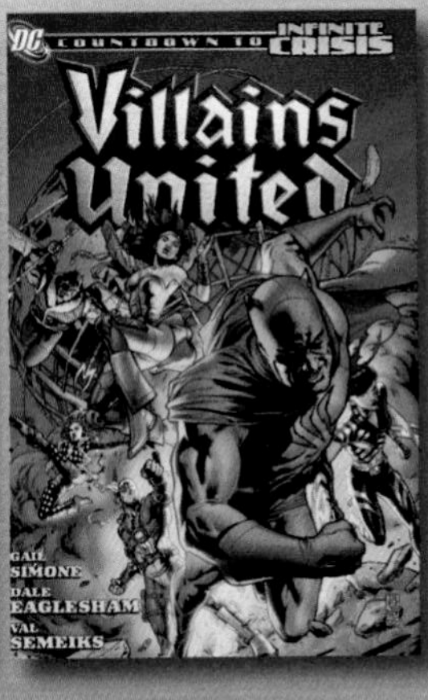
COUNTDOWN TO INFINITE CRISIS
Villains United
GAIL SIMONE
DALE EAGLESHAM
VAL SEMEIKS

GAIL SIMONE
DALE EAGLESHAM

DAY OF VENGEANC

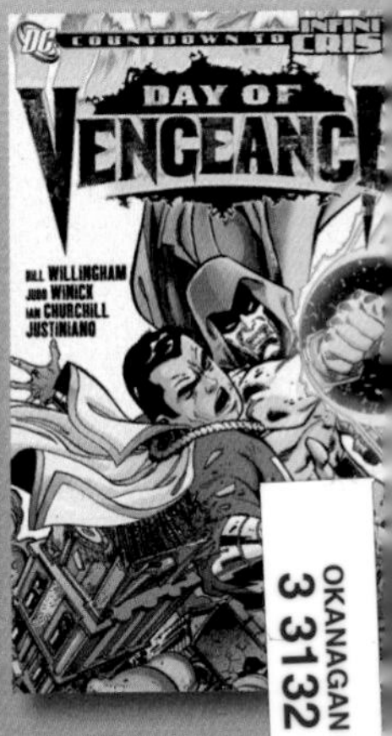
DAY OF VENGEANC
BILL WILLINGHAM
JUDD WINICK
IAN CHURCHILL
JUSTINIANO

BILL WILLIN
JUSTINI

SEARCH THE GRAPHIC NOVELS SECTION OF
DCCOMICS.COM
FOR ART AND INFORMATION ON ALL OF OUR BOOKS!